THE VOICE AND ITS DOUBLES

THE VOICE
AND ITS DOUBLES

Media and Music in Northern Australia

DANIEL FISHER

DUKE UNIVERSITY PRESS *Durham and London* 2016

Designed by Amy Ruth Buchanan
Typeset in Minion by Westchester

Library of Congress Cataloging-in-Publication Data
Names: Fisher, Daniel (Daniel Todd), author.
Title: Thev oice and its doubles : media and music in
Northern Australia / Daniel Fisher.
Description: Durham : Duke University Press, 2016. |
Includes bibliographical references and index.
Identifiers: LCCN 2015042543
ISBN 9780822360896 (hardcover)
ISBN 9780822361206 (pbk.)
ISBN 9780822374428 (e-book)
Subjects: LCSH: Communication in anthropology—Australia,
Northern. | Aboriginal Australians in mass media. | Radio—
Production and   direction—Australia, Northern. | Sound—
Recording and reproducing—Australia, Northern. |
Communication and culture—Australia, Northern. | Politics and
culture—Australia, Northern.
Classifi ation: LCC P94.5. A852 A8 2016 |
DDC 302.23/44089991509429—dc23
LC record available at http://lccn.loc.gov/2015042543

Cover art: Satellite dish, Northern Territory, Australia. ©
Deco / Alamy Stock Photo.

CONTENTS

ACRONYMS

ABC	Australian Broadcasting Corporation
ALPA	Arnhem Land Progress Association (Uniting Church)
ARDS	Aboriginal Resource and Development Service
ATSIC	Aboriginal and Torres Strait Islander Commission
ATSIS	Aboriginal and Torres Strait Islander Service
BRACS	Broadcasting for Remote Aboriginal Communities Scheme
CAA	Council for Aboriginal Affairs
CAAMA	Central Australian Aboriginal Media Association
CBF	Community Broadcasting Foundation
CMAA	Country Music Association of Australia
CREATE	Culture Research Education and Training Enterprise
DET	Department of Education and Training
DOCITA	Department of Communications, Information Technology and the Arts
IHHP	Indigenous Hip Hop Projects
NIRS	National Indigenous Radio Service
NTER	Northern Territory Emergency Response
NWA	Niggaz With Attitude (hip-hop group)
TEABBA	Top End Aboriginal Bush Broadcasting Association
YYF	Yothu Yindi Foundation

ACKNOWLEDGMENTS

I have been working on this project and thinking about the political and pleasurable imbrication of music, sound, and technology for a long time. Across ten years of research, travel, and teaching, many people and places have left their mark on my thinking and encouraged me along the different threads of musical and vocal sociality I draw together here. I extend my greatest appreciation to the many broadcasters, producers, musicians, and activists in Australia whose work drew my attention and whose efforts are insistently tuned to the horizons and futures of Indigenous possibility. Their efforts, their many successes, and the friendship they extended to me are at the heart of this book. In Brisbane Tiga Bayles, Alec Doomadjee, Daniel Kinchela, Wayne Blair, and many others answered questions and shared music and stories, all the while drawing me into 4AAA's daily routine and seasonal travels. In Darwin the crews at TEABBA and Radio Larrakia and the members of Darwin's Long Grass Association gave generously of their time and, just as importantly, gave me room to ask questions, to work across organizations, and took me with them on their travels. They need not have done so, and this willingness to cart me along made everything else possible. Rico Adjrun has for a full decade proved an enormous font of energy, great humor, and even better music. I also thank Tiga for his permission to reproduce my photograph of him as figure 4.1 and Jedda Puruntatameri for her permission to reproduce my photographs of her father and other family members in figures 5.2 and 5.3.

Several cotravelers in Top End media whom I here call Tracy, Gary, and Karen proved steadfast friends in the wake of a serious automobile accident on the Stuart Highway. The project might have stalled then and there but for the care and hospitality they offered in a moment of existential crisis. Robert Graham, Mary Laughren, and Murray Garde deserve special thanks for their enormous generosity and hospitality both in Brisbane and Darwin.

This project has its genesis in graduate studies in the Department of Anthropology at New York University. I often reflect on my good fortune to arrive at Smith Hall and the Culture & Media Program when I did. As constant models of rigorous and experimental scholarship as well as key mentors in this project's formative moments, Fred Myers and Faye Ginsburg were and continue to be more generous interlocutors than I would have thought possible. In another stroke of good fortune I was lucky to attend Steven Feld's seminars on sound, the senses, and cinema. I owe Steve special thanks for helping me begin thinking what a sounded ethnography might be and for his continued generosity and friendship. Tom Abercrombie and Bambi Schieffelin were sharp and enthusiastic interlocutors at NYU, and I can't thank them enough for their assistance as I got this work off the ground.

Kristin Dowell, Luther Elliot, Aaron Glass, Elena Kim, and Susie Rosenbaum saw some of this material in its earliest stages in our dissertation writing group and helped me greatly with generous and genuine engagement. Thanks as well to Elise Andaya, Lucas Bessire, Melissa Checker, Cheryl Furjanic, Laura Harris, Bill Horn, Mariana Johnson, Toby King, David Novak, Dawson Prater, Lisa Stefanoff, and Leshu Torchin for conversation, musical dialogue, and filmic companionship. Laura Ryan on East First Street and Lisa Bohnenstengel in Williamsburg, the many people I met through New York's Coalition for the Homeless, and the members of the Hungry March Band all helped me see and hear a bigger New York and to think ethnography in new ways.

The research on which this book is based was supported by an International Dissertation Field Research Fellowship, a program of the Social Science Research Council (SSRC-IDRF), with funds provided by the Andrew W. Mellon Foundation (2002); by a fellowship from the Social Science Research Council Program in the Arts with funds provided by the Rockefeller Foundation (2002); by a National Science Foundation Dissertation Research Fellowship, Behavioral and Cognitive Sciences 0210981 (2002–2004); by the Wenner-Gren Foundation for Anthropological Research, dissertation research grant numbered 6944 (2002); and by a number of additional grants and fellowships from New York University's Department of Anthropology.

In Sydney Jeremy Beckett proved a remarkably generous interlocutor during my first antipodean travels while Clinton Walker and Gayle Kennedy lent their ears and stories to my thinking as I finished the book. In Brisbane John

Hartley, Jo Tacchi, Jinna Tay, and Ellie Rennie were enormously collegial in my first months, while the Queensland University of Technology provided me with my first institutional base in Australia. In Canberra, Francesca Merlan and Alan Rumsey proved more than generous, and I thank them in particular for introducing me to Canberra and the ANU. I have also been fortunate to meet a remarkable group of Australian musicians and music lovers whose contributions to my work must also be noted here. Michael Honen and Mark Grose at SkinnyFish music gave of their time and their deep musical knowledge of the Top End; thanks as well to Tony Gray for continued conversation and shared stories.

The manuscript that led to this book has been in progress at several institutions. I first sketched its outline and core ideas while a Mellon-funded postdoctoral fellow at Cornell University's Department of Anthropology, and I especially thank Jane Fajans, David Holmberg, and Terence Turner for their support in this early stage and also am grateful for the collegial conversation of my cotravelers in postdoctoral research Johanna Crane and Francis Cody. At Rutgers University's Center for Cultural Analysis my thinking was sharpened by conversation with Biella Coleman, Lisa Gitelman, Beth Povinelli, and Michael Warner. In Australia, my colleagues at Macquarie University provided the best kind of supportive challenges to early ideas. In particular I thank Greg Downey, Chris Houston, Kalpana Ram, Jaap Timmer, Lisa Wynn, and the late Ian Bedford for their collegiality and insight. A sabbatical spent as a visiting scholar at Columbia University's Department of Music in 2013 greatly assisted in completing the manuscript. I thank Aaron Fox, George Lewis, Miya Masaoka, Meg McLagan, and Brian Larkin for their generous welcome. My arguments also benefited from the collective attention and engagement of audiences at Cornell University; Columbia University's Department of Music; the Department of Anthropology at Sydney University; the Anthropology Department at UT, Austin; the University of Technology, Sydney; Reed College; the Center for Cultural Analysis at Rutgers University; and UC Berkeley.

My colleagues at UC Berkeley have been enormously supportive and generous with both ideas and friendship as I completed the book, while students in my courses and seminars at Berkeley have likewise proven important and stimulating interlocutors. At Duke University Press, Ken Wissoker and Elizabeth Ault have been wonderful editors, encouraging and engaged at each step, and I am truly thrilled that this book found a home at Duke. I also thank the two anonymous reviewers who read the draft manuscript and provided crucial textual interlocutors for the final stretch of writing. Any faults that remain are, of course, my own.

Chapters 1 and 3 revise and expand on arguments first explored in essays published in 2009 as "Speech That Offers Song: Kinship, Country Music, and Incarceration in Northern Australia," *Cultural Anthropology* 24(2): 280–312; and in 2012 as "From the Studio to the Street: Producing the Voice in Indigenous Australia," in *Radio Fields: Anthropology and Wireless Sound in the 21st Century*, ed. Lucas Bessire and Daniel Fisher (New York University Press).

A special shout goes out to my family, who heard the music in this book first and whose conversations and laughter animate its pages. My parents, Paul and Linda Fisher, encouraged me from day one with their confidence, their love, and their strong sense of what truly matters. A million thanks also go to John and Lyn Tranter, who continue to extend their amazing hospitality in Sydney, allowing me to feel a part of their extended family. Kirsten Tranter has been a constant cotraveler from the first page to the last. She accompanied me for much of the research, through the lows of high-speed car wrecks and the highs of Christmases in Clovelly, New York, and California, and for the past decade has shared with me the great joy of parenting Henry and now Maximilian Fisher. Kirsten, Henry, and Max this book is for you.

Laurel and I sat in the cinder-block broadcasting shed at the radio desk. It was our third day in Barunga, a small Indigenous settlement in Australia's Northern Territory, broadcasting live radio from their renowned annual sports and music festival—five days of concerts, contests, and football games that drew Aboriginal and settler Australians from across the Northern Territory. Laurel, a Yolngu radio broadcaster and translator from northeast Arnhem Land, was playing country and gospel tracks and reading out the occasional request that was passed into the shed on a handwritten note or called in from the council office via the rotary phone stationed on the broadcast desk. And I was keeping her company, both of us taking a break from the insistent sun and dust outside.[1]

An old man came into the shed, wearing a plaid cowboy shirt, jeans, and in bare feet. Would we send news to his niece in Galiwin'ku, he asked, to let her know that her uncle had won the spear-chucking contest? I'd seen him throw an hour earlier, following some tourist's efforts that, though earnest, went far astray. His was indeed an impressive shot, putting the spear into a powerful low arc, carving it down a grass fairway of sorts and right through the heart of a cardboard box standing perilously close to some colorful polyester dome tents. Well-known Indigenous actor and raconteur Tom E. Lewis was holding a microphone and MC-ing the festival events. His voice led the loud collective cheer that followed through his handheld PA, distorting its megaphone and amplifying our collective excitement. Lewis had been working hard to keep up the enthusiasm as tourists struggled to bring the wooden spear within some proximity of the target. Everyone was thus thrilled to see the old man display such skill, his technique and strength directing the spear through the air as though with magic. Back in the studio Laurel opened the radio microphone to share the news. She knew the man and his family in Galiwin'ku, and put the news of his success across in Yolngu Matha, their shared first language, before playing a country track from the American singer Charley Pride.

In the days prior I had traveled south from the Territory's capital city, Darwin, through the large regional town of Katherine and on to this small central Arnhem Land community with a radio broadcast team from the Top End Aboriginal Bush Broadcasting Association (TEABBA).[2] We arrived at the festival site on a Friday, set up a tarp and tent, unfolded camping tables underneath for the outdoor broadcast gear, and strung extension cables into the cinder-block community broadcast studio. The initials NWA, acronym for the famed, seminal rap group from south central Los Angeles, were spray-painted against a low brick wall inside (figure P.1). This LA-based musical collective, the launching pad for celebrity rap artists and producers Dr. Dre, Eazy E, and Ice Cube, is as popular in many of the Northern Territory's remote communities as in Australia's southeastern cities. The broadcast equipment was housed inside a second room, behind a locking door. There a table with a microphone and small mixing desk sat in the middle of the room, while in the corner we found the rack-mounted tower of electronic equipment.

The crew had been promised lodgings near the radio facilities for sleeping and storing audio equipment. On arrival we found that the house we'd been allocated was the last available accommodation in the community, a derelict structure, abandoned after its previous occupants had moved several months prior. When we saw the hundreds-strong swarm of cockroaches scatter away from the open door and its sudden blast of sun, we instead decided to sleep on the floor of the more regularly occupied radio studio, unrolling swags alongside the graffiti and audio cabling. That meant a midnight visit from the community bullock, sticking its head up to the chain-link gate that served as a studio door, and a lot of talk late into the night in the shared, smaller space of the studio.

On Saturday we began broadcasting music, requests, and interviews with performers and politicians from the festival grounds. All day long Laurel, the association's manager Donna, and other Indigenous broadcasters and technicians had been running radio shows from the edge of the ceremonial ground that doubled as the dance hall, its leveled red dirt stretching away from a long

P.1 Graffiti adorns the brick wall of a radio studio, Barunga, Northern Territory.

semi-trailer-mounted bandstand. I spent the morning between the broadcast desk and the spear-throwing contest, and in the afternoon went with a video camera to tape local pop music luminaries Yilila Band as they did their sound check. Front man and lead singer Grant Nundhirribala and Yilila's tour manager, Tony Gray, used duct tape to bind a microphone to the end of a Yidaki, then Nundhirribala began pumping out a drone over the PA for the sound desk (figure P.2).[3] The yidaki was well traveled, cracked on one end, and adorned with a bright blue TEABBA radio bumper sticker.

Just past dusk a rising star took the stage. Jessica Mauboy, then fifteen, sang soul numbers to a prerecorded backing track, her melismatic delivery, carefully pinned hair, and spangle-studded blue jeans refracting the stage lights across the dusty faces, board shorts, and long floral dresses of her audience. She had recently won an award at the Tamworth country music festival for the virtuosity of her contemporary country vocal delivery, and her debut single, a country and western cover of Cyndi Lauper's "Girls Just Wanna Have Fun," had garnered enough attention to earn funding for a commercial music video. But this performance at Barunga marked a generic shift in Mauboy's musical persona. It now echoed the new soul and R&B sounds of Beyoncé

P.2 Duct tape holds a microphone to a yidaki, Barunga, Northern Territory.

Knowles and Britney Spears and showcased her powerful voice as a virtuosic instrument—a virtuosity foregrounded all the more by the lack of a backing band; instead a CD track provided her accompaniment, staging her voice as the focus of our appreciation. The audience gave her a rapturous welcome, anticipating the international success she would soon achieve as an R&B singer and feature film actor in films such as *Bran Nu Dae* (2010) and *The Sapphires* (2012)[4] before a star turn in the 2014 Eurovision competition. The show finished up with dancing as Nundhirribala's Yilila Band took the stage: eight people with guitars, bass, drums, and yidaki crowded onto the trailer-cum-proscenium and put their voices together over a driving dance groove. These were local heroes, hailing from the community of Numbulwar just down the road on the Gulf of Carpentaria, and were themselves soon to tour Europe and Japan promoting their first record.

After the bands wrapped up for the night, Laurel, Donna, and I turned up the powered speakers and let the music continue late. About twenty children stayed near TEABBA's broadcasting tent, dancing energetically under the spotlit tarps that shielded the transmitters, CD players, and powered speakers from rain, however unlikely such precipitation may have been in July, the height of tropical Australia's dry season. A few clutched after a ball, taking advantage of TEABBA's bright spotlights to scrabble together a game of Australian Rules football. Parents and visitors drifted by in the night, just out of reach of the lights. The association's signal goes out each year from this and other cultural festivals held in remote communities across the Top End. Their broadcasts reach out through remote community transmitters from Nauiyu, Galiwin'ku, Barunga, Maningrida, Oenpelli, and more, sending out requests, country music, news, and interviews with a range of Aboriginal public figures—actors, musicians, and intellectuals. At times they also record local bands and local battles of bands, songwriters, and young performers. These recordings fill their broadcasts in later months—occasionally becoming classics of a kind— cherished and repeatedly requested by listeners across the Northern Territory.

TEABBA's broadcasts are themselves the sonic zero point of a large, regional community broadcasting network. Their signal travels through consoles and tie lines, satellites and antennae, eventually to be transduced as sound emerging from radios, computers, and even the phone systems of Indigenous corporations in Darwin and Alice Springs. At Barunga and other on-location broadcasts, TEABBA's radio booth fills with children from local communities and Aboriginal Australians from all corners of the country who stop for cups of tea and talk, possibly putting out a request on-air while they sit and have a yarn. And those requests take a particular shape, speak to others in terms of kinship and family connection, and frequently rely on genres of popular music—country, rock, and increasingly hip-hop and R&B. For the "ethnographic present" of this book, roughly the decade running from 2002 to approximately 2012, the voices on air moved across a spectrum of sung and spoken language—including the cosmopolitan African American sounds of the Fugees, Beyoncé Knowles, and Mauboy herself; the country music of Slim Dusty, Charley Pride, and Roger Knox; and the voices of radio requests and song texts spoken and sung in Yolngu Matha, Northern Territory Kriol, and Aboriginal English. And in festivals like Barunga, voices also emerged from microphones and powered speakers, from battery-powered megaphones and radio speakers. The voice in northern Australia, this is to say, is always already mediatized, staged by a broad range of musical genres and sound technologies.

When I reflect on the research that informs this book, these days at Barunga also stand out for making tangible the density of exchange between sonic form and social relation that Aboriginal audio media entail. In walking over to the broadcast studio that afternoon and allowing a recording of Charley Pride to celebrate the victory, the spear-throwing contest winner trod a well-worn path, engaging in a widespread, familiar practice that draws together voice, technology, and musical sound. That path has a highly politicized, often surprising history of activism and institutional politics in which what has been at stake is how mediatized expressive forms will speak to, for, and of Indigenous Australia. Audio media have long been at the center of Australian Indigenous rights and cultural activism, activism that sought to craft space in the broader Australian imagination for Indigenous histories and concerns. But it also emerged to address fears that the arrival of satellites, radios, televisions, and popular musics in northern Australia would mean the end of Australian Indigenous cultural difference and distinction—that popular culture and satellite TV would entail a catastrophic displacement of Aboriginal singularity by ersatz culture and the commodities of the distraction factory.[5] These concerns drew together Aboriginal activists and non-Indigenous advocates aiming to enable the self-determination of Indigenous people, and also attracted the concerns of a range of state actors and advocates whose sporadic attention led to funding support for organizations such as TEABBA and radio and television production equipment for communities such as Barunga. Begun in activism and advocacy, such media soon began to receive the (inconsistent) support of the state in the form of money, policy formation, and research.

Such figures of activism and the imprecise attention of the settler state do not in themselves account for the layers of politics and affect that audio media entail as sound. The establishment of Aboriginal radio stations and recording studios have met the immediate aims of enabling the Aboriginal production of media and also exceeded them. The stories I engage with in the following chapters emerge from a remarkable and rich media world—one that has fostered the growth of an Indigenous Australian music industry as well as the broad circulation of transnational forms of popular music: American country music stars Faron Young and Charley Pride join Australia's many Indigenous rock, country, and R&B acts on the radio playlists of northern Australia. It has also led to what I term the mediatization of Aboriginal expressivity more broadly, a consequential imbrication of sociality and audio media that matters greatly for my Indigenous interlocutors.

Jessica Mauboy, staging her voice above the polished groove of a CD backing track, participates in a long history of media activism and advocacy that today allows a voice such as hers, singing commercial soul and R&B musics, to be heard in a remote Aboriginal community as at once "black" and "Aboriginal." As mediatized avatars, such celebrity voices have themselves come to inhabit people's own voices and expressive repertoires, not just when they speak and sing about Aboriginal experiences, but in ways that fundamentally shape the value, politics, and historical significance of those experiences. Barunga provided an extended engagement with this mediatized voice, a voice staged "onstage," in radio, and against the drone of a yidaki, and also against broader, Afro-diasporic genres and self-consciously black musical sensibilities. While this book will suggest that the voice is always already staged to the extent that we speak both in our "own" voices and in the voices of others, I am here preoccupied with a productive tension between a heightened reflexivity around what Mikhail Bakhtin called "heteroglossia," what Erving Goffman figured as reported speech, and what Jacques Derrida approached as the iteratability and citationality central to speech and to the mediatization of voice as sound.

All these terms can evoke aspects of how my interlocutors and I often speak our bodily voices as our own, yet also equally frequently require and stage the voices of others with our own mouths and bodies, animating a series of sonic avatars in prosodic, musical, poetic, and vernacular facets of speaking (and singing) together. In asking Laurel to send a message over the radio, the old man I introduce above entrusted her with his voice, making himself the author, perhaps, of speech that Laurel animates (Goffman 1981). She then did so with a mode of address that performs intimacy and kin relatedness in public; that both "sends a message" to a listener from her uncle and also performs that relation for an audience, the public of Indigenous radio that is entailed by this message and that can also hear itself there, staged in sound. So if Aboriginal audio media at times bears the signature of the state, in such moments of collective self-abstraction it can also unsettle, doubling an Indigenous world in sound and creating there the possibility for shared pleasure, reflection, and critique. This joining of publicity, interpellation, and audition outlines the mediatization of the voice as sound that is the topic of this book—a removal of the voice from the body in a series of technical, expressive, and institutional endeavors that gather together technology, musical sound, and forms of desire and aspiration.

INTRODUCTION

This is a book about the Aboriginal production of audio media. It explores how the mediatization of voice and sound have come to animate Indigenous life, how audio media draw the interest and investment of the Australian state, and how such media move people and matter in the lives of Indigenous Australians. Like so many places across the globe, northern Australia is awash in electronically mediated sound, with radios and electric guitars joining microphones and mobile telephones in the circulation and amplification of music and voice. These audio technologies entail a durable politics of indigeneity and liberal government, a shared concern with eliciting Indigenous voices that brings together Indigenous and settler agencies, and also a series of arguments about how best to do that, and why and how such voices might matter. While audio media sound of Aboriginal history, its producers are also drawn into the orbit of the state's interests in Aboriginal media and associated forms of fiscal and institutional discipline. Sound and voice, that is, are sites where forms of affect, aural culture, and audit culture collide. This book asks what is at stake for Indigenous Australians in this collision, and in so doing endeavors to better understand the powers of audio media and affecting sound in contemporary northern Australia. To tell the story of Indigenous audio media in Australia is thus to explore an ontology of the recorded voice, the moving character of speech and song in their mediatization, and also to register the centrality of audio media and the voice to an aporia at the heart of liberal government in the early twenty-first century.

Beginning in the early 1980s, Aboriginal Australians found in radio, music production, and film and television the means to transform the terms of their engagement with a broader Australian polity and to insert themselves into the center of Australian political life. The activists behind such media built radio stations and music studios and found technological and institutional forms through which to take some control of the satellite and telephone networks then spreading across northern Australia. They did so by crafting request shows from country music and cassette-taped recordings of Aboriginal gospel, country, and rock bands singing in local languages. Such efforts sought not to sequester Aboriginal people from a global mediascape but, rather, to shape the contours of the media world they would inhabit, to enable forms of visual and aural sovereignty in a new, mass-mediated domain. In the chapters to follow I analyze the mediatized world that has since taken shape, focusing on the distinctive work of music production and broadcast radio, and analyzing the close proximity of media technologies, the voice, and those public expressions of intimacy and kinship that suffuse Aboriginal Australian social life. One of my arguments is that this history of media production and media politics has led to a particular sedimentation in sound of a rich politics, one that draws voice, race, and agency together in distinctive ways, yet also tears them apart in forms of discursive contest, expressive performance, and technological work with wired sound.

That these different media can today seem unremarkable in northern Australia is itself, from a historical perspective, quite a transformation, and one that began with radio technologies and cassette tapes and the hopes they embodied. Over the course of the 1960s and 1970s a number of Australian politicians and Indigenous activists and advocates had seen in radio broadcasting a means of amplifying Indigenous participation in Australian political life. H.C. "Nugget" Coombs, advocate for Aboriginal interests and bureaucratic champion of a then-new turn toward policies of self-determination, considered the feasibility of creating a northern broadcasting network for Aboriginal people, one modeled on the use of radio as governmental communication in colonial Papua New Guinea.[1] Coombs and his associates imagined this as a means by which Aboriginal people could be informed as citizens, enabled with news and political information to participate in a broader Australian society, but to do so on their own terms. While one might argue that this endeavor was part of an effort to devolve governmental labor onto Aboriginal corporations, a form of Australian "indirect rule" (see, for instance, Batty 2003), one can also see in Coombs's interests a technical and ethical approach to Indigenous political aspiration, a dialogue with Indigenous activists such as Pastor Doug Nicholls, Bill Onus, Charles Perkins, and other advocates in their efforts to make Aboriginal people full members of a broader Australian polity.[2] However one figures such governmental interests in Indigenous broadcasting, these hopes for remote Aboriginal radio were still, at the end of the 1970s, unfulfilled.

Ultimately Aboriginal and Torres Strait Islander activists and their allies organized around radio and music production, producing media in forms of oppositional political activism and creating the historical conditions of possibility for the diverse media world that one finds in contemporary northern Australia, a world constituted by a series of Aboriginal media institutions and Aboriginal-managed media infrastructures. Today's Indigenous broadcasters include remote satellite networks such as the Top End Aboriginal Bush Broadcasting Association (TEABBA) and the Pintubi Anmatjere Warlpiri radio network, larger regional broadcasters such as the Central Australian Aboriginal Media Association's (CAAMA) 8KIN FM, and more urban stations operating under community broadcasting legislation, such as Radio Larrakia in Darwin and 4AAA "Murri Country" in Brisbane. Over the last decade this institutional field of cultural production has been complemented by a digital and fiber-optic infrastructure. Cell phone access is widespread across remote Australia, Internet-based media and tablet technologies are commonplace in Northern Territory communities, and pop music from Lady Gaga to Ludacris can be heard on phones and boom boxes throughout the North. This is a complex sound world by any reckoning, shaped by the musics and material culture of contemporary audio media, but it remains one to which a series of Aboriginal-run media institutions are central. These have a long history as sites of political activism and have encouraged the growth of a significant Indigenous music industry; as places in which people reflexively attend to the voice both discursively and through practical work on wired sound, Aboriginal radio stations and music studios foster an appreciation of music and voice both as a social fact—emerging from distinct Indigenous expressive traditions and histories of colonial relationship—and as a technical one, amenable to extensive manipulation and refinement. This contemporary media infrastructure thus entails forms of voice consciousness to which audio technologies, governmental institutions, and Indigenous political action are central.

The following chapters explore this mutual involvement through a series of ethnographic and analytical questions: What are the particular musical, historical, and institutional routes by which sound and the voice have come to play such primary roles in the lives of Aboriginal Australians? How has mediatized sound become a stage for intra-Indigenous political life? And why might such sound so powerfully attract governmental efforts to resolve a supposed Aboriginal problem? What is at stake for Indigenous Australians and for the state itself in producing the voice in northern Australia? How, that is, do contemporary concerns with voice and voicing draw together the distinct, frequently agonistic interests of Aboriginal activists, cultural institutions, and the varied agencies of the settler state? To grapple with these questions is also to address the historical complexity of Indigenous media as a political instrumentality and the different metapragmatic foci that such production entails.

Three key imperatives underwrite Indigenous audio media production: giving voice, sounding black, and linking people up. These imperatives have shaped the politics of voice and expressive sound that course through media institutions and provide the key metapragmatic and aesthetic terms of debate about what audio media should do and how they should sound. The imperative that Indigenous media give voice, for instance, joins vocality to widely circulating, historically overdetermined tropes of expressive agency that rest on the powers of media to entail forms of collective or mass subject through distinctive forms of broadcast address. While such efforts to give voice have often been understood to enable agency, authority, and Indigenous peoples' latter-day participation in a settler Australian polity, they can also be figured as a key means by which the legitimacy of the Australian state is itself secured in its guise as a secular, liberal democratic, and maximally inclusive polity (cf. Batty 2005; Michaels 1994). Sounding black, however, provides instead an underdetermined rubric for both the valorization and critique of expressive speech and musical sound. Globally mobile, Afro-diasporic figures of blackness have come to resonate deeply for Aboriginal Australians. In their juxtaposition with an emergent local valorization of and metacultural concern with blackness as a signifier of Indigenous identity, these figures can elicit talk and argument about how Aboriginal music, speech, or radio ought to sound. Finally, linking up provides a locally significant gloss on the imperative that Aboriginal media must do more than represent, but also must draw together an Aboriginal public as the bearer of a new cultural future. The phrase "linking up" entails a charge in Indigenous Australia, one that draws together durable Indigenous ontologies of relatedness with the repair of relations ruptured by colonial violence and settlement. Linking up as metaphor therefore describes a pragmatic and normative, rather than representational role for audio media: Radio, music, and media activism, that is, should do something with sound, should (re)create and animate forms of relatedness assaulted and ruptured by violent colonization, settlement, and assimilationist government.

Each chapter of this book explores an expressive, technological, or institutional complication entailed by these imperatives. Throughout I seek to demonstrate how a fundamental indeterminacy in the relationship between these imperatives and the sounds of Aboriginal media can lead to reflection, conversation, and forms of intra-Aboriginal contest around the meaning and power of sound itself. These are moments in which music, radio, and the voice itself can come unstuck, when the ontological stability of both a collective subject and its expressive apparatus appear under negotiation by individuals and institutions alike. Radio and music production offer privileged points of entry, then, not only into the ways that Aboriginal people have made a cosmopolitan musical culture their own, but also into the constitution of an Indigenous historical agent through sustained, reflexive consideration of musico-vocal mediation, and through expressive work in and with sound itself. This is a story, in other words, about making audio media in Indigenous northern Australia and the imbrication of this work with modes of kinship, affect, the material qualities of phonographic and radiophonic technologies, and the shifting and imprecise attention of the settler state.

How such metapragmatic and aesthetic imperatives are translated into the sounds of radio or into musical form by Indigenous media producers can be a source of intra-Indigenous disagreement. That is, the consequences of such imperatives can be understood as relatively underdetermined, and indeed, these distinct but mutually implicated frameworks that I group together here under the rubrics of voicing, blackness, and relatedness elicit evaluative reflection in the radio and recording studio, and often work to denaturalize the collective Indigenous subject implied by particular forms of vocal expressivity. They are also a source of excess, of a fundamentally creative preoccupation with voicing that spills beyond the music and radio studio and comes to inform the historical subject of Indigenous politics as an institutional concern, its nonreducibility to the settler state conditioned not solely by a foundational alterity or ontology but by this dynamic, at times contested relation between a mediatized vocal sociality and the historicity of Australian indigeneity. What I here frame as imperatives are thus the metapragmatic frameworks by which Aboriginal producers reflect on the aims and ends of their work, how they orient and think about its value and consequence for Aboriginal communities, and how they reproduce their distinction within a broader settler-colonial society. As such, I approach these as recursive principles that feed back into the poetic contours and musical sounds of Aboriginal audio, informing those vocal and social practices through which audio media, its Indigenous subjects, and the Australian government have become entangled in northern Australia.

In Aboriginal Australia the capacity to speak is itself inflected by a charged political culture around representation. Indigenous Australian activists and the communities they have come to represent express a profound concern with who can speak. For those seeking to speak for Aboriginal communities or institutions, for instance, their authority is frequently circumscribed by a representational project and sense of obligation and responsibility toward those represented. Such relations are lent a particular charge both by the long history of colonial violence and displacement experienced by Indigenous Australians and by the frequent moments in which non-Indigenous Australians and settler governments have been heard to speak for them. This is joined by a more diffuse restraint, a performative hesitation to speak beyond one's own mob when conscious of the many and diverse people that cohere as "Aboriginal Australia." In contexts of music production, cultural festivals, and radio programs, such intensely focused consciousness around representation leads to a question: How ought such authoritative or representative voices be staged? Many of my interlocutors also ask, following this line of questioning, With what kind of voice and in what kinds of musical genres might one speak as, for, or to Aboriginal Australians? To put it differently, questions of who can speak for or as Aboriginal are also deeply tied up with questions of how one should speak, and with questions about what kinds of sounds and musics and expressive idioms ought to be considered representative, and which inappropriate or even dangerous for Aboriginal Australia. To approach Aboriginal audio media, then, is to reckon with the question of authority as a representational and political issue, but also as an aesthetic, technological, and historically durable and generative problematic as well.

On one hand, the mediatized voice can be understood as a series of sounds placed at a remove from particular bodies and social moments and put into circulation. This is a voice at once of a self and other to it, a site of technical labor and expressive virtuosity, and also an object of discourse and practical labor around which congeal arguments and debates about blackness, political agency, and representation. These sounds also resonate in more abstract figures of voice and musical genre that circulate as data and argument in boardrooms, grant applications, and governmental audits. As I suggest in chapters 5 and 6, this voice may also be elicited by the state as an index of citizenship or required by governmental powers who constitute their sovereign authority on principles of democratic participation and inclusion. And, finally, it may be figured institutionally as a commodity, an auratic figure of audience to be transacted within an institutional economy as market share.

Such forms of expressivity, elicitation, and institutional exchange course through the voice when it is made both a site of political mobilization and expressive agency by Aboriginal people and Aboriginal advocates, and a site of intense interest and investment by a range of governmental, institutional, and juridical powers. For instance, liberal forms of sovereignty grounded in ideals of democratic participation, frequently figured in terms of "voice," have in Australia come to inform broader governmental efforts to "recruit" or otherwise support the production of an Indigenous voice (Batty 2005; cf. Attwood 2004). Informed by the efforts of Aboriginal activists and advocates such as Doug Nicholls, Bill Onus, Charles Perkins, Faith Bandler, and many others, policy makers and advocates[3] in the Council for Aboriginal Affairs (CAA) sought to create the conditions through which Aboriginal participation in Australia's political life could be assured. One outcome of such aims was the legal and policy apparatus of "self-determination"—juridical instruments and commonwealth-funded institutions that over the course of the 1970s and 1980s enabled the formation of distinctly Aboriginal corporations, and funding and representative structures designed to cultivate and enable an Aboriginal voice. One of the most immediately germane consequences of these efforts was the Aboriginal Councils and Associations Act (1976), parliamentary legislation that provided the legal and fiscal infrastructure for the corporate organization and rationalization of Indigenous media production.

This shared interest in recruiting an Indigenous voice also presumed its status as medium, indexing the manifestation of both political will and subjective interiority writ large. This can be parsed more finely, even troubled by other analytic approaches to voice that historicize and its colloquial and scholarly apprehension as media. John Durham Peters's (2004) parsimonious gloss on the mediatization of voice highlights five distinct categories by which we might consider the voice a "modern medium."[4] These include the voice as a trope for power and agency; a medium for language and site of linguistic interest; an object of aesthetic interest or poetic reflection; an embodied physicality—a biological process; and a psychic object, a focus of desire and at times erotic interest.[5] My aim in the chapters to follow is not so much to add to this list as to think about how such categories spill beyond liberal understandings of voice as media, asking how these are distilled and remixed in social practice, how they are inflected, conjoined, and differently constituted across uneven relations of power and racialized privilege.[6] It is also to extend the latter figure of voice as eros back through the prior categories in order to hear in the voice a series of incommensurate state, settler, and Indigenous interests.

We can give this figure of mediatized sound and voice as a domain of shared interest greater nuance by drawing it through what Jacques Lacan (2004) termed the *objet petit a*, a concept Michel Chion (1998) and Mladen Dolar (2006) translate as that "small otherness" of which the voice partakes in forms of signification and subject formation.[7] As a historically emergent product of intertwined histories of political action, media production, and musical sociality, the voice here is neither simply transparent to relatedness nor inert, a "thing" around which separable individuals gather. It is at once an index of sedimented relations, a feelingful and charged expressive medium, an "affecting presence," and the means and ends of difficult political labor.[8] As such voice might be considered a provocation: even where it receives maximal reification or objectification, we should understand the consequential and lively thingness of the voice as a "common stumbling block" of the different institutional and Indigenous agencies for which it is a focal point, a figure of desire, or an object of work; as an opaque instigation to shared interest, it may also be a source of incongruence and differentiation.[9] As the following chapters will describe, the voice can often seem elusive, emerging in unexpected places, hard to quantify or enumerate in the small but deeply significant corners of a music recording or radio request (see chapters 2 and 3). If the particular aims of many of my interlocutors to produce the Aboriginal voice could emerge as a sedimented politics (see chapter 2), they could also seem swallowed by forms of institutional labor and bureaucratic compromise (chapter 5) and the sounded voice deferred or displaced—pushed to the future through frequent grant proposals, or figured as past accomplishment in those audits, surveys, and grant reports with which Aboriginal organizations are so often forced to contend (chapter 7).

In the chapters below I endeavor to untangle the technological, institutional, and expressive forces within this media world that push and pull at the Aboriginal voice in its mediatization, de- and renaturalizing its expressive powers in order to better understand the character of those diverse sounds and media artifacts animated by Indigenous audio media. So although the book does not venture far into a psychoanalytic field (see Gordon 1997: 41–42), it does focus its analysis on a politics of desire, aspiration, and hopeful praxis that in Australia has been pegged to the mediatized voice itself.[10] In Australia that politics takes shape in a series of historically specific relations—between kin, between institutions, between different Indigenous peoples, and between Indigenous people and the state—that are as much the subject of this text as the mediatization of sound. When I write about the particular kinds of nostalgia that country music thematizes and elicits for Aboriginal listeners, I tie that work to the crafting of kinship relatedness in the face of state discipline and administration, and when I explore conflicts between agencies of the settler state and Indigenous broadcasters, I aim to understand the ways that what exists in the world might be a consequence of what people have aspired to, what they worked together to create, even when what has come to into being can seem so very different from prior imaginings.[11] In the story I tell here, aspiration and desire, in both their fulfillment and frustration, are ingredient to the mediatization of music and sound.

The Vocal Uncanny

The deep connection of radio and recorded music with voice and affecting sound make audio media a premiere site for expressive projects that tie mediatized sound to a political project. To foreground the mediatization of voice in northern Australia is therefore both to register a globally consequential ideology of voice as index of power and self-presence and to confront a fundamental reflexivity and self-consciousness around voicing. This requires attending not only to the consolidation of an ideology of voice to which a broad scholarly literature so strongly testifies,[12] but also to the voice as sound and to its frequent de- and renaturalization in such contexts of cultural production. In these ways the voice might be approached through the figure of the vocal uncanny, a way to understand the voice as something both of and other to my interlocutors, a power at once deeply familiar but, as the nodal point of at times competing interests, also a site of defamiliarization, struggle, and unease.

My own engagement with these questions began at 4AAA radio, a hugely successful Aboriginal country music radio station in the southeastern city of Brisbane whose call sign, "Murri Country," derives from the regional and valued ethnonym for Indigenous Queenslanders. In my first six months of research I joined young Murri men and women as they underwent training in radio and music production. I found that their training, ostensibly focused on producing vocal sound for broadcast radio, included a broad range of other objectives as well. Vocal training occurred in constant commentary on recordings; in metapragmatic discussions between Aboriginal broadcasters around how they might reach an imagined Anglo-Australian listener; in technical pedagogy around the visualized sound of a digital timeline undergoing the "normalization" of audio compression; and on the telephone, learning to "speak professionally" and sell an advertising spot. In each of these different moments, the effort to produce a professional sound involved a corresponding aesthetic and pragmatic effort to produce a respectful representation of Aboriginal competence, and was also a highly technical operation, using software tools and visual icons of audio signal in a computer timeline to normalize the volume frequency of a prerecorded radio program. Here, as I detail in chapters 3 and 4 below, expressivity, technology, "blackness," and professionalism all became entangled in conversations and technical pedagogy around the voice and its relationship to the music with which it is conjoined in a broadcast. And it did so across a broad array of practices that spanned technical work, paperwork, and a lot of talk.

My young interlocutors in Brisbane in this first stretch of research spent much of their day seeking to reach others on the phone, in a production studio crafting a public service announcement, or in a classroom following the lesson plan of a technical instructor. They then documented these activities in worksheets and forms of written assessment geared toward displaying their training for governmental auditors. The voice here emerged as a goal of expressive and technical labor, a mediatized force to be audited as sound, and also an object of institutional reporting, a figure on the page. In my first months of fieldwork, then, assisting in the training of young Aboriginal men and women in producing Aboriginal radio, I was drawn to understand the voices they produced as a number of related avatars signifying, minimally, a broad Aboriginal collective subject, the institutional fulfillment of governmental requirements, and the education and capacities of these young producers. In such work, the "Aboriginal voice" was both evoked as an aim and dispersed as technological skill, expressive technique, and the abstract "product" of institutional labor and governmental investment.

In these terms the voice became layered with political struggle, with the interests of the settler state in its role as auditor, and also with a range of charged and highly valued forms of Indigenous political engagement and representational authority. In the recording studio, at the radio desk, and in the office cubicles and political meetings that mark much life in Aboriginal Australia, the voice inspired reflexive consideration and occasional unease that resonates with a series of familiar, modern figures of media's productive power, its capacity to enable forms of collective self-abstraction, to amplify senses of collective identity and political agency, and to evoke an alterity, one's "self" returned as the voice in the machine. Analytics of self-abstraction (the capacity to hear oneself as part of or membershipped into a broader collective "self") or of the uncanny (hearing a sound that is both of and other to oneself, impelling distance from the sound and that collective self) each single out the excess that media animate in social life, underscoring how media avatars may distill the relations of their production in forms of sensory engagement or spectacular object.[13]

My consideration of the ways that sounds take on such powers, however, should not be read as marking a mystically inclined Indigenous alterity. Rather, this is to reckon with the capacity of modern media more generally to spectacularize and animate objects, images, or sounds emerging from specific social relations (Debord 1972; cf. Briggs 2007). As Michael Taussig (1993) and Andrew Jones (2001) have argued, the magic of technological reproduction strongly inheres in a Euroamerican fascination with media across the twentieth century, a fascination that accounts in part for the primitivist staging of that magic by colonial powers in charged domains of the global South in what Taussig describes as a form of "frontier ritual" (1993: 208; see also Jones 2001: 11; Weheliye 2005). This overdetermined assessment of a supposedly primitive engagement with media might better be understood as a form of projection by which analysts have returned magic to media technologies by routing it through a putative non-Western alter.[14] Furthermore, in northern Australia phonographic, filmic, and broadcast media have a lengthy history prior to their deployment by Indigenous activists. Film and photography famously played a central role in frontier engagements as Aboriginal people have been subjected to regimes of cinematic surveillance and specular fascination (see Berndt 1962; Bryson 2002; Deger 2004). Beginning in the 1950s in Arnhem Land and the 1960s in Australia's central desert, Aboriginal people sought some say in the ways they were pictured by ethnographic filmmakers. Aboriginal people also have long been consumers of filmic media—theaters in Darwin and Alice Springs, as well as in small country towns and in the larger cities of Melbourne and Sydney, counted Indigenous people among their audiences from their first moments. Vinyl records and cassette tapes also circulated widely in Australia and make up a part of the material archive of Indigenous history in northern Australia. As I recount in chapter 2, country music on tape and in performance has been a marked feature of remote northern Australian life since the late 1950s, and this history of media consumption informs how people remember the past as well as how they make that past significant for present musical and other concerns. One aim of my analysis of the mediatization of sound in northern Australia is to understand this as historically contemporary with Euroamerican, so-called metropolitan histories of media consumption and thus to approach the emergence of Aboriginal media as coextensive with this longer durée, not simply emerging, ex nihilo, in the last decades of the twentieth century.

Unpacking the term "mediatization" provides a first step toward understanding the sustained reflexivity of my interlocutors in their relation to modern media and its avatars. In recent scholarship across communications, art history, and anthropology, mediatization describes a distinct form of metatheory—a way of tracking the significance of modern media's institutions, technologies, and mobile artifacts beyond or before any specific moment of reception or production (Briggs 2011; Couldry 2008; Hjarvard 2013; Schulz 2004). Here the objects of media attention do not simply exist in the world, but are in important ways made by, for, and through their mediatized circulation, taking shape in relation to media technologies, institutions, and modes of circulation as "communicable" (Briggs 2007; Briggs and Hallin 2007; cf. Agha 2011). The term can also be differently traced genealogically into literary theory and the "postmedium" moment of art critical writing (see Osborne 2013), and from there to a North American conversation around "new media." Fredric Jameson (1990) thus describes "mediatization" as a medium's awareness of itself as one component of a broader system, an insight taken up by David J. Bolter and Richard Grusin in their work on remediation (1999); that work is itself inspired by Marshall McLuhan's interests in how new media "consume" old (1964). These writings inform recent scholarship in anthropology that seeks to theorize relations between different forms of media (Gershon 2010) and between media and those other forms of social mediation with which anthropologists have long been fundamentally concerned, such as ritual, kinship, and exchange (see Mazzarella 2003, 2004).[15] In these works, media are said to "remediate" one another, to acquire their meanings and capacities through their correlation and to gain a form of self-consciousness in that mutual relation. To address the mediatization of the voice is thus to foreground the extension of the embodied, human voice into other forms and agencies, the taking of voices into circuits of transduction and circulation, and also the use of vocal sound and metaphors of voicing to figure expressivity, representation, and social power. It is to see "voice" as fundamentally preoccupied by media technologies and thus made a site of reflexive consideration, manipulation, and judgment.[16]

This dynamic of de- and renaturalization can be figured against Walter Benjamin's accounts of the aura in his widely read essays on mechanical reproduction and the history of photography (1968 [1936], 1999 [1931]). For Benjamin the auratic aspect of an original seems both to attend and to be destroyed by the advent of new technologies of pictorial reproduction and serialization—a paradox that Samuel Weber characterizes well: "What is clear in Benjamin's discussion, even if he does not say it in so many words, and what has been increasingly evident ever since, *is that aura thrives in its decline* and that the reproductive media are particularly conducive to this thriving" (1996: 101, emphasis in original). Reproducibility, in short, provokes reflection on singular things and originary moments as media supplements take on constitutive powers.[17] A similar underdetermined relation links voice and audio media. Historically durable language ideologies that link presence and interiority to speech are implicated in the anxieties surrounding the power of recording technologies to take voices from bodies and confront auditors with a form that speaks at once intimately and abstractly, unsettling the givenness of both audition and expression.

The Euroamerican history of broadcast radio, for example, is one in which radio sound has indexed a great expansion of the audible domain. In this moment radio figured as both an icon of technoscientific modernity and an occult, almost magical practice. To hear through a wireless was not simply to hear a voice or piece of music, but also to sense domains beyond the immediately perceptible, beyond the frequency range of human audition, and also beyond the parameters of human life itself. And this twinning of technology and magic, of enlightenment and the occult, suggests an aural kinship with Benjamin's optical unconscious. To listen through the ether, that is, also could mean listening to the ether, drawing on radio's auditory prosthesis to animate domains beyond the immediately sensible with desire, imagination, and anxiety such that radio signals could speak from beyond the grave (Sconce 2000; Sterne 2003). Radio's early static and hiss also could index affective, seemingly opposed experiences of a newly audible mass public—both the claustrophobia of being immersed in an unimaginable crowd and the loneliness of great distance, of a vast and shared isolation (Sconce 2000).

This focus on perception receives a different emphasis in analyses that background reproducibility in favor of prosthesis and affordance, describing the ways that media extend the senses, becoming submerged within the sensory horizon and field of agentive possibility this can entail. Friedrich Kittler's writings build on Heidegger to describe the imbrication of radio technologies with Euroamerican perceptual horizons, suggesting that radio's uncanny magic quickly receded to the limits of awareness as broadcast technologies were naturalized as a technical accomplishment, transparent to their content. Radio, that is, allowed—or, better, demanded—a new kind of hearing. Kittler draws on Heidegger's brief references to radio in *Being and Time* to describe radio's spatial magic underscoring how remote things can become "ready to hand" by means of broadcast technologies (see Heidegger 2008 [1962]: 140). "With the radio, for example," Heidegger writes, "Dasein has so expanded its everyday environment that it has accomplished a de-severance of 'the world'" (1962: 140). The world is at once closer, yet also set at a remove as an object toward which a subject may act. Radio here typifies for Heidegger a modern sensory prosthesis with reflexive consequences for the constitution of the modern subject (Heidegger 2008 [1962]: 141). Heidegger's subsequent discussion of eyeglasses makes this proposition of technology as prosthesis more clear: though perched on one's nose, they disappear, making the distant wall available to a myopic subject. Just so for radio, insofar as it makes far-removed sounds seem themselves closer to hand than the very receiver that brings them close, which for both Kittler and Heidegger serves as more an affordance for being-in-the-world than a focus of attention.[18] The mediation of sound thus disappears to the extent that audio media themselves are naturalized as transparent, technological prostheses—less magic, and more machine.

Yet such figures of the transparency of radio sound and the backgrounding of mediation that it can entail are consistently problematized in Australia by an institutional politics of representation and forms of pedagogy around the voice in radio work and sound engineering. The mediatized voice is a lightning rod for talk and reflection about cultural authenticity, appropriation, expressivity, and agency. It is also a site of expressive virtuosity and technical expertise. And its metaphorical resonance means that voice can stand for the sonic, even visual representation or pragmatic locution of an Aboriginal collective subject—voice becomes avatar here, its doubles encountered across a range of media forms: images of singers, numbers in an audience survey, and even, or especially, in the visual representation of sound displayed in a graph of tonal values at a digital audio workstation. To this we must add recorded voices, the voices of radio DJs, news stories and analysis, as well as the sounds of song—traditional and commercial alike. And finally we might include the numbers of an audience survey or the sociospatial representations of broadcast signal on a radio station's promotional materials. In Australia audio technologies rarely vanish to the voices and agencies their mediation supplements, and this productive capacity of media, its power to occasion concern with the ontology of its referent, is at times itself in the frame.

In Australia producing the voice as recorded and broadcast sound has led to a conjuncture in which specific voices must become aware of themselves as instances in a broader system of mediation, and as such susceptible to logics of remediation. Such remediation can be formal, evidenced by the aesthetic form of an expressive or media practice as it takes the shape of another media, one homologous or alike in some way. It can mean the ways a particular media becomes the content of another, such as when music is made into film, or singing voices animate the apprehension of still images, or it can be a form of media ideology in which the way one uses or thinks about a particular form of media derives from a relational, multiply mediated environment and the social and cultural protocols that inflect the valence of their relationship to one another. Finally, that awareness can extend to arguments about the ways that media might remediate social phenomena that historically have not been seen as media per se, such as kinship (chapter 1), ritual (chapter 4), or the voice itself (chapters 2 and 3).

As I detail in later chapters of this book, the voice in northern Australian media production must also be understood as an object of institutional desire, a site of governmental interest, and the raison d'être of a broad range of broadcasting institutions, funding bodies, and governmental departments. I thus approach the voice in such domains at once with attention to its embodied expression, its mediatized transduction as radio or musical sound, and the power of its varied avatars in the institutional labor dedicated to cultivating, soliciting, or eliciting an Aboriginal voice. Surveys and seminars, audits and governmental policies all come to evoke and set out the voice as both a power to be reckoned with and a quality or quantity to be reckoned, an object of bureaucratic desire and a focus of frequent enumeration and statistical characterization. And in the context of such different interests in sonic media, encounters that empower are tempered by encounters that evoke unease. Indeed, what Mladen Dolar terms the "bare life" of voice, itself evoked as a possibility by the voice's mediatization, can seem swallowed by these different technical and institutional apparatuses and their avatars as quickly as it becomes apparent. The successful self-abstraction of Indigenous belonging by means of such indices of indigeneity, then, may be accompanied by encounters with a vocal uncanny, ghosts of power or phantoms of the state shadowing the mediatized voice.[19] One of the primary arguments of this book, then, is that the "ideology of voice" that one encounters across northern Australia, and perhaps across much of the world, must be drawn through audio media's power to both amplify and unsettle the voice and the character of its bearer.

Sounding Black

Conversations around the voice and its avatars are also implicated in a local concern with what blackness itself ought to sound like in this particular, Aboriginal place. Blackness is a historically variable, charged racial ascription in Australia. Its targets have been vilified, policed, and dispossessed on the basis of an ascribed racial difference that has been marked (in part) by skin color and by efforts to reckon degrees of distance from a putative "whiteness." Over the course of the twentieth century, however, this ascribed and stigmatized category was refashioned and revalorized, upended to become a point of pride and belonging, a resource in political struggles over rights and recognition. Writers, activists, and historians such as Kevin Gilbert, Oodgeroo Noonuccal, and Gary Foley embraced blackness as a necessary aspect of Aboriginal identity and political power. Gilbert in particular, a playwright, novelist, and poet, gave literary form in works such as *The Cherry Pickers* and *Black Like Me: Blacks Speak to Kevin Gilbert* (1977) to an experience of blackness that both decried the racism of a broader settler society and celebrated the particular experiences of black Australians across the continent, building on the foundation of an ascribed racial category the ground of a shared identity. In Gilbert's plays, poetry, and nonfiction writing, the experience of racializing subjugation became the crucible for a collective subject amid the diversity of Indigenous Australia. Such works participated in a broader, cosmopolitan diaspora inflected by the thinking of Frantz Fanon, the Black Power movement, and the successes of American civil rights activism. The activism and exploration engaged by Gilbert, Noonuccal, and others might thus be understood by reference to a kind of antipodean "double consciousness" (Du Bois 1903; Gilroy 1993), with which I gesture here to a form of self-reflexivity that recognizes a racial identity ascribed through settler-colonial rule and turns this racialization on its head by way of a cosmopolitan identification of shared subjugation, a manifest assertion of solidarity and identity with the Black Power of North America and anticolonial movements of West and South Africa (Attwood 2004).

The founders of Sydney's Radio Redfern, a station I introduce more completely in chapter 4, thus placed themselves at the vanguard of Australia's anti-apartheid activism, seeing the extension of welcome by the Australian state to the South African rugby team, the Springboks, as turning a blind eye to the violence of South African apartheid rule. Tiga Bayles, Radio Redfern's co-founder, recalled funneling into the stadium in a small crowd of activists, sitting in the bleachers and unfurling placards condemning the actions of South Africa's apartheid state. They were greeted with racializing insults and aggressive police, and ultimately helped occasion a government-imposed state of emergency that sought to quell Australian anti-apartheid activism.[20] Such world historical events arrived in Australia through forms of mass media, galvanizing Aboriginal activism around a transnational movement and asking people to reckon their own situation by reference to broader, global dynamics of racialized rule. The global character of anti-apartheid activism and the Australian resonance of American Black Power and civil rights movements, that is, have long informed Australian efforts to reckon race beyond what Fanon called the "double narcissism" of a racialized dependence of black on white (2008 [1952]: xiv); to embrace blackness as a shared, structured aspect of diverse Aboriginal and world historical situations, and to seek remedy for those situations.

One can understand the possibility of such contestation and identification in terms sketched by Cornel West (1990), Paul Gilroy (1991, 1993), and Stuart Hall (1993). Focusing in particular on what Gilroy famously terms the Black Atlantic, these scholars tied the emergence of blackness as a global cultural value to three coordinates: the displacement of "high cultural forms" and a European Enlightenment inheritance as universal models of culture; the emergence of the United States as a global political power in the post–World War II period and an associated shift toward the United States as a global source of cultural production "in its mass-cultural, image-mediated, technological forms" (Hall 1993: 104); and finally, and critically for this book, the decolonization of the Third World and the broad attraction and publicity that accrued to the civil rights movement, Black Power, and forms of stylistic Afro-centrism.[21] Aboriginal political struggles, most frequently understood through the lens of a global movement toward Indigenous rights, must also be understood within this global moment of postcolonial struggle in its mediatized constitution. What this broader framework has brought to the mix in Australia is the centrality of colonial legacies and postcolonial relations to a range of musical cosmopolitanisms, the inversion of racial dichotomies, and the awareness of whiteness as itself a historically unmarked but powerful racializing category (see also Warwick Anderson 2006).

This matters in distinct ways in relation to sound, sound recording, and radio. Musics coded as black have been a central feature of both sound recording and radio since its inception. John and Alan Lomax not only took sound recording gear across the United States, recording and revalorizing the musics of an American racial underclass; Alan Lomax also brought "black sounds" to a national radio audience beginning in 1939 (Szwed 2010). The first popular musics, first sound film, and early national radio audiences were in part constituted around the sonority of black voices, then understood as favored by emergent technologies of audio reproduction (Donald 2008; Weheliye 2005). Critical theoretical scholarship on the history of sound recording technologies thus suggests that forms of black cultural production have shaped Euroamerican understandings of audio technology, even as they have often been staged as each other's antithesis (Taussig 1993). Of equal importance, those same technologies quickly became part and parcel of a broad range of black cultural production itself, instruments in musical counternarratives of a black future.[22] If the history of audio technology builds on a foundation of racial presupposition, such technologies acquire unforeseen life in the futurist composition and improvisatory bricolage of racialized peoples. They find their apotheosis, one might say, in their redeployment in the "cut 'n' mix" of diasporic musical culture and in the compositional practices of a black avant-garde.[23]

Much of the scholarship describing and exploring such relations between race, sound, and audio technology has been manifestly concerned with a geographically distinct Afro-diasporic cultural formation, a "sonic afro-modernity" (Weheliye 2005), its improvisatory bricolage (Hebdige 1987; Veal 2007), and the signal dilemmas that diaspora and minstrelsy present to the diverse communities constituting the Black Atlantic (Gilroy 1993, 2010; cf. Edwards 2004). This powerful critical historiography, however, does not apply transparently to an Australian embrace of black popular culture. Many of my Australian interlocutors identify themselves as "black but not African," seeing the many similarities in their experiences and collective history with racialized populations across colonial domains yet also questioning the relevance and ubiquity of Afro-diasporic cultural forms across Australia. As I describe in chapter 4, the tension between a racialized identity as black and the firstness and distinction of indigeneity, alive in the political reflections and strategies of activists through the 1960s and 1970s, were swayed toward the latter in the tenor of public discourse and activist endeavor beginning in the early 1970s. Yet the powerfully attractive, exciting images and sounds coming from North America, South Africa, and the Caribbean all sounded as strongly for Aboriginal Australians through the 1960s and 1970s as they do today and often give form to the ways that technology itself is understood as musical instrument or to how the voice should sound, how a song ought best be sung. In dialogue with scholars who have traced the resonance of African American expressive idioms beyond the communities of a contemporary Black Atlantic and into China and Japan,[24] this book thus explores the emergent significance of blackness as a musical sign of value and power, an aural and actual embodiment of revalorized alterity with resonance for my interlocutors, and a deeply felt problematic that draws together race, sound, and relatedness across what might be termed a Black Pacific.

To return to the events recounted in my prologue, when Jessica Mauboy sings soul and R&B musics in northern Australia, she is heard to overtly perform blackness as a positive facet of her own and her Northern Territory audience's shared identity as "blackfellas" in a settler-colonial Australia, but also to take a position within Australia at the popular musical vanguard as a commercially viable representative of an antipodean soul tradition. In Australia, country music has for decades stood as the paramount, iconic genre of Aboriginal popular music—singing powerfully to Aboriginal people, resounding on radios, and dominating request programming and performance practice. More recently, musical genres of R&B and hip-hop have joined country as a means to link up with peoples elsewhere, to perform blackness as a positive value against a long history of racial vilification. In 2004 and in the Northern Territory, Mauboy could do so both with a country cry-break against an acoustic guitar or with the wide vibrato and creaky voice of commercial R&B—and each generic musical signifier could also cross over from a politicized, affecting performance of blackness and indigeneity for an Aboriginal audience to a broad, commercial and white audience in Australian cities and suburbs around the country. Yet in the studios and radio stations of Aboriginal Australia, as I describe in more detail in chapters 2 and 3, the broad challenge to country music by more overtly "black" musics of soul, hip-hop, and R&B has not proceeded without comment. While one radio host at Sydney's Koori Radio argued that black music speaks to a black experience, and embraced the musics of Africa, America, and Australia alike as speaking equally well to the experiences of Aboriginal people, other music and radio producers in Queensland argued that such musics participate in the racialization of

Aboriginal people—and that their efforts should instead be toward underlining the history of colonization and dispossession, to foreground the particularity of Indigenous historical experience and expressive tradition. We move further away, then, from the sensory prosthetics of Kittler et al., to understand audio technologies in Australia as always already problematized by a politics of sound.

Linking Up

The mediatization of voice and the imperative that audio media sound black both attend historically overdetermined and highly charged concerns with relatedness that I gloss here as the third imperative underwriting Indigenous media production as political praxis: that such media "link people up." In Aboriginal Australia linking up means more than simply making a connection; it evokes a profound suturing and repair of ruptured social relations. Its historical resonance rests in the ways it has come to signify bringing families together who had been separated by colonial violence and the predations of an assimilative state. The phrase itself comes from efforts to identify and reunite children and families forcibly separated when children were placed in homes and missions, taken from their families and communities as members of what has come to be known as the Stolen Generations (Read and Edwards 1989; cf. Attwood 2004). The premiere organization responsible for much of this work and for publicizing and advocating on behalf of people affected by these policies was called simply *Link-Up*, and this now names a national network of organizations dedicated to assisting people who have been separated from their families and communities.

One must also situate linking up in terms of a historically durable Indigenous understanding of and value in relatedness more generally. Relations that anthropologists figure as kinship are a foundational a priori in much of Australia and provide a normative charter for both intrahuman and human—nonhuman relations, linking people to one another through country and its nonhuman inhabitants as well as through geological formations, aspects of climate and seasonal transformation. Across Australia, that is, kinship reckons social relations and ties those relations to forms of cosmogenic authority and ancestral precedence. Kinship also provides a foundational icon of Aboriginal difference within settler-colonial society, a means by which Indigenous people valorize and understand their distinction from others, as a people who "have kinship." As I detail in chapter 1 this adds considerable weight to historically charged desires for reconnecting people profoundly impacted by colonial settlement with their kin. To see in media an imperative to "link up" is thus to underscore a further, overdetermined site of political and affective investment in Indigenous social priorities, one drawing on but not reducible to durable Indigenous Australian forms of "relational ontology" (Myers 1986; Poirier 2008; cf. Strathern 1988).

In these terms, linking up has been about reestablishing the founding ties of a kinship polity, bringing people back to their families. As I discuss in chapter 1, linking up is the master trope for media as a political and social instrumentality. By linking people up, radio and other forms of Aboriginal media put parents and grandparents into connection with children, link incarcerated men and women to their communities and kin groups, and create a broad, intimate public around a powerful, historically resonant figure for kinship connection. But media production also links up producers from urban, southeastern cities with northern remote and rural towns and communities. Linking up, that is, tropes the broader cohesion of an Aboriginal public in a historically charged, value laden form. This effort has been a constant across diverse forms of Aboriginal media work, and was given poetic form by Aboriginal poet Oodgeroo Noonuccal in her "Black Commandments." One of these commandments, the imperative to "gather thy scattered people together," amplifies this metapragmatic norm in poetic form, lending it weight as a kind of sedimented social history.[25]

Understanding the particular overdetermination of this value of linking up means broaching the broader history within which media has served as a premiere site of cultural activism that brings together an endeavor of representation with one of pragmatics, a performative effort to reanimate relations torn by settlement and colonial policies that quite literally took children from families and broader kin and clan relations. By the close of the 1980s, music and radio production were widely understood as powerful instruments for political liberation, a means to "take voice" and achieve self-representation by Aboriginal cultural activists. Aboriginal producers and activists found such ideas through their partnership with peace activists and were encouraged by the experience and writings of the Italian anarchist radio movement. Engaging with the progressive political scenes of the day, Aboriginal activists sought to make such ideas about public intervention and civil rights activism work in changing their position in Australia. Much of how Aboriginal media have come to matter are directly related to this overtly political and anti-colonial project.

Perhaps the high water mark of this instrumentalization of audio media as central for a liberatory, Aboriginal politics occurred in 1988. Over the preceding two decades media technologies had taken a central place in forms of anti-racist, Aboriginal activism across the southeast of Australia. In Sydney, Auntie Maureen Watson and her son, Tiga Bayles, began in the early 1980s to ally themselves with peace and queer activists on a local community station, Skid Row Radio. From an initial several hours a week on Skid Row, Auntie Maureen and Tiga managed to secure an independent community license for a dedicated, Indigenous station, called Radio Redfern and located in the urban Aboriginal community Redfern. In 1988, Sydney Harbor provided a stage for confrontation as the commonwealth staged a symbolic reenactment of the arrival of the First Fleet, a confrontation to which Radio Redfern was central. For Aboriginal activists, to celebrate the settling of Australia meant a radical erasure of their experience and the violence of colonization that accompanied the First Fleet. Activists gathered in their thousands around the shoreline of Sydney Harbor in protest. And they also took to the airwaves, broadcasting from a Redfern terrace house that doubled as a hostel for people traveling from other cities and towns. Radio Redfern is today remembered for the ways in which the space of its studio acted as a kind of meeting point for Aboriginal people coming from outside of Sydney to demonstrate, and for the ways in which its sounds spoke of and to a collective political subject. Radio Redfern's signal consisted of black music, telephoned requests, and topical interviews on the politics of the day, and its example continues to provide a template for activists and advocates of how Aboriginal radio can bring together voice, sound, and black politics in ways that reshape public discourse about Australian history and the place of Aboriginal people in a more just Australia, and do so in a way that is also maximally efficacious in bringing Indigenous Australians together, moving listeners both affectively and quite literally, bringing bodies onto Sydney's streets.

While stations such as Radio Redfern were staging forms of urban political action, more remote communities and smaller towns in the North and West witnessed other forms of radio activism. In the central desert and northern tropics activists were beginning to make radio and video that encouraged the ongoing use of local language, and that sought to counter the threat of cultural imperialism, largely through the imposition of a satellite footprint that threatened to begin broadcasting television and radio from Australia's settler-colonial media industry and, more alarming at the time to all concerned, to begin broadcasting American soap operas and mass cultural commodities.

In the Northern Territory, Indigenous media organizations have been supported most frequently by commonwealth funding and been run by Indigenous and Torres Strait Islander cultural workers who answer to a governing board of remote community Indigenous elders. In these terms, Aboriginal media production has often emerged as a form of cultural brokerage, advocacy, and/or Aboriginal representation in a doubled sense—both in the sense in which representation entails a kind of political advocacy, by and on behalf of Aboriginal people with respect to non-Indigenous interests, and in the sense that representation entails the production of representations—textual, visual, performative, sonic, or other forms by which Aboriginal people can also represent themselves to themselves.

This representational project has been not only concerned with intervening in dominant representations of Aboriginal people, but has also been about building linkages between urban and remote Aboriginal communities.[26] In her account of Aboriginal film and video production, Aboriginal academic and activist Marcia Langton notes the heterogeneity of Australian Indigenous experience, and suggests a corresponding diversity in the kinds of media that might be termed "Aboriginal" (1993: 11; cf. Ginsburg 1994, 2012). Langton's discussion puts this diversity in historical and political terms, drawing out the ways in which relatively remote and relatively urban Aboriginal people have been set on different cultural paths by historical circumstance with respect to the trajectory of colonial settlement, by policies of assimilation that aggressively removed and resettled so-called half-caste children, and by their ongoing differences of location in relatively urban, suburban, rural, or remote communities. For example, Indigenous populations in urban northern Australia include members of the Stolen Generations and their children, forcibly relocated to an array of missions and camps during the first half of the twentieth century. They also include what Peter Sutton (2003) has termed "families of polity," extended families with locally recognizable claims on what have become "settled" Australian urban and town spaces. Alongside these networks of extended families, individuals from rural and remote groups move through cities and towns, visiting kin in boarding schools, prisons, and hospitals, and perhaps also looking for the excitement of shared grog and the diversions that urban Australia presents (Fisher 2012, 2013). These differences in Indigenous social experience have been central for the politics of identity and kinds of cultural difference that inform Indigenous cultural activism in Australia and are also key features of media work and the field of cultural production within which such work occurs. From its beginnings, then, concerns with the impact of media on the ability of Aboriginal people to control the means of their own cultural reproduction have been joined by practical efforts to craft not just a power against the state, but also relationships across forms of intra-Indigenous difference.[27]

These kinds of Indigenous difference, however, are highly politicized in Australia and have been amplified by vexed efforts to entitle Aboriginal people on principles of their cultural alterity and firstness with respect to the settler state. Regimes of land rights and native title are only the most prominent of a range of governmental measures that seek to empower Aboriginal people but which also must discern those Aboriginal peoples who can be entitled—leaving many doubly deracinated by rubrics that can seem, by politicized criteria of authentication, to reaffirm the dispossession and displacement of colonial settlement (and this often despite the express intentions of the architects of these legal regimes to enable Indigenous entitlement and recognition). Much analysis of these dynamics emphasizes the significance of state practices and legal regimes (see Gelder and Jacobs 1998; Merlan 1998; Povinelli 2002), but the complex process of adjudicating cultural difference cannot be reduced to juridical recognition (Fisher 2012). In the first instance, cultural recognition in practice entails a degree of indeterminacy as Indigenous people face several competing regimes of recognition in the forms of land rights tribunals, education systems, sacred sites authorities, and the juridical instruments of land rights tribunals (Povinelli 2006). Such recognition also enters into and inflects a world cross-cut with a range of Indigenous identities and social groups. It is not merely the state that legitimates and constitutes forms of Aboriginal identity—indeed, for many people it is the recognition of neighbors, extended kin, and others that matters for their self-understanding, their performances of identity, and their legitimation as black people, as Indigenous Australians, or through forms of localized language, clan, or "tribal" identity such as Yolngu, Arrernte, Burrara, Larrakia, Warlpiri, and so on (cf. Dussart 2004; Fisher 2010, 2012).

The benefit of placing such observations beside audio media and its metapragmatic entailments in northern Australia is that these can cast light on the ways that mass-mediated Indigenous public culture has created possibilities for intra-Indigenous forms of relatedness and recognition. "Linking up" also brings media producers into sustained, meaningful relationship with remote communities and a range of Aboriginal peoples across Australia—surmounting the kinds of difference amplified by uneven, at times divisive forms of cultural recognition and entitlement. One entailment of this effort to link up and "cross borders" (Ginsburg 1994) has been to enable what I have come to understand as an intra-Indigenous cosmopolitanism—an interest in and valorization of relatedness across forms of localized identity (see also Beck 2010 and Werbner 2008). As will become evident, this diversity within Indigenous experience and the cosmopolitanism of many Indigenous people inflects both the cultural poetics of audio media and the intercultural and intra-Indigenous relations that motivate such media's production.

A Mediatized Cultural Poetics

> Here's a song, here's a song you can listen. You mob listen! Here's a song, I'm gonna request it myself. I'm gonna request it for all the Barunga council, for all the Barunga people who works hard for doing this. Thanks to them. And I'm going to sing this song for all the Barunga staff that works, from shop, to school, to plumber or whatever. Here's a request for you, that always ask me for smoke, and I say *Yaka Bayngu*! Means "nothing!"
> —GEORGE BURARRWANGA, Barunga festival music stage

A recorded performance of an Aboriginal rock band at Barunga's popular cultural festival, repeatedly broadcast on radio across Australia's Top End, provided my own (often very loud) opening onto some of these issues. In 1999 a radio and recording crew from the Central Australian Aboriginal Media Association (CAAMA) traveled north from Alice Springs to Barunga, the same small Aboriginal community about an hour southwest of Katherine that I visited with Laurel, Donna, and TEABBA in 2004. Once there they set up microphones and recording gear, much as TEABBA would do five years later, and taped the music performances taking place on the Barunga stage. Alongside the Hermannsburg Choir, the Letterstick Band, and Lajamanu Teenage Band, the Warumpi Band took the stage with its iconic, guitar-focused sound and its legendary front man, George Burarrwanga. Burarrwanga is often recalled as the Mick Jagger of Aboriginal music, a captivating, energetic front man for Warumpi's loud shows whose stature has not diminished since his death in 2007. He began this performance with the shouted request and command that is this section's epigraph. "You mob listen," he yelled, hailing an audience made up of local Aboriginal people, Aboriginal and Torres Straight Islanders from other parts of Australia, and a sizable non-Indigenous crowd. He was also, crucially, addressing a radio audience—speaking and singing to a wider, nonpresent "mob"—the listeners to CAAMA, TEABBA, and 4AAA. To do so

George draws on the most highly marked form of radio speech, the radio request, and dedicates his song to the Barunga people, its council, and its staff: "You mob listen! Here's a song, I'm gonna request it myself. I'm gonna request it for all the Barunga council, for all the Barunga people who works hard for doing this. Thanks to them."

On the recording "Yaka Bayngu"'s shouted verses also echo a radio DJ as George narrates his travels from Darwin through Katherine and out to Barunga. Each stanza ends with a declamation caught between singing and shouting, "Yaka Bayngu!"—"No, nothing!"

> I arrived from Darwin last week, on the bus from Darwin. And you know, when you're on the bus or in the bus, you're on the road, you don't smoke do you? You can't smoke in the bus, hey! Well, I have to wait until I get to the Katherine terminal and get out and have a smoke. And there's some people there sitting down! [I've got] one package. They asked me for smoke and I said, I turned around, and I said, [Guitars begin] "Yaka Bayngu!"

Burarrwanga's *Yaka Bayngu* is a phrase in Yolngu Matha, a language spoken by Yolngu people of northeast Arnhem Land and George's own first language. *Yaka Bayngu* combines a simple negation, "no" (*yaka*), with a noun, "nothing" or "none" (*bayngu*), that together can be glossed simply as an assertion, a "no"—as in one sense it does in the song lyrics as Burarrwanga responds to a request for smokes with a negative. But here he does something a bit more complex, avoiding a flat-out refusal by dissimulation—not "no" but, rather, "No, I haven't got any." Nonetheless, he ends up sharing those cigarettes in the second stanza, where George describes giving them away.

> Well, I gave them [cigarettes], and my packet got empty. I went across to get orange juice. And I went and got orange juice, and there's a mob of people just behind me looking at my hands. They ask me for money. "Hey, can you give us one dollar, we chuck in for cask." And I turned around, I said, [guitars begin] "Yaka Bayngu! *Rupiya* [Money]!"

His *Yaka Bayngu* is perhaps not to be taken at face value as a negative assertion, but rather as an attempt to not say no, to in fact avoid an abrupt and dispreferred negation with dissimulation. Indeed, saying no is an intensely strong, potentially relationship-ending stance in Indigenous Australia, while dissimulation is a frequently accepted and common measure of retaining both one's autonomy and one's relatedness with others (see Myers 1989; Petersen 1993).[28]

"Yaka Bayngu" can also work socially as a linguistic icon of a language group, an identity marker for Yolngu people based on the way they, as speakers of Yolngu Matha, say no. In this sense "Yaka Bayngu" works also a kind of indexical entailment of social identity, a way of identifying a social group in a heteroglossic landscape filled with other Aboriginal groups. The song thus tells a story about mobility and sociability in contemporary northern Australia, while also singing from a particular readily identifiable place. It describes the movement of a linguistically emplaced ego through a socially diverse landscape.

The song was also offered by George to parts of his audience in a kind of expressive exchange. This was a dedication, modeled on radio requests, and these often speak in idioms of kinship and familial connection across great distance. Call-in requests are perhaps the single most recognizable feature of Aboriginal radio, and on request programs songs are frequently dedicated to a long list of sisters, brothers, cousins, and extended family. Radio requests, that is, are something you do publicly for kin, and kin are those with whom you share identity. George draws on this resonance to deftly bring his audience on side.

This seemingly simple sung performance, three short stanzas that rapidly move an ego across northern Australia, is in fact dense and rich in interpretive possibility and in terms of a pragmatic, social poetics. In dedicating his song to all the Barunga people, and the staff that made the festival possible, Burarrwanga echoes a familiar language of radio requests and evokes the mediated space of a radio broadcast. But he also begins, in the stanzas, to narratively describe recognizable forms of Indigenous mobility and stranger-sociality. George's performance stands for me as an icon of the voice's mediatization in northern Australia by evoking how electronic media pervade a great range of Aboriginal expressive practice, and inform new intercultural arenas for Indigenous performance and belonging. It is radio's broad, intra-Aboriginal address and the abstraction of a kind of lived cosmopolitan sociality and the collective subject it allows that makes sense of this performance both to northern Australian and other listeners. "You mob listen" works as an icon of this mass subject, entailed, potentially, as "all one mob" (cf. Taylor 2002; Warner 2002). The performance itself remediates a musical technology, making radio's mass mediation a part of its very address, and then goes on to narrate the experience of travel and a distinct form of stranger sociality in northern Australia. That it recurs daily on radio in the Northern Territory even today, as the recording is played and replayed on air, suggests that its performance has become iconic of the public that George's musico-vocal address entails.

The recording itself is all the more significant insofar as Warumpi Band is one of the first Indigenous acts making music for an Indigenous radio public in the Northern Territory, and their music (and this track itself) continue to be in constant rotation on Aboriginal radio across the country. Warumpi Band were founded in 1980 in the central desert settlement of Papunya by Burarrwanga and Neil Murray, a non-Indigenous man from Victoria, then teaching in the community, and two other young local Indigenous men, Sammy Butcher and his brother Gordon. The band wrote rock songs in English and Luritja and was approached by CAAMA radio's Philip Batty in the early 1980s for cassettes to play on the air. Batty was then looking for music in local languages that could speak directly to their listeners and also work to keep those languages vital against the impending onslaught of commercial English-language media from elsewhere (Murray 1993; cf. Wendy Bell 2008). One could say that CAAMA and Warumpi Band's music gave each other a leg up, much in the same way that radio and popular music have been mutually implicated across the world. This has echoes in Peru, where radio stations and Indigenous musical performance are closely intertwined, both in highland community stations and in urban Lima broadcasts (Martin Barbero 1993). It also resonates in the interanimation of radio and popular musics in South Africa (Gunner 2012), and of course in Memphis, where performers like Johnny Cash, Elvis Presley, and Loretta Lynn all relied on radio airplay—as radio relied on them—in the emergent popular cultural landscape of mid-twentieth-century North America. John Szwed (2010) has recently described the centrality of radio in making folk music into popular music, and performers such as Woodie Guthrie and Burl Ives into durable icons of American Identity. Popular music and radio broadcasting have always seemed each other's historical cotravelers, each creating an important condition of possibility for the other.[29] CAAMA's 1999 Barunga recording performs this relationship in a new register, staging a public, popular Indigenous music tradition and also creating a legend of its foundation.

Listening in fifteen years later, I now hear a collection of performers and voices that have become legends in northern Australia. In addition to Warumpi Band the cassette includes tracks from the Hermannsburg Choir and Letterstick Band, as well as Saltwater Band, the Lajamanu Teenage Band, and Coloured Stone—all Indigenous rock and gospel groups whose repute has only grown with the passing of time. Today these recordings are a mnemonic cornerstone of a growing edifice of Aboriginal public culture. Indeed, rock music recordings, hip-hop battles, and country song are all marked features of Aboriginal social life in northern Australia, gathering a public around their exhortations, exclamations, and amplified yet still intimate address. And that address achieves its power by taking media into its very core, introjecting its circulation and addressee in a recursive model of its own success. Like "Yaka Bayngu," the most powerful of such work stirs listeners by calling them out and including them in its celebration of travel and a broader Northern Territory public culture.

Aboriginality and Publicity

How do such audio media build an Indigenous public for themselves? How does that potential public shape the poetics and musical forms that are made to circulate on Aboriginal radio? And what are the political entailments of these popular musics and the mediatized voices in this (very particular) place? The term "public" is perhaps dangerously imprecise insofar as it has animated such a diverse range of scholarship focused on media as democratizing forces (Habermas 1989; Calhoun 1992), on subcultural and/ or counterpublics as sites of political transformation (Fraser 1992), and on the formal, aesthetic, and pragmatic means by which media "texts" gather publics to themselves through their modes of address (Lee and LiPuma 2002; Gaonkar and Povinelli 2003; Warner 2002). The capacity of media to entail and make visible (or audible) a mass subject or collective historical agent has fascinated scholars and media producers that include Dziga Vertov and Sergei Eisenstein (Buck-Morss 1996), Frantz Fanon (1994 [1965]; see my chapter 4), Benedict Anderson (1983), and a range of developmental projects that seek to give voice to and empower marginal social groups through the development of community media (as in Freire 1973; cf. Bessire and Fisher 2012; Fardon and Furniss 2000). This scholarship is so huge, and so entwined with a range of media, cultural, and postcolonial studies as to defy reductive characterization.[30] Yet what these literatures share, to varying degrees, is an interest in the relationship between formal and aesthetic features of mediatized address and forms of historical consciousness and collective subject formation. So while it may seem so broad that we lose the specificity of Aboriginal Australian media, to consider how forms of public culture gather audiences to themselves is also to ask how their particular forms of address may entail consequential abstractions of broader social groups, audiences, or publics.

Yet in Aboriginal Australia the abstract objectification of intra-Aboriginal society embodied in ideas like "public" and public culture have emerged despite some seemingly profound ontological and cultural hurdles (see Michaels 1994; Deger 2004; Langton 1993). These hurdles relate primarily to the distinct ways that many forms of Indigenous expressive culture are decidedly not public. Proscriptions apply to the circulation of forms of secret/sacred knowledge, often figured as "law" across Australia, that have been handed down by powerful ancestral beings.[31] At once secret/sacred, indexically linked with the foundational actions of ancestral powers, and historically valued, scarce cultural property, much traditional Aboriginal cultural production has been or has seemed to be quarantined from circulation.

The ancestral precedence of such law, the restrictions on access to country, story, and lore that give it shape within and between Indigenous groups, and the frequent disregard of such restrictions by outsiders, have meant that Indigenous people have had to take great care in how they record, produce, and distribute forms of Aboriginal song and story. Indeed, many ethnographers have documented the negotiations, occasional conflict, and generally steep learning curve that Aboriginal communities have faced as forms of ritual practice, expressive culture, and design have entered into broad circulation. And instances where Western normative ideas of "public" and "publicity" run afoul of an Indigenous normative regime of restricted circulation fill the literature on Aboriginal expressive practice.[32] Yet it would be a mistake to overstate the ontological problems this represents for Indigenous people. Indigenous communities, advocates, and media producers have found a number of ways to navigate the new domains of cultural production that electronic media have opened, and they have done so in dialogue with filmmakers, anthropologists, musicologists, governmental institutions, and each other.[33]

Indeed, to stress the difficulties that Indigenous people face perhaps inadvertently exaggerates the parochialism of Aboriginal Australians, even as it is against this that so many have demonstrated the flexibility of Indigenous practices, a capacity to negotiate, even embrace change, and the profound capacity to reimagine media from the starting point of Indigenous ontologies of mediation. Images of deceased persons, references to proper names and even nicknames, restricted forms of story and totemic charter, even images of significant features of the landscape have all at times seemed obstacles that in negotiation and consultation have been turned into opportunities for intercultural communication and various projects aimed at cultural reproduction and political action.[34] And the radical circulation that these opportunities can entail has meant that some forms are reimagined as no longer secret (Berndt 1962), while others are walled off entirely from circulation—separated radically from more "public" forms of nonrestricted song, dance, and ritual expression (see Corn 2009; Toner 2005).[35] At other times, producers and local communities obscure the features of a story, providing a bare outline while keeping key details opaque (see especially Anderson 1995; Deger 2004; cf. Morphy 1991). And finally, some find in their sense of a broader Aboriginal public the possibility that ritual expression might live on as explicitly public forms of intra-Indigenous performance (Dussart 2004; cf. Berndt 1962).

While these restrictions most clearly have impacted "traditional" cultural forms, they have also been consequential for the forms of popular culture that animate my own analyses. For instance, a well-known and widespread practice with the potential to limit circulation and reproduction is the restriction on names or images of deceased persons. Some gloss this restriction as an effort to keep the spirits of deceased people from hanging around too long, causing trouble. Others will tell you that this is to keep the living from feeling the loss of kin too keenly—to see a photo or hear a name recalls that person to the living and causes distress. That such regimes are amenable to generational change (Deger 2004) and can be negotiated through forms of protocol and consultation with Indigenous communities (Michaels 1994) has been central to the participation of Aboriginal people in television production over the past three decades. And the ubiquity of preprogramming announcements on Australian television warning of the possibility that programs depict deceased Aboriginal persons is testimony to the ways that Australia's broader public culture has, in some small ways, been indigenized by media activists and Aboriginal sensibilities (see Bell 2008; Ginsburg 1997). Indeed, the Warumpi Band's front man, George Burarrwanga, was not known as such in life but instead carried a different surname. In death, his family and community recognized that his charismatic persona and musical legacy are not likely to be forgotten easily and that, as he did in life, his music, film clips, and repute will move well beyond Yolngu country and will live on in a range of media. They thus deploy one possible solution by providing an alternate name to allow us to continue to speak (and write) about Burarrwanga without referring to his name in life, thus attending both to the fact of his continued media presence and significance in a broad, intra-Aboriginal cosmopolitan North and to a normative, still valued proscription on the proper names of deceased persons.

Yet the uncertainties that can face producers when publicizing forms of secret-sacred ritual or expressive culture, with the need for repeat negotiation and discussion with regard to traditional forms with ancestral precedence, have created an opening for new kinds of popular culture to fill. Today, much of what moves people in Aboriginal Australian media are forms that do not speak from ancestral precedent, even as they traverse and reconfigure Indigenous ontologies of mediation. Forms of popular music and local voices singing in Yolngu Matha, Murrinh-Patha, Warlpiri, Pitjantjatjara, as well as in English, Aboriginal English, and Kriol (among others) occupy the airwaves, tell stories, and address a mass audience with a contemporary vernacular. They draw on electric guitars, microphones, antennae, and receivers, and on computers and software designed to manipulate and sculpt digital audio. These are forms that, like Burarrwanga's performance of "Yaka Bayngu," pragmatically entail a listening public in mixing metapragmatic discourse, direct address, and expressive sound. When Burarrwanga exhorts his audience to listen, he interpellates that diverse audience as a "mob," both presuming and entailing a valued, collective cultural subject.

Mediatized Ethnography

I want here to prefigure the spatial expansiveness that marks the chapters to follow and also to signal the diversity of Indigenous peoples, languages, and places drawn together here, as well as the different settler Australians and institutions this media world involves. I do so not simply to outline the geographically dispersed character of my ethnographic object, but also to signal the ways that my research was itself mediatized—made aware of the constitution of locales in their relation to other places, certainly, but also made aware of the doubling in sound of my own objects of interest in the interanimation of movement, sociality, and media. As Weiss (1995), Adorno (2009), and many others have written of radio and other audio media, they draw great dispersal and radical intimacy together in catachresis. We have encountered audio media's peculiar distribution here almost before we have begun, its far-flung places and different peoples drawn together around, through, and within forms of mediatized sound and intimate address. This unsettled the spatial fixity of my research, making a form-sensitive attention to media and the historicity of its movement crucial for understanding the relations and institutions I describe here. Following forms of technological connection ethnographically meant following my interlocutors' aspiration for relation; it meant traveling with people in their media work, and also following media

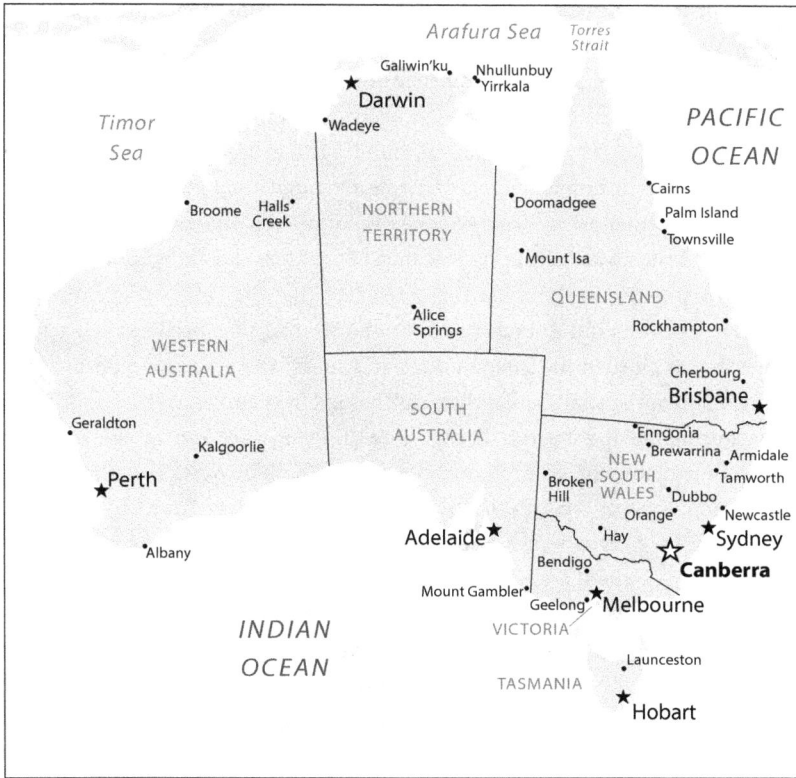

```
Arafura Sea        Torres
                   Strait
        Galiwin'ku.   .Nhullunbuy
      ★              *Yirrkala
      Darwin
Timor   *Wadeye                    PACIFIC
 Sea                               OCEAN
                                 *Cairns
  *Broome  Halls*   NORTHERN    *Doomadgee    .Palm Island
           Creek    TERRITORY                 *Townsville
                              *Mount Isa
                                   QUEENSLAND
                    .Alice
                    Springs        Rockhampton*
 WESTERN
 AUSTRALIA                                Cherbourg.
                         SOUTH           Brisbane ★
.Geraldton               AUSTRALIA      *Enngonia
     .Kalgoorlie                     *Brewarrina .Armidale
                                  NEW
  ★Perth                    *Broken SOUTH    *Tamworth
                            Hill  WALES *Dubbo
                                   Orange*   *Newcastle
                    Adelaide★    .Hay   ★Sydney
 .Albany                        Bendigo.   ☆Canberra
                    Mount Gambler*      Canberra
                       Geelong* ★Melbourne
 INDIAN              VICTORIA
 OCEAN                              .Launceston
                     TASMANIA
                             ★
                             Hobart
```

MAP I.1 Australia

forms themselves as I sought to constitute mediatization as a site of ethnographic understanding.

This meant a spatially dispersed but not arbitrary ethnographic praxis. I began research in Brisbane, the capital of the eastern state of Queensland (see map I.1). As a graduate student in New York I had seen a series of remarkable films about Indigenous activism in Australia, including Sharon Bell's documentary *Radio Redfern* (1988), whose production I describe in detail in chapter 4. The energy and anger jumped off the screen, music and talk echoing through the theater. I really needed to meet these remarkable people. In 2002 one of the DJs featured in that film, Tiga Bayles, was running a country music station in southeast Queensland. This was an urban station, a hugely successful Indigenous media project with an enormous local audience of both Indigenous and settler Australians, and Tiga allowed me to contribute my own labor to their radio project in exchange for the chance to join a group of young Murri trainees learning to produce radio and engineer sound. These students thrust themselves into a broad Aboriginal domain both literally and figuratively—literally in travel for live recording and remote broadcasts, and figuratively through work on sound, building that domain's avatar in audio media and contending with its social heterogeneity and heteroglossia, as well as its entanglement with forms of state oversight.

As I became aware of the significance of that broader Indigenous domain for media making in Brisbane I also realized that the space of my research would need to expand to include communities much farther west and north, places drawn close in the imaginations and sound worlds of my interlocutors in Brisbane, but spatially quite distant. That led to me to Darwin, a four-hour transcontinental flight from Brisbane to the very top end of the country, where I ultimately recentered my research in the Northern Territory. Work here entailed yet more travel, now alongside producers from the Top End Aboriginal Bush Broadcasting Association (TEABBA) as they maintained the technical infrastructure and social relations of a regional remote media association. TEABBA is the largest association of remote Indigenous broadcasters in Australia, both in terms of the number of communities it brings together and in terms of the geographic area and degree of intra-Indigenous cultural and linguistic diversity it accommodates. I spent a further year working with TEABBA, and this entailed many trips beyond Darwin to communities and cultural festivals: south to Katherine, a three-hour-long drive down the Stuart Highway; east along unsealed roads into communities from Barunga to Yirrkala in northeast Arnhem Land, one to two days eastward by Toyota troop carrier; and also to communities spread across the Daly River region of the Northern Territory's northwest coast, a half day's drive on unsealed roads southwest of Darwin (see maps I.2 and I.3).

These remote trips were often occupied by the routine labor of technical training and equipment repair that TEABBA engaged in as they supported the work of Aboriginal broadcasters in remote areas of the Northern Territory. Multiple languages, great distances, and movement through forms of socioeconomic and institutional negotiation are central to daily life for TEABBA's media makers and central to the sounds they produce. Although initially it seemed as though I was following a network, moving within an institutional and technological infrastructure, I came to understand this movement as an effort to trace the different vectors of Indigenous interest and governmental desire, following Sydney- and Brisbane-trained Indigenous media makers in

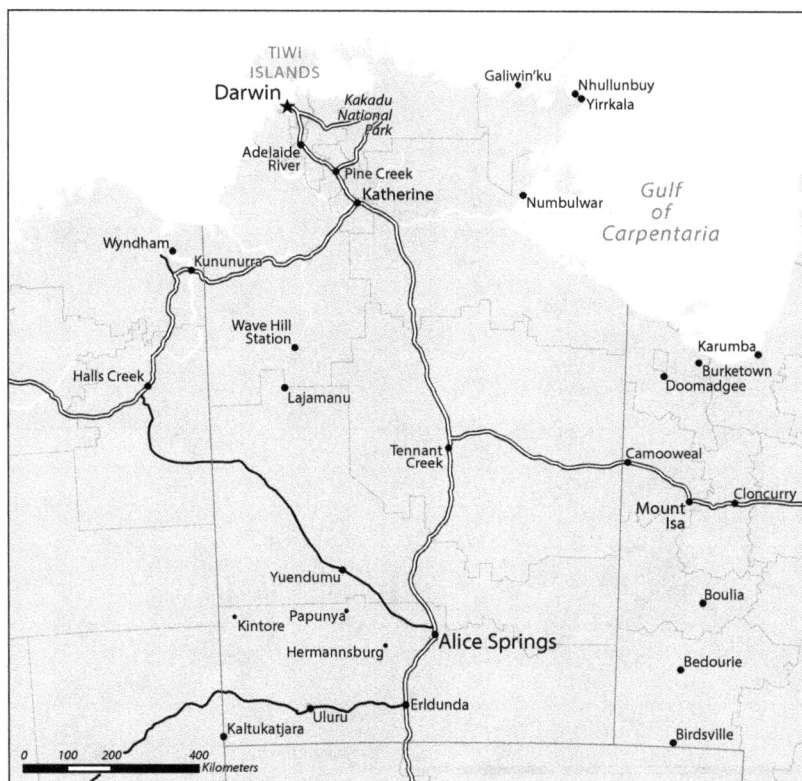

TIWI
ISLANDS
Darwin
Kakadu
National
Park
Adelaide
River
Pine Creek
Katherine
Wyndham
Kununurra
Galiwin'ku
Nhullunbuy
Yirrkala
Numbulwar
*Gulf
of
Carpentaria*
Wave Hill
Station
Halls Creek
Lajamanu
Karumba
Burketown
Doomadgee
Tennant
Creek
Camooweal
Mount
Isa
Cloncurry
Yuendumu
Kintore Papunya
Hermannsburg
Alice Springs
Boulia
Bedourie
Kaltukatjara
Uluru
Erldunda
Birdsville
0   100   200   400
Kilometers

MAP I.2 Northern Territory, Australia

their efforts to link themselves up with communities and kin groups else-where, and tuning in to the power of affecting sound itself to draw together a disparate series of communities and countries. If the book's empirical center of gravity is marked by what can seem a spatial entropy, this frequent move-ment traces the mediatization of its object.

The arguments I pursue here, then, are indebted to a series of relationships built through shared travel, shared media making, and shared listening. In other words, the ethnography from which I write is one that took place in motion together with a group of highly mobile makers of sound and media, people who understand their work as an endeavor to craft relations. By pro-ducing radio and recording music I learned something of the technical and aesthetic imperatives animating my interlocutors' work, many of which speak directly to these broader aims. And from a number of interlocutors who soon

Introduction   35

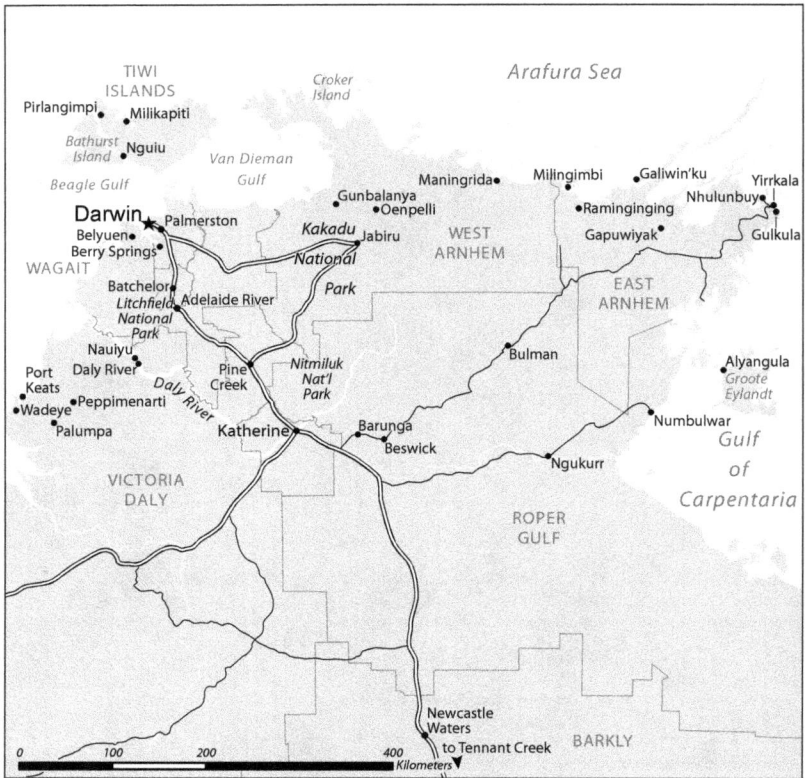

MAP I.3 The Top End of the Northern Territory

became friends I grew interested in the significance of relationship more broadly to this work, the ways in which relations are a fundamental aim of this practice, ingredient to the kinds of travel it entails and to the kinds of worlds it gathers together in sound. While I might have chosen a different way to tell this story, one based primarily in and among the producers and family groups in Darwin that I came to know well, to do so would have made the kinds of relations they embrace with other peoples across Australia opaque and would have perhaps obscured the formative, central place of mediatization to this particular Indigenous world. I have thus chosen to make mediatization the focus of my account here, one that tracks the movement of my interlocutors as tied closely to the voices they value and the sounds they set in motion.

Structure of the Book

In thinking about how to account for the diverse ways the voice is staged in Australia, about the different ways that the voice becomes preoccupied by media, and about how a series of metapragmatic imperatives inflect the mediatization of politics in northern Australia, I have been helped by the opposition Althusser stages (2005 [1965]) between Hegel and Marx and the resolution Althusser finds in Lenin's historiography. For Althusser, "expressive totality" describes the relation Hegel posits between an inward "spirit" and its expression across a range of manifestations—all of which refer back to a core "consciousness" of an age. In this perspective, famously, a unified core essence determines the shape and variety of these diverse manifestations. This is, in part, a frequently critiqued feature of cultural essentialization, and is an idea of historical process that Althusser challenges by elaborating on the concept of an "overdetermination of contradictions." This was Althusser's way of rethinking the Marxist historical problematic—understanding what it meant for Marx to extract the dialectic from its Hegelian idealist problematic. While this book does not pursue an overtly Marxian analysis of the agents of historical change, the idea of overdetermination powerfully captures the multiplication and mutual articulation (Hall 1996: 325–326) of quite diverse arenas in which Aboriginal expression and representation are problematized, and also suggests how institutional, technological, and expressive dynamics collide to overdetermine the charge carried by those avatars of voice with which my interlocutors and I are preoccupied.

This provides a way of understanding the structure of this book as well, in which each chapter pursues different arenas within a broader field of Indigenous cultural production to suggest how it is that the voice has become at once the paramount icon of Aboriginal agency yet also a site of reflexive denaturalization and speculation about such agency. Each chapter explores related institutional, performative, and historical facets of Indigenous vocal cultural production. In each I ask how my interlocutors reckon with a range of avatars of the voice, forms of sound, institutional evidence, and indices of political will. These are the ghosts in the machine that speak as an Aboriginal collective subject, and also the expressive powers retaking a media apparatus that, to borrow Samuel Weber's figure, for years "saw" Aboriginal people for a settler Australian audience, yet could not accommodate them as the subjects of such mediation itself (1996: 103–106). This maximally tropic figure of voice as power, however, is matched by an underdetermined debate that informs each chapter about the shape this voice ought to take, about who or what it might index, and how its production might proceed.

Chapters 1 and 2 begin by foregrounding sociolinguistic, expressive, and performative dimensions of Aboriginal audio media, historicizing the musical genres and forms of circulation from which it emerges. Here I describe both the deep historical purchase of commercial country music and the distinct way this provides a politicized nostalgia and affective ground for figuring the distinction and firstness of Aboriginal Australians vis-à-vis settler society. Chapter 1 describes relationships between a long history of Aboriginal incarceration, the geographic dispersal of kin networks, and emergent expressive idioms entailed by radio request programs. These programs draw together recorded speech with the spare poetics of country music to link up kin dispersed across the prisons and hospitals of Australia's North. In so doing they provide affective vehicles of an Aboriginal social imaginary, giving people the means to both entail and reflect on the value of Aboriginal cultural distinction. Request programs also conjoin speech and song, tying expressive speech to recorded musics, and using forms of intertextuality between a spoken address and a song's lyrics to affect listeners. This chapter's analysis draws on sociolinguistic frameworks of social deixis and person reference to open an empirical, ethnographic window on two interdependent axes of Indigenous radio's performative staging of the voice: its imbrication with networks of kinship relations and local epistemologies of "networked relations"; and the creative, expressive labor required to secure the immediacy of satellite radio's mediation.

Chapter 2 continues to explore the significance of country music for Aboriginal people. Here the focus turns to the ways that the genre has shifted in value from a primary domain of commoditized pleasure to an icon of a past public through the remediation of musical nostalgia in filmic and online social media. The chapter describes how country music's Australian career began in Sydney's suburban hotels and pubs, circulating through the remote communities and small towns of Aboriginal northern Australia as non-Indigenous performers sought new audiences in the bush. As settler Australian country bands from southern cities began to tour the outback towns and communities of the North, a number of Aboriginal performers themselves turned to the genre, penning songs that drew on country music's well-known pastoral tropes of loss to speak to the distinct situation of Aboriginal people in Australia. The relative ease of securing such records and cassette tapes in remote Australia also meant that country music recordings contributed to a nascent Aboriginal consumer culture in the country towns of rural Australia. The chapter concludes by arguing that country music, the first commercial music shared across Aboriginal Australia, finds new value as a sign of twentieth-century tradition in its remediation as a distinctly black music in Indigenous film and other televisual media.

Drawing on research with young Aboriginal radio producers-in-training, chapter 3 looks more closely at some of the experiential and political consequences of radio's particular production technologies. The chapter explores the ways that the digital manipulation and malleability of sound in studio production divorces the voice from any necessary relationship to speaking subjects, and describes the arguments, anxieties, and insights this has entailed for Indigenous radio and music producers at 4AAA. Here I examine regimes of vocal discipline and musical imagination as well as metapragmatic reflections on the voice in performance that these entail in radio and music production. I juxtapose two distinct idioms of vocal practice that intersect in the work of Aboriginal radio production: on-air broadcasts and the conjoined vocal and musical mediation of politically charged senses of loss they entail; and the improvisatory, verbal "battling" of Aboriginal hip-hop performance. In these domains Aboriginal radio producers negotiate multiple tensions between a practical understanding of the voice as a plastic, technologically malleable site of expressive play, on one hand, and as the foundation of Indigenous political agency, on the other. In this context I also begin to explore how the imperative to give voice informs a reflexive apprehension of the relationship between the materiality of the voice and the sociality of voicing.

Where these first chapters outline a social poetics of the mediatized voice, subsequent chapters explore its institutional production and the different forms of desire, aspiration, and political will that coalesce around understandings of voice and voicing. Most media work has as much to do with bureaucratic labor and institution building and its associated politics as it does with laying hands on images or sound. Chapter 4 focuses almost exclusively on the former and argues that it is in such institutional, often highly routinized and bureaucratic labor that the voice achieves a profound form of abstraction, reification, and a corresponding denaturalization. Empirically this chapter outlines the complications faced by an Aboriginal organization that seeks to shift the terms of its fiscal dependence on the state and its funding and administrative oversight. Education has been at once a means to secure the potential for Indigenous social reproduction, a core aspect of the station's explicitly antiracist broadcasting work, as well as a means to find financial support outside the politicized framework of self-determination. Yet this endeavor also implicated this organization in numerous additional regimes of fiscal and managerial oversight. The chapter thus outlines the complications faced by an Aboriginal organization seeking to move into a more entrepreneurial relationship to the state.

In chapter 5 the book's focus moves north to contrast the situation of 4AAA with the different circumstances facing producers in remote regions of northern Australia, focusing in particular on the work of the Top End Aboriginal Bush Broadcasting Association (TEABBA). This organization manages a remote satellite network of thirty Indigenous broadcasting facilities across five distinct language groups in the Northern Territory. The chapter describes the distinct moment in the organization's history when its producers were asked to refigure their remote Aboriginal constituents as a market under state-driven demands that Indigenous media embrace commercial modes of production. The tensions such brokerage entails become apparent in two seemingly incommensurate rituals of recognition: one a widespread ceremony that draws the media institution into the kinship and ritual circuits of remote Australia, and the other the very different bureaucratic recognition afforded by the collection of statistical data and the enumeration of listeners as market share. As TEABBA's producers were drawn into relationships figured on lines of kinship and ritual responsibility, forms of intra-Aboriginal recognition (smoking ceremonies) and governmental recognition (statistical enumeration) began to work at cross-purposes.

Chapter 6 continues this discussion, but turns to describe a range of institutional interests in their interaction. The chapter provides an ethnographic account of representational conflict between a missionary-derived radio network developed to serve the specific interests of northeast Arnhem Land's Yolngu people, and TEABBA's interest in representing a larger and more diverse number of Indigenous groups that includes Yolngu people. While the Uniting Church–funded Aboriginal Resource and Development Service (ARDS) network sought to cultivate Yolngu language news readers, to speak of broader affairs in a resolutely local register to a localized, Yolngu audience, TEABBA sought to speak in the voice of a shared regional Aboriginality— broadcasting in a mix of local languages, Aboriginal English, and standard Australian English and producing music from and for this broader population. While the politics of representation this conflict indexes had existential consequences for each institution, the terms of debate revolved around who was best able and best suited to represent Indigenous interests in northeast

Arnhem Land. How should the collective subject of those interests be drawn? And in what kind of voice should it speak?

The chapter's analysis draws on a close account of a meeting between these two institutions and a group of Yolngu people in the community of Yirrkala and focuses on the differing visions of what should constitute the "audience" for northern Australian Indigenous media—particular, individualized country and language groups, or a diverse and regional intra-Indigenous domain? On the basis of this ethnographic narrative, the chapter argues that what are often derisively figured as a problematic "black politics" should instead be understood as an index of a vibrant, increasingly complex field of Indigenous cultural production.

In my conclusion I suggest that the acute forms of voice consciousness that preoccupy the preceding chapters emerge in part from the interanimation of highly technologized expressivity and the politicized dynamics of representation and social relatedness that suffuse Aboriginal cultural production. The frequent oscillation between the de- and renaturalization of voice, a voice taken from bodies and made a focus of self-conscious speculation, institutional labor, and technological manipulation, enters here into the poetics of Aboriginal expressive culture itself and provides a rubric for understanding the radical mediatization of Aboriginal political life in the twenty-first century. That mediatization entails a doubled logic, one that produces relatedness between Indigenous Australian peoples while also amplifying reflection on those forms of alterity and distinction that emerge within this field itself.

| Mediating Kinship

Radio's Cultural Poetics

Never has there been a genuine cultural institution that was not legitimized by the expertise it inculcated in the audience through its forms and technology.
—WALTER BENJAMIN, "Reflections on Radio" (1931)

Switch on the radio, twist the dial, and tune in your local Aboriginal station, and whether you are in Sydney (Koori Radio 93.7 FM) or Brisbane (4AAA "Murri Country" 98.9 FM), Alice Springs (8KIN 100.5 FM) or Broome (Radio Goolari 99.7 FM), you'll soon hear radio requests, music directed by a caller to friends and family, often given voice by a DJ who relates their message word for word, transmitting terms of endearment as reported speech. Aboriginal Australians from across the country draw on radio to address kin with messages that bring together intimate speech and music on a public stage. On Sundays one can tune in to *The Mary G. Show* coming from northern and western Australia, in which radio personality Mark Bin Baker takes on the persona of an Indigenous auntie, Mary G., to field requests and greetings from listeners across Australia and to spin the sounds of country music and Aboriginal rock bands. Mary G.'s flirting and innuendo with male callers and her constant willingness to entertain requests and send dedications garner Mary G. a national audience, one she has cultivated through request-based programming for more than a decade. In Darwin, capital city of the Northern Territory, radio producers at TEABBA host a weekly request show that seeks to link the bush communities of Australia's Top End with the hospitals and prisons of Darwin's suburban sprawl. In southeast Queensland, 4AAA continues its long-standing practice of producing a three-hour program dedicated to requests. That program, like many others, began life as a means of allowing incarcerated Aboriginal men the opportunity to speak to their families. Such radio programming remains significant even today, when mobile phones and online social media might supplant radio as cornerstones of Indigenous communications infrastructure.

Indigenous call-in request shows are such a routine and expected feature of radio programming that they practically define the medium in Australia. These programs provide a foundational framework for audio broadcasting and, understood by their producers in terms of the kinship connection they enable, are frequently said to be the functional raison d'être of Aboriginal radio. In these terms such programs are where Indigenous broadcasting achieves what Theodor Adorno called ubiquity (2009: 93), an idea that draws together the formal, expressive standardization of commercial radio with its mediated dispersal, its capacity to be everywhere but also nowhere in particular. For Adorno this taken-for-grantedness in spatial dispersal perhaps occludes how ubiquity also depends on repetition and reproduction, and as he tropes the standardized broadcast of symphonic music against the repetition of the advertisement, both gain a kind of power in their reduplication.[1] Request programs, however, are also a place where Indigenous Australians exercise a particular expertise, in Walter Benjamin's (2015) terms, displaying a practical mastery in bending broadcast technologies to the politics of kinship. Understanding radio's significance in Indigenous lives, unpacking how radio sound comes to matter so deeply to people, depends on grappling with this imbrication of kinship and broadcasting, on understanding the specific expertise that lies at the heart of Indigenous radio's ubiquity.

The institutional and technological network such programming animates consists of sizable Aboriginal radio stations in a half dozen cities, and smaller Indigenous broadcasters and retransmitting facilities in another hundred remote settlements and country towns. And while these latter occasionally operate autonomously to produce local programming, they also link together by means of satellite networks and telephone relays, frequently convening a national, intra-Aboriginal audience for shared broadcasts.[2] On each broadcast one hears the sounds of country music; one always hears family members addressing one another as kin in requests that both evoke and transcend geographic and institutional distance; and each program relies on digital technologies of sound production and the material technology of satellite and telephone networks to shape its signal and to address a broad, intra-

Aboriginal audience. These programs address populations whose frequent movements across Australia follow institutional routes; through hospitals and prisons, government-sponsored conferences, and ritual and ceremonial gatherings, and across geographically dispersed networks of kin. And it is this dispersed, heterogeneous, and mobile population that becomes, in the address of radio DJs, "all one mob." The networks I describe here are thus less about the communication of information and more about the manifestation and revivification of Indigenous distinction and difference through the rubric of kinship relatedness, a mode of imagining mediation that has, over the past two decades, come to characterize radio itself, turning broadcasting technologies toward Australian ends. The transduction of vocal and musical sound by radio technologies accomplishes then the mediation of mediation, an amplification of kinship address and reference in a sonic, mass-mediated, densely technologized, and reflexive form.[3]

The networking of Indigenous radio broadcasters begins, however, with the sudden expansion in the 1980s of Australia's satellite broadcasting capabilities. In 1979 the Australian government established a national broadcasting company, AUSSAT. Until its privatization in 1991 AUSSAT served as the national satellite broadcasting corporation, managing Australia's investment in forms of orbital communications infrastructure. Its first satellite, the AUSSAT A1, was launched from the space shuttle *Discovery* in 1985 and commenced operations that same year, joined later in 1985 by AUSSAT A2 and in 1987 by AUSSAT A3. Together the footprint of these satellites stretched across some of the most remote and difficult-to-reach areas of central and western Australia. These events were a cause of concern in Australia, as many began to worry early on about the negative consequences that might accompany the introduction of satellite broadcasting across remote Australia, and their potential to displace local languages through English-language, mainstream Australian (and American) programming (see Ginsburg 1994; Molnar and Meadows 2001; Michaels 1994; cf. Batty 2003; Featherstone and Rennie 2011). This led to efforts to prepare and protect Aboriginal people from what many saw as a tidal wave of English-language, commercial programming that would swamp the small, localized languages and cultural practices found across the remote Northern Territory and western Australia.

The advent of satellites and the commercial broadcasting they would bring also instigated the employment of American anthropologist Eric Michaels, who conducted research with the Warlpiri community of Yuendumu in the Northern Territory from 1982 to 1986, working closely with Warlpiri man

Francis Kelly in a series of videotapes produced in accord with forms of local social organization and demonstrating how Warlpiri people might produce a distinctively Aboriginal television (see Michaels 1994; cf. O'Regan 1990; Molnar and Meadows 2001).[4] In addition, the commonwealth government commissioned a report on possible responses to the impending introduction of satellite broadcasting, Eric Wilmott's *Out of a Silent Land* (1984). As Faye Ginsburg has suggested (1993), Indigenous control over satellite networked broadcasting gained further traction in practical terms through the actions of Indigenous media activists themselves. CAAMA, for instance, then largely a radio and music initiative in Alice Springs, successfully proposed to take on regional Indigenous television broadcasting and subsequently established the Imparja TV service, while urban activists in Townsville and Sydney, whom I describe in more detail below, turned to community radio legislation to establish local, terrestrial stations and began to advocate for such control more broadly. In part informed by Wilmott's report, in part by the ongoing work of Kelly and Michaels, and in part by a series of radio and video experiments at CAAMA in Alice Springs and in community stations in Townsville and Sydney, remote Indigenous participation and production became the preferred response to these events.

Following the suggestions of *Out of a Silent Land*, from 1987 remote Indigenous communities began receiving equipment under a governmental scheme designed to counter the imposition of English-language broadcasting. The Broadcasting for Remote Aboriginal Communities Scheme (henceforth BRACS) aimed to provide remote communities with the capacity to produce and insert their own programming, lending them control over the kinds of audio and visual media their communities consumed. By 1996, 103 communities in all had received equipment including a small video camera, radio microphones, and broadcasting gear. Yet none of this gear came with training or local infrastructure, and it occasionally arrived in a remote community without any prior warning: Governmental support for the program's implementation, then, was haphazard and ad hoc. Soon, however, a new generation of satellites (the Aurora series) began broadcasting, and with the amplification of broadcast reach they brought from 1992 came a second program, the BRACS Revitalization scheme, which aimed to upgrade and repair equipment and train local people in its use. As part of this second scheme a series of eight Remote Indigenous Media Organizations were granted funding. Many of these organizations, however, had already been incorporated under the Aboriginal Councils and Association Act (1976), including CAAMA in Alice Springs, as well as TEABBA, which was incorporated in 1989 to assist remote communities of Arnhem Land and the Daly River region with training and technical support for the BRACS equipment they had begun to receive. Between the early 1980s and early 1990s, then, a satellite-based Indigenous broadcasting infrastructure took shape around Australia.

This story, grounded in technological investment, corporate institution, and governmental policy, provides one narrative through which to grasp the emergence of remote Indigenous broadcasting. And while it may be hard to overstate the impact of the AUSSAT satellite services on the worlds of remote Indigenous Australia, these developments are not adequate to account for the durability and distinction of Indigenous broadcasting in Australia, the ways it draws and holds together a technological infrastructure, an institutional network, and a series of conventions and meaningful expressive forms to which kinship has become central. This chapter analyzes this mediatized Aboriginal domain, exploring the productive interaction between these forms of satellite-networked broadcast media and the geographic dispersal of kin networks. In part, I show that radio's significance for Aboriginal people has been overdetermined by the charged value of Indigenous kinship in Australia. Following a century of state policies that removed children from their communities and families, and after several decades of activism and public debate on the meanings of those policies in the present, "Aboriginal kinship" labels a contentious, politicized focus of postcolonial governmentality and public discourse—one that for Aboriginal people raises specters of familial loss and the violent rupture of cultural belonging. As I describe more fully below, Aboriginal kinship has also taken center stage in new, publicly charged debates over how, and to what extent, the Australian state should effectively govern Indigenous family life.

Today these links are further troubled by the disproportionate numbers of Aboriginal people incarcerated in Australia's prisons. In 2004, for instance, Aboriginal people made up approximately 21 percent of Australia's incarcerated population, but just over 2 percent of its total population (ABS 2002, 2004).[5] In 2011, these numbers appeared yet more stark, with Indigenous Australians accounting for 26 percent of Australia's prison population, though now 3 percent of Australia's population (ABS 2011). A recent review by Don Weatherburn, director of the New South Wales Bureau of Crime Statistics and Research, underscores that even in an era when the overrepresentation of Indigenous people in Australian prisons is widely understood as a social justice issue and as manifestly inequitable, the numbers continue to grow:

The problem is getting worse. Between 2001 and 2011, the Indigenous imprisonment rate increased (on an age-standardised basis) by more than 51 per cent, while the (age-standardised) non-Indigenous imprisonment rate in Australia increased by less than four per cent. The ratio of Indigenous to non-Indigenous imprisonment rates rose from 10.2 in 2001 to 14.8 in 2012, an increase of more than 40 per cent (ABS 2012a, p. 56). . . . We may reasonably suppose that many of those who do not have any contact with the criminal justice system in any one year have had contact with it in the past or will have contact with it in the future. (Weatherburn 2014: 3–4)

High levels of incarceration also affect children whose parents, grandparents, or elder siblings may be incarcerated, certainly, but these levels also directly index children's own encounters with the agents and institutions of Australia's criminal justice system. Weatherburn again digested the statistical evidence:

On an average day in 2009–10, only one in every 1886 Australian juveniles (0.4 per cent of young people aged 10–17) were in custody. The custody rate for Indigenous young people (1 in 146), however, was more than twenty-four times higher than the custody rate for non-Indigenous young people (1 in 3626). In 2009–10, Indigenous young people were being taken into juvenile justice custody at the rate of more than fifty a month. As with adults, the rate of entry into custody is increasing. In the four years to 2009–10, the number of Indigenous young people sentenced to a term of detention rose by 25 per cent. (Weatherburn 2014: 6)

One consequence of the mass incarceration of Indigenous Australians can be seen in the frequent separation by both geographic and institutional boundaries of Indigenous people from their kin and communities. Such incarceration plays a large role in the family histories and memories of many of my interlocutors, and also in Indigenous expressive culture, with young men penning songs about jail time and request shows seeking to gather together dispersed family members locked away in jail. As Weatherburn also notes, such frequent contact with prisons also means that the stigma that might accrue to a stint in jail for a white Australian is much less marked within Indigenous Australia. But it is the relation between kinship and incarceration that is so important for the history of radio and that I focus on here.

Making requests (and making request shows) are cultural practices through which the work of radio and the work of kinship turn into one another. "Linking people up" is what radio is held to do in northern Australia, and as such the technology resonates with a broader, two-decades-old project of linking up families, communities, and dispersed members of Australia's "Stolen Generations": those Indigenous people taken from their families and communities and sent as children to state institutions and foster homes over much of the twentieth century. It also resonates with media activists' efforts to link up incarcerated men and women with their families and communities. The idiomatic distinctions between these different senses of "linking up" are often erased in practical terms as radio producers and listeners create broadcasts that center on connections between spatially and institutionally dispersed kin. In the course of this productive erasure, radio request programs celebrate kinship connections, while kinship itself comes to typify the kinds of immediacy, intimacy, and connection that radio enables. Kinship thus (pre)occupies radio, lending the medium value within a politically charged history of Aboriginal loss and at a contemporary moment in which linking up has taken on a value of its own that my interlocutors often felt to be self-evident.[6] In brief, then, this chapter analyzes the "comobilization" of broadcast media and kinship in northern Australia.[7] The mediatization of kinship's mediation, I argue, enables its contemporary, recursive value as an icon of Aboriginal distinction and grants its ubiquity a metacultural character.

One thread of my account here draws on the significance of kinship for the character taken by a mediatized Aboriginal social imaginary to suggest that kinship reference provides a particularly powerful metacultural language by which Aboriginal Australians both reflect on and reproduce their relationships with one another, and by which they maintain their distinction from a broader Australian society. That language is not merely given by Aboriginal traditional practice; it emerges from the intercultural, technology-rich contexts of postcolonial Australia. Another thread focuses on the interweaving of speech and song that radio production entails in order to place its affecting character and distinct poetics in social historical context. And a third, closely related thread concerns the importance for Aboriginal communities of the high rates of incarceration for young Aboriginal men and the particular, perhaps surprising responses of their communities and families to the institutional and geographic dispersal of kinship relations that this can entail. Together these provide empirical coordinates for tracing the ways that radio has been given value in Aboriginal Australia in its networked form and that kinship relatedness, as a generative cultural resource, has become newly available for the normative evaluation of Aboriginal personhood and identity.

The mass-mediated, Indigenous public culture I draw attention to is shot through with figures of kinship, amplified by historical narratives of loss and state-mandated dispersal, and given a sense of immediacy through the affective, musically framed, and nostalgic evocation of familial relations. But chock-full of commercial hits (from country music to hip-hop and R&B), featuring DJs speaking primarily in Australian and Aboriginal English, and violating the boundedness of discrete remote settlements, Indigenous radio often, paradoxically perhaps, lacks what might be termed appropriate "Aboriginal content" (Michaels 1994). In these ways it challenges the ideals of early policy makers and Indigenous media activists by embracing the commercial, often American musics that so worried early policy makers and advocates. For many activists and Aboriginal people themselves, "culture" resides in other forms—in Indigenous languages, for instance, and in those forms of ceremony and performance that are markedly sacred and were the first target of media's conservative project to retain Indigenous cultural practices rather than supplant them with commercial media from beyond Australia's shores.

These self-conscious interests in and valuations of culture have led to important, novel forms of media production across Indigenous Australia and elsewhere (Christen 2009; Deger 2006). Jennifer Deger's long-term work with Yolngu people in northeast Arnhem Land (2004), for instance, or digital database projects such as the Ara Irititja project in southern Australia (see Thorner 2010; see also Christen 2009; Christie 2008) have developed forms of Indigenous cultural protocol, aiming to grant control over the mediatization and conservation of cultural values to Aboriginal Australians themselves. Yet the forms of radio that interest me here do not transact in culture in quite the same fashion as ceremony or dreaming story or the indigenizing of a database or filmmaking relationship. As Samuels (2004) describes with regard to much contemporary Apache expressive culture, radio request programs register "Aboriginality" in ways that sidestep indexical relationships between a single, stable expressive form and any given social identity. Dependent on regional networks of Indigenous audiences, unfolding in the mundane spaces of building sites, cars, office buildings, and prison blocks, and entailing new forms of relationship between Indigenous producers and communities, Aboriginal radio has not provided objects that can be abstracted from, or easily circulate outside of, an Aboriginal domain.[8] This has perhaps contributed to the relative paucity of scholarship on Indigenous Australian broadcast radio, but it also has meant that activists and radio broadcasters have had maximal control over programming, have been able to develop this media in their own interests under legislative rubrics of community broadcasting and articles of incorporation set out by the Aboriginal Councils and Associations Act (1976), and initially, at least, were able to pursue their aims relatively undisturbed by state broadcasters or bureaucratic oversight.

Media Networks and the Public of Requests

Today TEABBA coordinates the technical and broadcast capabilities of approximately thirty settlements spread across the Top End of the Northern Territory, making it the largest such network of Aboriginal media facilities in Australia. The settlements in TEABBA's network are culturally diverse, and although the association has frequently been dominated by energetic individuals from the Yolngu communities of northeast Arnhem Land (see chapters 5 and 6), the network also includes the Tiwi Islands to Darwin's north, Arnhem Land to its east, and the communities and associated language groups of Wadeye, Palumpa, Peppimenarti, and Nauiyu to its south and west. These latter are active listeners, frequently calling TEABBA's Darwin studio with requests or messages for friends or family in Darwin.

TEABBA was established in 1989 to support Indigenous people in the use of broadcasting gear that had been distributed to remote settlements under a poorly managed governmental program, the Broadcasting for Remote Aboriginal Communities Scheme (BRACS), during the previous year. Initially an administrative, advocacy, and technical support organization, in 1994 TEABBA also developed the capability to take a radio signal from any one of its member communities and then retransmit this over satellite to all the rest, or even across Australia through the soon-to-be-implemented National Indigenous Radio Service (NIRS). In so doing, TEABBA became a de facto regional broadcasting network, joining several other such networks in central and western Australia.

My work with TEABBA involved assisting the organization of regular broadcasts from their Darwin studios, then located in one of the city's older northern suburbs, and in the production of remote broadcasts and arranging technical training in the communities that make up TEABBA's broader network. One afternoon in 2004 I was given the job of minding the reception desk. I was alone in the building with Gary Bennett, the organization's assistant manager and also a regular and loved DJ whose program *Gary's Classic Gold* was one of the mainstays of TEABBA broadcasting. During Gary's show requests came in with some frequency, called in from any number of communities across Arnhem Land, and often looking to send a song and a shout-out to someone in another community. I'd taken a few already this afternoon, writing down a message and a song title on a scrap of paper and carrying this into the sound studio. Although I had just taken a request for the Black-Eyed Peas hit "Where Is the Love" (then in heavy rotation on both commercial radio and music television), it was more usual to receive requests—particularly on Gary's show—for an Aboriginal rock or country music group, like this request from the woman who called me next.

"Do you have anything from Peppimenarti?" she asked.

"We do have a Peppimenarti CD," I responded, referring to a CD recorded in the Aboriginal community of Peppimenarti by TEABBA technical aides and an Aboriginal apprentice in sound engineering. These recordings, undertaken successfully with funding by the Community Broadcasting Foundation (CBF) of Australia in the year before, 2003, had become wildly popular in TEABBA's member communities.

"Yeah!" she responded emphatically. "Can you play number 6? That Peppi band, Peppimenarti band!"

Her enthusiastic response transformed a general request for something generically local into something much more specific: She knew exactly what she wanted played—track number 6, a song about getting out of jail and going home to Peppi—the shorthand name for the community of Peppimenarti, southwest of Darwin in the Daly River region. I moved on to the next question, which always requires an answer with respect to requests: "Who's it going out to?"

"Going out to my cousin Robbie at Berrimah Prison, at Berrimah!"

"Yeah, who's it from?" I continued.

"From all his sisters and cousins. And nephew, Tracy, and his daughter Charlene. When will you put that on? Can you mob put that on right away, please? Yeah, that Berrimah Prison one?"

Berrimah Prison is a major site of interest for Aboriginal people in the Top End, as they are brought there from across the Northern Territory on a variety of charges—for offenses often (but not exclusively) related to some combination of excessive alcohol consumption, driving, petty theft, and/or assault. In part owing to excessive policing, in part to their incarceration for offenses for which many white Australians receive monetary penalty, Aboriginal men are proportionally overrepresented in Australian prisons more generally and dominate Northern Territory prison populations.[9] So it is perhaps unsurprising that although many of the commercial recordings from the Top End evoke sounds of "traditional" Aboriginal Australia and are produced through institutional and activist efforts to foreground aspects of Aboriginal cosmol-ogy, much of the music that matters locally speaks directly to experiences of prison or is made to do so through radio requests that evoke distance, loss, and longing.

When I took this request to Gary in the studio, he said in mock exaspera-tion, "Oh no, not another one, I haven't even gotten to the first one yet!" He then commented, "That's for Friday, you know? That's for the link-up with Radio Larrakia." I didn't understand what he meant, and asked him to explain.

"That's when we link up with Radio Larrakia, when Donna does her show in town too. He can't hear it now," Gary added.

Radio Larrakia is Darwin's Indigenous community radio station, and it broadcasts solely within Darwin's city limits. TEABBA, as an association of remote Aboriginal community broadcasters, does not broadcast to the urban environs of Darwin at all except when these different Aboriginal institutions link up for the purpose of relaying requests between relations—a practice aimed squarely at bringing the Aboriginal inmates of Berrimah Prison into contact with their remote kin. What Gary meant was that Robbie, then incar-cerated at Berrimah, could not have tuned in to TEABBA's broadcast signal. On Friday, though, TEABBA's manager, Donna Garland, would link city and bush in a single broadcast as Radio Larrakia joined TEABBA's satellite-linked network. In such moments, request programs are the form by which local media recruit a broader public.

Despite the value of temporal immediacy such programming suggests, it is also important to note that had Gary played the request, some aspects of the caller's purpose still could have been achieved. As I will demonstrate more fully below, in requesting that a song be played for one's cousins or "rellies," one airs a relationship, performing it in a heightened, public context, em-placing kinship in a social, institutional, and geographic landscape. This public airing of social relationship can be fleshed out by further discussion of telephones in the Territory. Although telephones are readily accessible, Aboriginal residents of remote settlements do not, in general, have telephones in their homes. Nor have mobile phones become quite as taken-for-granted a technology in such remote settlements as they have in much of the rest of Australia.[10] When people call TEABBA to make a request, often they do so from the public spaces of settlement council offices or schools. Radio broad-casts are also heard in these council offices, or in the garages, machine shops, and other institutional spaces of Aboriginal settlements, and less frequently on a verandah or in a car. Broadcasts are also heard in the space around a remote broadcasting facility itself, which often include an outdoors loud-speaker bolted to an external wall. In general, then, radio in northern Australia is perhaps best understood as what Brian Larkin terms a "public technology" (2008: 48) insofar as the act of making a request from a remote settlement often occurs in spaces that are both electronically convened and spatially shared. The privative model of the isolated listener in a domestic space or automobile is here atypical.

Request Programs at the Advent of Aboriginal Radio

The origins of Aboriginal radio can be further parsed by sketching and drawing together two parallel narratives of radio activism and the mediatization of Aboriginal expressive culture. On one hand, efforts of Aboriginal activists to develop community radio in urban and town locations followed models of activism and overt resistance from Italy, North America, and South Africa as Aboriginal activists join forces with a broad coalition of activist movements making strides in challenging normative modes of exclusion in Australia's cities. In Australia's Southeast, Aboriginal activists began broadcasting on non-Indigenous community radio stations, often at the invitation of DJs involved in the peace movements of the 1970s and 1980s, and themselves inspired by the anarchist, oppositional politics of European, particularly Italian, free radio. On the other hand, the growth of activism and subsequently cultural policy to promote remote Indigenous broadcasting—initially within a framework of cultural survival and language maintenance—found support in governmental policy aimed at encouraging the participation of Aboriginal Australians. In relatively remote areas of Australia's North and West, and in response to the advent of satellite broadcasting across the Northern Territory, activists, academics, and policy makers saw in radio and in then-new video technologies a means to intervene in the kinds of media to which Aboriginal people would be subject. As noted above, if governmental concerns in the 1970s had to do with self-determination, by the early 1980s such concerns were focused on stemming a feared cultural imperialism, the displacement of Indigenous cultural practices by foreign (particularly American) cultural commodities.

But while these two domains—one urban, the other rural and remote—constitute seemingly distinct domains of media activism, they share a key feature in their interest in addressing incarcerated Aboriginal people. Early on radio producers in both urban and remote or regional locations began visiting prisons, making cassette-recorded greetings that could be played on air from the studios and taking telephoned requests to be broadcast into nearby jails. However, early programming most frequently was produced locally, only occasionally drawing on cassette-recorded programs distributed by the post from the ABC. It thus was rarely heard interstate as a form of "national" Aboriginal media. Aboriginal radio's expansive spatial reach began with the networking of remote broadcasters in the 1990s and with the 1996 establishment of the National Indigenous Radio Service (NIRS). These technological developments led to the possibility of national broadcast programming and mark the relatively recent arrival of a national, mediated space and the intensified circulation through Aboriginal communities of Australian, American, and Latin American media forms.

For many remote Indigenous communities the most obvious ramifications of these developments have been, paradoxically, the establishment of uninterrupted radio and television broadcasts and the organization of regional associations to manage community broadcast facilities and personnel. While policy makers hoped to replace international media signals with Aboriginal content, ironically the communications networks set up to enable this have in fact ensured that English-language soaps, pop music, and commercial advertising reach the remotest Aboriginal communities. This has fueled popular perceptions that such media have been less than completely successful in their aims, undercut further by the different channels by which commercial media—not least pornography and pop music—come to be consumed by young Aboriginal people (see, for instance, Toohey 2007). In 2004, on learning that my research was focused on the Aboriginal production of media, a local non-Indigenous Territory Government bureaucrat calmly informed me that the whole project had been a failure. All the kids listened to was rap music, he told me, and all they looked at were pornographic videos. As I note below and in subsequent chapters, some Indigenous media producers share this sentiment.

For my interlocutors, however, this perspective can seem dismissive, can seem to overlook the centrality of kinship relatedness to the project of making media Aboriginal, and this suggests thinking differently about the work of radio as a form of cultural activism and about the ways that radio can be apprehended as a condensation of family connection. In part this view of radio as an icon of kinship takes shape as nostalgia. Indeed, we are now several generations into the electronic mediation of Indigenous public culture—so far, in fact, that radio stations can be apprehended and represented in nostalgic terms by Indigenous filmmakers. Warwick Thornton's short film *Green Bush* (2005), produced by CAAMA, casts an affectionate eye on the prison request program of the same title, produced at CAAMA radio over the past two decades. Chronicling one night's broadcast, Thornton uses the request program as a frame for the relationships between the "cultural" mob who live in the camps of Alice Springs and take shelter and cups of tea in the radio station's studio, and the broadcaster, called Kenny, who is English-speaking and perhaps from a family dispersed by state intervention in previous decades.

In following Kenny through his busy night, the film speaks to the desire of many Indigenous Australians to craft such relationships, and to both the difficulties and rewards their pursuit can entail. As the film's DJ spins records and sends out requests, the station fills with Aboriginal people from around town. First one older man, friendly and clearly familiar with Kenny, appears at the door, asking for a cup of tea. Then others arrive, occasionally accompanied by small children, and the DJ finds himself as busy in the kitchen preparing tea as he is in the studio, spinning records. Eventually an older woman arrives, bleeding. When it becomes clear that her son or grandson is also her likely assailant, this greatly disturbs but does not surprise Kenny, and he calls an ambulance. In dramatizing such episodes, Thornton's narrative depicts how calling an ambulance, making tea, and convening an Aboriginal public make up the daily round of radio production, suggesting that the work of Aboriginal radio is an exercise in cultural brokerage and intracultural connection. Thornton explained Kenny's work for the *Green Bush* press release:

He is called on to be policeman, counselor, protector and cup-of-tea maker. Kenny is young and inspiring and he has to be strong and try and hold it all together and he keeps coming back despite the difficulties of the job. He gives people access to their family and friends in jail. By doing the show and linking up these families makes Kenny feel strong and links him firmly with his Aboriginality. It gives him identity within the community.[11]

"Linking up" and looking after kin are as much a responsibility of radio production as spinning records is. And while the explicit interest in Aboriginal kinship finds iconic expression in CAAMA radio's call sign, 8KIN FM, Thornton's reflexive narrative also suggests the fraught character of those links that media producers cultivate.

Thornton's representation condenses a great deal of what interests me in this book, though in the narrative, visual, and formally distinct poetics of the screen. *Green Bush* also allows us to see that Aboriginal engagements with media now take place in a multiply mediated domain, where filmmakers figure one medium (radio) as the locus of "community" and intra-Indigenous relationship from the formal domain of a second (film). Further, his representation suggests thinking about the social spaces opened up by Indigenous media in ways that exceed the preservation of linguistic diversity, as valued as these are, and include new forms of Indigenous public culture and political distinction. In the following section I turn to the individuals who are given cinematic representation by Thornton and whose production work gives this social imaginary its shape.

Kinship's Mediation

In November 2002, Aboriginal radio producer Charles Dale began visiting prisons in southeast Queensland in preparation for his annual Christmas request broadcast. Over the course of several visits to Queensland's Woodford Prison and the Brisbane Correctional Centre, "Uncle Charlie" recorded dozens of greetings and song requests from incarcerated Aboriginal people. Carting his minidisk recorder back to the studio in suburban Brisbane, Dale transferred the recordings to the archives of a large computer server, where they waited his later attention as a series of digital files.

As a radio producer and host of a weekly request program on the Aboriginal country music station 4AAA, Dale had worked for more than a decade bringing together an interest in bridging institutional and geographic distance between families with his activist, representational aims to foreground the folly of racist discourse and to counter "mainstream" representations of Indigenous criminality. He did this by eliciting and broadcasting the declarations of solidarity, hope, longing, and loss between men and woman incarcerated in Australia's prisons and their families and mobs spread around Queensland. I introduce three such recordings here as I heard them first: as spare, unadorned vocal recordings, yet to be framed by music, by Dale's friendly voice, or by his "station identification":

> Yeah, I'd just like to say hello to Mummy, out in Alva there, uh Merry Christmas Mum and I hope everything goes all right for you this year. Let my nephews and nieces know that I said hello and send my love. Also for my cousin Sara and all the Nowla crew, hope to see youse in the new year.[12] Take care and be strong, love yas, bye.

> This is just a Christmas greeting from Grant here at SDL. I want to send a shout out to all my family, too numerous to mention. Hope youse are thinkin' of me.

Hello, my name is Les and I'd like to say a big hello and a Merry Christmas call to all the fellas at Bourke and Gunyah and especially my mother and father there at Bre'.[13] And I wish that I was home there with youse there now and I miss yas all and, uh, I wish I was home there with youse now. So, yeah, so I'd like to say Merry Christmas to youse all at Bre' and Gunyah and Bourke there. And I'd like to put over a big hello to Judy over there. And you wanta keep strong, and be happy, and you'll be out soon. So for all the best of Christmas and New Years, my baby, from your sweetheart always, Les.

Dale subsequently employed audio production software tools to weave together these recordings with short advertisements and country songs, producing a three-hour, prerecorded program for broadcast over Australia's national Indigenous satellite radio network.

While Dale's Christmas program focuses on the voices of incarcerated men and women, another DJ's work at the same station suggests how prisoners' relatives' voices are made to animate country song, how requests entail both forms of intimate address and also normative exhortation, and can also make more clear the broader societal context in which such requests circulate. 4AAA producer Marissa James opened her Sunday program with a pointed interweaving of speech and song, inaugurated by a recorded voice reproduced from the 4AAA answering machine:

From Nanna Evie. I love you, my boys, no matter what happened in the past you're still my grandchildren and I pray every day for you. May God be with you and watch over you while youse are there on holiday. Love you boys.

The grain of Evie's voice is quite pronounced, carrying bodily indices of age and emotion as well as digital clipping and distortion added by the telephone's poor signal. Recorded digitally from an answering machine dedicated to such requests, the rough production of this segment (in which the producer has retained the click of the telephone receiver closing off) evokes distance and foregrounds the mediated character of Nanna Evie's connection to "her boys." These material indices of technological distance and emotional charge give way to the mournful tones of a fiddle sliding up a major third, layered with the "crying" comment of a pedal steel and the voice of North American country singer George Jones:

I've had choices
Since the day that I was born

There were voices
To tell me right from wrong

I should have listened
'Cause I wouldn't be here today
Living and dying
With the choices I've made.

The relevance of these lyrics to Evie's grandchildren is clear to any atten-tive, local listener. For my friends and interlocutors at 4AAA, her euphemistic "on holidays" located her grandchildren in jail. Clued in to this euphemis-tic figure of incarceration, listeners can then hear George Jones's "Choices" (framed by Evie's message) as an expression of both her mournful regret and as a pointed scolding. Importantly, the song itself also vocalizes the loss of an opportunity, insofar as its nostalgia speaks to a past chance to make good— to a poorly made choice. While the scolding echoes a locally robust, egali-tarian ethos and broad discourse of individual responsibility for one's social conduct, the regret is both highly personalized through the distance of these particular young men from their family and the backward glance over a life's wrong turns, and also evokes the more general, generational loss of many such young men to long stretches in Australian prisons.

Indeed, most listeners to the request show will be aware of the high num-bers of Indigenous deaths while under police custody and an associated, commonwealth-wide investigation in the late 1980s—the Royal Commis-sion into Aboriginal Deaths in Custody (Johnston 1991). Between 1987 and 1990 this body investigated the deaths of ninety-nine Aboriginal people while in police custody, many of which were the result of suicide. And while the commission did not find these deaths to be due to deliberate po-lice brutality or violence, it did foreground the disproportionate numbers of Aboriginal people in prison, and alleged a general deficiency in what the final report termed a "duty of care" to Aboriginal people in custody (see Johnston 1991).

In today's non-Indigenous Australian media, Aboriginal incarceration is most frequently represented in polarized terms of either excessive or inad-equate policing of Aboriginal young men. An instance of the former may be the death of C. Doomadgee in late 2004 at the hands of a Queensland police officer, severely beaten while in short-term custody for alleged public drunkenness. His spleen severed in two, Doomadgee perished in a cell, his death recorded by video and his injuries unattended. Doomadgee's violent death led to a renewed outburst of concern at the excessive policing of Aboriginal men. Frequently, however, mainstream forms of tabloid journalism also identify a "feral underclass" freed from productive labor and societal obligation by welfare payments and running amok in rural towns and Aboriginal communities (see Sheehan 2007; cf. Hooper 2008). Such narratives thus place the locus of violence and suburban crime in the laps of young Aboriginal men. When police violence ends in killing, as it did here, the cause is imagined to inhere in the wildness of remote locations, a wildness that police officers must embrace to survive and successfully administer their charges (see Hooper 2008).[14] As suffused with publicity as this case became, I want to foreground the frequent and familiar relations between police and many Indigenous people across Australia, as well as a prevailing sense of injustice at the overwhelming overrepresentation of Aboriginal men and women in prison.

As I hear Nanna Evie, however, this broader social issue is well in the background, and she draws on neither a framework of excessive policing nor a critique of a "welfare culture" and its enabling of black social pathology. Rather, the intimacy of Evie's request and her own personal loss are complemented by a public scolding as she singles out her grandchildren for their poor judgment and the "choices" that have led to their incarceration. This scolding is softened perhaps by its indirect voicing—that is, not by Nanna Evie, but by George Jones (through his song "Choices"), and perhaps by the show's on-air host, Marissa James (who likely chose to pair this particular song with Evie's request). Indeed, this indeterminacy with respect to the source of the song underscores for me a normative attribution of responsibility. In its employment of both speech and song, the request directs a sophisticated, multilayered message, putting some responsibility squarely on Evie's grandsons' shoulders that in other contexts Aboriginal activists and advocates would also (and rightly) direct to the broader, structural inequities of race and class.

In foregrounding her grandchildren's agency, this multivocal request also implicitly calls on the many other men in Queensland's prisons to reflect on the choices that led to their imprisonment, bringing into play two aspects of a critical discussion on Aboriginal incarceration—the structural character of its seemingly punitive, violent discrimination against Aboriginal men, on the one hand, and the individual misdirection and poor decisions made by specific persons, on the other.

Denaturalizing Radio, Rethinking Kinship

Aboriginal Australia is often (indeed, stereotypically) figured as a social field in which kinship relations pervade public life. As the primary frame for social relatedness in such distinct Indigenous communities as the suburbs of Darwin, the camps of Alice Springs, and inner-city Brisbane, it is clear that "family" is both a valued diacritic of Indigenous singularity and its form of social reproduction. Indigenous kinship also has been a significant site of intervention on the part of the Australian state. This can be seen historically in the removal of so-called half-caste children from Aboriginal families in the name of state-mandated assimilation, and in the charged demands on behalf of these Stolen Generations for governmental apology and redress. Beginning in the last years of the nineteenth century and extending as recently as the mid-1970s, children perceived to be mixed race were taken from Indigenous families and placed in forms of labor, institutional training, and foster care and adoption. These policies have led to current amplification of kinship as a site of cultural reproduction and political action. It also can be seen institutionally in the contemporary importance of genealogical research for activists and institutions (such as the Australian National Archives) who are now engaged in "linking up" communities, families, and now adult children dispersed by historical intervention.[15] Kin relations, genealogies, and family histories thus take on an overtly politicized caste, their value at once self-evident to my interlocutors, and also charged.

Second, under the Native Title Act of 1993, with its institutional invocation of genealogical forms of group formation, kinship has found new domains of significance as a means of recognizing Indigenous difference and reckoning its authenticity (Merlan 1998; Povinelli 2002). The capacity to reckon descent and to map Indigenous ownership through forms of genealogical reckoning also make kinship a primary means of reckoning temporal durability and forms of title in land. That is, kinship as genealogical descent matters greatly today as a route to title in land through such juridical instruments (see Povinelli 2002; Smith and Morphy 2007).

More recently, in 2007 the outgoing government of John Howard symbolically reaffirmed such intervention in its response to a report on the sexual abuse of children in the Northern Territory (Anderson and Wild 2007). In broad terms, the Minister for Indigenous Affairs shelved three decades of institutional self-determination and asserted the commonwealth's interest in intervening in Indigenous families. This ostensibly aimed to stem the sexual abuse of Aboriginal children by banning alcohol and pornography from Indigenous communities across the Northern Territory and by managing welfare payments to ensure that these were spent on children (otherwise, it was argued, the funds would be spent on alcohol and/or gambling). In addition to a number of other controversial entailments (see Kowal 2008; Lea 2014),[16] these maneuvers underscored the status of Aboriginal kinship for many Australians as suspect and as potentially subject to further state disciplinary intervention. The people from whom children needed protection, it implied, were their own parents and close kin.

Though increasingly figured as socially pathological in both popular and policy discourse, relations reckoned by kinship and haunted by loss, charged by a historical rupture, have become key icons of a broad Aboriginal social imaginary. In the context of these overlapping social and historical preoccupations, Australian kinship has assumed a charged character and value as both index and vehicle of Indigenous cultural distinction and survival. For many Aboriginal people, kinship is the paramount means of grasping the shape of an Aboriginal polity and of understanding its distinction from non-Indigenous Australia. In its mediation, then, forms of kinship as address in audio media take on performative powers, reproducing and amplifying that to which they seemingly only refer, extending concerns with kinship into institutional mandates and expectations about what media are and ought to accomplish. And in modes of kinship address, Aboriginal people are interpellated as members of a broader Indigenous domain.

This is emphasized in the ways that younger Aboriginal people are trained to become media producers. Charles Dale, whose work I touch on above, is one of the first generation of Aboriginal media producers whose experience was gained through early programming experience on non-Indigenous, community radio stations. This generation frequently learned to produce from one another, from other non-Indigenous media activists, and through their own experimentation. Over the past two decades, however, Aboriginal media has become institutionally rationalized as its producers have won both recognition and state funding for their media work. Today, the children and grandchildren of this first generation of producers are more likely to be formally trained as producers within Aboriginal radio stations, often by elder Indigenous producers such as Dale. Producers and activists such as Dale and the others I introduce here provide both models of practice and metacultural rationales that explicitly figure the work of radio as a work of linking up Aboriginal kin.

For instance, Auntie LW, a founder of 4AAA "Murri" radio in Brisbane, made family the focus of metacultural comment in a lecture given to young Aboriginal media trainees in 2003. Asking students to reflect on their difference from non-Indigenous Australians, she posed and then answered a rhetorical question:

What do Murris do when they first meet each other? They ask each other, "Where are you from? Who's your mob? Who's your family?"

She continued her lecture by describing forms of Aboriginal English as further foundation for distinguishing contemporary Aboriginal cultural practice. For LW, Aboriginal English terms such as *gammon* (which can be glossed as "fake," "fraudulent," or "broken") join a normative stress on kinship as shared "frames" of Aboriginal interaction—the ways that students craft points of connection and practically define themselves in distinction to the normatively unmarked character of non-Aboriginal Australian kinship. LW directed our attention to kinship affiliation and its frequent evocation in forms of distinctively Murri interaction in a disciplinary context, lecturing young Aboriginal people assembled for the purpose of learning to produce Indigenous media on the matter of their distinction.

Kinship also remains a key register for performing and reproducing Aboriginal distinction in Australia in intersubjective, intra-Aboriginal contexts. In urban communities where people feel keenly how a broad range of cultural practices have been attenuated by colonial subjugation and settlement, and where people often feel doubly deracinated by discourses of authenticity that subsequently challenge their indigeneity as inauthentic shadow of something now past, obligations to family expressed in idioms of kinship carry a great deal of weight in affirming one's cultural identity as properly, "authentically" Aboriginal. In this charged context, the willingness to look after one's kin can itself provide an ethical stance by which to authorize oneself as properly Indigenous. Kinship thus carries both iconic and normative burdens, mediating postcolonial arguments about identity, authenticity, and behavior in an intercultural domain.

As a form of direct address and of pronominal reference, what Garde (2013) and Zeitlyn (1993) figure as the social deixis of person reference, categories of kinship relatedness emerge in the substance of greetings and in terms of respect and affiliation between people beyond the general scope of Euroamerican practice.[17] In the Southeast, English-language kin terms and some marked local derivations are the preferred form of address, closely followed by nicknames and personal names. "Bruz," for instance, conjoins both "cousin" and "brother" in a markedly Aboriginal vocative pronoun, and openings such as "How ya goin', bruz," "G'day, brother," or "G'day, sis" populate conversations between people who may be genealogically distant from a Euroamerican perspective. In addition to its ability to stand as an icon of Aboriginal social distinction, "bruz" also entails an additional reflexive, social indexical aspect by drawing attention to itself as Aboriginal lingo (as do the collective nouns "rellies" and "lations"—relatives, relations). When speaking of other parties not present, my interlocutors used terms that spoke of relatedness and respect. "My cousin," "my auntie," and "my uncle" thus frequently moved beyond genealogical relatedness and into registers of respect and friendship figured in a familial idiom. In the example above, LM drew students' attention to the particular, distinctive character of such interaction and affirmed the particular distinction of Aboriginal mobs vis-à-vis whitefellas as a matter of everyday practice—a practice that 4AAA DJs, and others around Australia, enshrine in broadcast production.[18]

Stanner's (1937) description of Aboriginal "modes of address" in the Northwest, chief among which was kinship category, lends some historical insight into these practices and their continued relevance across the remote settlements of Australia's North. Stanner noted the charge that his interlocutors accorded proper names, and he argued that proper names were not simply referential signs but, rather, were considered consubstantial with persons—and thus sites of potential intimacy and probable danger. Stanner argued that kin terms were part of a broader range of circumlocutory means by which people avoided the use of personal names, and he documented the greater ability of individuals to accurately reckon kin relationships than to recall others' personal names (cf. Dusset 1997). More recently, Garde (2013) reframes such interests and circumlocutions as social deixis, focusing on the poetic possibilities that features of biography, genealogy, and classificatory kinship enable for person reference in Bininj Gun-wok: indeterminacy and circumlocution, he argues, allow for forms of expressive triangulation and hermeneutic play that speakers take pleasure in exercising.

In more abstract terms, it is an anthropological truism that kinship relatedness provides both egocentric and sociocentric means for ordering social life.[19] In addition to granting the ability to reckon others' relationships to ego, or to enframe social relations through moiety or classificatory means, kinship systems also can themselves become iconic and metacultural and therefore signs of group distinction relative to others. Therefore people with elaborate subsection systems (as one finds across Australia's central desert) and/or who classify parallel cousins as "brothers" and "sisters" (a practice widespread across Australia) may see in these practices the substance of their distinction vis-à-vis a broader society, and as media for shared identity with other Aboriginal groups.[20] Abstracted from social context and indexical specificity, and placed into circulation as metacultural icon, kinship reference thus matters in new ways as a vehicle of Indigenous cultural reproduction.

It should not be surprising, then, that in Australia these various aspects of kinship relations and their mobilization in social interaction and public discourse have come to pervade Aboriginal media as a social practice. Weaving together prerecorded telephone calls with country music hits, named places, and the performative language of radio DJs, Aboriginal radio is imbued with vocative pronouns that index intimate relations, as well as constant third-person reference to family members, family networks, and their associated communities, and one of my suggestions here is that this performative interweaving of speech and song provides a stage for both affective and reflexive aspects of Aboriginal kinship. In these terms, kinship animates an intra-Aboriginal radio network and finds recursive purchase as the appropriate rubric for describing the value of that network.

Anthropologists have repeatedly found kinship to be central for these forms of contemporary Aboriginal cultural production. Anthropologist Eric Michaels found kinship in the viewing practices of Warlpiri—most famously in their tendency to foreground kinship relatedness and what he called their need to fill in "missing content" when viewing "Western" narrative film. For Michaels, Warlpiri must provide this "missing content" when watching Western feature films such as *Rocky* by speculating on "where Rocky's grandmother is or who's taking care of his sister-in-law" (1994: 92). Michaels also found kinship important to the organization of Warlpiri video production, where subsection and moiety membership dictated production relationships. Together these specific ethnographic instances from Michaels's writings have become iconic of the imbrication of Aboriginal social values with media practices. More recently Hinkson (2004) argues that radio has enabled the formation of a gendered Warlpiri public in radio greetings that travel between distant Warlpiri settlements, generally produced by and exchanged between related Warlpiri women.

As significant as such interventions in representing Indigenous social life have been, one can also learn a great deal from asking how the distinction of particular Indigenous groups may be vouchsafed in its display to other Aboriginal groups, performed in a technologically mediated intra-Indigenous domain. Françoise Dussart has recently explored this issue with respect to women's ritual and its transformation into forms of intracultural performance as Warlpiri women perform for non-Warlpiri Aboriginal peoples (2004). I seek to address Aboriginal kinship and media in a similar register, as they increasingly presuppose the colonial history of northern Australia, the broader intra-Aboriginal domain suggested by Dussart's work, and as they both cross and reaffirm such distinct Aboriginal identities as Warlpiri, Yolngu, Larrakia, or Koori. Both Dussart and Hinkson place emphasis on the performative dimensions of Indigenous kinship relatedness and Aboriginal forms of distinction, and their analyses suggest that one should approach expressions of such relatedness in radio requests in terms of their performance, asking how these both presume and accomplish kinship relatedness and entail its public value.

The Value of "Country": What the Song Brings to the Request

Country music brings its own particular features to request programs and country songs and celebrities can be mined by a transgenerational, intra-Aboriginal audience for their expressive potential in articulating the complications of individual agency and structural discrimination brought together in the many particular Aboriginal experiences of imprisonment. Country has a lengthy history in Australia, stretching back at least to the importation of recordings by American performers Jimmy Reed and Hank Williams (Beckett 1993; Smith 2006). This early engagement with country music led in several generic directions—toward the bush ballads and Anglo-Celtic styles of Australian performers Slim Dusty and Tex Morton, and into the performance repertoires of Aboriginal singers who crafted locally resonant songs by substituting their own lyrics for those of the songs they used as templates. Over the past several decades, the number of Aboriginal musical stars has grown as Australian country itself has emerged as a significant cultural industry, and their biographies have become narratives available for broad circulation and retrospective celebration.

The singer Vic Simms was a young Aboriginal pop star of the 1950s who gained exposure by touring with the non-Indigenous Australian pop group Col Joye and the Joy Boys and recording several early 1960s hits. At the age of twenty-two, at the height of a short but successful career, he was sentenced to seven years in prison at Bathurst Jail in New South Wales. While incarcerated he recorded his now legendary album *The Loner* in a single two-hour recording session in 1973, and this recording led Simms to further performance tours across New South Wales, singing inside correctional institutions, but also performing in high-profile venues such as the Sydney Opera House (see Walker 2000). Although the recording and these early tours were organized by the New South Wales Department of Correctional services in a bid to put a positive face on the prison system, the songs he recorded have gone on to fame as some of the first Aboriginal protest songs. Today Simms's smiling face and snapping fingers have found new value for Aboriginal media producers (and for non-Indigenous advocates for Indigenous rights) as a historical icon of Aboriginal resilience and social activism. In retrospective reviews across a range of Indigenous media (from radio programs to newspaper articles) he is made both to stand as Australia's Johnny Cash and to evoke the figure of Elvis singing "jailhouse rock"—two of the more recognizable vocal characters of country and pop music in Australia as in the United States, and two performers famously (if differently) associated with prisons.[21] Simms's biography is far from the only instance of Aboriginal country's prison-centric iconography. Utilizing early Aboriginal pop stars like Simms, record labels such as New South Wales's Enrec Records and numerous radio stations provided media for an emergent Aboriginal public domain in the 1970s and 1980s. In these new sites for Aboriginal performance and representation Australia's first generation of popular recording artists drew on Elvis Presley's country-tinged rock for their own work. For instance, a well-known collection of prison songs recorded by Aboriginal country artists features a cover in which performers Vic Simms, Roger Knox, and Mac Silva gaze on an original pressing of Elvis's *Jailhouse Rock* (figure 1.1). This image can be seen as a recognition of musical debt, a humorous nod to "Jailhouse Rock" (one of the more famous "prison" songs), and an acknowledgment of Elvis Presley's status as a central figure in an emergent Indigenous public culture.

In these terms the image is difficult to see outside its staged appreciation. Yet the collectible vinyl pressing also suggests a form of cosmopolitan desire for participation and identification beyond the boundaries of Australia's public culture and in a broader, transnational field of rock-and-roll commodities and cosmologies. It is also hard not to reflect on the sense of the original recording's character as itself an artifact of intercultural mimesis, appreciation, and appropriation insofar as Elvis and Sun Records founder Sam Phillips put

KOORI CLASSIC
VOLUME FOUR

KOORI CLASSIC
VOLUME 4

Lonesome Jailhouse Blues
I Fought The Law
Muddy Water
Malabar Mansion
Goulburn Jail
Branded Man

Riot In Cell Block No. 9
Folsom Prison Blues
Midnight Special
I'll Break Out Again
I Want To Be Free
Jailhouse Rock

ENREC
ENC 044

GOULBURN JAIL	Roger Knox
BRANDED MAN	Vic Simms
MALABAR MANSION	Mac Silva
LONESOME JAILHOUSE BLUES	Mac Silva
I FOUGHT THE LAW	Vic Simms
MUDDY WATER	Vic Simms
RIOT IN CELL BLOCK NO. 9	Vic Simms
FOLSOM PRISON BLUES	Roger Knox
MIDNIGHT SPECIAL	Mac Silva
I'LL BREAK OUT AGAIN	Roger Knox
I WANT TO BE FREE	Roger Knox
JAILHOUSE ROCK	Vic, Mac & Roger

WITH THE ENREC STUDIO BAND: STEVE BERRY, ANGELIKA BOOTH, ANDREW CLERMONT, DAN DUFFIN, PETER GRECH, MATT HARRISON, PAUL HENDERSON, DEE LANE, STEVE NEWTON, KEN POPE, RANDALL WILSON, LAURIE D., D.K.? FROM BERRIGANS MUSIC.

COVER SHOT: VIC, MAC & ROGER EXAMINE AN ORIGINAL 1957 COPY OF ELVIS PRESLEYS "JAILHOUSE ROCK"

PARTIALLY FUNDED BY THE AUSTRALIAN BICENTENNIAL AUTHORITY TO CELEBRATE AUSTRALIAS BICENTENARY IN 1988.

ENGINEER: STEVE NEWTON
PRODUCERS: GOULBURN JAIL, MALABAR MANSION, LONESOME JAILHOUSE BLUES, MIDNIGHT SPECIAL PRODUCED BY LAWRIE MINSON. FOLSOM PRISON BLUES, I'LL BREAK OUT AGAIN, I WANT TO BE FREE, PRODUCED BY PAUL GREEN. ALL VIC SIMMS TRACKS PRODUCED BY MICK LIBER. JAILHOUSE ROCK PRODUCED BY ED MATZENIK.

National Bicentennial Aboriginal and Torres Strait Islander Program

1.1 Cassette cover for the Enrec Studios release "Koori Classics Volume IV: The Prison Songs" (1984).

the styles of Jimmy Rogers and Bill Monroe together with the blues of artists like B. B. King—or, perhaps, as Phillips repackaged forms of African American rhythm and blues (music that Phillips himself adored) in a young, white icon for an emergent radio-listening, record-buying market (Guralnick 1994; cf. Gordon 2013).

These recordings were also produced with an eye to an emergent record-buying and radio-listening Aboriginal audience. Yet there is something more canny in these performers' appropriation of Elvis, and of country and rock musics more generally, as they draw "classic" jail songs into conversation with the particulars of Australian prisons and their Aboriginal inmates and purposely evoke homologies between specific incarceration and a broader Aboriginal experience of settler-colonial Australia. Jeremy Beckett argues that in the songs of his friend and Indigenous interlocutor Dougie Young, written and recorded in the late 1950s, Young had "taken back the image of the anonymous, stereotypic 'drunken Aborigine,' making him—it is a 'him'—once again a human being with a name, friends, and the gifts of music and laughter" (1993: 37). The counterpublic reclamation of persons from stigmatized identity and experiences are palpable in Aboriginal country and rock musics, and they resonate in requests such as Evie's rehumanizing of her grandchildren through the disciplinary attribution of personhood, and in the narrative celebration of

Indigenous country celebrity by reference to such international stars as Elvis Presley and Johnny Cash.

While incarceration occupies a central place in country music's iconography, 4AAA's Sunday night request program is also occasionally punctuated by hip-hop, soul, and R&B recordings. Occasionally such recordings reference Indigenous incarceration, and many of the concerns of the young Indigenous producers of these musics also revolve around issues of Aboriginal identity; around what Indigenous Australians share with a global, cosmopolitan black experience; and around what makes black Australians distinct. Yet these musics make only sporadic inroads into request programs.

One prominent Indigenous DJ's perspective may shed some light on why. In 2003 a popular hip-hop producer in the Brisbane area, DS, was working at 4AAA and hoping to build a career as a sound engineer and performer. When it came to discussing what sparked his interest in music, DS often put together the Aboriginal country music of his youth with the cultural and media activism of his family:

> Growing up I listened to Knoxie [Roger Knox] with my mum. . . . He's a countryman of mine—we're both from the same country in New South Wales.
>
> I grew up with all black music, pretty much all Koori music and Murri music. I've been in radio all my life. Like I used to sleep at a radio station in Canberra, 2XX. And then we moved out to a farm and all the famous Murri, Koori bands back in them days used to come there and stay with us.

DS's recollections, in accord with Beckett's insights into country song in 1950s and 1960s New South Wales, suggest the historical depth to identification with cosmopolitan forms of public culture such as reggae, R&B, and of course rap and hip-hop. DS also addresses the importance of country music for what request programs are designed to encourage:

> Even if there's people in jail, even over in western Australia, if they're taking NIRS [the National Indigenous Radio Service] . . . Brisbane can send a shout-out over to them. So that's the idea, giving the brothers and sisters inside, you know, they still can hear their mob. . . . 'Cause often they mightn't be allowed to get so many calls in a week or day, but then they know Sunday night, they'll hear music that'll bring their spirits back up.
>
> Because it's what we all know. Like we all know country, we all know Charley Pride, we all know the Murri music and the Koori music, and all

the different Indigenous music. So it brings back that home feeling again, you know.

When I related my encounters with requests that bring speech and powerful song together, the Aboriginal writer and poet Gayle Kennedy, a confessed "country music tragic" and one of my most eloquent interlocutors around the power of country music's vocal sound, added her own recollections— recollections that moved from early moments of requesting songs on rural, non-Indigenous radio stations of New South Wales in the 1960s and the scene at home, when the "family rogue" came home from prison:

> GK: Well, that's what we did when I was a kid, we'd send requests out to all our relatives. You know, Mum would get me to write the letter and I would: "And this is for Auntie Chookie and this is for Auntie Lois," or "This is for Auntie Dolly, from "Bebby," which was Mum's nickname.
>
> I remember that my Uncle Claude used to get in a lot of strife. And my grandmother used to play the mouth organ and sing. And I remember him coming home from jail. And we were home in Ivanhoe, in these humpies I guess you'd call 'em. They'd have several different rooms and everything, and they were quite sophisticated really! [Laughing]
>
> I'd always remembered him coming in in the gloom after getting out of jail, and this song that Granny Esther used to play was the Slim Dusty song "You Can Never Do Wrong in a Mother's Eyes?" [laughing] So I always remember, I always associate that song with him getting out of jail. You know, he was a great singer and guitar player as well.
>
> And quite often you'll go, "This song is for you". I mean, we all have different songs that we play for different people in the family. This is your song, or this is your song. Or "I always think of you when I play this song". . . . A lot of country songs have real pointed messages. Even though he'd be in strife with the rest of the family, to Granny Esther he was her son. He was the family rogue, you know. But he had a beautiful voice!

While I discuss Slim Dusty's career and his popularity in Aboriginal Australia at greater length in the next chapter, it's worth pausing for a moment here to hear these lyrics with Gayle. Dusty's song is minimalist in its narrative, a chronicle of allusions to misdeeds and accidents seen primarily through the pain they cause the mother of the song's second-person addressee. A country waltz built around a five-one chord progression, the song is nonetheless up-beat, and you can practically hear Slim Dusty's smile as he sings. The nostalgia is palpable too in the opening line, repeated across the song's 2:30 seconds, "You can never do wrong in a mother's eyes"—a musical aphorism drawing place, family, and sentiment together in the memory of a few bars:

> You can never do wrong in a mother's eyes
> No matter what you may do
> She will always forgive any wrong you've done
> And she'll open her warm heart to you
>
> Though you've been the cause of her tears she's cried
> When you've strayed the straight narrow bar
> Oh, you can never do wrong in a mother's eyes
> For she sees her son through her heart
>
> She knelt by her bed many lonely nights
> While waiting for you to come home
> And prayed to the Lord to keep you right
> And guard you wherever you roam.

Two aspects of requests come through in Kennedy's recollection. The first is the association of a particular tune with an identified family member, such that the song calls that person to mind as a relation. The second is the motivation that directs the song's lyric as a normative exhortation and lament, much as with Nanna Evie's request described above. Both bring together prison, poor choices, and maternal forgiveness, amplifying aspects of biography and relatedness through poetic and musical redundancy. And these aspects also sketch the structural forces that confront Aboriginal families, the separation of parents from children and the importance of prison as a widely shared aspect of individual biography and family history.

While hip-hop beats and rhymes are increasingly important for DS's gen-eration, marking their sense of shared identification with, and distinction from, a broader transnational black experience, country music draws all lis-teners together, young and old, urban and remote.[22] Charley Pride, Elvis, and country music's Indigenous interpreters such as Roger Knox, Jimmy Little, or Warren Williams can elicit nostalgia and invoke desire for belonging fig-ured in terms of kinship connection and the requests themselves can evoke singular memories, such as Gayle's uncle's voice and her grandmother's love.

Dusty's song speaks across generations with a pointed message, its refrain sung following a catalogue of bad behavior: "You can never do wrong in a mother's eyes / For she sees her son through her heart." Just so for DS too, for whom radio gathers its widest Indigenous audience around country music's ability to evoke and recollect shared senses of home and family: "It's what we all know."

Networking an Indigenous Public

In part such figures of home and family are themselves products of request programs and the ways they place Aboriginal families in a social geography. As a pedal steel guitar faded to silence at the close of "Choices," 4AAA presenter Marissa James read a series of other requests, thank-yous, and more general shout-outs that together mapped an extended family spread across Queensland and northern New South Wales.

> George Jones with "Choices" here on Murri Country, 98.9 FM. G'day to Greggie Heart there, thanks for the letter. Also the Henry Brothers, Justin, Steven, and, um, who's the other one? Travis. Sorry, yeah, Justin, Steven, and Travis, thanks for your letter. And a few shout-outs here. I'll read them out while I'm onto 'em.
>
> First of all it says "Happy Birthday to my brother Steven. [From] Metaka Henry."
>
> "Justin, my big brother, stay strong over there. Maybe one day we can be together once again, hey? From your brother."
>
> Also, "to my Auntie, thanks for the card and the twenty-eight bucks. Auntie Vicki take care and I hope to hear from you again sometime." That's from Travis Henry.
>
> And, uh, "to my Grandmother and mother, hello, love youse, hope to hear from you or see youse when youse come up. Good-bye and love yas, Tyrece, Betty, Kelly, and Karalee." And that's from Travis Henry. . . .
>
> Alrighty, we've got a track coming up next going out to Gregie Heart, Magpie, Dusty, Garnie, and David. And also one on the message bank, that's "Cherbourg Boy," [by] Lance O'Chin and friends, here on Murri Country, 98.9 FM.

Following a recitation of familial affection and displacement, James's voice introduced another digitally recorded telephone request "on the message bank," which she had culled from the many left by callers through the week. As with

Evie's previous request, this also carried the material index of its transmission in the static hiss of the phone line:

Good afternoon, this is Auntie Cleary. I'd like for you to put a request over for Boy Morgan of Palm Island, uh, Happy Birthday for tomorrow, Monday the 17th from your brother Dion, Kurt, DeWayne, and Garnie M. of Woodford Prison. "Cherbourg Boy."

As in other programs, James's production work brings together distinct voices and forms of speech, from the digital recordings of actual shout-outs to James's own, often lengthy reiterations of other requests collected on paper or recorded earlier. In her completed broadcast, James spins requests into a narratively coherent performance, mixing direct and indirect discourse such that the words and voices of callers mingle with her own. These requests, filled with family names, terms of endearment, and place-names, ground country songs such as Lance O'Chin's "Cherbourg Boy" in a social geography animated by the poetics of kinship reference. In this way, the nostalgic themes of travel and loss that course through country music become tropes of Aboriginal dispersal.

One can hear aspects of family history brought into play through euphemisms such as "on holiday" as well as through the textual and affective themes of particular songs. Particular choices made or places left behind animate the songs' more general tropes of distance and leave-taking. Country music's generic poetics of loss and nostalgia are thus made to speak to an Aboriginal modernity in which travel and distance are frequently framed by what Goffman (1961) termed the "total institutions" of prisons and hospitals.[23] This poetic evocation of distance also finds an echo in repeated, phatic references to the mediatized channel itself in the framing language of shout-outs, "sending a message," and "putting a song over." As iterative passages from kinship's technological mediation to its vocative performance of immediacy, such features of radio discourse evoke the distance that speech and country music transcend. In these terms, radio animates two distinct domains of networked connection: one emerging from the historically overdetermined and pragmatically secured "immediacy" of satellite and telephone transmission, the other from the vocative interpellation of kin, itself amplified by the genealogical memory of colonial governmentality, a ghost that haunts kin relations in Australia. The road between country (as music) and country (as place) thus traverses social history, marked features of Indigenous expressive culture, and the audio technologies that give form to listening, calling, singing, and speaking publics.

Request programs make clear that an intra-Indigenous domain has emerged that must be described in terms of its technologically mediated character and by reference to those vehicles of public affect that give it shape. In approaching this here I have been helped by the attention of ethnographers to the ways media entail particular kinds of audience. For instance, Mazzarella (2004) and Kunreuther (2014) draw on Althusserian understandings of interpellation in order to foreground the particular manner by which broadcast media may produce those audiences, publics, or listeners to which they seem merely to refer.[24] Importantly, their work attends both to affective and reflexive vehicles of public making, and to the metapragmatic labor involved in the production of immediacy in mediatized public cultures (see also Gaonkar and Povinelli 2003; Hirschkind 2006).[25] These accounts suggest the value of bringing together the distinct material characteristics of media, local understandings of their efficacy, and the particular forms they animate in order to understand how they may entail certain forms of social transaction.

These approaches also provide a means of understanding media's historical purchase as indebted to the signifying practices of media producers. Unlike film and other media in which producers may be figured as auteurs and whose labors have therefore received a good deal of attention (both celebratory and analytical), broadcast media frequently carry ideologies of communicative transparency that may abet the potentially novel, constitutive social transactions I discuss here, but may also obscure the creative labor by which such transparency is purchased. This everyday disappearance of production labor in broadcast media may be abetted by theoretical accounts that emphasize the immanent power of media as extrasocial agencies—as determinant of social formations (as in Kittler 1999 and Virilio 1989; see also McLuhan 1964) and/or as disruptive of a more primary, prior social domain.

While Aboriginal radio producers rarely figure themselves as auteurs, and in fact downplay their creative agency in the studio, their investments in shaping radio programming and placing valued forms of social relatedness at its center are nonetheless key for the phenomena I describe here. It is in the deployment of minidisk recorders, in the use of audiovisual timelines of sound-editing software (which closely resembles contemporary film-editing software), and in the metapragmatic, poetic attention to the interanimation of speaking and singing voices that radio producers amplify kinship as an icon of Aboriginal distinction. Analyses of Indigenous media's recursive, performative character—its ability to invoke an audience through its presumptive address—thus require a perspective that draws at once on the forms of creativity and expressive practice involved in media's instrumental deployment, on the immanent possibilities of particular technologies, and on the particular social and historical domains within which media are deployed in postcolonial, intercultural domains.

Insofar as Aboriginal radio only acquires "objectness" and social value around relatively distinct preoccupations and sedimented social practices, it remains helpful to consider it less a firm object and more a congregation of distinct practices, materials, and relations—a network in Latour's terms (1991, 1993) that has resonance with contemporary efforts to rethink kinship within anthropology. This rather distinct understanding of network resonates with the ongoing revision of kinship within anthropology (as in Carsten 2000, 2004; Franklin and McKinnon 2001). Edwards and Strathern (2000) foreground the collation of narrative and biotechnology in English practices of making (and delimiting) kinship relations. They understand the value of contemporary network thinking in how it extends one's understanding of social relatedness beyond dichotomies of "nature" and "culture" and into the historicity of kinship, technology, and politics, and figure the contemporary, dominant understanding of "network" as follows: "Networks are not just relations between persons: they are, like the Net, both the effect of vehicles mobilized to carry messages and the resultant passages and translations which comobilise different orders of phenomena" (Edwards and Strathern 2000: 162). In critical, if appreciative conversation with Actor-Network theorists, Edwards and Strathern ethnographically foreground the narrative aggregation and disaggregation of the biological, technological, and the cultural in Euro-American kinship, suggesting that the networks thus built are bounded by "the very constructs that carry them" (ibid.).

In Australia, it is in this passage between kinship networks and radio networks that Indigenous radio acquires its coherence, value, and durability. As a means by which to reflect on the complications of individual biography, incarceration, and dispersal, Indigenous media conspire with Aboriginal preoccupations and sedimented social practices in the amplification of an Aboriginal polity. Much as Nanna Evie's request for her grandchildren departs dramatically from the standard poles of Aboriginal delinquency and structural disadvantage, many other requests foreground the roles of incarcerated Aboriginal men and women as brothers, sisters, cousins, and grandchildren, emphasizing both their agency as persons and value as kin. In such moments radio becomes a significant site for the widespread circulation of kin address and family networks as diacritics of an Aboriginal domain critically intertwined with the intercultural, postcolonial relations of northern Australia.

Yet in today's Australia, to foreground agency is also to evoke a distinct, publicly circulating figure of responsibility. As the objectives of state policy have turned toward empowering Indigenous communities as entrepreneurs of their cultural selves and have overwhelmingly rejected past policies of self-determination as a form of pathologizing quarantine, a broad public discourse now deploys figures of "shared responsibility" and "mutual obligation" to invoke proper state-subject relationship (Kowal 2008; cf. Pearson 2000). It is interesting to note that the language of callers and imprisoned listeners resonates with this broader neoliberal interest in eliciting Aboriginal subject-citizens as self-creating and self-governing participants in a multicultural Australia. Yet this resonance has limits. Mediatized requests to kin entail normative figures of agency, choice, and responsibility that, by foregrounding personhood and intra-Aboriginal social relationship, reframe Indigenous personhood in an oblique relationship to liberal discourses of economic responsibility and obligation. In the social imaginary of Aboriginal radio, and in the cultural activism of its producers, the social deixis of kinship reference and its affecting modes of interpellation thus run counter to the pathologization implied by this broader public formulation and craft possibilities for cultural distinction "outside the defining limits of law and policy" (Ginsburg and Myers 2006: 29).

In a number of ways, then, Indigenous request programs and the historicity of Indigenous kinship demonstrate the value of keeping together what are too often distinct analytical perspectives on media—the agencies of producers whose creative labors as cultural activists initiate and give form to radio request programs through distinct, Aboriginal poetics of voice and sound; the agencies of networked media themselves as entailing forms of social imaginary, modes of address, and genres of musical commodity; and, last, the recursive significance of both kinship and radio as normative models for connection and communication. In northern Australia this demands working at the interface of two domains of mediation: the networking of radio and the reckoning of kin. Radio here comes to be understood through the particular kinds of connection and relationship that kinship exemplifies, and kinship to be understood as a form of linking up. Radio and kinship turn into one another in ways that evoke some recent efforts to understand media in reference to the various media ideologies by which it is both understood and made to do social work, and also through the social interpolation of different media technologies. This allows us to see radio remediating kinship, and kinship remediating radio, such that the two must be understood as cotravelers in contemporary Aboriginal Australia.

A Digital Coda

Today my most frequent encounters with radio requests take place in the domain of Facebook and other social media, where my Indigenous interlocutors bring together digital speech and song and continue to use country's musical archive to give expression to bittersweet romance, as well as to express nostalgia for country itself. Friends from northwestern and southeastern Australia alike curate Faron Young, Jim Reeves, Charley Pride, George Jones, and Slim Dusty, many proclaiming the "classic" status of their distinctive voices and the songs they sing. In postings to Facebook they occasionally mix comments on the music with reflections on their current emotional state or the state of their relationships, perhaps relating when they first heard the tune, or how it was a father or mother's favorite. Alongside a range of other musics—heavy metal, hip-hop, R&B—country is thus made to sing of particular sentiments, to elicit the past, and to perform kinship in ways that continue to move people though now in relatively new domains of online, so-called social media.

Radio itself cannot be understood without reference to this broader media ecology to which forms of social media, cell phones and smartphones, and a range of online networks themselves remediate radio. In 2011, while visiting Darwin, I found myself texting back and forth with one of my Aboriginal friends and interlocutors—someone who now works for the Australian Broadcasting Corporation, the ABC, producing a national radio magazine on Aboriginal issues. Vic had been up for several days working almost nonstop on an extended radio documentary about the 1966 Wave Hill Walk-Off, a famous strike by station workers that helped lead to equal wages for Aboriginal people in the territory and is also seen as a foundational action in the movement to attain self-determination. The strike itself found support from a series of union officials and socialist supporters in Darwin and involved the ferrying of supplies from Darwin, down the Stuart Highway, and across to the Wave Hill station. I was looking forward to hearing about the project, which centered on the heritage listing of a famous Bedford flatbed truck used by union organizer and Aboriginal rights advocate Brian Manning to bring supplies and letters from Darwin to Gurindji Strikers at Wave Hill. Vic's story seemed a communication about communication, a radio show about an early infrastructure, and a comment on the deep history of Indigenous communications infrastructure and its political possibilities in northern Australia.

As interested as I was in this story, arranging a meeting was difficult. Vic's attention was elsewhere: his girlfriend had just left for a job in Perth and he didn't much want to talk. Vic is an inveterate user of Facebook, with several thousand "friends" and followers, and while we were texting he also began making a series of postings on his Facebook wall. I knew all was lost when he shared there a YouTube music video attached to a status update. The text of Vic's posting was entirely drawn from the song's lyrics, "Don't you try to tell me that it's rain," and this was written over a YouTube video, a televised performance of American country star Faron Young singing the chart-topping hit "Hello Walls," embedded within the Facebook posting. "Hello Walls" is a widely known 1950s release from Young, a song about a man losing his mind, talking to the walls, ceiling, and windows of his room after his lover has left him. The "rain" on the windows is imagined here to be tears, the house itself grieving in the hallucinatory delusion of the song's protagonist. The semantic interdependence of text and country song seemed clearly to echo the artful use of requests to make kinds of intimate statements in public. I thus immediately heard Vic's posting in this register as remediating radio through a request that at once performs and qualifies the status of a relationship.

This was confirmed a few moments later when Vic put a second status update on his timeline: "Put your sweet lips a little closer to the phone," it read, and it accompanied a video of Jim Reeves's huge country hit from 1959, "He'll Have to Go." This song thematizes the difficulty of telephonic communication, of long-distance relationships, and possibly jealousy. The reason that the alter of this line has to put their lips a little closer to the phone is that the ego of the song's lyric is in a bar and can't quite hear the voice of his lover. As the song's spare, lyricized narrative proceeds, it becomes clear that she's with another man. The song ends:

I'll tell the man to turn the jukebox way down low,
And you can tell your friend there with you, he'll have to go.

This seemed at once unusual (unlike most of my Aboriginal interlocutors, Vic doesn't much listen to country music) and also completely formulaic—participating in a form of musical communication that reaches across Aboriginal media, giving "voice" to Facebook as a sounding medium, an extension of radio's power to stage the speech-song continuum. But it also centered his reflection on the troubles that media can entail—drawing together telephones, radio requests, country music, loud jukeboxes, and video—suggesting the nontransparency and unsettling potential of mediatized communication. It's this trouble, this sense of unease—which can extend beyond troubled love to the character of one's own voice—that Vic's posts also brought to the music and media mix. When I asked Vic's permission to use his posts in this book and asked after his motivation, he chuckled. It was a breakup, Vic affirmed, and he added something of a local truism—that Aboriginal people love their country music because it was a part of everybody's family life: "we all grew up with that."

Vic's remediation of radio's address on Facebook can also suggest something of the complexities of voice consciousness in the space of its mediatization. In this sense, I want to hear Vic's post through the history of Aboriginal engagements with radio and country music, as an effort to link up, but one that also, and characteristically for Vic, expresses an engagement with the troubles that technology can bring. Here radio is apprehended nostalgically, as the voices of country stars are couched in its characteristic address, paired, that is, with a message. These two concerns, the affecting voice of country song and the troubles that technology can involve, the reflection it can elicit around the voice, stage the concerns I take up in chapters 2 and 3 with how musics are made to sound both black and Indigenous and how this process asks people to reflect on and denaturalize their own voices.

CHAPTER 2 | Aboriginal Country

In every corner of Australia country music matters deeply to Aboriginal people. Country has provided the musical counterpoint to Aboriginal urbanization, labor migration, and incarceration, and to other complex forms of movement and mobility. People listen to it both with a sense of this historicity and with a kind of pride, a sense of generic ownership and often incisive appreciation for the expressive nuance and technical skill of its performers. In this chapter I provide a historical and ethnographic account of this Indigenous intimacy with country, describing how its nostalgic address speaks to Aboriginal Australian forms of movement, migration, and institutionalization, and explore how country provides a significant and deeply felt historical cornerstone for contemporary Aboriginal media. The story of Aboriginal country demonstrates the long-standing significance of commercially produced musical media for Aboriginal people and asks that we rethink how popular musics stage race and place in sound.

Contrary to the naturalization of its sounds in North American popular culture as "white," in Australia the genre has come to sound loudly as an Aboriginal genre, something that everyone knows to be cherished by Aboriginal people, a stereotypically "black" popular music. That identification occasionally elicits the (misapprehended) commonsense notion, to which I alluded in the previous chapter, that country music transparently maps onto Aboriginal understandings of "country." The racialization of country music in North America, further, has been critiqued in a range of recent music scholarship. That work takes a critical perspective by asking a powerful historical question: how is it that country music has come to sound so white, given the large African American contribution to its origins and industrial production?[1] A related question animates scholarship on the popularity of country music in Native North America: how does a "white" music so closely associated with a cowboy hagiography become so significant and speak so profoundly across Indian country?[2] Such questions multiply when we tackle the significance of country music genres across the globe, the ways its chronotopes of loss, its devotion to memory, and its deep commitment to sentiment can sound so powerfully from Brazil to South Africa to Australia (cf. Dent 2009). The analogous critical questions in Australia might be, how does country sound black here differently than other popular musics, such as soul, R&B, and hip-hop? How do these different generic forms mediate each other's significance in today's Australia? And finally, what do historical accounts of country music's Australian career accomplish today?

To address such questions requires understanding both how country music sounds in distinct ways to Aboriginal people and how country has animated those fields of (Indigenous) cultural production that mediate its meaning. While an Aboriginal affinity for country does entail what Will Straw terms a "long-term and evolving expressivity" (1993: 370),[3] country also comes to mean by virtue of the specific ways that country music has traveled to Indigenous people; how, where, and when it has been sung; what kinds of perspectives on social life its form encourages; and, one of my primary concerns below, how it comes to mean in relation to other genres. As a generation of scholars of public culture have suggested, to answer a hermeneutic question about country's meaning also requires asking a pragmatic question about what country music does and a related social and metapragmatic question about how it comes to circulate (Gaonkar and Povinelli 2003; Ginsburg 1994; Mazzarella 2004; Novak 2013). This is to underscore that in Aboriginal Australia, as elsewhere, this form comes to "mean" in its mediation and in the modes and media of circulation its movement both builds and borrows.

Yet while I begin with the broad question "How has country come to matter so deeply for Aboriginal people,"[4] just as often I hear another question: "Does Aboriginal country music still matter?" As an Australian ethnomusicologist once asked me, "Isn't that all done with? Isn't it all about hip-hop now?" Indeed, it is hard to talk about country music today without some (occasionally anxious) reference to hip-hop's usurpation of country as the iconic Aboriginal sound, or to celebrations of hip-hop's contemporary significance as "black" music. And certainly the dense networks of Aboriginal musical performance and recording I sketch below exist today in a different form, encourage different genres, and depend on a different relationship to their audiences and recordings than they did in the 1960s, 1970s, and 1980s. My younger interlocutors in Brisbane and Darwin were deeply immersed in digital media, rarely purchased music offline, and heard their lives echoed in words, sounds, and worlds of hip-hop and R&B. Hip-hop in particular offered a stage on which to exercise ideas about blackness, indigeneity, and the relation of Indigenous Australia to white Australia. And if these young people did still know "their" country music, responding strongly to its affecting appeal, this response was often in an overtly nostalgic mode—one overdetermined, perhaps, by the form's address itself. For this younger group, hip-hop and its related visual styles and modes of bodily comportment were the terrain in which they understood themselves and through which they sought contemporary forms of distinction, identification, and prestige.

In some respects discourses of country's own demise as a popular musical form have accompanied the genre from its first popularity in Australia (cf. Smith 2005). Understood as a remnant of a past, rural way of life that was itself under threat, country and folk musics stood as survivals, elegiac icons of a disappearing world. This iconic status can be amplified by the prevalence of tropes of loss and displacement within the music itself; country as a genre often sings mournfully of a time just past. Further, an early Australian interest in "hillbilly music" celebrated its rural nonmodernity and its capacity to give voice to a nostalgia for a recently passed outback existence (Hayward 2003; Smith 2005). And, too, the power of early country's voice in Australia drew on the variably deployed, class-marked rurality that "country" evokes in opposition to the city, made to figure a past idyll against which the present compares poorly (cf. Dent 2009; Fox 2004; cf. Williams 1975). Furthermore, Australia is a famously urban society, clustered in several large cities along its coastal South, that has long built its myths of national identity on figures of the bush and the frontier. Country music's seemingly rural voice thus found a ready-made audience in an urban and suburban post–World War II Australia.

Country music's particular chronotope, its backward glance and nostalgic evocation of a recent—often rural—past has also been a powerful aspect of its appeal to Aboriginal people, for whom categories of racial difference have been imposed in tandem with a class-marked derogation. Country's working-class cultural iconography resonates with many Aboriginal people whose working lives run through paddocks, trucking routes, and the many and varied forms of labor and loss that mark an Aboriginal and working-class modernity. There are also striking similarities in this story to the popularity of country music in Native North America, where cowboy songs have come to matter greatly and where the voice's sonic character resonates with a distinct politics of indigeneity and settler-colonial history (Jacobsen-Bia 2009; Samuels 2004; cf. Dueck 2013). Scholars of country's significance in Native North America have tied this in part to the midcentury reach of radio across the American Southwest and to the significance of live performance. As in Australia, in Native North America the genre has been given life by native bands covering beloved songs from country's commercial pantheon and indigenizing the genre by deemphasizing country's "twang" and through the textual substitution of local place-names, making the world evoked by these songs a local landscape (see Jacobsen-Bia 2009; Samuels 2009). This layering of poetic, prosodic, and toponymic specificity also inflects the sounds of Aboriginal country across Australia, creating a kind of affective redundancy where voice, place, and country's "chronotope of loss" (see Dent 2009; Fox 2004) resonate powerfully across different Indigenous domains.

In seeking to understand some significant shifts in how country has mattered for Indigenous Australians, I first attend to country music's formal features, its distinct sounds and stories, and how these have been heard by Indigenous Australians. Country's beginnings in Aboriginal Australia are most frequently located in the traveling performance tours of non-Indigenous musicians and early, non-Indigenous country recordings and the ways these included Aboriginal people as both a key audience and a prototypical subject of song. This also set the stage for the appropriation of the genre by Aboriginal performers and by the institutions—activist and governmental—that subsequently encouraged, recorded, and distributed Indigenous performers' works within a field of Indigenous cultural production centered on music. But as in North America, the circulation of country is equally mythologized as an affair of new technology and the commodity form—and, indeed, radio's broad reach and the nascent market for vinyl records and cassette tapes were critical for the constitution of Aboriginal Australian audiences for country music and for the ways it is recalled today. I conclude the chapter by discussing the broader, generically rich world of contemporary musical media, in which country's status and meaning as "tradition" have been consolidated both within a commercial domain and against transnational genres such as hip-hop and R&B. Although country music remains a cornerstone of this Indigenous public's ground of possibility, it does so within an increasingly complex Aboriginal public culture.

Slim Dusty and Aboriginal Country: A Chronotope of Loss?

On September 19, 2003, Australian country singer and songwriter Slim Dusty passed away at the age of seventy-six. Dusty's career began in the 1940s with recording, radio, and suburban theater performances in Sydney, where he continued to work as a plasterer while launching his career as a musical performer. Dusty continued to perform over the next five decades in caravan tours of remote and regional Australia, taking in some of the more remote and difficult-to-reach towns and communities of northern Australia. As Dusty described it, his caravan troupe would send a motorbike in advance, booking halls and putting up posters before the band's arrival (Dusty and McKean 1996). These annual tours, like those of many other country performers, took in Aboriginal reserves, settlements, and communities, as well as small country towns, mining centers, and mission stations. Over the years Dusty and other performers such as Buddy Williams, Slim Newton, and Johnny Chester returned to these communities, and in tandem with country music radio programs and record sales, these tours enabled Aboriginal people to regard Dusty's music as their own. Dusty himself is rivaled only by the American country performer Charley Pride and Indigenous gospel and country singer Jimmy Little in the instant recognition and affection his name and his songs can elicit.

Dusty was eulogized and celebrated by all of Australia's major newspapers, recognized in Parliament, and given a state funeral at Sydney's St. Andrew's Cathedral, but perhaps the most touching eulogy was by Gayle Kennedy, a writer, poet, and member of the Wongaibon clan of the Ngiayampaa-speaking nation from southwest New South Wales. She writes:

> I don't think there's a blackfulla alive today who hasn't listened to Slim (whether you liked his music or not). My earliest memories are of Dad coming home with the latest single and playing it over and over again on the old battery operated gramophone.
>
> We kids would all be lying in bed praying he'd had his fill of "Trumby" or "Saddle Boy" and just when we thought he had, you'd hear him say to Mum "whack'er on again, Beryl" and you knew there was nothing left to do but cover your ears and pray for sleep. (Kennedy 2003)

Kennedy closes her eulogy with a poetic, place-based evocation of the meaning of Slim's music:

When I came to Sydney as a teenager, I discovered blues, soul and jazz and somehow thought Slim wasn't good enough any more. The funny thing is, though, when I'd get homesick or things were going wrong, I'd sit up all night getting drunk, crying and listening to his music.

The next day I'd be hung over but cleansed and strengthened. Because Slim was red dust, clay pans, saltbush, river banks, corrugated iron halls and dusty football fields. He was Mum and Dad and family. He was, is and always will mean home to me. (Kennedy 2003)

Although I quote Kennedy at such length because her remembrance so deftly evokes what country music has come to mean for Aboriginal people across Australia, the deep affinity of Aboriginal people for country music her words suggest is not mysterious or surprising to most Australians. Country music, that is, is widely understood in Australia to be Aboriginal music. Perhaps the popular association of Aboriginal people themselves with "country" as place conspires with the valorization of the Aboriginal stock worker in Australian popular culture to make the association of Aboriginal people with country as music even seem natural, particularly appropriate. But despite this form of Australian common sense, or perhaps because of it, musicologists and anthropologists of Aboriginal Australia have been slow to tackle the deep connections.[5] Indeed, such homologies do not capture the historically deep practices by which country has come to stand as Aboriginal tradition, to signify indigeneity so deeply. Nor do they capture how country has supported the development of a broad, intra-Indigenous public culture.

Kennedy's remembrance itself suggests that to approach an Indigenous affinity for country music solely through the lens of stock work and the privileged association of Aboriginal people with "country" as place may in fact obscure the numerous pathways by which country has become meaningful as Aboriginal history—both the distinct poetic and pragmatic features of how country has acquired the capacity to move people and also the histories of urbanization, institutionalization, and labor migration within which it has come to matter as a kind of Aboriginal tradition itself. As I'll suggest here, the affinity for country and the collective Indigenous subject to which it sings and speaks are historically inextricable. Several themes merit further discussion, including the movement of people from rural to urban spaces, a subsequent renewal of appreciation and even abiding love for country music, a sense of the negative, déclassé character that country might have in these new spaces, and an almost defiant embrace of country as a key to one's own history, a means of recollecting family members and celebrating a shared cultural identity.

As I hope to demonstrate, that country sings of a place and time both outside of and prior to an urban present is its key asset. Country's elegiac discourse exists both within songs like Dusty's "Trumby" and exceeds them in the kinds of discourse and ways of talking that quote the song and surround the music itself (Fox 2004; cf. Williams 1975). On reflection, it is also not surprising that country itself is so densely and poetically evoked as in Slim Dusty's Indigenous obituary. Kennedy's remembrance of Dusty resonates with the musical intertexts of "Trumby" and "Saddle Boy" by which Dusty's music is remembered. These two songs both share an elegiac discourse with this obituary, and the latter itself becomes a vehicle for performing country's "chronotope of loss." Like Nanna Evie's use of George Jones, Gayle does expressive work here, evoking song within her text.

With "Trumby" and "Saddle Boy," Kennedy's obituary evokes two of Slim Dusty's most mournful songs, rather than the hundreds of others (such as "Pub with No Beer" or "Duncan") that celebrate drinking with mates, trucking, or outback places. Both "Trumby" and "Saddle Boy" are stark lamentations, and for those who know these songs, they become intertexts for her obituary itself. "Trumby" catalogues its hero's sympathetic relationship with the country, its cattle, and his horse as it recounts the story of an Aboriginal ringer who dies from drinking at a poisoned water hole. "Saddle Boy" is also a story song, narrating the tragic death of its young, eponymous hero, killed with his horse in a flash flood. It's possible that in their moment such songs participated in a broader settler-colonial sensibility about Aboriginal belonging—as well as voicing an ode to a country under threat—and a regret at its (perhaps "necessary") passing. Indeed, songs like "Trumby" are difficult to listen to as an anthropologist without some sense that they place Aboriginal people at the margins of modernity, in the country and the past, overcome—even exterminated—not solely by individuals or settlement but by a racialized notion of progress to which they cannot belong. In this way they echo broader primitivist tropes of Indigenous demise that themselves have been widely critiqued by anthropologists—a mode of representation that presumes the demise of that which is described (see Fabian 1983; cf. Beckett 1996; Ivy 1995; Stewart 1988). So country's generic privileging of a nostalgic past suggests two immediate questions: How can Slim Dusty provide a fundamental note of Aboriginal modernity? And how might songs that seem to trope the passing of Aboriginal people come to mean so much to Aboriginal people themselves?

In Kennedy's appreciation and in the ears of my many interlocutors who love and curate country music and occasionally mourn country music's own passing, such songs create the possibility of making other sorts of claims to those that I initially heard in their sung stories. This has been clearest, however, when Aboriginal performers craft their own country songs with different sorts of lyrical narrative and lamentation. Well-known examples of country ballads that bring a critical perspective to colonial tropes of settlement include the Country Outcasts' two odes to place, "Blue Gums Calling Me Back Home" and "Streets of Fitzroy." Other songs that share in this elegiac mode memorialize the loss of family, describing the removal of so called half-caste children from Aboriginal parents. Bob Randall's "Brown Skin Baby," for instance, describes the loss of a child to governmental agencies—and has become an anthem to the Stolen Generations—while Herb Laughton penned country songs about the Alice Springs Bungalow, where removed children, including Laughton himself, were institutionalized.

The loss these Indigenous country songs evoke differs from the elegiac form that animates the lament of "Trumby." In part this difference emerges in the individualization of country's chronotope through autobiography and kinship relations. Kennedy's own particular memories, for instance, gather around Dusty's songs. She sketches her own biography through rural–urban movement and evokes the organization of familial care by reference to the battery-operated gramophone—binding a time to set of valued social relations through both Slim's songs and an (old) technology. When I spoke with Gayle about country music in 2012, she underscored the deep connection to movement and migration that such sounds abetted. Her sense of displacement on arriving in Sydney was strong, and the sounds of Slim Dusty provided important solace, one tied to a sense of racialized isolation:

When I first came to Sydney, I came down here to go to school at Queenwood. And I was the only black kid there and I was so far away from my family, and I remember "Old Dogs, Children, Watermelon Wine" by Tom T. Hall? That was a really big hit and they played it on the radio all the time here in Sydney. And every time I heard it I was home.

And every time I played country music records that I brought with me I was home. They were my link to home and they still are. Like if I am lonely, and I mean, even though I've lived away from home for a long, long time now, whenever I play country music I am home. It's my way of connecting with home. And I know that, like, relatives or other Kooris that have come from the bush, when they come to the city they bring their country music with them and they feel the same. They bring their country music, which means that they bring part of home with them. You know, it's always home to me whenever I play Slim. I'm always home, you know, I just close my eyes. I can't stress enough how important it is.

Another modality of country's Indigenous distinction and the ways that country's loss is given a political voice can be found in the lyrics of those recordings that many of my interlocutors held up as iconic of the ways the genre has been indigenized. Such a recording is the Country Outcasts' "Streets of Old Fitzroy":

Oh those city lights are drivin' me crazy
As I walk the lonely streets of old Fitzroy
How I wish that I was back there in the dreamtime
In the country where there's always peace and quiet

Oh, I wish that I was back in the dreamtime
Hear the didgeridoo dronin' in the night
Where the corroborees are seen by firelight
Far away from the glow of city lights

Now Gertrude Street it makes me feel so lonely
For the gum trees and the taste of porcupine
I see my brothers and my sisters here in Fitzroy
Torn apart by government ways and city life

Yes, city lights are drivin' me crazy
As I walk the lonely streets of old Fitzroy
I know that someday I'll be called back to the dreamtime
Where the white man's ways won't bother me no more.

For many people in the 1960s and 1970s, Aboriginal activism entailed intensified relationships between urban Aboriginal activists, many of whom were taken from natal communities and kin groups as part of Australia's policies of child removal, and Aboriginal people in remote northern and western Australia. Such encounters could be bittersweet—charged with potential to craft a new, historical Aboriginal voice and agency, and also redolent with what many people taken away from their communities and families felt they had lost—their family, their language, an easy sense of belonging. Country music, through artists such as Bob Randall and Harry and Wilga Williams, became one way to sing about the particular terrain of loss and sorrow that could so mark Aboriginal lives in the city. To sing of gum trees and porcu-pines from Melbourne's Indigenous inner city is not simply to evoke the coun-try, but to evoke a lost mode of being in the world, one that can only be found in death—when one is "called back to the dreamtime." And, of course, this is also an overt critique of "government ways and city life."

But the textual politics of country song, as powerful as they may be, do not encompass country's affecting form for Aboriginal people, the ways that it endures as an "affecting presence" (Armstrong 1972) in people's lives or that country sounds can themselves become like persons—with distinct voices and country stars as cotravelers in the biographies of many of my interlocu-tors (cf. Fox 2004: 300–315). When I asked Gayle about her sense of country's specificity, its distinct power for Aboriginal people, she initially looked to the stories such songs often relate:

> It's because we love stories. And country songs have a story. And there's a country song for any occasion, really, isn't there? And you know, they celebrate a lot of things that are important, not just to Aboriginal people but to a lot of people. They celebrate things like wedding anniversaries and the birth of children, and they celebrate old-fashioned values, you know?

These thoughts on story echo widespread understandings of the power of Ab-original media more generally, its capacity to tell Aboriginal stories and to insert these into a broader mediascape. They also echo tropes about country music's love of narration—its songs are indeed stories, from the spare, almost comic despair of the protagonist of the Willie Nelson–authored hit for singer Faron Young, "Hello Walls," who speaks to the walls, windows, and ceiling of his empty house, imagining that it shares his grief at the loss of his lover, to the vocal personification of a song's lovelorn protagonist by George Jones, who will "never be the fool I was before." Gayle introduced me to Faron Young's catalogue, and both Young and Jones feature frequently in Aboriginal radio: Their songs are both cherished and sung by many of my interlocutors.

Kennedy herself took to country's sounds very young and when she was a small girl, would be set atop the kitchen table by her aunties to sing songs such as "Don't Sell Daddy Any More Whiskey" and "I Want a Pardon for Daddy"—an image about which we laughed long and loud in 2012, sitting outside in the Balmain Bowling Club and talking country music over chips and soda. Her stories, if they capture hurt, do so with a comic irony: no doubt her aunties were themselves rolling about in tears of laughter and appreciation at Gayle's youthful performances.

When Gayle turned to the voice, though, she moved determinedly to capture how these voices grab her, how they bring her to tears, and how that always brings her back home. In particular, she singled out country's "cry-break" in her account of what to her makes for a strong country voice:

> I always say it's got a little bit of heartbreak in it. You know, there's just a little break in it; I think that there's a little sob in it. There's something about them about their voices that breaks your heart. You know, like George Jones only has to open his mouth and I'm in floods of tears [laughing].

This perfectly describes the range of vocal techniques and expression that together sound as a "cry-break" in country song and that are analyzed in detail by Aaron Fox in regard to South Texas honky-tonk performance (Fox 2004: 280–283; cf. Feld et al. 2004). Such effects are achieved by restricting the voice in mid-articulation: the voice "breaks" and resumes, and can (as Fox also describes) be followed by a further crying effect—a "little sob," Gayle calls it—amplified as broad vibrato. The cry-break is that transportable, embodied lament that country song transmits as aesthetic accomplishment.

While Kennedy evokes sobbing in country's American recordings, that cry-break also features prominently on some of the more iconic Aboriginal country recordings as well, most notably perhaps in Roger Knox's "Koori Rose" from 1986. This song's opening phrases announce its theme of loss in a series of crying effects that begin with a move from the bass register, stuttering up to the baritone over seven syllables in a clear reference to Elvis Presley's signature, much-imitated vocal inflections (famously on display in the opening lines of "Blue Christmas," where he gives each syllable of the first line two stuttering beats—this effect is echoed in Koori Rose's first vocal moments). The second line establishes a pattern to which Knox adheres throughout, breaking the lyric with subtle closures of the throat, and an attendant coarse, affecting break in the melody—here amplified by the resonance of the body in the voice as Knox vocalizes from his chest:

> Oh this_a_lo_onely heart keeps reminding me of you,
> And how I miss you he_aven knows.
> This hurt inside keeps telling me it's over.
> But I still love you, Koori Rose.

His lyric also draws out the long, hard vowel of "rose," but here staying relatively clean and clear, lacking vibrato yet resonating with a polished control as the melody moves up a major third, a movement that draws together deep feeling and total control. This is indeed how Knox is recalled in conversation, as the "Black Elvis" and Aboriginal country's widely esteemed technical king.

As Kennedy's reflections suggest, its capacity to gather to it feelings of intimacy, to elicit memories of family and to evoke romantic love, and to do so in ways that also attract aesthetic appreciation and reflection on the qualities of particular vocal performances have been central to how country has sung to Indigenous Australians. But its connection to "old-fashioned values" is also key to how it matters in the present, as is, paradoxically, the temporality of country's address. Its power to move people to tears and its relevance to Aboriginal people in the twenty-first century depend both on the time-space of its form and on the sobbing vocalized cry-breaks in its performance. In the next section I place these particular southeastern and urban relationships to country's powerful chronotope alongside a broader, historical development of a mass-mediated Aboriginal public, a development to which country music has been central.

Country's Aboriginal History

Beginning in the 1960s, country recording artists like Dusty made a practice of including Aboriginal communities in their national tours. Indeed, while radio was crafting broad public audiences for country music in the United States, some of this same work was being accomplished by touring caravans of country performers including Dusty, Tex Morton, Buddy Williams, Slim Newton, Smokey Dawson, and more recently John Williamson (Dusty and McKean 1996; Smith 2005). While Sydney provided the industrial center of country music recording and record production, rural and remote tours, often as part of larger touring circuses and rodeo shows, lent it a beating heart and built up a public for country music that included Aboriginal communities and country towns. By 1964, Slim himself was spending ten months of the year on the road, covering as many as thirty thousand miles of Australia each year by car and truck (Dusty and McKean 1996).

Steve Newton, founder of Enrec Studios and one of the more significant non-Indigenous producers of Aboriginal country music in the 1980s, recalls that his first experiences with Indigenous people occurred during seasonal outback tours with his father Slim Newton[6] and Rick and Thel Carey. When I spoke with him in 2008, he identified a small group of performers who cultivated Aboriginal communities as a core audience:

Buddy Williams is the man that went really the furthest. He's the man that toured mostly remote Aboriginal areas, reserves, settlements, communities. From the middle [of the continent] out he did it the hardest of all. There's a real benefit, of course, because you're killing your competition, no one else can get out there. They'd take caravans and some of the caravans would be destroyed. The roads are rough and so Buddy Williams, he probably went places that some of the others didn't quite go. Brian Young, and certainly Slim Dusty would. Slim Dusty before Brian Young, really. When they were young people, Slim and Joy and some of those artists that would travel with them, Chad Morgan, Brian Young, Rick and Thel Carey.

Kennedy also remembered attending these touring country shows when I spoke with her in 2012:

People like Slim would play up in the Territory, out at the actual missions and that, but they'd all go to the halls, the country halls. Like I saw most of them at the Hay War Memorial hall, but out at Ivanhoe they'd go to the hall out there or maybe sometimes the football oval and play out there.

That's how they made their living, you know, they had to travel. And they'd take lots of merchandise. Like there'd be photographs, you'd take your photograph with them. And they'd sell their records, they'd sell autographed photographs, and I think later on they'd sell their tapes. But that's how they'd sell their records. So all the country artists traveled.

Though relatively few shows toured the more remote communities of northern and western Australia, these few managed to corner a market and secure a very loyal audience. Selling cassette tapes at performances and playing in the informal spaces of school verandas, tennis courts, and sports fields, country acts performed in sunshine and rain and with instruments that were sometimes as dented and worn as the caravans themselves. Newton recollects this moment when country's urban audiences had dwindled and country music's popularity seemed confined to these remote settlements and country towns:

These are largely unknown artists. Country music at that time wasn't a big part of the market. And so of course by getting out in the remote areas, by default, you're the only one they know about. And that's how they built up this following, by going to places where other artists simply wouldn't go because they didn't feel they could get to.

And look, there's a number of venues that immediately spring to mind. The tennis court on the community (they call it now—at the time they called it missions). You'd be on the veranda of the school with people on the ground in front of you, or you'd be on the tennis court 'cause it's the only bit of flat ground that's workable, or you'd be out on a sporting field. I mean, um, one time we were on the back of a truck, and I have a strong feeling it was Hermannsburg community, probably 1978. Look, the roads are hell, it's bull dust, and it takes all day to get a couple hundred miles. Well, we set up and it's started to rain and you're not going anywhere, so we did the entire concert, audience and show, no cover in the open rain.

Speaking on film to folk performer and Aboriginal advocate Ted Egan in 1979, Wilga Williams also described the loud, energetic audiences that greeted her and the group she fronted with her husband, Harry Williams, during a tour of central Australia. She echoes Newton's recollections of both the difficulties of playing in these spaces and the rewards they offered country performers:

Sometimes the places where we've had to perform are in tin halls, and the electric sound we've got with our instruments seems to bounce everywhere in the hall. But if we all had acoustic guitars and acoustic instruments it would be ideal, but with electric equipment it was very bouncy, sort of coming off the walls and that. Well, we were performing last night, Harry got all the dust down his throat and he couldn't sing loud 'cause he was coughing too much. But it made no difference to the show itself and the kids really had a ball. We had them onstage, it only took one child to get up onstage and then the whole stage was packed with children wanting to dance and really swing it up![7]

If in the 1960s country found a steady audience in remote and rural Australia, country's rurality spoke first to an expanding, postwar suburban audience. Graeme Smith (2005: 92–93) argues that the turn to such rural and remote touring was in fact impelled by the advent first of television and then the growing popularity of rock music in the cities where country artists had initially been supported by a large, suburban performance circuit. The demise of a steady audience in the suburbs, that is, led country artists to seek new audiences and new performance circuits.

Indeed, Sydney was an important first crucible for country music recording: EMI and later Festival Records recorded Australia's first stars and subsequently some of its first Indigenous performers as well. Indigenous country star Jimmy Little initially found success in 1955 when he moved to Sydney from rural New South Wales and started performing in a thriving urban and suburban country scene, ultimately also recording with EMI (Walker 2000). And Indigenous country music performance and early Aboriginal activism came together in inner-city suburbs of Redfern in Sydney and Fitzroy in Melbourne—both of which were significant crucibles for a generation of Aboriginal political activists and country musicians, such as Harry and Wilga Williams, Candy Williams, Alan Saunders, and Jimmy Little.

In Australia, non-Indigenous performers "Australianized" country by looking to Indigenous place-names and Aboriginal themes. In part this included songs about Aboriginal stockmen, like Dusty's "Trumby," but more frequently drew on Australian place-names such as Peppimenarti and fauna such as blue gums (eucalyptus). And while settler Australian singers were finding ways to make country music speak to an Australian landscape, so too were Indigenous Australians recrafting country's lyrics, making existing tunes reflect Aboriginal phenotypical norms—replacing standard lyrics in songs to make the eyes of Johnny Cash's teenage queen, for example, not "blue" but "brown"—and also writing new songs that used the genre to speak to specific Aboriginal experiences.[8] In his writings on Dougie Young, Jeremy Beckett describes the humor and ironic refusal of the stigma that fell on the shoulders of Aboriginal people (1993). Beckett met and recorded Young in Wilcannia, but Young traveled across NSW and Queensland, gaining attention for his humor, irony, and wit. Young's songs also circulated on their own as people performed them across New South Wales in the mid-1960s.[9] In this period, country music—and Young's songs in particular—accompanied men and women moving across a landscape as drovers, laborers, truckies, and through institutions like prisons, missions, and hospitals.[10] Here country spoke of contemporary experiences in an industrializing rural landscape—one in which a generation of Aboriginal people were emerging (or escaping) from state institutions and emplacing themselves with a secular knowledge of that landscape derived from experiences of both adversity and adventure (see Beckett 1996; Gilbert 1973).

This was also the period in which recordings of American country stars began to find mass-mediated circulation as vinyl records and, importantly, cassette tapes. These latter were the preferred mode of circulation in the Northern Territory—the material route by which a great deal of American country, and by the early 1980s Aboriginal recordings as well could circulate here. Charley Pride's recordings, for instance, which began to emerge following his 1962 major label debut, were distributed by RCA in Australia. The massive scale of their distribution combined with the relatively small roster of stars in their catalogue to make Pride a household name in Australia. Though his blackness is often referred to today as the most important contribution to his popularity in Aboriginal Australia, one must equally consider the ways his songs themselves sung to Aboriginal people (and how they sing now), and also the ways their availability as cassette tapes in great numbers abetted their movement across the North as part of an industrial effort to create a mass market. In small towns across the country in this period, people were also beginning their record collections and favoring country music in their selections. Gayle Kennedy's own introduction to country came from her father's record-buying habits, and so too did her own early record collection. As he moved on to a new favorite, brought home from the music store in the small New South Wales town of Hay, Kennedy would appropriate his cast-offs. She chuckled at the memory, relating this time to me in 2012:

> GK: Well, he would collect singles, 45s, and he would learn the songs. And once he'd played the shit out of them and he'd learnt them, then they'd get put away and I often purloined them. But I was the one who collected records. So like every fortnight, when the other kids would get, you know, on Dad's payday, they'd get something, you know, I'd get a single. But it used to be books, Little Golden Books, and then later on I'd get singles. I had one of Dad's friends used to buy me albums. And one of the very first ones that I wanted, when I was about seven, was a Jim Reeves album. And I've still got it! [laughing]
>
> DF: How'd you get them, at the record shop?
>
> GK: We used to get them through catalogues. But the bloke who used to get me the presents, the LPs, he used to travel around a bit, so he'd buy them, he'd buy them from record stores. And we had other friends who came from Melbourne. And they would bring up a whole stack of the latest albums, like at Christmastime. So they introduced us to people like Charley Pride and Merle Haggard. They'd bring up their albums.

While touring caravans of country music performers laid the foundation for a broader Aboriginal public culture, Kennedy's obituary for Dusty and the absolute centrality of 45-rpm records and cassette tapes in our conversations and her recollections suggest that Aboriginal country music matters as much in recorded form as it does as live performance. Yet the recording of Aboriginal country performers did not emerge spontaneously from these tours or from any natural affinity of Aboriginal people for country music. Indeed, the early commercial recordings by Jimmy Little, Col Hardy, and others were soon joined by a great range of other recordings that depended in part on the rise of Aboriginal activism, on an Aboriginal counterpublic, and on the rise of Indigenous media institutions and governmental efforts to encourage Indigenous cultural production—including Aboriginal country music. Alongside a grassroots tradition, country in Australia has a distinct industrial history—tied to Indigenous activism and to governmental funding for Aboriginal cultural production.

In the Southeast, after initial commercial recording ventures by EMI and Festival Records, the Australia Council's Aboriginal Arts Board played an important role in country's expansion by providing funding for performance festivals and recording projects. The Outcasts thus found funding in 1976 to begin a long-running series of Aboriginal country music festivals and eventually to produce two records that now are widely esteemed as foundational Koori country recordings. In 1979 the Arts Board also funded the central Australian tour by the Country Outcasts I draw on above, joined by Mac Silva on drums and Ted Egan as tour manager and opening act. Other artists, including Roger Knox, took this Arts Board funding to private studios in efforts to craft commercial recordings.

The sound of the Country Outcasts, polished on record, practiced and professional, closer to their contemporaries recording in Nashville than to the rough, bush ballad styles of guitar and laconic voice so pronounced in the recordings of Slim Dusty or Buddy Williams, has itself become a marker of a particular southeastern sound. Alive most clearly in recordings by performers like Auriel Andrew, Roger Knox, and the Country Outcasts, this production aesthetic was shaped in part by Enrec Studios, a production house that was heavily influenced by a Nashville sound. Based in Tamworth, NSW, Australia's "country music capital," Newton and his partner, Ed Matzenik, noticed the increasing availability of Aboriginal Arts Board funding, but also that it rarely provided enough funding to carry a record through recording, pressing, and distribution. They thus pulled together the artists they had come to know through their recording work—Roger Knox, Vic Simms, Mac Silva, Bobby McLeod, and others—and began applying for funding themselves for bigger recording projects. From these efforts came a number of single-artist recordings and a series of "Koori Classics" albums—seven records total, each built around a different theme running through Aboriginal country music. These included a recording of prison songs, "the Girls" (composed entirely of women's performances), a record of trucking songs, and a rockabilly collection.

These projects were interspersed with recordings of performers who have become household names across Aboriginal Australia, of which the most significant may have been Enrec's two projects with Roger Knox, "Give It a Go" and "The Gospel Record." As Newton describes it, Knox has something of Elvis Presley's presence and a huge popularity across Indigenous Australia, and in recording Knox, Enrec acquired a recognition in Indigenous Australia that led to the studio's producing records for groups from all around Australia and even New Zealand.

Look, we were lucky that Roger Knox came along as the first person, because he is, still, almost a household name amongst Aborigines. So as soon as we recorded him, they all talked and everyone knew about us, and as we continued to record more Aborigines the name spread. So that was very easy to get the name out in the Aboriginal community.

Alongside this southeastern growth of an Indigenous country music industry, central and northern Australia were also being transformed in the 1970s and 1980s by Indigenous media activists and advocates. The first and most successful of these was the Central Australian Aboriginal Media Association (CAAMA; see Ginsburg 1991, 1994, 1997). Its founders, John Macumba and Philip Batty, began seeking tapes of music in central Australian languages as properly Aboriginal content. And when these radio producers first began to put music on the air and to seek materials that would allow Aboriginal languages to find space on radio, they looked initially to country music and rock (see Batty 2003; Murray 1993; Ottoson 2006).

Aboriginal Australia is famous for its rich and varied regimes of secrecy that shepherd sacred knowledge and lend it power through restricted distribution. It might seem as though these could occlude the possibility of a true public built on the circulation of Indigenous media, preventing the development of the broad stranger sociality (Warner 2005) on which modern publics depend. It is certainly the case that concern about the circulation of secret-sacred images and stories has been a significant structuring condition in the production and circulation of Indigenous film, video, painting, and photography and in the mediatized sharing of stories and traditional knowledge (for instance see Deger 2004; Myers 2004; Michaels 1994; Chris Anderson 1995). Music recording has also addressed these issues, in part through the sensitivity of Indigenous producers behind recording projects and their interests in encouraging popular musics performed in Indigenous languages, and in part because of the sophistication and care taken by Indigenous performers—much like that taken by painters and Indigenous filmmakers—when recording or performing songs with an ancestral precedent (cf. Toner 2005).

Country as an Indigenous popular music escapes the situatedness and particular political meanings of a great deal of Aboriginal music and can thus sing to, and of, the broadest range of Indigenous experience. In relying on country musics CAAMA producers encouraged the growing reputations of performers like Gus Williams, Isaac Yamma, Herbie Laughton, and later a younger generation including Warren Williams and Frank Yamma, as well as a huge range of country and rock bands from across central and northern Australia (Batty 2003; Murray 1993). These bands often sang in local languages, and over the past twenty-five years CAAMA's recording studio has produced hundreds of recordings and provided a broadcast platform for Indigenous popular musics to thrive in the Northern Territory (Ottoson 2006). And this growing archive of Aboriginal music quickly began to feature in request programs and to thereby "link up" families dispersed by the dislocations of institutionalization, incarceration, and urban migration. As I described in the previous chapter, country music's affective appeal was put to pragmatic use here, helping to creatively entail the very public it presumed.

Country, then, much like kinship, must be understood as entwined with Aboriginal modernity. In one form it reached its apotheosis in request programs that broadcast country musics, often sung by Aboriginal people and addressed to Australian places, alongside kinship and social relations across a landscape that was increasingly structured by labor migration, urbanization, and the institutional dispersal of Indigenous people. In another, country's absolutely public, nonrestricted character endowed it with the capacity to facilitate forms of stranger sociality and through its deployment alongside kinship address on request programs facilitated forms of collective identification as Aboriginal. In the next section, however, I turn to think about this story of Aboriginal country music in its remediation by Afro-diasporic musical genres such as soul, R&B, and hip-hop and its historicization and celebration on film.

Country Music and Cultural Intimacy in *Samson and Delilah* and *The Sapphires*

When I began my own fieldwork with Indigenous radio and music producers, this broad narrative seemed as though consigned to history. There are now scores of professional Aboriginal country recordings, dynasties of performing families, and regionally distinct styles of country performance, and Aboriginal country performers themselves play an increasingly significant role in mainstream Australian country music festivals. The very radio activism, recording projects, and Indigenous media associations that served these early musicians and activists so well have led to a media landscape in which country is but one of a number of genres, and some feel that country music suffers in the context of this generic heteroglossia. While country music found its apotheosis in prison request programs, today hip-hop and R&B increasingly find space in such programming, and governmental and arts funding targets hip-hop as a developmental expressive practice with an insistence that has global significance. And, too, while radio remains central to country's Aboriginal social life, it is joined by festival performance, feature films, and YouTube's archive—each of which provide insight into the discursive and generic "remediation" of country's value—jostling alongside hip-hop, R&B, soul, and other sounds and formal principles of an Afro-diasporic musical explosion.

But perhaps "consigned" is not quite the right way to talk about country's historicization. Publics often exist primarily in the media by which they are encountered, as expressive or textual form (see Cody 2011; Warner 2005). And publics can be entailed by forms of address and representation—much like the ritualized poetic performances of radio requests. But this mode of existence also can make certain kinds of public into the focus of nostalgic regard. One might thus recognize my representation of an Indigenous public captivated by country music's affecting appeal as itself a nostalgic image—and, indeed, it is a description that many of my interlocutors look *back* on, as in, "Country music *has been* important to Aboriginal people." Indeed, the Indigenous public built around request shows and founded on country music's enduring broad appeal can in fact seem like a kind of proposition about how things ought to be, rather than how they in fact are. In part, this nostalgia for a country music public has been sharpened by the sense of a generation of people that hip-hop has usurped country music in the playlists of young people and has therefore undone something fundamental, has displaced something considered authentic to Aboriginal people as their twentieth-century tradition.

I close this chapter by looking at two films, each of which tells a distinct story and stages country music as a powerful twentieth-century tradition while relating the genre to newer, Afro-diasporic forms. While the two films make different sorts of claims about country music and the Aboriginal voice, both position country as fundamental to contemporary Aboriginal lives. Country's black history as told and valued today rests closely on the ways that it can evoke and stand for a collective public, but also for the particular ways that country comes to signify family.

Samson and Delilah

In 2009 Warwick Thornton's film *Samson and Delilah* took the Palm d'Or for best first feature at Cannes. Thornton's film, starring Rowan McNamara as Samson and Marissa Gibson as Delilah, was deservedly celebrated and acclaimed around the world. This is a remarkably rich production that will doubtless inspire a great deal of critical interpretation and commentary. As an introduction to my own questions and concerns, both here and in the following chapter, I wish to focus almost exclusively on its soundtrack and on its evocation of a particular Aboriginal world of sound.

Briefly, the film tells the story of a young central Australian Aboriginal man and woman, the former sniffing petrol and seemingly aimless and alone, the latter despairing after the loss of her grandmother. Feeling cast aside by and alienated from their relatives following the death of Delilah's grandmother, they flee their remote community, steal a utility truck, and drive to Alice Springs. There they encounter terrifying indifference, deprivation, and physical abuse at the hands of settler Australians—with Samson all the while sinking further into a petrol-induced fog. The film's Dickensian misery and stark account of Aboriginal lives at the internal margins of Australia's settler colony is relieved first by the affection and care these two encounter in another Aboriginal camper in town (played to great effect by Thornton's elder brother), and then through an improbable saving grace that follows a terrifying accident. As the film closes, Samson and Delilah leave Alice and, with the support of Samson's family, escape to a remote outstation where Delilah cares for Samson away from petrol in a kind of Aboriginal bush rehab.

Music and sound are key to this film's narrative momentum and affective power. Thornton has stated that all of the film's musical sound was scripted into the work prior to actual production and has also suggested that a significant part of the film's budget was dedicated to securing rights for the reproduction of several huge commercial hits. Its opening sequence begins with Samson waking below a sun-drenched, sheet-covered window. As the frame speed shifts from a slowed 48 frames per second (fps) to a standard 24 fps, the image acquires a surreal, dreamy calm, interrupted by the brief static of an untuned radio, and then the bright sounds of a pedal steel guitar. These are the opening licks of Charley Pride's "Sunshiny Day," its lyrics proclaiming the power of love to cast sun in the darkest corners of one's life. As sunshine spills around a fluttering sheet at the window, Samson reaches for a tin of petrol and buries his face in its open top. While his left hand clutches the open tin of petrol to his face, his right begins drumming along with the insistent downbeat, allowing the audience to hear the music as diegetic, as does a radio that sits at the head of his mattress. For the film's soundtrack, "Sunshiny Day" is pitched upward by a half step from the key of A to A-sharp, and the tempo is slightly accelerated with the downbeat brought forward into the mix and more out front than in Pride's original 1972 release. The bright, positive stereo spread of "Sunshiny Day" creates a sharp, ironic juxtaposition with the images on screen, but it heralds the film's broader tale of redemptive, unjudgmental, "necessary" love, in Thornton's words. As Thornton describes for the popular Australian online media blog *Crikey* (Buckmaster 2009), the juxtaposition of a slowed, surreal evocation of a petrol sniffer's addiction with the bright music aims to establish the film's sense of place and to disturb.

Ten minutes into the film, and after we have been introduced to both characters, we see Samson back on his mattress, tuning his radio. This time we hear a DJ's voice announcing CAAMA radio's Green Bush Prison request program. The voice is recognizable as the actor David Page, reprising his role from Thornton's earlier short film *Green Bush* (2007) in an intertextual reference to that film and a historical reference to the actual request program at CAAMA's 8KIN FM. This voice also establishes the significant place of radio in central Australia, and for the filmic audience it establishes central Australia as the diegetic location of this film. An audience can hear the broader central Australian world just offscreen through this sonic representation of a broader, Aboriginal public.

The film's closing scene shows Samson and Delilah at relative peace, together in her desert country and listening to the subdued reggae progression that has been a kind of diegetic theme song for Samson throughout the film, at times played by his father's band on the front porch or emerging from the radio. The progression here ends with a request sent to Samson from his father, which has the effect of making both Samson and the viewers part of a radio audience. And after Samson's joyful laughter hearing his name and his father's request (and perhaps the announcement that his father has only "six more weeks" to go in jail), the reggae progression gives way to Charley Pride's "All I Have to Offer You Is Me," which moves from the diegetic radio speakers to the broad stereo spread of nondiegetic film music as the credits roll.

Before you take another step
there's something you should know
About the years ahead and how they'll be
You'll be living in a world where roses hardly ever grow
'Cause all I have to offer you is me

There'll be no mansion waiting on the hill with crystal chandeliers
And there'll be no fancy clothes for you to wear
Everything I have is standing here in front of you to see
All I have to offer you is me

These lyrics have their own intertext in Pride's "Crystal Chandeliers"—*the iconic Pride song* for Aboriginal Australians. Charley Pride is, to outsiders, perhaps an unexpected figure to serve as an icon for Aboriginal Australians. And in some ways his power in Aboriginal Australia, his capacity to give intimate shape to a radically politicized form of public identity, rests in his resolutely commercial status in Australia during the 1960s and 1970s. His records were distributed in Australia by the international media conglomerate RCA, and his enormous popularity in Australia benefited from the relatively restricted variety of international musical popular culture in this period and the extremely wide availability of such commercial recordings. RCA records were everywhere.[11] And as importantly for the circulation of Pride's music across northern Australia, RCA did a brisk business in cassette tapes—the favored medium for musical consumption and circulation in the bush. Many Aboriginal people had battery-operated cassette players in this period, further aiding a musical culture built on the materiality of plastic and acetate. But there is more to this popularity than the simple fact of circulation. Many of my interlocutors, when asked, generally look surprised at the question and respond along the lines of, "Well, of course, he's black!" Pride's blackness and the ubiquity of his records within an already vibrant commercial country music soundscape can thus seem to overdetermine his great popularity across Aboriginal Australia.

Perhaps more obviously, however, the lyrics here speak directly to the situation of the film's protagonists, ensconced in a rural outstation, where a single tin shed and a functional windmill frame Samson's recuperation. While I initially understood this film to suggest a nostalgia for country itself and its privileged mode of circulation in radio request programs, "All I Have to Offer You Is Me" is also a promise, voicing figures of romantic love that address the future. The film thus deploys Pride not as an elegy, but as a promise, as Pride sings in the subjunctive mood and allows Thornton to figure the redemptive power of love. We are returned only in part to pastoral, then, as the film itself takes the form of a country song. If only, it suggests, we could return to our outstation, away from the urban ills, away from the whitefella's ways in Fitzroy and Alice Springs, and away from the grog and the petrol and the violent disregard of a broader Australia.

This soundtrack also suggests a portrait in sound of the Alice Springs Thornton remembers as a younger man. It shares in country's pastoral tropes by evoking this temporal distance, when Alice Springs was, in Thornton's words, still a small town. Responding to a question for the popular Australian media blog *Crikey*, Thornton describes how Alice Springs today differs from the town in which he grew up:

> It's a much darker place now. Back then everybody kept an eye on kids all the time and doors were open. We never had a lock on our door when I grew up. Now the fences have got higher, the dogs have got cheekier and there's two locks on your door. It's better the devil you know and when we grew up we knew the devils. Nowadays you can't pick them in a sense. When I grew up Alice was quite small, tourism was quite small, and today tourism is this mega cog in Alice Springs and so the dark issues are swept under the rocks to keep tourists happy because it's a trillion dollar industry.

However, the film's narrative choices also suggest that other issues bedevil Central Australian Indigenous public culture. In Beck Cole's documentary film *Making "Samson and Delilah,"* we meet Rowan McNamara in his first screen tests with Thornton, dressed in a basketball jersey emblazoned with a FUBU logo. Likewise, the other young men and women we meet as the production crew seeks a cast all wear various forms of contemporary sports clothing. These are markers of contemporary central Australia, differentiated in generational terms by sartorial as well as musical choices. Thornton responds to an interview question about filming teenagers:

> Our kids in Central Australia are caught in this incredibly hard world. There is Aboriginal Law and Culture, which fights to stay strong and there are the pressures of capitalism with rappers 50 Cent and P. Diddy and all the illusions that go with this scene. (Phillips 2009)

In the context of the opposition Thornton evokes here between culture and capitalism, between indigeneity and illusion, the film can be seen to posit country music as something truly and powerfully Aboriginal. Who better,

Thornton suggests, than Charley Pride to give a hopeful voice to the complexities of central Australian life?—and, in light of the complex intercultural and intra-Indigenous politics of Australian country, to sing in a way that can move both Aboriginal and non-Indigenous audiences?

Country's chronotope seeps into the film's broader narrative as well. If we begin with the irony of Pride's "Sunshiny Day" as the soundtrack to petrol sniffing and despair, by the time we reach the conclusion, again with Charley Pride, this irony is replaced with an overriding sentiments of promise, hope, and joy. Samson laughs in pleasure hearing his name in a request tied to a song. Highly crafted, the soundtrack displays clear, almost didactic purpose—it is not merely evocative, but central to the architecture of the narrative. Both in the remarkable irony of the opening sequence and the sense of promise elicited by the film's closing sequence, country music and its radio-mediated public are a central subject of this film. Indeed, the film might be considered a model form of country's expressive remediation.

The Sapphires

Despite the ways these genres can seem generic opposites, and are positioned as such by Thornton here, the sounds of R&B and country musics share an origin story. These different genres share some imaginary space in North America's South, some real studio spaces in what Charles Hughes terms the "Country Soul Triangle" of Memphis, Muscle Shoals, and Nashville (Hughes 2013; cf. Robert Gordon 2013), and they have been North American cotravelers from Al Green's 1970s ventures into the country song book (Awkward 2013) to the more recent recordings of the Hacienda Brothers, who dipped into the soul songbook assisted by pedal steel and baritone guitars to create what they termed a "smoked blend of stone country and old school R&B" and that was received by industry critics and fans as "western soul." As Aaron Fox (2004) and Diane Pecknold (2013) have suggested, the possibility of such transgression and genre mixing depends on the construction of each genre as "black" or "white," on the kinds of social work that distinguish each as the other's racialized alter.

If in North America this cohabitation of soul and country requires some argument and can seem strongest in such idiosyncratic moments as Green's country borrowings or the Hacienda Brothers' genre-bending western soul, in Australia the shared spaces of country and soul are less obscured, and to the extent that both genres can here figure as "black," their juxtaposition can seem less sociologically problematic for many of my Aboriginal interlocutors. This juxtaposition is revisited in another film that, on its face, thematizes soul music and its power to sing of the experiences of black Australians. Wayne Blair's Australian feature film *The Sapphires* (2012) tells the story of an Aboriginal girl group touring Vietnam in the late 1960s, entertaining military troops and finding a sense of affirmation and acceptance both as singers and as black women. Starring Deborah Mailman (as Gail), Jessica Mauboy (playing Julie), Miranda Tapsell, and Shari Sebbens (as Cynthia and Kay, respectively), and with Chris O'Dowd as Irish band manager Dave Lovelace, the film is adapted from the 2005 stage production, directed by Wesley Enoch and written by Tony Briggs about his mother and auntie, who themselves toured Vietnam, Thailand, and the Philippines as backup singers for a soul band in the late 1960s and who had, prior to these travels, performed in Melbourne as the Sapphires, singing soul covers under the direction of Maori band leader Pinky Te Paa.

The film paints a loving portrait of these women and thematizes a meeting of black Australia with the Afro-diasporic musics of American soul and R&B. The problem of blackness constitutes the film's comic and tragic subplots. One of the sisters, for instance, is taken as a "half-caste" child from the family at a young age, and this event drives much of the tension between the sisters and a recurrent contest within the group over who might or might not be a "real" blackfella. But this question also applies to Lovelace, the Irishman who helps build the group, managing their audition and tour through war-torn Vietnam. His character is what Australians might call a soul music tragic, and his love for the genre is deep. We first meet Lovelace as he wakes outside the country hotel where he works; the sounds of "Soul Man" provide an ironic theme song as he stumbles out of his car and through the bright sun to the pub, clad in underwear and carrying his pants. Early in the film when one of the girls asks crudely, "What would this dopey whitefella know about soul music, anyway?" he objects: "Hey! I might be a little pale on the outside, but my blood runs Negro, woman!"

The film's humor often comes from this narrative play with the disjunctive fit between its protagonists' identities as Indigenous and Irish and the musics that move them most.[12] At the outset, the sisters are country music singers, performing for their family and singing a Merle Haggard tune for a local talent show at the pub where Lovelace works as an MC and accompanist. Musical genres loom large in this film and are almost characters themselves. The distinction between country and soul, for instance, is rehearsed early in the film when the band's Irish manager, Dave Lovelace, questions the capacity of the girl group to entertain US troops. Lovelace asks the girls, rhetorically:

OK, just for fun, let's say that you do go to Vietnam, what would you sing? Because this may have escaped your notice, but you're black. And you're singin' country and western music. It's just wrong.

Deborah Mailman's character, Gail, responds to this line of questioning testily: "We don't sing that kind of stuff," she argues. Jessica Mauboy's character, Julie, quickly adds, "We like Charley Pride."

In the Sydney theater where I first saw this movie screened, the audience laughed long and loud at Julie's seeming naive interjection here, registering, I thought, the inside joke—the sense that this love for Charley Pride's music will register to non-Australians as bizarre, out of place, yet also that this is the moment in the film when the "truth" of Aboriginal identity is laid bare. This staging of Charley Pride in opposition to the "soul" needed to please "the brothers in Vietnam" lends country music a special, backhanded distinction as a kind of secret badge of belonging that evokes, almost covertly, strong memories of family and place, characterizing, as it also does for Thornton, a valued Australian black public. In the film, however, Lovelace responds bluntly to the singers' protestation: "If you want to perform for the brothers in Vietnam, you've gotta give them soul."

While the film charts the success of these women and the ways they overcome differences among them through the power of song, staging a strong Australian blackness through the sounds of an Afro-diasporic genre, it also manages through such understatement to make country music itself a black music, more affectively Australian, more intimate: something that if on a global stage might seem out of place, embarrassing, is the precise music for singing to one's kin and community. Such apprehensions of country music position the genre within a broader economy of genre distinctions, such that hip-hop, R&B, and soul do public, performative work while country music, its performance and the unabashed love that it can elicit, occupies a space of what anthropologists might recognize as cultural intimacy. I draw this term from the work of Michael Herzfeld (1997) and Andrew Shryock (2004), for whom it describes forms of cultural practice around which gather forms of self-conscious affection and identification such that the practice becomes iconic of cultural identity. Significantly, in their analyses, these are practices that are felt to attract the negative assessment of outsiders, but which despite, or perhaps because of, this marked character are also routes for the performance of cultural identity and in-group modes of identification. It is particularly appropriate in the case of Aboriginal country insofar as it also speaks to the most intimate domains of contemporary Aboriginal life and to that which has received such profoundly destructive, colonial attention. It is a place where intimacy, kinship relatedness, and a self-conscious apprehension of the voice come together.

For instance, the passage of the singers from young girls under the care of their mother to women in control of their own destinies is mapped by a shift in their repertoire from country music to soul and R&B, and from an audience made up of their family and community to a transnational, black audience for Afro-diasporic expressive forms. There is, here, a tension in the estimation of country's presence and in the form that blackness takes in Aboriginal voices that is given aesthetic treatment, but that is also a site of metapragmatic and aesthetic discourse and argument in radio and music studios—to which I turn in the next chapter.

Gayle Kennedy considered these qualities of the voice in our conversations, and she drew an explicit, feelingful link between the cry-break that marks the country she loves and the kinds of "crying effects" and expressive idioms that move her in soul and R&B:

> I like lots of kinds of music. I like blues. I like jazz. But even in blues and jazz I like the soul, a soulful sound. My favorite singers are people like Shirley Horn, you know, Nina Simone, people with that soul, they've got that heartbreak in their voice too.

Later on Gayle added that "they've got more sex in their voice too." She heard these different genres as registering different kinds of desire, different forms of want, one around loss, the other around lust.

The Sapphires stages this shared space of country and soul, a place where the aching of loss indexed by a broken voice sounds now with desire. Some of the film's most powerful moments stage this desire in the voice of its standout musical performer, Jessica Mauboy. Her character's performance of two different songs early in the film draws Afro-diasporic and American musical circulation into an Aboriginal story, the musical curation of the film's producers evoking the generic complexity of twentieth-century Aboriginal musical culture. In the first performance the girls sing the Haitian song "Yellow Bird" a capella with their mother, making a sonic link to the Caribbean and overtly evoking a Pacific affinity for the sounds of a Black Atlantic. This is nostalgia and sisterly love. Later, in the musical center of the film's first act, the sisters again sing together in a country hotel talent show, performing the Merle Haggard authored "Today I Started Loving You Again." Two of the sisters, Gail and Cynthia, played by Mailman and Tapsell, begin the song alone. They are joined onstage midway through by Mauboy's Julie, whose virtuosic performance lifts an already strong musical performance into three dimensions as three voices join in the chorus. Mauboy, already a star in Australia, plays the youngest sister, full of talent and aching to perform. She brings the song to a conclusion with a melismatic cadenza, harmonizing with her coperformers, yet bending pitches to hint at the pentatonic tonality and melisma of an R&B vocal delivery. This performance, moving from country to hint at the potential of the singers' voices to produce a soulful sound, heralds the musical trajectory of the film's narrative from the cultural intimacy of country music to electric performances for, and romantic trysts with, American soldiers.

Genres of R&B and country can be heard here in the same voice, inflecting single passages with the generic intertextuality of country and R&B. In part this echoes a much broader dynamic in popular music at work both in Australia and North America, in which features of soul and R&B—their "blue notes," melisma, and a throaty vibrato—have taken center stage in varieties of commercial country musics. Widespread forms of commercial music consumption and critique revolve around melisma itself, which grants a ready point of access and assessment for viewers of talent contests such as *American Idol* and *Australian Idol*.[13] In both Australia and the United States melisma provides an icon of R&B performance, the sonic signature of black performance histories in their popular circulation. One might be able to tell the story of contemporary popular music as a kind of gospel minstrelsy in which melisma has moved from the black church across a broad range of popular, commercial musics (see, for instance, Heilbut 1971).

Such minstrel performance has a distinct Australian history. A young Betty Fisher, for instance, was among a group of so-called half-caste children evacuated in 1942 from the Methodist mission on Croker Island, approximately 160 kilometers northeast of Darwin, and then sent far south to a second Methodist mission in suburban Sydney. After three years there Fisher performed for the nationally broadcast radio program *The 2UW Australia Amateur Hour* and won the contest with her rendition of the minstrel song "My Curly-Headed Baby." This was written by the London-based Australian composer George Clutsam in 1897, and later made famous by Paul Robeson's HMV recording in 1932[14] and again in 1948. Blackface minstrelsy was popular across Australia and New Zealand, and Clutsam began his own career as a pianist in a black-face group touring Australia and New Zealand. The choice of tune may also have been inspired by the Australian tenure of the Fisk Jubilee Singers, who themselves traveled through Sydney frequently from the 1890s through the 1930s on a series of Pacific tours.[15] Fisher's own aspirations to sing professionally were dashed when mission officials forced her to return to Croker Island to finish schooling on the mission. At the time her talent and her plight received national attention and a public outpouring of interest in securing her freedom to pursue her musical performance ambitions. By 1948, at age seventeen, she had found the support of a foster family in Sydney and planned to return.

While this suggests the lengthy history of Afro-diasporic and American contributions to antipodean Indigenous performance, it also highlights the ways they come alive in Australia in movements through other places: England, New Zealand, and North America all contributed to the phenomenon of public concern evoked by Fisher's predicament. The story grew perhaps more complicated in the second half of the twentieth century, when record distribution relied on economic projections of market prospects that were based on what was happening with music sales in England. As Australian music journalist and historian Clinton Walker recalled, in the 1960s and 1970s New Zealanders provided a route for a range of black musics that were not felt by record companies to be as marketable to Australian audiences. In the 1960s and 1970s marketing divisions for labels such as RCA and EMI kept their eyes on the English charts, deciding on the basis of success in the United Kingdom which records to import into Australia's much smaller market. This meant that only a few recordings would circulate in official, commercial channels in Australia. In New Zealand, however, Walker recalled that one could find a greater range of American imports, as the black market for imported recordings was less strictly policed there than in Australia. Several observations follow from this divergence. First, Pinky Te Paa and other musicians can be understood as conduits for the circulation of Afro-diasporic musics into Australia. As significantly, these sounds echoed across the Pacific in specific moments of performance, accompanying soldiers and the broader apparatus of American and Australian war efforts in Southeast Asia. Black soldiers from America, Māori band leaders from New Zealand, and black singers from Australia meet in the camps and bases and bars of Vietnam. In *The Sapphires* these meetings are narrated as romantic encounters in which Aboriginal singers attract the desiring ears and eyes of American servicemen (and an Irish soul music tragic) and provide a kind of "foundational fiction" (Sommer 1993) for contemporary Indigenous public culture—a narrative that tropes diasporic intimacy as romantic love.[16]

Mauboy's own commercial break came from her turn as a finalist on the popular talent show *Australian Idol*, not unlike Betty Fisher in her 1945 success. For Mauboy's audition, televised in 2006, she sang Whitney Houston's "I Have Nothing" in a remarkable performance filled by repeated crescendos, pitch-sliding into the melody, and a broad voice devoid of nasality but replete with phrase-initial laryngealization (instances of "vocal fry" or "creaky voice") followed by clear, broad vibrato and the expressive constriction of the throat around the larynx. These techniques have long provided gospel and soul singing their particular emotional timbres and famously inflect soul voices with a simulacra of the loss of control, a hypercontrolled expressivity that sounds as a crying out or a scream (à la Sam and Dave's shouts in the song "Soul Man"—which in *The Sapphires* plays from Lovelace's radio in the sequence immediately preceding Mauboy's performance of "Today I Started Loving You Again").[17] Alongside such melisma and vocal fry, in performance Mauboy employs a wide, controlled chest voice that at once advertises virtuosity and registers emotional engagement.

In Blair and Briggs's film country and soul are made to relate, their shared social space staged narratively and musically by these remarkable singers in their performance of a Merle Haggard cover, a performance coded here as maximally "black," feelingful, and replete with the true virtuosity of artistic accomplishment. The story thus does both narrative and musical historical work, drawing "soul" back through Aboriginal music history while amplifying viewers' awareness of Aboriginal Australia's long-term musical cosmopolitanism and the skill of its practitioners, represented here through the (semifictionalized) story of an original Aboriginal girl group. In my viewing, the film registers both the cultural intimacy that sounds in and as Aboriginal country and an interest in an Indigenous musical cosmopolitanism that recognizes and aspires to relatedness with a global black diaspora. Through the manifest technical skill of its performers and the high production values of the film itself, it also provides something to which its audience might aspire. In promoting the film, Blair expressed his interest in reaching an audience of young Indigenous women in a form that might make them proud, might give them a sense of their own possibility.

Today both country music and R&B are enjoying an Australian renaissance. In addition to the popularity of *The Sapphires* and its chart-topping soundtrack, singer Emma Donovan's recording "Daddy" sounds like a reverential ode to the Stax record label. The song was recorded in Melbourne in 2014 with a white backing band, the Putbacks, and draws an overtly nostalgic line to 1970s recording culture, its guitar lines transformed by a germanium-chip fuzz pedal, and its quick 4/4 tempo driven along by conga drums. Donovan's sessions also look backward with nostalgia to a prior era's technologies and were recorded with the Putbacks in a single room on analog 8-track tape. "Daddy" has received accolades in the Australian press and in the US-based magazine *Wax Poetics*, while Donovan herself has drawn comparisons to American virtuosic soul revivalist Sharon Jones.

The Sapphires' soundtrack also was produced with spare, period-correct arrangements. The track "What a Man," for instance, sounds much closer to its 1968 Stax prototype, originally sung by white American Linda Lyndell, than it does to either Mauboy's other contemporary recordings or to the 1994 Salt-N-Pepa version of the same tune. An onscreen cover of Otis Redding's 1962 Stax recording "These Arms of Mine" also receives the spare accompaniment of guitar and piano, but its sung performance takes contemporary form through pitch-sliding, quickened tempo, and melismatic delivery. Such techniques perform complicated temporal work with genre and should be heard at once as the sonic counterpoint to the filmic realism of Blair's production, as well as part of a broader politicized nostalgia, of which Donovan's "Daddy" also partakes.

Donovan's family, however, much like the filmic Sapphires, has a history in country music. Her parents and their siblings made up the Donovans, a popular country and folk group, and in her childhood she traveled annually to sing at the Tamworth Country Music Festival with her mother. Donovan herself went on to cofound the Stiff Gins, a well-regarded vocal trio of Indigenous women, and sang in the Black Armband, a music and theater company made up of some of Australia's best-known Indigenous musicians. Donovan's generic and performance interests are, much like Mauboy's, quite broad. Reflecting on comparisons with forms of soul revival elsewhere for *Wax Poetics*, Donovan differentiated her musical signature. She recalled growing up performing country music and exploring the sounds of the musical legends that filled her father's record collection, where she remembered finding Etta James and Laverne Baker alongside Aboriginal groups such as No Fixed Address and singers like Archie Roach. Each of these musical projects relates a story about the Black Pacific and does so in sound, lending a historical resonance to Black Australia that speaks to the shared space of country and soul in a local acoustic imaginary.

2.1 Betty Fisher introduces the Croker Island Mission to reporters from *Australian Women's Weekly*, March 26, 1946.

SHOWING our representatives round the Mission grounds with other girls, Betty sang with unconscious pathos, "Don't Fence Me In."

It is this sonic imagination, a doubling in sound of a social relation, that I hear in *The Sapphires*, in Emma Donovan's soul revival, and in a range of other contemporary forms of R&B and hip-hop across Australia. This dialogue with the musics of North America also, in both its aspiration for relation and its self-awareness, asks us to recall Betty Fisher. In 1946 the *Australian Women's Weekly* magazine visited Croker Island for a photographic feature celebrating Fisher's plans to return to Sydney. They brought a photographer who documented Fisher giving the reporters a tour of the mission. A striking photograph in the magazine depicts Fisher smiling, arms akimbo, and striding along a path, her mouth open, singing "with unconscious pathos," we are told in the caption, Cole Porter's well-known cowboy song "Don't Fence Me In" (figure 2.1). The image is arresting, a photograph that indeed resonates with song. But I find it difficult to imagine that Fisher would not be keenly aware of the tropic potentials of Porter's famous tune, of the near impossibility of hearing it without attention to its figurative pathos (or perhaps droll humor).

Attention to the power and pathos of song preoccupies all of my contemporary musical interlocutors, as does a frequent and sustained reflection on the implications of musical sound and sung text. From Nana Evie's laserlike aim with George Jones's "Choices" to the musical sophistication that occupies Mauboy in her renditions of contemporary R&B, music and the voice provide stages on which people both produce and reflect on the social in sound. The politics of racialization this sound world evokes are complicated by forms of governmental elicitation and liberal recognition, themselves bound up with a historically durable ideology of voice as expressive interiority, autonomy, and agency. In the following chapter I turn to ethnographic work in a contemporary Aboriginal country music station to explore the ways that encounters with a mediatized voice can evoke forms of voice consciousness to better understand the particular extensions of social imagination that musical form entails in Indigenous radio and music studios and to explore the politics of such reflection on sound. The ideology of voice as expressive agency must be drawn back through the capacity of the voice to double social relations, to make these an object of reflection, praxis, and politics.

CHAPTER 3 | From the Studio to the Street

Let's go back along this country track a little further, returning briefly to *Samson and Delilah*, focused less now on its remediation of country music and more on its filmic interest in staging the voice. Thornton describes this film as a central desert love story, and its narrative does, in part, travel the road of its protagonists' mutual desire and the obstacles they must overcome in order to be together by story's end. But *Samson and Delilah* is also notable as a story about the challenges of living in a particular place and time. Visually, it works with the contrasts of the desert sun and landscape to emplace its characters in a beautiful desert space, yet also brings its audience into the various institutional and intimate spaces in which its characters dwell—bedrooms, cars, a dusty mattress on a front porch, a drinker's camp below a bridge. The realist imperative that brings local, untutored actors to the screen also inflects the screenplay's minimalism and perhaps keeps the staging of the remarkable central desert landscape from overwhelming the "hard love" that Thornton seeks to explore. The soundtrack, largely keeping to this imperative, draws heavily on the diegetic space of the screen narrative for its sources. The film's spare Warlpiri dialogue is joined by the music of American country singer Charley Pride, a central desert reggae band, and the Mexican singer Ana Gabriel, as well as the sounds of radio, the cafes of Alice Springs, and the daily soundscape of a remote community. This film's sound world is diverse and rich.

Yet for all the attention to sound here, the communication between Thornton's two protagonists occurs largely through sign language, an aspect of the film that can be read as a realist gesture, one that reflects the widespread use of sign languages across central and northern Australia. The immediate material reasons for this, however, are specific to the film's casting. Thornton and his coproducers were intent on producing the film primarily in Warlpiri language—and they remain proud of the film as an award-winning Warlpiri-language production.[1] However, Thornton's lead actor Rowan McNamara does not speak the Warlpiri of the other central cast member, Marissa Gibson. With an otherwise spare vocal soundtrack, voiced largely in the Warlpiri language of central Australia, and with two main characters whose communication is frequently silent, "voiced" with sign language, the film's musical media thus do expressive work where dialogue cannot, amplifying the affective aspects of their relationship and suggesting the complexity of these characters' interior lives. We are shown this complexity, asked to feel it, through sound.

Thornton was also critical of the representation of Aboriginal and adolescent interaction in other filmic works. His aim with his own screenplay was for a more accurate representation of the nuances and rhythms of adolescent interaction, enabled perhaps by his need to rely on sign language and the broad media ecology of central Australia. And this also inflected the minimalism of the film's scripting. Asked in an promotional interview about the spare dialogue of the film, Thornton's first response addressed the representation of adolescent love:

> That's realism to me. When you're fourteen you don't talk about love like you're a forty-year-old who's been through two marriages. When I was growing up, if I liked a girl I threw a rock at her. I also think that audiences should work as well. It's easy for a writer to have his characters say "I'm happy," "I'm sad," write that into a script and then have an actor say it. It's much harder when you have to play it without words.

Indeed, its two central characters do largely "play it without words," and this marks the experience of watching the film profoundly.

For me, these circumstances of production and careful, realist representation lead to a different sort of question: How might it matter that the most lauded Aboriginal film of the past decade, the paradigmatic icon of success of a thirty-year-long effort to give voice and attain recognition, must ultimately background speech itself? With only a few exceptions, in this film people's voices come from outside bodies—from cassette decks and car radios. And if the radio voices a request for Samson from his father, implying to the audience that the latter will be coming home from jail, the song then seems taken up by Samson, "speaking" with it to Delilah as they share a smile. In this mechanized, iterable expressivity—a request from a father to a son taking shape as reported speech in a voice that reaches out from radio—radio's foundation poles of intimacy and self-abstraction find remediation in cinematic form, ventriloquizing an Aboriginal public with a radio voice (see Bolter and Grusin 1998; Mazzarella 2004). What can we learn from the near-literal equation of media with voice in this film, with its diegetic mechanization and musicalization of the voice?

Thornton here literalizes metaphors of prosthesis that subtend many discussions of media and modernity (Mills 2012) by presenting a subject who physically cannot speak, who relies on media's capacities for his powers of speech. Thornton also opens a window onto a local apprehension of the social and technical distribution of vocal agency. In broad and widely analyzed tropes, to "have voice" is to be an autonomous, political subject. In the film, however, this particular equation is both reaffirmed and problematized. The film suggests, for instance, that the voice is something Samson's difficult life takes from him. It is through key forms of kin relationship and romantic love that Samson may in fact regain a voice lost to petrol sniffing and despair. The film thus tropes the capacity of musical sound and radio broadcasts to speak as a mediatized collective Aboriginal subject, even as it begins to question where the voice might itself be found. *Samson and Delilah*, then, can figure here as an aesthetic index of a "voice consciousness" (Feld et al. 2004) widely prevalent in music and radio studios in both northern and southeastern Australia, one that involves the de- and renaturalization of media as voice in forms of vocal media.

Analyses of Radio as a Vocal Technology

In this chapter I return to 4AAA, Brisbane's technology-rich, highly successful Aboriginal country music radio station, with these questions of the voice's mediatization and remediation in the foreground. I want to explore features of this institutional voice consciousness and to address the relationship between a broad, transnational discourse of voice as agency, and the highly reflexive, maximally technical work of Aboriginal radio production. How is a local apprehension of the voice's materialization and plasticity as "wired sound" conditioned by understandings of the voice as a meaningful figure of agency and identity? I demonstrate that while "voice" has been a paramount icon of

Indigenous agency and political power, and occasionally a fetish of policy discourse (Batty 2003; Michaels 1994; Sterne 2003), it is also persistently denaturalized in forms of technical labor, vocal performance, and in the discursive give-and-take of Aboriginal radio production and musical curation. Indeed, in the increasingly industrial, digitally mediated work of Indigenous radio, the voice can at times seem a material object, external to particular bodies, and an effect of technological intervention and manipulation.

The chapter draws on these poles of Indigenous voice consciousness to craft some ethnographic coordinates for understanding radio as a generative site of Indigenous self-fashioning. Following a brief analytical discussion and short sketch of Aboriginal radio's historical emergence, I explore three interrelated domains in which ideas of voice are produced and given life. These include the visually dense, historically charged environment of urban Aboriginal radio production; broader discursive fields in which icons of "black" identity inflect local vocal styles and ideas of expressive propriety; and governmental media programs and cultural policies geared toward eliciting and encouraging Indigenous expressive practices. In framing Aboriginal radio as a site of cultural production, the discussion foregrounds the voice as a place in which blackness and indigeneity are negotiated in practice and through metacultural discourse. Throughout I consider how radio's contexts of production as wired sound might reframe how we think about the interaction of different domains for "voice"—as icon of agency, index of copresence, site of affective and aesthetic investment, and object of social critique.

That radio may amplify the voice's social meaning as index of collective agency is an idea with a distinguished history. Frantz Fanon's writings on radio are prescient in their interest in the uncanny social power of a "voice" that is never heard in its "calm objectivity," but rather in light of colonial social relations, violence, and new kinds of national subjectivity. Anticipating Marshall McLuhan, and preceding Benedict Anderson's provocative *Imagined Communities* by twenty-five years, Fanon writes of the changing meaning of the radio voice in Algeria over the course of the revolution—from being a voice of colonial power to one of national subjectivity and a way to affectively participate in the revolution, in which owning a radio meant "buying the right of entry into the struggle of an assembled people" (1994 [1965]: 84). Vocal sound occupies a paradoxical place in this important chapter in Fanon's writing, at once central to it but curiously absent. The more the French colonial forces sought to jam the insurgent broadcasts of *The Voice of Fighting Algeria*, and the more difficult it was to actually hear its broadcasts, he argues, the more powerful it became as an icon of Algerian independence and national identity.[2]

In psychoanalytic and deconstructive writings, the voice figures as excessive to language, foundational for all meaning, and yet meaning nothing in itself (Derrida 1976; Dolar 2006; Salecl and Žižek 1996). In a prominent psychoanalytically inclined conversation, voice and the gaze emerge as sites of volatility, structuring absences around which desire seeks coherence (see Copjec 1996; Salecl and Žižek 1996). Similarly, though in the form of historical narrative, Fanon describes a radio voice that exceeds linguistic, prosodic, or poetic analysis. It is foundational for a sense of Algerian national subjectivity, yet as one seeks to tune in, it remains static and noise. In Fanon's Algeria the radio voice emerges as a social Rorschach, an aural instigation to a listener's historically primed psychic life. Through this figure of noise as an opening onto desire, Fanon's brief historical account provides a psychoanalytically informed account of the mediatization of politics at midcentury, an early evocation of the mediatized voice as itself political power, its own end.

An obverse instance of the close connection between political power, radio, and the voice is analyzed by James Siegel (1998), recounting Sukarno's annual Indonesian Independence Day address from 1963. Here Sukarno himself figures his own voice in its broadcast mediation as an "extension of the tongue of the people" (in Siegel 1998: 23). To address the people here is expressly performative: it calls forth that to which it refers in what Siegel terms a promise. But it also exceeds the discursive, sociological relation that would make Sukarno an originary source of such performative power, as he is himself possessed, made a medium through the address. The figures used to evoke his mediumship are at once electric and sonic: Sukarno titles his address "the resounding voice of the Indonesian people," and Siegel shares that the idiomatic figure for voice here means, literally, a "bell," a cowbell. Sukarno's address is dense in figures of electrified sound animating a national people through his mediumship: "Everything in my body seethes (or overflows); my thoughts seethe, my feelings seethe; my nerves seethe, my emotions seethe. Everything in my body then vibrates, becomes spirited and shakes and for me, fire is as though it is not hot enough, the sea is not deep enough, the stars in the heavens are not high enough" (quoted in Siegel 1998: 25).

This passage describes the shift from a familial authority to that of the state as Sukarno's vocalized address, broadcast by radio to the people, produces the people as its body; it is the obverse of Fanon's image inasmuch as the voice of authority emerges as an electric loop, oscillating between the collective body

and the personification of authority from which it springs. Uncannily resonant with Fanon's account of radio's animation of a collective, fighting Algeria, Sukarno's address looks past the revolutionary moment to its postcolonial
consolidation in which, broadcast by radio and television, his voice "claimed
to bring the revolutionary forces into the nation" (Siegel 1998: 29). A mediatized voice here thus animates authority as a postcolonial negation, a populist
assertion of nationalist autonomy (see also Mrázek 2002).

Such historically charged enframings of radio technology—bound tightly
in both Fanon's Algeria and Siegel's Indonesia to almost erotic figures of the
voice's mechanized displacement—continue to shape how we think about
radio today and are deeply embedded in its ideological evolution over the
twentieth century in postcolonial and national projects. These ideas and
tropes also echo through the politics of Australian community radio broadcasting and advocacy and into the ways that people talk about Aboriginal
radio more generally. In Australia, radio has been celebrated and deployed as
an affordable, durable form of small media through which Aboriginal people
can speak to one another and create a kind of community. It also has been understood as at once a means to enable and enlighten Aboriginal communities
through health education and political information, and a means by which
diverse Aboriginal groups can become a people—culturally empowered in the
face of forms of transnational media commodity and an encompassing society's
damaging representations. Yet in the studio radio animates voices such that
they exceed any natural, ahistorical ontology, becoming entangled with the
racial and cultural politics so alive in the margins of the settler colony.

To talk about encounters with the voice in the language of the uncanny
is therefore not to amplify the strangeness of the voice to my interlocutors
but, rather, to underscore the ways in which the voice arrives in these different institutions through a series of avatars which are resolutely historical
and social, the product of distinct and specific relations and institutions, and
in which are invested a series of specific historical and political aspirations.
Here, then, I want to divorce the uncanny from its foundation in Freud's "spe-
cies of fear" (cf. Masco 2006) and instead tie the strangeness I at times found
in my interlocutors' engagement with the mediatized voice more directly to
struggle and contest; to the pervasive sense of care and uncertainty that so
marked practices of media production in the institutions where I worked;
and to the shared and at times agonistic forms of interest and desire that
gathered around the voice as a site of social aspiration. This is to follow both
Fanon and Siegel, to hear sounds as haunted, perhaps, by things that are

not necessarily manifest but through which our ears are drawn as to a "blind field" (Barthes 1980), a zone of concern resting in the experiences, interests, or preoccupations of an auditor. In this specific way the mediatized voice might be understood as a "phantom power," to play on the term for the electrical current provided to the condenser microphones resting above radio desks and cluttering up the recording studios of northern Australia. It is present, a material agent in the history of Aboriginal Australia, yet is also something that does not simply secure identity but also solicits contest and the cultural work to which such contest can give rise.

Here I ask what it means for my Indigenous interlocutors to produce actual Aboriginal voices for radio and musical circulation, to speak into a microphone, edit vocal sound on a computer monitor, and argue about the matter of the voice in a radio station's conference room. The stakes of such vocal production are high. For the Aboriginal cultural producers with whom I work, such media production has become a crucial site for Indigenous cultural reproduction and activism. The broad publics and intra-Indigenous relationships that radio production entails have transformed the character of Indigenous social life and are a key feature of daily life across Aboriginal Australia—and the outcomes of such arguments, the place where participants fall in understanding what the voice is and from whom it emerges, can seem immediately consequential. At once an effort to intervene in popular representations of Aboriginal people, a means of finding new, intercultural forms of address that might reach both settler Australian and Aboriginal audiences, and the stage for increasingly diverse forms of Indigenous popular culture, radio stations are places where people attend in a heightened fashion to expressive features of the voice more generally.

Together these practices constitute a local domain of voice consciousness, and I share many concerns with the scholars discussed above. But in describing the vocal features of such industrial sound production in Australia—where racially marked forms of music and a contested politics of recognition suffuse radio production, music, and other forms of Aboriginal cultural production— I seek to foreground the charged, maximally heteroglossic, perhaps dangerous or exciting power that occupies certain expressions and expressive practices and can seem to inhabit the voice itself in contexts of Aboriginal media production. More generally, to take up a radio voice, speak into a microphone, and edit sound visually on a computer monitor is also in some sense to alienate one's own voice—to become other to it.[3] In these terms a radio voice might acquire an agency of its own and resonate with something inexplicable yet powerful, and this may contribute to one's sense of its power (see Fisher 2010). However, one might also see that power domesticated by technologies, brought to heel by the magic of technological manipulation, the processing power behind digital editing technologies translating at times into the naturalized reification of "voice" as simply a communicative instrument. Yet if we too quickly see magic turn to technology, we elide the risks and sense of consequence that attend such technologized vocal production. If Indigenous radio production and vocal training may allow the voice to become an object, it is one of a special kind—one that by the seeming ease of its technical manipulation, its transformation to a visual icon on a computer screen, and by the risks entailed in adopting particular voices of racialized others, encourages people to reflexively consider its contours, boundaries, and social ramifications.

These are thus sites of highly reflexive and collective self-fashioning in two senses: that of "standing for"—reminding others, particularly settler Australians, of the historical firstness of Aboriginal people to Australia—and of "speaking for"—acting in a politically representative fashion as part of a broader, settler Australian democratic project.[4] The Aboriginal audio media I focus on here should thus be seen through the lens of a long-standing struggle both to assert Aboriginal sovereignty, occupation, and belonging—the firstness of Indigenous Australians vis-à-vis the state and a settler Australia—and an interpellation by a range of state agencies and governmental interests in soliciting forms of Aboriginal participation. An awareness of so many divergent investments in the voice was not always readily articulable by my interlocutors, but did emerge in contexts of argument around the cultural, Aboriginal, and at times racialized character of the voices they were tasked with producing. It is this layering of interest in the voice that can inform a sense of anxiety, disfluency, and antagonism toward particular media projects, scripts, and institutions.

Programming and Digital Production

Let me briefly return to and renarrate the emergence of Aboriginal-produced radio, tying it more closely now to the early prevalence of request programming and governmental concerns with the cultural threat of satellite broadcasting. The advent of Indigenous radio production can be located in the early 1980s in two related developments: first, the efforts of Aboriginal activists to develop community radio in urban and town locations, and second, the growth of activism and subsequently cultural policy to promote remote

Indigenous broadcasting—initially within a framework of cultural survival and language maintenance. In Australia's southeast Aboriginal activists began broadcasting on non-Indigenous community radio stations, often at the invitation of DJs involved in the peace movements of the 1970s and 1980s, and themselves inspired by the anarchist, oppositional politics of European, particularly Italian, free radio. In relatively remote areas of Australia's North and West, and in response to the advent of satellite broadcasting across the Northern Territory activists, academics, and policy makers saw in radio and in then-new video technologies a means to intervene in the kinds of media to which Aboriginal people would be subject (Ginsburg 1991, 1994, 1997; Langton 1993; Michaels 1994). The impending arrival of the AUSSAT satellite in 1985 informed a range of political endeavors to amplify remote Indigenous Australian involvement in media production, while in southeastern cities, broader policies of self-determination and Aboriginal participation led to efforts to make space in national media organizations for Indigenous voices.

Early on radio producers in both urban and remote or regional locations began visiting prisons, making cassette-recorded greetings that could be played on-air from the studios and taking telephoned requests to be broadcast into nearby jails. Yet early programming most frequently was produced locally, only occasionally drawing on cassette-recorded programs distributed by post. It thus was rarely heard interstate as a form of "national" Aboriginal media. Aboriginal radio's expansive spatial reach began with the networking of remote broadcasters in the 1990s, and with the 1996 establishment of the National Indigenous Radio Service (NIRS). These technological developments led to the possibility of national broadcast programming and mark the relatively recent arrival of a national, electronically mediated Aboriginal domain. As I discuss in chapter 4, 4AAA's choice of country music as its primary genre offering was at once historically overdetermined by the great popularity of country music in Indigenous Australia and also politically strategic. Not only did this allow 4AAA (or Triple-A) to reach a large non-Indigenous audience; it also gave them access to a great deal of Aboriginal music, provided them with a potential commercial base by filling a niche then underdeveloped in Brisbane's broadcast market, and involved them with a number of industry organizations and a wide, potentially national, Aboriginal audience. Today 4AAA seeks to reach both Aboriginal and non-Indigenous audiences through a shared musical genre, avoiding confrontation in favor of bridging an intercultural chasm and historical point of conflict. Aboriginal radio's sounds, then, have been mediated from the start by the historical popularity of country music globally, across Indigenous and settler populations.

But there is more to the mechanics of this mediation than programmers' broad attention to their growing pan-Australian audience. In addition to the broad focus on a shared musical genre, 4AAA's country music programming is joined by broadcast projects ranging from public service announcements and audio "bulletin boards" (addressed specifically to Brisbane's Indigenous population) to request programs geared toward those who have been incarcerated in southeastern Queensland's prisons. And it also entails training Indigenous young people in the various skills involved in radio production, from presentation and journalism to telephone sales, marketing, and social networking. This inclusion of trainees in 4AAA's broad range of broadcasting projects meant that radio production was a frequent topic of technical discussion and manipulation at 4AAA, and also a framework for thinking and talking about the voice itself.

The Stayin' Strong project provides one example of radio programming, active during my research at Triple-A, in which discussions revolved around forms of vocal address and within which young Aboriginal producers were trained to reflect on their voice as a media instrument. Funded by a state program geared toward suicide prevention, the Stayin' Strong project aimed to provide information to Indigenous "youth," a charged category and focus of increased governmental and developmental attention in Queensland as elsewhere in Australia. While primarily a program targeting Indigenous suicide and seeking to reduce the prevalence of this phenomenon in Indigenous communities around Australia, according to a flyer handed out to staff explaining the goals of the project, it also aimed "to provide positive messages alongside information about community organizations and resources people can access both in times of crisis and to improve their lives in general."

During twice-weekly production meetings, trainer Matthew Simms would lead a group of Murri men and women from their late teens to their early twenties through various tasks associated with producing this prerecorded program. Short segments on depression, youth suicide, drug use, and education incorporated statistical information and interviews to construct a magazine-style public service announcement aimed at Aboriginal youth. These were conceptually divided into four types of messages: "Service Provider Profiles," giving information on Aboriginal and Torres Strait Islander organizations such as health, employment, housing, education; "Inspirational Messages" from community elders; "Issues-Based Interviews" that explored in more

3.1 Maestro software and broadcast hardware, Radio Larrakia studios, 2004.

depth issues around suicide prevention, as well as other issues affecting Indigenous youth; and what station management termed "Community Voices"—"an opportunity for everyday people in the community to deliver positive messages or talk about their own experiences." Produced, digitally mixed and mastered, and finally presented by young Murri trainees, programs such as Stayin' Strong were one primary focus of training—training that included both technical and expressive, vocal components.

In 2003 and 2004 the inclusion of trainees in such station programming relied heavily on 4AAA's capability to prerecord and digitally schedule radio programming. The station is unusual among Indigenous media organizations for its enthusiastic embrace of digital programming technology. An Australian-authored software program, Maestro, allows DJs to preselect songs from a digital library and to schedule programming, including the forward- and back-announcing of songs, commercial advertising, and public service announcements (figure 3.1). Such production work is also highly visual, run through the digital interfaces of Microsoft Windows–based software such as CoolEdit or SoundForge, and has as its formal aim the construction of a "live" community and the experience of copresence.[5] While a good number of

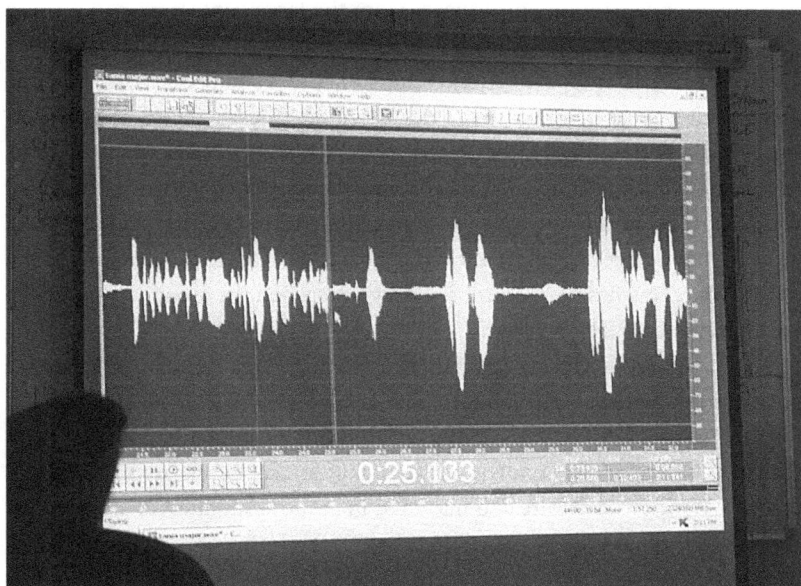

3.2 Students learn to normalize the voice using digital compression in CoolEdit Pro software.

Aboriginal stations had moved to digital libraries and to the Windows-based control panel of Maestro, few, if any, had so completely embraced the digitization of the DJ's audience address. This was understood as a professionalization of 4AAA's operation, and the extremes of digital manipulation this entailed informed the great extent to which broadcast technique and vocal technologies became sites of discursive and practical consciousness.

During the course of my fieldwork, the sixth and eighth floors provided a home for 4AAA's broadcast work, and the sixth was most frequently dedicated to media training. A large conference room occupied the main center of the floor and was in use daily as meeting room, classroom, and workshop for the various digital tasks associated with broadcast training. Scattered around its edges were long tables and desks for PC workstations. These were constantly in use—sometimes for manipulating the sounds that make up 4AAA's broadcasts, and at other times to search the Web for MP3s, to look at hip-hop and R&B fan sites, and to produce the beats and hip-hop rhymes that were a constant focus of interest for the young men training at 4AAA (figure 3.2).

This large room was flanked by smaller offices, each containing one or two PC workstations also networked into 4AAA's large server. At the end of a long corridor separating office spaces from the large conference room stood a complete digital studio, called studio C in reference to broadcast studios A and B, the on-air and production studio's on 4AAA's main, eighth floor. The broadcasting desks of these three studios brought together a traditional mixing console with a desktop PC wired to 4AAA's institutional server. Soundproofed and outfitted with mixing console, microphones, and another digital workstation, studio C was often occupied by 4AAA staff producing training recordings, conducting interviews with guests for later broadcast, or putting the finishing touches on prerecorded programs when the broadcast studios of the eighth floor were occupied.

Radio production at 4AAA thus exemplified what Porcello and Greene have termed "wired sound" (2005). That is, the "object" of Triple-A labor and the manifest focus of much training exists as information and electricity, signals tonally shaped through a visual digital interface. Levels are manipulated through Windows software and mastered in a studio situation using a professional audio program that "normalizes" audio levels through the compression of signal peaks and audio drop-out to achieve a signal even in amplitude and polished for a smooth, broadcast friendly signal. In 4AAA's studios, the actual sounds of radio production emerged only sporadically from desktop speakers, wired into the Windows-based digital workstations, and 4AAA's broadcast signal itself was generally heard only in the background, coming through the small speakers of the telephone intercom system and quietly battling with the tinny sounds of headphones and the spontaneous hip-hop rhyming and verbal play of Murri trainees.

But sound was always an object of talk. While it is possible for a particular recording to be downloaded to the digital library, "normalized" visually through CoolEdit, and sent to air through the Maestro scheduler without ever actually sounding in the space of 4AAA, the form of that signal—its sound, shape, and substance—was always a topic of conversation. Sound was a constant, if hushed, presence. While students were being trained in the conference room to prepare a community service announcement free of digital clipping and without sudden surges of volume, others were discussing how best to script an appeal for volunteers or learning to insert a musical "bed" beneath a prerecorded interview. Indeed, at times employees and trainees found this aspect of radio production an affront to their sensibilities as to what radio should entail, and station management themselves continued to seek a comfortable balance between live-to-air radio and digitally produced programming. For example, the significance of copresence was a frequent point of discussion among station managers and DJs. Although 4AAA did not advertise its digital disc jockey, some DJs felt that the lack of actual liveness was a liability for the station—"canned" programs were felt to be less dynamic, less able to draw listeners in. Perhaps in response to this pervasive sense that liveness was critical to the character of good radio, my period of fieldwork also corresponded with a series of changes in the live-to-air schedule including an overnight show geared toward "truckies" and live on-air DJs monitoring the signal throughout the day.

Most days at 4AAA were thus filled with several kinds of ongoing radio production. In the mornings one might find AJ in the on-air studio, announcing country hits, sharing news and weather, conducting interviews, and occasionally bringing live performers in for brief on-air sets. Across the hallway, Marissa James might be found prerecording and programming a Sunday night request show, while in the newsroom special reports were written and taken into Studio B for production, prerecording, downloading into the digital library, and adding to the scheduler for later broadcast. These industrialized production practices draw attention to the more general status of radio's liveness and immediacy as semiotic and representational conventions as well as the object of a good deal of social labor (Meintjes 2003). On the one hand, 4AAA works to produce this sense of liveness with digital schedules and prerecorded programming technologies, and on the other, it achieves this effect through the rebroadcasting of telephone requests and recorded "back-announcing" in which a DJ lists the songs just heard and perhaps comments on the material. The close interweaving of song, speech, and call sign are highly crafted, programmed streams that work to entail copresence and to grab the attention of listeners who, my interlocutors frequently remarked, might switch the channel at any moment.

When questioned, however, Bayles tells visitors how this digital approach to media production allows Triple-A to provide a twenty-four-hour broadcast signal. This itself is a significant and rare achievement in chronically underfunded and understaffed Indigenous community radio stations. An example of how such programming has been significant for 4AAA can be seen in the Sunday night broadcast, which began with the "youth program" *Girrabala*, a one-hour music magazine that ran from seven until eight, and continued with a four-hour request program dedicated to broadcasting music that had been requested by listeners who recorded telephone messages left on the station's dedicated voice mail. *Girrabala* was produced each week by senior trainees, who selected music, prerecorded back-announcements and interview segments, sought commercial sponsorship, produced public service announcements, and made sure all of this was mixed, mastered, and scheduled onto Maestro by Thursday evening. These kinds of hands-on tasks gave trainees a focus for their work that ran side by side with both the official media production curriculum proffered by commonwealth educational bureaucracy, and an education in the political history and politics of urban Aboriginal cultural production (and which I discuss more extensively below). Here, however, I wish to foreground how the technology of digital broadcasting allowed a single staff member to draw requests from an answering machine, pair these with songs drawn from the digital library, and construct a sonic representation of copresent listeners sharing their attention through 4AAA's signal—and to do so from the confines of a suburban office, hours, days, or weeks before the program was sent to air. As in many commercial broadcasters in mainstream Australia, in the process the voice achieved reification and manipulability within a loose circuit of techniques, technologies, and broader suppositions about how a radio voice ought to sound. In the next section I suggest how that circuit opens onto an Aboriginal social world as well.

From the Studio to the Street: Radio Sound and Social Mediation

If vocal sound is a constant focus of talk and technical practice at 4AAA, its politics and the meaning of an Aboriginal voice emerged from the streets of Brisbane as much as from the studio.[6] This was most apparent in the ways that the lives of my trainee friends trailed into production studios and conference rooms—spinning out from their anxieties about, interests in, and aspirations for the world outside.

This is easiest to demonstrate in terms of musical genre. The efforts by 4AAA trainers and Indigenous managers to cultivate a strong, professionally competent Aboriginal voice overlapped with the interests of their younger trainees in hip-hop performance and the cultivation of its particular vocal skill set. Indeed, while the young broadcasters I worked with valued their participation in the professionalization of Aboriginal cultural production, they also drank from a very different pool of musical commodity and ideas of expressive empowerment—and displayed a markedly greater interest in hip-hop and R&B—than the older trainers and station managers.[7] For many of the young men I knew at 4AAA, the technical skills provided by 4AAA's production training were thus put to service manufacturing "beats"—the rhythmic, musical foundation for the verbal contests and hip-hop performances that spontaneously broke out in 4AAA's training studio—and my younger interlocutors at 4AAA sought skills in rhyming and the competitive poetics of hip-hop improvisation. And these interests led them to pressure Bayles and other senior 4AAA staff to include more hip-hop, more R&B, more "black" music in the station's broadcasting menu.

This, however, entailed some expressive dilemmas, as became clear to me in a relatively rare, informal public performance I attended in 2003; not in the studio, then, but in the street—in the places where expressive culture and forms of identity and difference were negotiated in interpersonal, occasionally violent intercultural spaces. In early March, I met 4AAA DJ and radio producer DS and several of his friends at Currie's, one of the many nightclubs and cafes located in Brisbane's Fortitude Valley—but one of the very few that opened their doors to young, mostly white men for hip-hop battles, bourbon-based drinks, and beat-based vocal display. In general, the performance venues for Aboriginal hip-hop were then few, small, and informal—most often such performances occurred in homes, small parties, and radio studios. But something that everyone agreed was special happened when DS found a lively public open mike at the nightclub Currie's. Thursday nights featured "bomb shelter"—a weekly event dedicated to "freestylin'," improvisatory rhyming battles. DS was coming down to take a turn at the mike, putting in a second performance after a wild first visit several weeks before.

Earlier DS had told us how that previous battle had gone south when two rappers got too serious, "dissing" each other to the point where verbal boxing broke out into proper violence. Fists flew, he said, and then a large empty planter found its way into the combatants' hands, breaking over a head and spilling blood.

> DS: When I got there, there's all these gammon rappers, hey.[8] So I walked in there, and I was about to grab it [the microphone], and I was thinking, how many Australians are in here? 'Cause they were all talking American accents, and all that talking about killing people and all this stuff, and "M-F this" and "M-F that." And I just heard that and I said, "Nah, I'm not going to rap, man." And then everybody started battling each other. I looked at 'em, just let it go I thought to myself, and then the next minute, they started into it—they got into it, bruz![9]
>
> TK: Started punching 'em?

DS: Yeah, bruz, over a battle. And then one guy nearly got killed, bruz. Hey, blood everywhere! It was far out. Friday night in the battle.

In recounting this outbreak of violence, DS provided a primer in what a proper Aboriginal performance should avoid, emphasizing the American accents put on by white Australian rappers, the frequent swearing of "gammon" rappers, and the aggressive, tense atmosphere that dissuaded him from picking up the microphone.

Now several weeks later, waiting just inside in the doorway of the nightclub for DS to arrive, I watched the rain outside as young, white men gathered in circles under the awning of the club entrance—bouncing and waving their arms to the beats pouring out of the DJ booth. Bobbing up and down, they took turns laying down rhymes and amplified the intensity of their lyric both verbally and physically with flattened hands that danced back and forth inside the circle of their bodies. Remembering DS's stories, I imagined these young men lyrically sparring their way into a proper fight, spilling through the arched entrance to the club and carrying each other into the wet street, disturbing the small clusters of drag queens passing out club invitations, the "Anglo" suburban clubgoers out for a night in the valley, and the very few small groups of older Aboriginal people, clustered in the covered causeway.

But this remained a storied side of Brisbane's hip-hop battles. DS soon arrived with several friends just as the MC took up the mike and welcomed the small audience to Bomb Shelter. The beats kicked up loud and the MC started in rhyming right away, concluding with a statement "I'm sick of all this battlin'!" Soon DS stepped up, his whole body bouncing in step with the rhythm, thumbs up, held above his head in strong affirmation. It wasn't long before the microphone cycled into his hands, and, asking the DJ to slow it down a bit, he performed a series of prewritten rhymes—proclaiming his pride in his Indigenous identity and his Murri community. He soon stepped back to where I stood watching with the others. "These are *real* rappers here tonight," DS said, grinning, his head rocking up and down with the steady beats from the DJ booth. Another DJ from the station, AJ, was critical, in a bad temper that seemed to be made worse by the onset of the music. He leaned in to me, shouting over the beats while a young white rapper held the mike, critiquing the white hip-hop artists for putting on American accents and swearing, but extolling DS's talent. As I would soon learn, AJ felt an ambivalence about the Aboriginal performance of hip-hop, and the identification it could elicit between Aboriginal performers and African American stars.

This Indigenous appreciation and production of hip-hop is not novel. Aboriginal hip-hop group Native Rhyme Syndicate, for whom DS was an on-again, off-again DJ, won an Australian Recording Industry Award (ARIA)[10] in 1998 for their performance, and the social worlds of Sydney's hip-hop scene extend back to the early 1990s (Maxwell 2003; Mitchell 2006). Yet despite the almost mundane presence of hip-hop in Australia, a persistent discursive dilemma runs through these practices and revolves around how one defines oneself by genre. That is, hip-hop comes to Australia with both national and racial connotations. Which of these connotations its proponents or detractors single out depends, of course, on context, but often these are linked aspects of critique, as in the following dedication opening the group Local Knowledge's first CD.

This goes out to these wannabe *Negro* Aboriginals, walking around thinkin' they're something special. We bringin' "Abo" hip-hop to our communities, we don't need your type, pretenders. We're representin' Aboriginal hip-hop 100 percent. Us Aboriginals own this, it's ours, like this fuckin' land.

Although Local Knowledge's swearing was not universally appreciated in the production rooms of 4AAA, such politically didactic music resonates strongly with local critiques of American-based hip-hop frequently voiced by an older generation at 4AAA—those in their late twenties to early thirties and older. For these people, the visual, verbal, and aural styles of global hip-hop were worrying—both for the ways the genre threatened to supplant country music and, more significantly, for its racial iconicity, and they would frequently remind younger Murris that they were neither "gangstas" nor "African" but, rather, "Aboriginal." As one older country music DJ angrily asserted in a meeting with younger trainees: "We are not '*niggaz*'! We're Aboriginal!" This charged exclamation itself deserves a further gloss. It is important to note the different registers to which these statements might speak. In the first instance, the word "niggaz" may emerge as a citation of hip-hop rhymes themselves, the counterhegemonic reappropriation by African Americans of a significant slur—one of the most charged words in today's American English (but see Hartigan 1999). However, it may also cite the young Aboriginal men who occasionally slip into patterns of speech and vocabulary adopted from American hip-hop recordings and popular culture.

For an older generation with its own distinct history of engagement with transnational black expressive cultural and politics, "blackness" and "indigeneity" label long-standing forms of transnational identification that have been in at times conflicting, and at times complementary, relationship in Australia. The historian Gary Foley, for instance, joined others to found the Black Panthers in Melbourne in 1968—an organization that overtly identified with the American movement and drew further inspiration from its aggressive posture and its visual styles. More broadly, over the course of the 1960s, organizations advocating for Aboriginal civil rights had debated the place of white Australians in their organization and increasingly figured their movement in racial terms. As the 1960s drew to a close, Aboriginal activists began to figure their identity and struggle in terms of blackness and in a newly aggressive style that resonated with their admiration for and sympathy with the North American Black Power movement and that also registered a concern with cooptation. In 1969 the activist and Aboriginal poet Oodgeroo Noonuccal drafted her "Black Commandments"—which began with the imperative "Thou shall gather thy scattered people together" yet also included number 4, "Thou shalt not become a black liberal in white society." Number 7 reads "Thou shalt meet white violence with black violence," and the poem ends with "Thou shalt think black and act black," number 10, and number 11, "Thou shalt be black all the rest of thy days" (330).[11] But while such sharp figures of Black Power resonated strongly with a global black politics, such figures were leavened and mediated by the growing movement for land rights. In 1971 the loss of the high-profile Yolngu land rights case in Arnhem Land and the Australian Black Panthers' move to establish the famous "tent embassy" on the lawn in front of Parliament—a bristling declaration of Indigenous sovereignty—helped propel the rhetoric of Aboriginal rights toward issues of culture and belonging.[12]

Today's ambivalent reception of hip-hop's sounds and styles echo the internal ambivalence and excitement surrounding the sounds and styles of Black Power in the 1960s and 1970s. In these terms hip-hop can occasionally raise a specter for older Aboriginal people—one of cultural dissolution, the racialization of Aboriginal kids, and a detrimental move from a politics of indigeneity into a politics of race. When 4AAA managers and elders express ambivalence about the Aboriginal production of hip-hop and underline the ways in which Aboriginal young people are Indigenous—heirs to land and law—they thus echo an older tension between a transnational identity as "black," antiracist activism and a specific identity as "Aboriginal."

Back in the studio, describing his first experiences performing at the Bomb Shelter open mike, DS further suggested to me how he negotiates these tensions and underlined the significance of clear lyrics and constructive, non-combative battling.

So we walked in and we bought a few drinks and sit down and listen to music, and there was people dancing, then they said, all right, "open mike," and some guys jumped up. . . . They were good lyrics, and a little bit of accent here and there, but that's their business. And I was getting more drinks into me and I thought, all right, I gotta get up there and I'll say my piece. . . . And when I started rapping, that's when people walking past started looking in. Because all them [other, non-Indigenous] guys they just [muffles his voice to imitate their rapping]—you know, they're not clear? But I jumped on the microphone and you could hear me word for word, you know, and I got a lot of respect for that.

For DS, his distinction from other, aggressive white rappers lay in this clear enunciation. Telling stories with clear rhymes made the practice acceptable, even respectable to his elders and peers insofar as it successfully evaded racialized markers of African American "gangstas."

This prominence of vocals, out in front of the mix and its clarity preserved apart from further prosodic or timbral coloration, is a marked feature of Aboriginal hip-hop, is also central to the performance and production of country music, and was a constant point of explicit discourse in the studio's at 4AAA. As a prolific white recording engineer and producer of Aboriginal country music stressed to me in 2008, the key to producing country, whether live or in the studio, rests in foregrounding the voice—lending it clarity. "Mix it [the recording] like you do for the house at a live performance—with the voice up front and center—if you don't have a story you don't move people," he said. This imperative drives his own production work with country artists such as Warren Williams and Roger Knox, two of the most notable, national country artists of Indigenous Australia, both of which are known for the smoothness and polish of their delivery. These descriptive terms describe a professional sound, one that emulates the vocal delivery of the American singer Charley Pride or Koori singer Roger Knox. This is a feature of country music recording and performance in the United States as well, preserved by engineers and front of house sound technicians who arrange the overall audio mix of performers leaving the middle frequencies clear for vocals, uncluttered by other instrumentation. Professional sound production and engineering takes such efforts further, using a broad range of technologies and practices (types of microphone, microphone preamplifiers, microphone placement, mixing boards, compressors, etc.) to give vocal presence forms of "character" and color, to situate a sound distinctly in a mix in relation to other sounds (see Porcello and Greene 2005).

This practical and technical attention to engineering clear, understandable voices is also a feature of commercial radio broadcasting as taught to these producers in 4AAA's studios. In addition to teaching students the rudiments of radio desk operation, 4AAA's Matthew Simms aimed to train the voices of these young Aboriginal men and women. To get respect on the mike, to sing an affecting story, or to sell an advertising spot you need to put clarity front and center in the mix. Simms's efforts to train young Murri men and women in radio production frequently returned to several themes: "Avoid hard language; watch out for the pops and whistles where the microphone meets the body; hold your mouth slightly away from the mike; careful with your 'ahs' and 'ums'; if prerecording, edit these out for smoother diction." When DS rhymes, he also holds the mike at a distance, keeping its diaphragm from oversaturation and the distorted sounds of a clipped voice. This is in marked contrast with the non-Indigenous hip-hop performers DS and I saw in the valley, who cupped the microphone close up, making use of the microphone's proximity effect to maximize lower frequencies, and also to greatly distort their vocal sound.[13] DS brings such technical sensibilities together with a social attention to the ramifications surrounding the sounds of black voices in southeast Queensland. Telling stories with clear rhymes was DS's way of making hip-hop an Indigenous form—and one acceptable to his elders and peers insofar as it successfully evaded racialized markers of African American "gangstas," and the swearing and aggression that my interlocutors felt marks a good deal of white Australian hip-hop. Seeming to draw on his production training and professional awareness of audio media technology, DS's musical aesthetics and his production practice thus sought to mediate contradictory discourses in Aboriginal public culture—balancing a lived tension between "blackness" and "indigeneity" for those making radio and curating hip-hop in 4AAA's studios. This tension however speaks to the reification of voice as a site of social concern as well as something that lives as an imagined alter—a place where dangerous kinds of difference struggle with valued forms of identification.

Such tensions continued to resist resolution and in spite of the expressive strategies of performers such as DS, and the critiques of their aunties and uncles in radio studios around Australia, many, many young people continue to listen to and emulate the commercial sounds of American hip-hop and its producers—an emulation that can be heard both in the music itself and the voices and promotional work of radio announcers and hip-hop fans. Listening to a late-night hip-hop show on Sydney's Koori Radio, *Takin' It Back*, I heard two presenters engage in a quick routine:

PRESENTER #1: You're listening to the *Takin' It Back* show, where we're takin' it back!
PRESENTER #2: How far back?
PRESENTER #1: All the way back, you know, all the way *black!*

What many people hear in hip-hop's sounds is a valorized, powerful, and aesthetically sharp "blackness"—indeed, this is what lends it prestige and power. The dilemma that DS and others face is that when brought into the radio studio and to the forms of technologically mediated public culture this involves, forms of "black" expressivity that in one domain are sites of desire and power, in another become sites of danger and representational debate.

While taking voice may give shape to community, the forms that voice takes may be at once of a collective self and other to it—in a word, uncanny.[14] This is to bring both psychoanalytic and heteroglossic understandings of voice and language to bear on vocal mediation—to focus on people's apprehension of outrageous or dangerous features of vocal practice, as well as on the ways they argue about, exaggerate, or perhaps deny such features.[15] In Australia, when Aboriginal people take on particular kinds of "black" voices they speak as Indigenous Australians recasting the local historical denigration of blackness in a positive, powerful light. They also draw on globally circulating forms of black expressive culture, particularly hip-hop. However, they also may risk censure from their peers if they seem to speak as other than themselves through the appropriation of North American, non-Indigenous accents and expressive language. The Aboriginal discourse on "voice" that emerged in the context of radio studio ethnography thus took on an uncanny cast in part due to the plasticity and vocal "schizophonia" introduced into Aboriginal media production by digital editing technologies (cf. Feld 1994) and in part to this historically unsettled character of "blackness."

For many Aboriginal media producers such forms of vocal cultural production entailed a kind of doubled reflexivity, due to their efforts to give voice to Aboriginal experiences—at times with forms of expressive culture marked as North American—but also due to some remarkable practical and professional features of radio production that make the voice a highly plastic medium. Producers are thus both speaking and "listening subjects" (Inoue 2003), regimenting Aboriginal voices in part by constituting certain expressive modalities as their alter. The practices and discourses I describe here, then, should be understood as part of a contested expressive regime, a mediatized crucible of Indigenous self-fashioning that gives voice while at the same time creating conditions that unsettle its a priori character. From the specific forms of self-abstraction entailed when an intimate address is made to speak of a broader public, to the iconic vocal markers of soul musics, expressive sound and voice are sites where alterity is made identity, and identity alterity.

From Expressive Agency to Governmental Elicitation

Despite the highly technical and reflexive attention to the voice that I encountered at 4AAA, it is worth recalling the truism that social identities are ascribed, negotiated, elicited, perhaps thrown off or rejected in forms of social relationship—relationships in Australia that emerge from a colonial situation and that continue to inform governmental policy. Much cultural production in radio stations has governmental support and emerges from forms of intercultural collaboration and institution. These receive funding from groups like the Australia Music Radio Airplay Project and the Australia Research Council–funded Local Noise Project. The interest in supporting, eliciting, and developing a distinctly Aboriginal voice has a genealogy that at once includes and also exceeds the interests of Aboriginal activists. I now turn to these features of voice as a site of historical governmental interest and investment.

Between the late 1960s and late 1970s, as the Australian state moved away from logics of assimilation and toward an official rubric of self-determination, Aboriginal advocates in national policy-making circles began looking for a means to secure Aboriginal inclusion in government, impelled to do so in great measure by the long-standing activism and efforts to effect such change by a series of campaigns led by a number of Indigenous activists, Oodgeroo Noonuccal, G. Yunupingu, and Vincent Lingiari among them (see Attwood 2004). H. C. "Nugget" Coombs—architect of Australia's postwar banking infrastructure, governor of the Commonwealth Bank, a former chancellor of the Australian National University, and founding head of the Australia Council for the Arts—was asked in 1968 to chair the newly created Council for Aboriginal Affairs, an advisory body that included Barry Dexter and the anthropologist W. H. Stanner and that was given the mandate to inform a new kind of Aboriginal policy. Coombs, who was instrumental in the changes to follow, sought to craft mechanisms that would elicit Aboriginal participation in national politics—to create the conditions that would foster what anthropologist Tim Rowse calls an "articulate indigenous leadership supported by culturally sustainable political structures" (2000: 8). Coombs came to believe that the way to empower Aboriginal people, to be fair and equitable, was to enable them to participate on their own terms. He immediately faced a quandary to do with the great diversity of Aboriginal people, their varying degrees of imbrication in settler life, and the radically different notions of authority and decision making both between Aboriginal and settler Australia and across Aboriginal communities themselves.

The council's efforts to secure Indigenous political infrastructure eventually led, under the government of Prime Minister Gough Whitlam (1973–1975), to the Aboriginal Councils and Associations Act (1976; the ACA), a mechanism for the incorporation of Aboriginal organizations and the administrative infrastructure by which they would receive commonwealth financial support. This might be seen, along with the Land Councils created in the same year and community broadcasting legislation begun earlier, in 1972, as a zero point of self-determination understood through the metaphoric rubric of "giving voice." For almost forty years now the ACA has given some body to Coombs's ideas by emphasizing autonomy at the local level for Aboriginal decision making, while also creating an administratively legible infrastructure for Aboriginal participation at a national level. The ACA also became the administrative backbone enabling the incorporation of a large number of Aboriginal media organizations, themselves now seen as crucial brokers between state projects and both remote and urban Indigenous people. While Indigenous activists, politicians, and community-based advocates were all pushing for the greater inclusion of Aboriginal people in Australian political life, I thus want to underscore the significance of legislative instruments to their efforts, and the durability and legibility that the ACA subsequently lent to this field of Indigenous cultural production. A governmental project to elicit and cultivate Aboriginal voices, both metaphorically as citizens and actually through infrastructures of administrative participation and broadcast media, also attended the institutional genesis of today's Australian Indigenous media world.

Such interests in empowering and "giving voice" also have a lengthy prehistory in state efforts to shape a national citizenry through the establishment of national broadcasters. Georgina Born, in her critical ethnography of the BBC, suggests that we understand such institutions as themselves "cultural states"—large, bureaucratically defined sites of governmental interest and institutionalized efforts to cultivate a responsible, "normalized" citizenry (2004: 66–67). The past thirty years have seen enormous transformations as such public institutions were made aware of fragmenting audiences and faced new demands for inclusion and participation from those previously considered marginal to a "national" public. In Australia, Aboriginal broadcasting and the emergence of community licensing in the 1970s and 1980s helped to draw attention to the limitations of a single national broadcaster and its structural presuppositions of singular national public when faced with a growing awareness of a multiple, culturally fragmented publics.[16] Philip Batty's (2003) historical analysis of the rise of Aboriginal media institutions makes a similar point, arguing that at least in the case of CAAMA, these institutions were the products of a complicity between Aboriginal activists and policy makers in need of partners in development. His historical analysis sees in such institutions a governmental apparatus that seeks to elicit particular forms of governable Aboriginal subject (Batty 1993; cf. Foucault 1991 [1978]). In the diversification and reorganization of a national broadcast economy we might see at once progressive attempts to maximize social inclusion and recognition and also a shift toward the governmental elicitation of Aboriginal subject-citizens.

In Australia these efforts exceed radio stations themselves and embrace a range of tactics for eliciting and encouraging vocal expressivity. For instance, several projects backed by non-Indigenous hip-hop fans and producers have toured Australia over the past few years seeking to elicit an Aboriginal voice—drawing on hip-hop's popularity and cultural prestige to encourage forms of self-expression and Indigenous self-esteem in remote communities. Prominent among these are:

- The "hip-hop workshops" of non-Indigenous DJ Morganics. Visiting remote community schools across Australia, Morganics coaches young Aboriginal students to author lyrics and produce beats on (relatively low-tech) production equipment that he supplies.[17] Several of his tracks found success on JJJ, the publicly funded national youth radio service. In 2009 he produced a track in collaboration with several small children from Wilcannia and British—Sri Lankan hip-hop star MIA.
- Operating out of Darwin, the Kid Hop project also worked in much the same way in 2003 and 2004, but focused on younger children in remote communities across the Top End, from northeast Arnhem Land over to the Daly River district. Much like Morganics, the two young non-Indigenous men who make up Kid Hop built rhythm tracks on the spot in school classrooms and coauthored rap scripts about family, fishing, traveling to see grandparents, or favorite camp dogs.

- The group Indigenous hip-hop Projects has made this a business model and has visited fifty-six communities to date, where IHHP brings hip-hop music and hip-hop dance to "confidence circles" and "expression sessions," and where they provide musical and rhythmic backing for students to generate rap lyrics. In their promotional video, one of the IHHP performers explains in general terms their aims: "Using the tool of hip-hop to deliver some really important messages, whether it's health messages, whether it's careers, employment . . ."

While the favorite topics of these school-focused productions are often about fun activities in the bush, about family and friends, the thrust of all this culture work is captured by an IHHP video clip in which a DJ elicits participation in a "confidence circle": "Who's going to go first?" he asks. "Come out and give it a go, come out and be leaders, come out and express yourself!"

Kid Hop's production, by two young men who would later achieve success on a national stage as members of Australian hip-hop collective the Herd, drew on the familiarity of one of its two producers, Chris Keogh, with the communities of the Top End. Keogh grew up in Nhulunbuy as the son of a teacher and was familiar with the broad social terrain of northeast Arnhem Land and deeply invested in forms of experimental music and sound. The Kid Hop project stands out as at once deeply concerned with "giving voice" but also is marked by the formulas that accrue to this project as a movement of development work. In their case, they took turntables and samplers to remote community schools. Once there they demonstrated the technologies in the schools, creating a rhythmic and musical bed over which the schoolchildren could compose rhymes. These were practiced, elicited from the group collectively, and placed on a whiteboard. The kids would then perform their rhymes over beats co-created with the Kid Hop producers. This project led to an independently produced CD that found airplay on Darwin's Radio Larrakia, with some of the more endearing tracks making the airwaves of TEABBA's regional broadcast.

In addition to Morganics, Kid Hop, and IHHP there are two other significant institutions interested in radio production as community development.

- The Australian Music Radio Airplay Project, a long-standing project funded by the Community Broadcasting Foundation. The project encourages young people's media production and has funded Aboriginal media students to take equipment into Queensland's prisons to record hip-hop performances of young incarcerated men and women for broadcast on the National Indigenous Radio Service and for distribution to

Australia's broad network of community radio stations. They have also supported the professional mentoring of young Aboriginal radio producers—two of whom have gone on to achieve national profiles as Indigenous broadcasters.

- The community arts group Information and Cultural Exchange works to encourage arts, media, and music production with Indigenous and new Australian immigrants in western Sydney and for the past seven years has put a good deal of energy into promoting, recording, and representing Indigenous hip-hop artists and training both Indigenous and young new immigrants in radio production.

It is significant that these intercultural performance and recording projects focus on incarcerated men and women as well as on schoolchildren and "youth" in remote communities—these are sites of both governmental intervention and public anxiety. But crucially, these are also domains of struggle and social transformation—arenas in which Aboriginal uncles and aunties, families, and communities have sought to intervene to expand the possibilities (and reduce the harm) that such institutions present to Indigenous people. Thus, much like trainers and managers at 4AAA, these different intercultural endeavors aim to cultivate expressive competence and expressive confidence as they also contribute to broader efforts to elicit forms of autobiographic narrative and personal story—efforts that ultimately seek to ensure the possibility of an Indigenous cultural future (Ginsburg and Myers 2006; cf. Attwood 2001, 2004). But they often do so in tandem with broader governmental projects, eliciting particular forms of voice and subject that are amenable to a broader settler Australian audience and that underscore "communication," expressive competence, and individual talent.

What Kind of Ethnographic Object Is the Mediatized Voice?

In describing how the production of Indigenous radio entails diverse forms of vocal mediation, I have endeavored to suggest how the voice in such places may become denaturalized and opened to heightened forms of attention and contest. These forms of mediation include the increasingly industrial and digital techniques by which voices are brought to air; the broader cultural politics of "black" cultural production in southeast Australia; and forms of governmental and institutional interests in eliciting Aboriginal expressive competence. These forms of cultural production are at once sites of expressive exploration, cultural activism, and governmental investment and instrumentality. These all work together to inform how cultural producers like DS and others imagine and negotiate the expressive possibilities and constraining features of a mediatized, Aboriginal voice.

My argument is not that Aboriginal radio can be reduced to governmental efforts or to the diverse audio technologies that increasingly support radio broadcasting. Rather, as a domain of cultural production, the study of Indigenous radio's Australian dilemmas and successes might also attend to the broad range of efforts made by Indigenous cultural activists to cultivate voices that will have some purchase in the world and to the entire situation in which such efforts take place. Such voices have been cultivated through structuring of radio broadcasts and in quite technical efforts to shape and reshape particular voices to distinct expressive tasks, from using a radio microphone to performing in a club. They have also been cultivated in the stories that surround the voice, in the potential and risk of battle or in the romance and imagination that labels like *black*, *Koori*, and *Aboriginal* carry. More than just a trope for representation, quite distinct voices have been the media by which race, indigeneity, and governmentality emerged in my fieldwork as an unstable matrix of desire, anxiety, and institutional labor.

In exploring how actual voices become media for cultural production I have found them unsettled and made uncanny to my Indigenous interlocutors involved in radio production. The remove from one's self that media may elicit has a rich history of problematization in media studies and anthropology. In addition to Fanon's discussion of Algeria's new national radio-mediated self, Susan Buck-Morss (1996) argues that early cinema gave audiences a new sense of themselves as a mass public and an agent of history,[18] and suggests that this mass "self" was made visible "to itself" by cinema's particular material and narrative technology as much as by political or economic forces. Friedrich Kittler (1999), attending to figures of transmission in Freud's writing as well as to Lacan's registers of the Real, Imaginary, and Symbolic, has suggested that psychoanalysis and its varied figures of the unconscious might themselves be considered a "historical effect" of the twentieth century's dominant media of telephone, film, and mechanized type (cf. Pazderic 2004).[19] These different but provocative accounts of modernity's mediatized subject, placed at a remove from itself by media's prostheses, perhaps overvalue the power of media technologies (Gitelman 2006). Yet they need not be taken whole to suggest a range of questions for how radio may make people's voices newly available to themselves. In southeast Queensland Indigenous radio stations emerge as institutions that encourage distinctly Aboriginal forms of voice consciousness; sites where the voice is de- and renaturalized in technological manipulation, metapragmatic discourse, and hip-hop's rhyming combat. The voice is thus not a straightforward index of agency, presence, or authentic being in these stations. Its status is always already susceptible to question, social critique, or contest. In the radio stations introduced here, this idea is more than an abstract, philosophical possibility: it is, rather, the grounds for frequent debate and discussion, an object of daily labor in dynamic relation to its deployment, less an inert instrument and more a site of contest and cultural poesis.

| From Radio Skid Row

to the Reconciliation Station

In Brisbane's wintery July and August, the mornings are cold. Each day in the first months of my research—winter in Australia—I climbed into a blue 1984 Range Rover. I'd bought this car cheaply in Sydney and driven it north, aiming to use its all-wheel-drive and raised suspension to go bush and leave the bitumen behind. And in the later stages of my research that car did ferry me and my friends and interlocutors over unsealed roads at the outskirts of Darwin, in the Northern Territory. But it clocked more kilometers commuting between the apartments and houses where I lived during fieldwork, and the radio stations and studios where I worked in exchange for the opportunity to conduct my research, and more time carrying people down city streets and highways, than it did in the bush. In the event it mattered more that the Range Rover had a good car radio than that it had four-wheel-drive, and in Brisbane I listened to hours of Aboriginal broadcasting while commuting between Highgate Hill and the suburb where the Brisbane Indigenous Media Association had their studios. That car thus looms large in my memory as a place of gathering warmth, musical sound, and the amplified voices of my interlocutors. On these cold antipodean winter mornings I'd fire up the big V6 engine and wait for the heater to kick in, listening to the radio and hearing the voices of those who had arrived at the station much earlier than I, often at four in the morning, ready to start their day and to greet their listeners—many of whom were, like me, climbing into cars and heading out to work. My entry into this ethnographic field was repeated in this way each day to the sounds of country music and Indigenous voices coming over a car radio.

Driving into Brisbane, tuning in to country music station 4AAA, I'd often hear Roger Knox's country hit "Koori Rose" segue into a George Jones or Merle Haggard song, followed by works from a new generation of commercially successful country stars, including Lee Kernaghan, Dan Sullivan, Troy Cassar-Daly, and Casey Chambers. I would also hear 4AAA's drive-time DJ AJ back-announce the songs, giving the artist name, title, and perhaps even the song's date of release. AJ often provided a bit more historical information for his listeners, telling them, for instance, that Roger Knox was one of the few Aboriginal recording artists that one could hear on Australian radio prior to the early 1980s. This world of sound, coming to me over a car stereo on Brisbane's streets, is something with a distinct and relatively recent history that can be traced materially to the early 1980s. From that point on, organizations like the Central Australian Aboriginal Media Association (CAAMA) and Enrec studios in northern New South Wales began recording in earnest and releasing compilations of Indigenous country and rock musics such as "Rebel Voices I" and "Rebel Voices II" (1980–81), Warumpi Band's "Big Name, No Blankets" (1985), and country records by southeastern performers, like Knox's "Give It a Go" (1983), often with the support of the nascent Aboriginal Arts board.[1] CAAMA and Enrec's recordings joined others produced independently in Australia's southeast by bands such as "Us Mob,"[2] and by a growing number of Aboriginal media associations, organizations founded under the relatively new Aboriginal Councils and Associations Act (1976). This was specifically intended to endow Aboriginal Australia with representative organizations as the latticework of Indigenous citizenship and an Aboriginal public (Attwood 2004; Batty 2003).

This level of pop music historical information didn't always come across in drive-time, competing with a range of community announcements and song-specific background; it was a feature of later programming, when young Murri radio trainees would host the "Murri Magazine," conducting interviews with their Aboriginal elders and focusing on aspects of Brisbane's Aboriginal community. The reflexive appreciation and cataloguing of this rich, contemporary music history was a central mission of such programming, certainly, but also spilled over into other kinds of discourse surrounding 4AAA's programming. AJ often celebrated Murri and Koori performers' identities, locating them in the history of Aboriginal country music performance that I describe above. But he also folded them into a larger transnational stable of country stars, speaking in a friendly, jocular voice to both a national Aboriginal audience (who likely needed no such overt signposts) and a more local, non-Indigenous group of Queensland's "country fans, truckies, and working blokes." As I listened more, heard AJ's stories on the radio and in person, and watched young Aboriginal producers create programs built around the voices of country music, the sense of strangeness that accompanied what I had once thought of as a prototypically "American" form slipped away and the sounds of country music came to index for me the historical depth and institutional complexity of the industrialized sound world I had come to study, as well as its imbrication with a longer history of Aboriginal engagement with commercial musics.

Despite the rich history of Aboriginal music and media production, hearing Indigenous music and music history at the center of the FM dial (98.9 FM) and in a southeastern Australian "capital city" is nonetheless a relatively recent phenomenon, occasioned by several decades of activism and major shifts in Australian Indigenous cultural policy. Tiga Bayles, managing director of 4AAA radio, remembers running midnight Aboriginal music shows in Sydney, scrounging for Indigenous music to play at a time when only a few select recordings were available. In Queensland and New South Wales, the 1960s and 1970s had seen a trickle of Aboriginal recording artists achieve some success, most notably the 1960s pop stars Jimmy Little and Vic Simms. CAAMA's recordings dovetailed with the emergence of Aboriginal rock music from central and northern Australia, most famously by Warumpi Band, perhaps due to their tour across Australia with the high-profile Australian pop group Midnight Oil (see McMillan 1989; Murray 1993). From Papunya, Warumpi Band was begun by Neil Murray of rural Victoria writing songs and singing, with George Burarrwanga from Elcho Island in the Top End as lead singer, Sammy Butcher on guitar and bass, and a number of drummers over the years, including Gordon Butcher, Sammy's brother, and American Allen Murphy, a former member of the pop group the Village People.

Much has changed in the intervening period and there are now many hundreds of hours of recordings of Aboriginal country, rock, R&B, and other contemporary musics. A developed Indigenous music industry also has come into existence alongside a network of radio stations, media associations, and training organizations spread across Australia. These are joined by independent record labels such as Enrec in New South Wales and SkinnyFish music in the Northern Territory, and by a number of small, remote radio and recording studios producing music on a more ad hoc basis. 4AAA "Murri Country" is an important agent within this network of institutions, enmeshed within

Queensland and New South Wales's country music industry, and closely allied with the National Indigenous Radio Service—a satellite network and news service based not far from 4AAA's studios in central Brisbane. 4AAA's signal now reaches Aboriginal radios as far away as Darwin in the Northern Territory and Cairns in far northern Queensland.

When I began research in 2003, 4AAA's management was concerned primarily with reaching Brisbane's Indigenous community, providing public service announcements on mental health, employment opportunities, and community events. And 4AAA took on as a foundational social duty the work of connecting kin across the institutional boundaries of prison walls and the often large distances between rural communities and former mission settlements like Cherbourg, and the many suburbs ringing Brisbane's city center. Yet 4AAA's managers had also kept their ears open to audience surveys and public relations statistics as additional means to assess their relationship with the tens of thousands of non-Indigenous listeners they also aimed to reach. Much of what occupied producers at 4AAA concerned their attempts to broker a relationship between opposing poles of Indigenous and non-Indigenous Australia, an aim they pursued in both the pragmatics of broadcast practice and the politics of institution building.

The story I tell in this chapter emerged from ethnographic work with young Indigenous trainees in 4AAA's recording and radio studios. In exchange for the opportunity to conduct that research, I helped to implement a standardized curriculum for radio production students and to assist station staff in managing their relationships with the funding and bureaucratic structures supporting Indigenous media training in southeast Queensland. Yet while I worked in a management-like position, an equally accurate depiction of my research would be that I occupied a structural position similar to that of the trainees. Through lectures and group workshops I joined young Murri radio trainees in sessions on the history of Indigenous media, the significance of Aboriginal English and family in providing "Aboriginal points of reference" for young Murris, on more technical aspects of digital production, and on producing Indigenous media with a strategic aim to represent Indigenous perspectives and to get that perspective across to an at times easily provoked, hostile audience. I also spent time alongside trainees as they learned digital sound-production software and as they contributed in practical ways to the daily cycle of Queensland Aboriginal radio.

The station's training entailed much more than broadcast skills; it also involved socializing trainees as Murri persons: 4AAA's directors sought to build trainees' capacities, hoping to encourage their employability in a broader, multicultural Queensland. Managers and trainers at 4AAA thus sought to give these young Murri trainees skills in navigating an intercultural institutional economy in which their participation was conditioned by the shifting ground of Aboriginal policy, on the one hand, and a hotly contested politics of identity and belonging, on the other. This chapter provides a bridge to join thinking about the social and cultural spaces that radio in Queensland shares with cultural production to the historically distinct development of broadcast media in the Northern Territory, which I turn to in coming chapters. My understanding of the pragmatics and public culture of Indigenous broadcasting began in Queensland, and this chapter provides a descriptive introduction to the institutional labor of making of "Murri Country" radio, and to the issues this labor raises for producers and for Brisbane's Indigenous community more generally.

Brisbane

Australian public culture and its myths of national origin frequently ground national history in the land—in cattle stations and stock work, as well as the mango farms and orange groves of the tropical North. Yet in spite of such figures of country life as prototypically Australian, Australia's population is overwhelmingly urban, with perhaps 80 percent living in the metropolitan centers and suburbs of Brisbane, Sydney, Melbourne, Adelaide, and Perth. One of Australia's major urban centers, Brisbane is located in the far southeast corner of Queensland, a short drive from the beaches and resorts of Surfer's Paradise and the Gold Coast. Brisbane's many universities, its busy city center, and its international seaport entail intense participation in a global network of other such cosmopolitan centers.

For many visitors, however, Brisbane is merely the urban gateway to Queensland's far north, a place to rest a bit before heading for the tropical beaches of Cairns and the backpackers' hostels and beaches that dot the coast in between. Indeed, another frequently cited Australian topos is built on the figures of the beach and the suburbs and Brisbane might also be understood as prototypical of this image of Australia, considering its proximity to the resorts of the Gold and Sunshine Coasts, and the fact that its relatively small city center belies a huge population, spread out over an enormous land area—primarily suburban and periurban in character. So I was somewhat surprised to hear many friends and Australians from outside of

Queensland refer to Brisbane in derogatory terms as merely "a big country town." In part this reflects Brisbane's history as a depot for stock and produce from Queensland's rural areas, but it also foregrounds Brisbane's status as the capital of Queensland and what some Australians call "the Deep North"—an epithet carrying the same connotations of religious conservatism, provincialism, and racism that "the Deep South" can carry in the United States. Such pejorative characterizations persist despite Brisbane's demographic status as the fastest-growing capital city in Australia, the profound transformation of its urban spaces, and a vigorous long-term effort by the former Labor Party government to promote a new, cosmopolitan Queensland.

A third popular take on Brisbane's history comes on the heels of the government of Sir Joh Bjelke-Petersen, Queensland's state premier from 1968 through 1987. His premiership left a popular sense of widespread corruption, rapid and poorly planned development, and a sense that political power was brokered in the dark corners of the pubs and strip clubs of Brisbane's inner-city suburbs (Wear 2002). This was confirmed for many by the findings of the Fitzgerald Inquiry. Begun in 1987, this investigation into police corruption lasted for two years and was finally completed alongside the Labor Party's return to power in 1989 (after a thirty-two-year absence). Occasioned by media reports of police involvement in prostitution, gambling, and drug trafficking,[3] the inquiry found unexpected degrees of corruption, extending to the highest ranks of the police and the political structure. As a review of the Fitzgerald Inquiry's successor, the Commission of Inquiry into Corruption, states:

> The Inquiry, which was initially intended to last for only a few weeks, ran for over two years, much of it in the glare of widespread media publicity. The Inquiry hearings and the report which followed revealed to Queenslanders that corruption and bribery had become so pervasive in the Police Service that it had developed into an organized protection scheme called "the Joke." (Butler 2001: 1)

The inquiry's status in contemporary public culture must also be seen as part of an ambivalent regard some Queenslanders maintain toward the reshaping of the city as Australia has increasingly sought to embrace the commercial opportunities and strategic alliances Asia represents. The historical periodization the inquiry enables additionally participates in the creation of a historical romance of Brisbane as a frontier town.

Brisbane has been a front line for engagements with an international political economic order for much of the twentieth century, as colonial capital, and later as southern staging ground for the Pacific engagements of World War II. The rolling fights between Australian and American servicemen in central Brisbane during World War II are a well-known early instance; the most famous is "the Battle of Brisbane" of November 1942. Such fights are popularly remembered as initiated by Australian soldiers' alarm at the prospect of relatively well-off American soldiers "stealing" Australian women. The sudden shifts of the 1980s and 1990s were distinct, however, and entailed a far different order of international engagement with the Asia Pacific region and a different understanding of Queensland's place in a transnational "cultural" economy. A frequently cited instance in this regard has been the opening of Australia toward Asia, which can be seen in the makeup of Queensland universities and their controversial moves to "export" an educational service for Malaysian and Southeast Asian students, whose years of study in Australia are an increasingly significant economic pillar of Australian universities more generally.

Like many other urban areas participating in the profound economic and social restructuring of the last decades of the twentieth century, Brisbane underwent a radical shift in its social geography. While stock work and the agricultural industries of rural Queensland receded in economic importance (and more recently have been bankrupted by a decade of drought and then further devastated by catastrophic flooding in early 2011), urban Brisbane has become a cosmopolitan center of cultural production, carried out in a large number of entrepreneurial corporate endeavors spotting the Fortitude Valley and in the institutions of its several universities. Whether playing a role in "global Hollywood" as affordable offshore locale for flexible strategies of feature film production (Miller et al. 2001; Rossiter 2004) or providing a home for online entrepreneurs and clothing design firms, southeast Queensland's economic focus is squarely on what have been termed their "Creative Industries" (Cunningham 2002; Flew 2014). On the heels of the development and influx of visitors during 1988's Expo (perhaps as salient a reference point for a historical break with "old Brisbane" as the Fitzgerald Inquiry), Brisbane's city council has sought to encourage tourist and leisure consumption in its inner city, refinishing the former treasury building into a massive casino, and turning the inner-city suburbs just across the river into the SouthBank development, replete with convention center, fabricated sandy beach and pool at riverside, and an extensive series of paths, pubs, and bridges connecting this area to Brisbane's city center. Beginning in the late 1990s, promotional videos on the Australian airline Qantas referred to Brisbane as "Bris Vegas" (a term with currency in everyday reference), and the luggage carousels at the Brisbane airport still feature enormous replicas of the paraphernalia of gambling—dice and roulette wheels.

These relatively recent shifts in the character of Queensland's public life are given a literary portrait in Andrew McGahan's novel *Last Drinks* (2000), in which, out of the murk of the Fitzgerald Inquiry and a century of authoritarian government, the darkened pubs and industrial breweries of inner-city "old Brisbane" have given way to sidewalk cafes and luxury apartments: "Everything was out in the open. All the things that had been kept unlawful, except for the privileged few, seemed to be anyone's now. And people had swarmed out of their houses and embraced it all. As if the old Brisbane, my Brisbane, couldn't be forgotten quickly enough" (McGahan 2000: 77). This is crime fiction as political allegory, and the death of Brisbane's past is mourned through the eyes of *Last Drinks'* protagonist. Eyes squinting as he emerges from darkened strip clubs onto café-lined boulevards, McGahan seeks to make sense of these changes through noir—the newly vibrant Brisbane retains its murky back rooms and seamy underside, but this now requires a different, international patina to survive the sunshine of international tourism and a growing sidewalk café–going urban middle class.

Concomitant with these transformations of Brisbane's economic geography has been the displacement of urban Brisbane's economic and racialized underclasses to the suburban fringe, and an accompanying shift in the property value in the city's central neighborhoods of New Farm, Highgate Hill, West End, and Spring Hill. Most of the young Aboriginal people I worked with, supported by some form of public assistance connected with their training at 4AAA, lived in distant suburban apartment units that ring the central suburbs of metropolitan Brisbane. The neighborhood of West End, just across the river from the city center and where 4AAA maintains a kiosk distributing literature on homeless shelters, soup kitchens, and left-leaning progressive political campaigns, was then witnessing rising property values and a slow shift away from the boarding rooms, brothels, and heroin trade of its recent history. Many of McGahan's Australian readers will be aware that New Farm Park, the central stage for much of *Last Drinks* and a formerly well-known heroin "shooting gallery" at one end of Fortitude Valley, has now become one of Brisbane's premiere "cultural precincts" and home to the Powerhouse Centre for the Arts.

Such changes run alongside broader political economic shifts that have transformed both the outward form of the city, as well as the ways that

Queensland government policy makers relate to Aboriginal people in Brisbane through institutions that have come to be understood through an influential English and broader European cultural policy initiatives, Creative Industries (see Caves 2000; Hartley and Cunningham 2001; cf. Miller 2004; O'Connor 2011; Rossiter 2004). In Brisbane, Creative Industries names a stress on cultural production as the backbone of Brisbane's cosmopolitan economy, a shift that has analogues in Sydney as well as across Europe, and that can be seen as a response to the growing importance of commercial cultural production to a local economy, and the growth of such work well beyond state-supported arts practice (see O'Connor 2011). The development of cultural precincts (by which educational institutions and industrial forms of design and creative practices are set in productive coresidence) and the apotheosis of Creative Industries as a guiding rubric for research and policy formation have had a decisive impact on the organization of Indigenous cultural production in Brisbane, as has an accompanying Australia wide shift toward the articulation of Indigenous cultural policy with neoliberal economic policy. Paradoxically, perhaps, a stress on enterprise led to more opportunities for funding Indigenous cultural production, yet it also led to a corresponding multiplication of oversight and audit.

In Queensland the valorization of these dynamics of creative enterprise has also depended on the applied aspect of cultural studies' revaluation of popular culture and its concomitant critique of the Frankfurt School devaluation of mass culture as commodity fetish (see also O'Connor 2011).[4] The stress on consumption and creativity as keys to success in a "new economy" in Brisbane shared cultural studies' valorization of active consumers and creative citizens, a discourse used to plot Indigenous success and citizenship within what were variously branded in Queensland policy discourse and press releases as a "smart state" and a "creative nation."[5] In this environment, social theory aiming to historicize and critically reassess the Frankfurt School era dismissal of mass cultural forms has come to underwrite new governmental initiatives that stress the significance of cultural consumption and creative production for Queensland's economy. During the late 1990s and early 2000s, these shifts came to have great importance for Indigenous media institutions. Both in the bureaucratic architecture used to rationalize state funding of Indigenous cultural production and in the ways that cultural policy draws on British cultural studies to refigure appropriate relations between Indigenous and non-Indigenous Australia, Creative Industries became part of the emergent apparatus of Queensland's Aboriginal governmental policy, drawing on the broad success of Indigenous visual art and film to see in the art market in particular a model by which Indigenous creative practices might generate economic self-sufficiency and social integration while supporting Indigenous political autonomy. Concretely, this meant governmental partnerships with local Indigenous entrepreneurs seeking to build digital databases and web-hosting services, support for Indigenous music and recording projects, and efforts to foster Indigenous scholarship and encourage the enrollment of Indigenous people in degree programs in Queensland University of Technology's Creative Industries Research and Application Centre. It also meant increased interest in research on the place of Indigenous media in a broader Australia and on the possibilities of making such media profitable.

For many of the young people I introduce here, Brisbane represented an urban location to which they came to find greater opportunities than existed in the smaller towns, cattle stations, and mission settlements where many were brought up. For others, these suburbs were a first home, from which trips to NSW or countryside Queensland were a novelty. Although Andrew McGahan's settler Australian antihero might stumble dazed past sunny cafes in New Farm and gaze in awe and ironic remorse at the new shops in Queen Street Mall, for many Aboriginal young people these are still dangerous spaces—holding the temptations of heroin, amphetamines, alcohol, and also the frequent threat of violence or abuse, as well as the constant surveillance of police and the private security hired by the mall itself. Furthermore, the shifts that account for reconfiguring the urban space of Brisbane in the early twenty-first century are also implicated in efforts to organize and direct their labor and to orient their aspirations and desires. The historical tropes by which non-Indigenous Australians objectify and circulate their experiences of this dynamic city take on a different cast in the discourses and organizational strategies by which Indigenous institutions rationalize themselves to state funders within a broad discursive valorization of enterprise but a constant interinstitutional stress on accountability. This discourse of enterprise and a corresponding amplification of institutional auditing are twinned forces that press in on the institutions in which young Murris are socialized into the labor of culture making.

Radio and Radical Politics: Early Indigenous Community Broadcasting

Looking at the playlist of 4AAA today, it might be hard to see the history of Indigenous political activism that lends this station its singularity, or to discern the networked families and kin groups with whom 4AAA has become entangled. For some, the commercial focus, use of audience surveys and questionnaires, and the station's computerized playlists might confound expectations of what an Aboriginal community radio station "should" be. In many parts of Australia, the efforts of media activists were embraced by bureaucratic government instruments in efforts to institutionalize and expand the gains of places like CAAMA, the Warlpiri Media Association, and Pitjantjatjarra Yakunatjarra Media in central Australia (see Batty 2003).[6] While the effects of this bureaucratization of Aboriginal media organizations are a controversial issue in Australian political life, it certainly has not diminished the political efforts of those in either remote communities or in urban centers such as Brisbane.

In Brisbane, as in the Northern Territory, the emergence of Indigenous media production has been characterized by a tension between institutionalization and bureaucratic rationalization, on the one hand, and the energies of individuals and families engaged in particular media projects, on the other. The station owes its existence both to community broadcasting legislation and to the radical politics of a small group of Aboriginal activists and advocates in the 1970s and early 1980s, and it emerges from Aboriginal programming that was made possible by the explosion of community radio in Australia during the 1970s and 1980s. Looking to the history of Aboriginal broadcasting, as well as the participation of 4AAA's management in founding Sydney's activist Aboriginal radio station, Radio Redfern, can historicize 4AAA's current focus as well as the political acumen of its manager, Tiga Bayles.

As Bayles tells it, Indigenous radio has independent origins in two places: Alice Springs, where CAAMA began broadcasting short programs on ABC local radio in 1979 and later acquired its own community license as 8KIN FM; and Townsville, at the Indigenous community radio station 4K1G and in the activist work of Florence Onus and brothers Bill and Mick Thaiday. In the early 1980s, the latter produced Indigenous radio in northern Queensland and today 4K1G broadcasts on the National Indigenous Radio Service (NIRS) with its talk program *Talk Black*—a play on the Australian term for talk radio, "talk back." Brisbane itself has been a center for the development of alternative and politically oppositional community radio. Community radio station 4ZZZ had its beginning here in 1974, just two years after the first community license in Australia was granted to the University of Adelaide's 5UV in 1972. The decade following was a time of exponential growth—with several hundred community radio stations going on-air across Australia as community broadcasting became a key feature of Australian broadcasting policy and practice. Today 4ZZZ has an established industrial presence for alternative rock as well as left-leaning political analysis, and community radio more generally has become a huge aspect of Australia's media landscape. In the early 1980s Aboriginal groups around Australia were among the applicants for newly introduced community licenses, with CAAMA radio in Alice Springs, the Thaiday brothers in remote Queensland, and 4K1G in Townsville as some of the first to broadcast under community radio licensing.

4AAA also operates under a community license. Its call sign, "Murri Country," speaks both to the regional appellation for Indigenous people who live in Queensland—"Murri"—and plays with the salience of "country" as a politically and affectively charged icon of Aboriginal belonging and as a label for the genre of music that is 4AAA's specialization—country music. 4AAA's broadcast studios occupy the top floor of the Barclay Mowlem Building, an eight-story structure looking out over suburban Brisbane and named for the construction and engineering corporation who owns the building and which occupies six of its eight floors. "Triple-A," as producers call it, also occupies one other floor of the building, a recent expansion by the radio station, acquired primarily as a space in which to conduct broadcast training for young Murris.

In 2003, the most public faces of 4AAA were Tiga Bayles; his mother, Maureen Watson; and his uncle, Ross Watson. They have been central figures in the development of Aboriginal media in both Brisbane and Sydney since the early 1980s. Founders of Sydney's Radio Redfern, Bayles and Watson began broadcasting Indigenous news and musics on Sydney community radio station 2SER in the early 1980s, following a visit Maureen made to Alice Springs and her encounter with CAAMA's 8KIN FM. Starting with a ten-minute spot on another presenter's show and quickly expanding the broadcast to a dedicated Indigenous program called *Black Perspectives*, Watson developed a weekly space for Indigenous radio in Sydney, bringing her son and other Koori presenters on board as well. Bayles himself went on to host a midnight-to-3 A.M. "black music show" on Sydney's radio station 2SER, and also to manage the band Us Mob and begin producing recordings of Aboriginal rock and country musics in a period when these were relatively scarce.

In an early 2003 interview with 4AAA radio trainees, produced and broadcast as part of 4AAA's Sunday evening youth program, *Girrabala*, Tiga described their subsequent move from 2SER to the more overtly political Radio Skid Row in 1983:

> Radio Skid Row offered the Koori community, Indigenous people, ten hours a week straight up. And because as Mum and myself and other members of—other Kooris in Redfern were doing this radio programming

on 2SER, they came to us and said that we've got ten hours a week over here, you know, "Get your mob together and come on over and let's start things moving."

We grew that to about forty hours a week and it was a real, genuine attempt by non-Indigenous people, those people controlling Skid Row, a collective of people made up of unemployed people, single mums, gays and lesbians, people out of jail, blacks, migrants, it was a whole range of people representing marginalized groups. So it was a real good feeling over at Skid Row, and it didn't take us long, I think it might have been three or four or five years, to grow to forty hours a week. I think it was only about three years. So that's where the radio thing started for me.

While Radio Skid Row initially offered to provide weekly broadcast time for Koori programming, by the late 1980s the station had moved to share its actual broadcast signal with Radio Redfern—an entirely Indigenous radio station named after the well-known Sydney neighborhood historically associated with the city's Aboriginal community.

Radio Redfern reached beyond an audience of Aboriginal and politically sympathetic listeners through the documentary *88.9: Radio Redfern*, broadcast on Australia's commonwealth-funded broadcaster, the ABC, in January 1989. This documentary was produced by anthropologist and filmmaker Sharon Bell (1990: 3), and a brief sketch of its production lends insight into the political acumen of Tiga Bayles, as well as an emergent sensibility with respect to Aboriginal broadcasting. The film itself was funded by the offices of Film Australia at a time when Aboriginal politics were the focus of great national interest. While Film Australia sought documentaries that could be marketable, it also sought representations of Indigenous communities that emphasized contemporary issues in the urban Southeast, as opposed to remote communities and traditional practices. Indeed, while Bell describes the genesis of the film as due in part to Film Australia's interest in work with broad public appeal and marketability, *Radio Redfern* also offered what Bell has called a "public window" into Sydney's Koori community. At the time this was a novel and attractive prospect to the producers and administrators at Film Australia.

If Bell's focus on Radio Redfern found bureaucratic support, she has also described the difficulty of her negotiations with Aboriginal activists during a period when Aboriginal political criticisms of academic and media representations were reaching a crescendo, particularly within the walls of Radio Redfern's studio:

In one studio situation two female announcers were having a heated discussion about cultural dominance, exploitation by academics and the burgeoning business of "Aboriginality." One woman was particularly down on anthropologists and my pulse quickened just slightly when she asked me my views on "bloody anthropologists riding to success on the backs of blacks." I probably mumbled something along the lines of "exploitative bastards," and survived another day. (Sharon Bell 1990: 37)

In producing Radio Redfern, Bell describes the mix of anger and canny political strategy she encountered among activists such as Gary Foley and Bayles himself. However, within the Aboriginal activist community there were differences of opinion on how best to achieve social change. While activist Foley rejected Bell's proposal to produce a film about Radio Redfern (on the basis that the production did not use Indigenous filmmakers), Bayles agreed to the Film Australia production but negotiated Indigenous involvement at each stage of production, postproduction, and distribution. In Bell's account of these negotiations one catches an early glimpse of Tiga's canny use of the project as a means to extend beyond Radio Redfern's signal and put forward an Indigenous image of the nation's bicentennial celebrations in Sydney Harbor to a broader Australian audience. Tiga's endeavor to reach a heterogeneous Australian audience with a particularly Indigenous perspective on Australian politics and social life resonates with 4AAA's broadcast strategy in the 1990s and 2000s.

The critiques of academic practice and media representation that informed Bell's filming also informed a broad rejection of the official celebrations for the bicentennial (refigured as "invasion day"), which included an official reenactment of the arrival of the First Fleet in Sydney Harbor. This bicentennial drama of national "discovery" galvanized a diverse group of protestors, and Radio Redfern and Radio Skid Row emerged as powerful centers for oppositional demonstrations and also as media outlets with critical and extensive coverage. Media activists were also becoming more cognizant of the place of media in political contests around the globe, and a reflexivity with respect to a new era of media activity informed the uptake of radio in particular. Tony Collins, a former organizer of Radio Skid Row, later a successful mainstream radio DJ and reporter, and in 2003 the manager of Warumpi Band lead singer, George Burarrwanga, described the place of radio during this moment, foregrounding a transnational vision of radio's political potential:

TC: We all had picked up a slogan from the Italian pirate radio stations—
"Radio is my Bomb." So that was the basic philosophy of what we were

doing there. We all had radical political views, it was the peace movement—as you know it was kind of at its peak in the '80s. There was a
big Aboriginal movement, a land rights movement.

DF: So you guys were tuned in to radical radio and free radio in Europe at
the time?

TC: Yeah! You know, the Barcelona stations and all that, the anarchists,
using radio to coordinate protests and all that. The 1988 celebrations
for the Bicentennial were a perfect example of that, where thirty thousand people came to Sydney to demonstrate against the celebrations
and there were huge protests and different groups of people—people
who wanted to do actions. And Radio Redfern, for the several weeks
leading up, while people were pouring into Sydney to take part in
this—it was like the radio was a PA system. It was like, "We need
blankets down here," you know, just a big coordinating kind of public
address system to say, "Right, we need, you know, we got people here
we need a bus down here." "Did the mob arrive from South Australia?
They haven't got any blankets" or, "People need clothes for the mob
from the territory" or, "Everyone's gathering out here for this protest"
or "There's a BBQ on here." . . .

People would come arrive in Sydney and just turn up at Radio
Redfern. So it became sort of protest headquarters, and in that way it
kind of fulfilled the function that we had been reading about five years
earlier, about what was going on in the early '80s, late '70s, in Italy.
People using radio as a political device and—you know, apart from
that we wanted to increase our audience and deliver a message that
wasn't getting through in mainstream media. And that was really the
modus operandi for the radio station—it was a propaganda machine
for our political beliefs. Probably that's why we had so much opposition and trouble—political trouble with the station—because we were
fairly blatant about our politics, and we were using this radio license as
a sort of liberation newspaper kind of thing. So that's where we were at
with Skid Row.[7]

4AAA and Reconciliation

The families and the Aboriginal activist politics at the center of Radio Redfern in Sydney were also catalysts for Brisbane's first Indigenous broadcasts.
In Queensland, Tiga Bayles's uncle and his mother, and several others began

broadcasting out of the studios of Brisbane's 4zzz in 1984, then located on the campus of the University of Queensland in the Brisbane suburb of St. Lucia. From the suppression of demonstrations by the state government of Joh Bjelke-Petersen to the clandestine preparations and excitement of public protest, older Aboriginal activists in southeast Queensland speak of their early experiences producing media in the same breath as activist performance, racism, and a deep anger at the social exclusion of Aboriginal people from public and political life. Tiga, for example, tells the story of 4AAA in part through his own biography, narrating his role as manager for the Aboriginal rock band Us Mob, and an early 1980s tour through rural New South Wales. Arriving at a Bowls club to provide musical entertainment at a festival, the band was forced out into the parking lot and onto the back of a trailer. According to Tiga the festival committee had failed to realize that they'd hired a "black band."[8]

Such stories had a marked place in the conference rooms and studios of Triple-A. They were told and retold to trainees in seminars and weekend outings, where the efforts of the Bayles and Watson families, and the eventual successes of Aboriginal broadcasters around Australia, are narrated for the edification of a younger generation who have grown up in an era in which Aboriginal media are a pervasive aspect of an Australian media landscape. For several weeks in 2003, production work on the sixth floor slowed as elder members of 4AAA's board lectured students, detailing aspects of 4AAA's history and their own biographies. Tiga narrated his movements from rural Queensland to Sydney, and back to Brisbane by way of a stint as chair of the New South Wales Land Council. Uncle Ross Watson described the difficulties of growing up in rural Queensland, a tale that Maureen Watson underlined, describing how she kept her own children from the officers of the state by pretending to be the family maid rather than its matriarch, when officials knocked at the door: "Oh, the games we would play!" she remembered ruefully. As I discuss in more detail below, for Triple-A's managers and educators, such stories are an intrinsic aspect of training, and they connect the political aims of 4AAA with histories of its family networks and individual biographies. Narrating 4AAA's existence activates a political history, told as a story of kinship ties and biographical narratives, and inculcated as values in the daily work of production training.

As with the early proximity and partnership between Radio Skid Row and Radio Redfern, radio production can be understood as a decidedly intercultural endeavor. During the period of my research, the training program at 4AAA was managed by Matthew, a non-Indigenous Australian originally from

Sydney who had previously been a volunteer at Triple-A alongside his wife Katherine. In many instances across Australia, sympathetic non-Indigenous broadcasters, technicians, and activists have played crucial roles in Indigenous media production. At 4AAA, Matthew was joined by Katherine and by Gerry Pyne, who as a technician and a manager of the National Indigenous Radio Service (also located in Brisbane) frequently helped maintain 4AAA's increasingly complicated studios.

If the Watsons' programming on 4ZZZ focused on "redneck bashing" and critiquing the structural and institutional conditions that made even nonviolent Aboriginal protests illegal, the successful application for a community license dedicated to an Indigenous station in Brisbane occasioned a different approach. Here, Tiga, Ross Watson, and Maureen Watson turned to a pragmatics of genre and audience to reach beyond the Murri community. "Twenty years ago we would have said 'Fuck non-confrontationist radio'; now we have cooler heads. We have a potential audience of almost two million; to reach them, instead of just preaching to the converted, we need a format that appeals to the mainstream" (Watson cited in Robson 2001). That format is country music. Popular with both Aboriginal and non-Indigenous Queenslanders, 4AAA's choice of genre was both strategic and historically significant. Not only did this allow Triple-A to reach a large non-Indigenous audience, it also gave them access to a great deal of Aboriginal music, provided a potential commercial base by filling a niche then underdeveloped in Brisbane's broadcast market, and involved them with a number of industry organizations and a wide, potentially national, Aboriginal audience.

Tiga frequently pointed out to me how they could reach a non-Indigenous audience with country music, avoiding confrontation in favor of bridging an intercultural chasm and historical point of conflict. This approach counters a popular stereotype of black-white confrontation in Queensland, critically articulated by Terry Lees, former general manager of Mt. Isa's MOB FM: "There was this concept about this part of the world, and the word that was commonly used was 'redneck.' It is often hard to define exactly what a redneck is, but I guess in the terminology of the time it basically meant someone who was not tolerant of any other culture or was perhaps classified as a racist. The comment had often been heard about Mt. Isa in particular—that there were a lot of racists up here" (Lees, cited in Foley and Watson 2001: 88–89). For broadcasters such as Lees and Bayles, these stereotypes emerged as obstacles in the way of communication, caricatures to be deconstructed and challenged through an inclusive broadcast practice. For example, radio host John Laws's extremely conservative talk-back program, broadcast in Brisbane between noon and one o'clock, competed for audience share with 4AAA. Triple-A's survey based audience research suggested that many listeners listened to his program until it finished at one, but then switched over to 4AAA for its afternoon program of country musics. During a board meeting in 2002, Tiga suggested moving 4AAA's own talk show, the "Murri Magazine" from a noon start time to 1 P.M. "They can hear John Laws and then when they switch over, we'll give them our point of view!"

For Bayles and others on the board of 4AAA, their strategy has thus been to take the broader political framework of "reconciliation" as a guide to the pragmatics of broadcast genre and the register of their audience address. Reconciliation was enshrined in Australian commonwealth policy in 1991 with the appointment of the Council for Aboriginal Reconciliation by then Minister for Indigenous Affairs Robert Tickner. The term itself comes from the 1990 *Royal Commission into Aboriginal Deaths in Custody* (Johnston 1991), the most public result of which was the official adoption of its final recommendation: "That all political leaders and their parties recognize that reconciliation between Aboriginal and non-Aboriginal communities in Australia must be achieved if community division, discord and injustice to Aboriginal people are to be avoided" (cited in Foley and Watson 2001: 11). Tiga and the board of Triple-A have embraced these ideals in the political aspects of their broadcasting practice. Bayles writes: "It is due to the utilization of the airwaves with its positive programming that 4 triple A has been referred to as 'the reconciliation station'" (in Foley and Watson 2001: 7).

Drive-Time Programming

AJ's breakfast show is perhaps the most iconic program format that 4AAA offers—the live DJ playing music, chatting, and perhaps reading the weather and public service announcements. This occupies an important slot in 4AAA's schedule, during which audience numbers are statistically higher than during other parts of the day, and in which the capital that audience ratings represent can be particularly valuable. When AJ arrived at 4AAA I found that the man I had met as an activist with a flair for storytelling and a forceful personality was also a polished radio announcer with a vast knowledge of country music. His drive-time programs and his interviews with Aboriginal and other Australian country music performers occupied a prime spot on 4AAA's programming, and his capacities as a reliable announcer with a charismatic voice and a noteworthy skill at creating an inclusive and inviting address were clearly valued.

In his early twenties when we first met, AJ grew up listening to Australian and American country stars such as Slim Dusty, Ricky Skaggs, and Charley Pride, as well as the rock sounds of AC/DC and Guns and Roses. Yet he describes his interest in radio not in terms of music, but in terms of announcing and his introduction to Aboriginal media production at Townsville Indigenous station 4K1G. He was taken there with classmates from Doomadgee primary school by a teacher, Philip Peachy, whom AJ credits with fostering his early interest in radio:

> The whole school used to have excursions, and then one year we went to Townsville. And he took us into a place there called 4K1G—which is an Indigenous station just like 4AAA. And I walked in there and that was it for me. I walked into 4K1G in Townsville when I was in year seven and I said, "Nah, that's what I want to do!' "

AJ described how Peachy followed up by helping his students put together mock radio programs, cassette-recording interviews with elders in Doomadgee, and then mixing these interviews with music and announcements over the school's PA system.

> And every Wednesday at lunch time, at school, we'd put the PA system out and play it to the school and act like we were in the radio. And we'd be sitting there and carrying on and on Wednesday nights, he'd take his time out after work and drive us down to the middle of the park in the community with the PA, and we'd put it on the back of the old school Dodge, old school ute there.[9] I would stand and act like we was on radio—me and about four other friends. And that was my first radio show.

In 1990, when AJ was in year 9 at school, the expansion of the Broadcasting for Remote Aboriginal Communities Scheme (BRACS) came to the attention of these young men in Doomadgee.[10] As AJ remembers it, his former schoolteacher, Philip Peachy, again brought this to AJ's attention:

> And he goes "Guess what, mate. The government's got this thing out called BRACS. The government along with Telecom have got this thing called BRACS which is Broadcasting in Remote Aboriginal Communities Scheme." He said we could apply for one of them, we could get a radio station here in Doomadgee. I said, "Really?" He said, "Yeah." He said, "All we'd need is a committee."

The need to have an organization through which to achieve official recognition, the need to "form a committee," is a recurring theme in Indigenous cultural production, and the Aboriginal Councils and Associations Act of 1976 was an explicit attempt to create the means by which the commonwealth could recognize and interact with an Aboriginal citizenship (Batty 2003; cf. Ginsburg 1997: 131). The ways in which Aboriginal media is almost always produced by a media association can be traced to this act and the policy discussions that led up to it. H. C. "Nugget" Coombs, an early architect of Aboriginal self-determination policy, saw in such corporations a means of reconciling liberal democratic participation with Indigenous rights and the politics of Aboriginal difference (Attwood 2004; Rowse 1992, 2000). In the current climate, in which Aboriginal autonomy shares discursive space with a neoliberal emphasis on privatization and "mainstreaming" of service delivery, the Registrar of Aboriginal Corporations is gradually attracting critical attention, even while remaining a significant organizational instrument for receiving funding and recognition as an Indigenous corporate concern (Rowse 2007). AJ continued:

> So us kids formed a committee at school. But 'cause we weren't old enough to be on a committee—like a proper Aboriginal organization, like what Triple-A is—we got some of the elder people in the community to come up and be like the chairperson and all that. We'd be like just little members on the side and they'd be the actual core of the committee. So we formed this committee, got it registered by the Aboriginal registrar in Canberra, and called it the Yandarinja Media Association.

AJ moved away from and came back to Doomadgee several times in his later teens and early twenties. This began with an extended visit to Brisbane in the early 1990s and was followed several years later with studies for a diploma in communications at James Cook University in Townsville. Here AJ moved outside of the curriculum to stay involved in radio production, working nights at 4K1G. Unsatisfied with the lecture basis of the curriculum, AJ returned to the Doomadgee to operate the BRACS station until deciding several years later, in 1997, to set out for Townsville and, he hoped, a job producing radio at 4K1G. As AJ describes it, he didn't make it past Mt. Isa, where he was given work at Indigenous community station MOB FM.

> I did everything, man—I was the program director there for the last two years of working there, for the first two years I was senior broadcaster. . . . I was doing Breakfast and, you know, producing and doing it all myself.

'Cause as you know, mate, we produce and do all our own stuff—we don't have sort of fifty people hanging around. I was doing Breakfast plus I was doing program director work, selecting the music and downloading all sorts of stuff, but that was for the first two years, and for the last two years I became the program director there. Because MOB FM is one of the only Indigenous stations in the country that are actually contracted to a non-Indigenous organization, they're contracted to Channel Seven. I wasn't only doing radio work, I was doing the news for Channel Seven, plus the ads for Channel Seven—so we were making [television] news stories that you see here in Brisbane on Channel Seven.

During the 2000 Olympic games, AJ was selected to act as part of the Indigenous press core covering the events in Sydney for national radio broadcasts over Indigenous community and remote radio networks. While there, he met Bayles and a number of other Indigenous broadcasters and journalists from around Australia. This led to an invitation from Bayles and 4AAA for AJ to try out for the early morning drive-time slot—which he took up in February 2002.

Festival Broadcasts and Live Production

While my mornings in Brisbane started with AJ's drive-time programming, 4AAA sought ways to move outside of the studio, taking its Outdoor Broadcasting van to festivals and live performances such as the Gympie Muster country music festival, the Woodford Folk Festival, and the Tamworth Country music festival. The numerous annual festivals, sports carnivals, and rodeos of Queensland and New South Wales provided sites where broadcasting focused on a "live" event and the representation of a spatially discreet, copresent audience. Tamworth is popularly held to be the world's largest single country festival, drawing anywhere from fifty thousand to one hundred thousand visitors annually, featuring thousands of live performances, music and dance workshops, and exhibitions over a ten-day period. Attending Tamworth provides 4AAA with a number of opportunities. In part this is a chance to achieve a visible presence with Australia's country music diehard fans, there in Tamworth to catch as many of the hundreds of country performers attending as they can. It also allows them to tap into a potential audience for Tamworth in Brisbane and across the country via the National Indigenous Radio Service. It is also an important training opportunity for young Murri producers: here they learn to run live sound and to produce a live, on-site performance of a large radio audience. The festival provides a large amount of recorded performances for later airplay, allowing the station to revisit Tamworth's Aboriginal performance stage in the months to come.

Tamworth is thus a key event on 4AAA's calendar and an extremely busy time for its staff, who record and edit music performances throughout the ten days of the festival. Triple-A's production team travels south to Tamworth en masse, renting a house and camping out there for several weeks. Carting down mixing boards, microphones, and other broadcasting and recording gear, Triple-A establishes a remote studio on the Tamworth show grounds, making one half of a mobile trailer into a live-to-air studio for the duration of the festival, and using the other half as a production suite and sound recording studio for producing and editing performances into broadcast-length segments that then go out over a phone line to Brisbane and Triple-A's link to the National Indigenous Radio Service, and from there to a satellite uplink. In 2003 their broadcasts included live recordings from the numerous Aboriginal showcases—concerts featuring a number of Aboriginal performers conducting short sets of four or five songs. It also included interviews and studio performances with both Indigenous and non-Indigenous recording stars such as Troy Cassar-Daley, Jimmy Little, and Paul Kelly.

As with the constructed liveness of much of Triple-A's digitalized studio broadcasting, producing festivals also requires a great deal of technology, effort, and skill. Rarely do performances receive truly live broadcast; instead they are recorded to a computer's hard drive for later mastering, editing, and broadcast. In the process, the "real" time of the performance and the festival itself are fit to the broadcast schedule and time frame of Triple-A's routinized programming. Festival production also relies on both corporate and state sponsorship and on the station's profile within Australia's country music industry. This latter is officially represented by the Country Music Association of Australia (CMAA) but is underwritten on an annual basis by large corporate sponsors such as Toyota and Telstra (Australia's recently privatized national communications provider). Broadcasts are often owned by public or commercial broadcasters who purchase exclusive rights to key events during the course of the festival.

In 2003, one exception to the routine of delayed live broadcasting was the Tamworth awards ceremony, the Golden Guitars. This marked the first time that Triple-A was able to broadcast from the ceremony, having been denied access by the Australian Broadcasting Corporation in prior years.

In 2003, Triple-A found a more willing partner in a commercial channel that had succeeded in acquiring the broadcast rights from the ABC and the CMAA. However, in the weeks that followed, Bayles expressed disappointment in the outcome of this arrangement, noting that they were forced to take a signal directly from the commercial broadcaster rather than having the ability to produce the event independently for their listeners. As Bayles later commented, this was understood as a real setback, in that the presenters were non-Indigenous and the focus of the event overlooked Indigenous involvement in both the country music industry and the audience. There were no "black voices" in the broadcast. Unlike other, prerecorded events, which are then edited and introduced by Triple-A presenters, the Golden Guitars award show went to air with minimal Triple-A editing and minimal Triple-A control.

If the Golden Guitars are the premiere event of the festival, less glamorous but no less valued musical performances take place on the street corners of the town itself. Despite extremes of heat and sun, Tamworth's main pedestrian mall is routinely filled with performers—from the honky-tonk dancing of urban Australian groups playing old-time rockabilly with an ironic wink, to young sisters performing earnest duets of mainstream country numbers from Australian radio's Top Forty. Every ten meters a temporary numbered stage has been reserved for a scheduled busker. On the last Friday morning of the 2003 festival, visiting musicians from western Queensland were scheduled on the mall and featured AJ singing songs with friends Brian and Noel accompanying. Appreciative listeners pulled up portable chairs, and as the band set up to play, Tiga, Matthew, and I set about documenting the performance. Tiga and Matthew checked their equipment, testing recording levels on their minidisc recorders before approaching the players. These were not strangers; indeed, the band had been camping in the backyard of 4AAA's house. Today Tiga interviewed Noel about his trip to Tamworth and his ambitions as a country singer, and Noel spoke of his admiration for Alan Jackson (and wore a T-shirt autographed by the American country star) and his hopes to secure a recording contract (figure 4.1). These interviews would be incorporated into a magazine-style format for broadcast.

As the band lit into their set, Tiga picked up his laptop computer and moved on to the town hall to prepare for recording the Aboriginal showcase occurring that afternoon. The band picked up acoustic guitars, welcomed a guest bass player from Adelaide rockabilly band The Fuelers, and began a long set of country covers. Songs by Johnny Cash, Australian Slim Dusty,

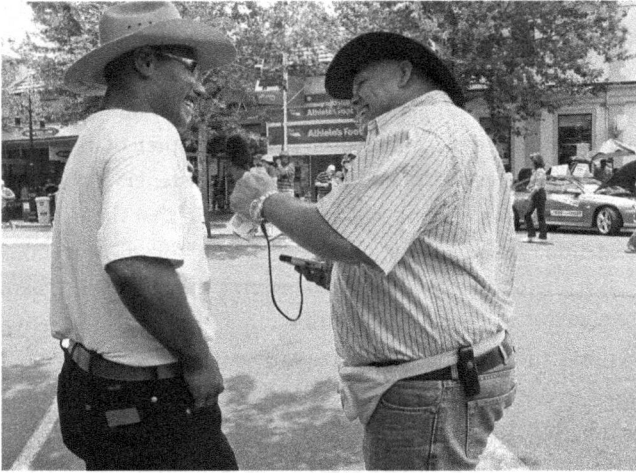

4.1 Tiga Bayles interviews a busker from Doomadgee.

and Waylon Jennings jostled for space in their set with pieces by Aboriginal country star Roger Knox, and people slowed to listen, gathering around the group. As the sun came up over the shade trees and band members started to sweat, an older non-Indigenous audience member went to fetch elongated, water-filled balloons, returning to drape these around the neck of each performer with the aim of preventing heat exhaustion. As the set wound up, I walked farther down the mall, listening in on other performers at adjoining busking stages. Before long I found a particularly eccentric singer who had brought along a series of homemade wooden signs and put them up for sale. Wearing a hat in the shape of a chicken coop (with a live chicken in residence), he sang bush ballads and country hits from Australian greats like Slim Dusty and Tex Morton. I was surprised to see his signs, constructed in the style of wooden plaques used to display house names in Australian suburbs, but mimicking the sounds of Aboriginal language to evoke a particularly Australian, working-class joke on the value of "grog" and a typically primitivizing representation of Indigenous languages—"didjabringyergrogalong."

Taken aback by this diminutive representation of Aboriginal languages, I was reminded that the former Independent representative from Oxley, Pauline Hanson, had come to Tamworth this year as the manager for a country singer and industry hopeful. Vocal in her anxieties over the so-called "reverse racism" of Indigenous rights, Hanson has been a frequently lampooned but significant political figure—and a favorite of conservative radio talk show hosts such as John Laws. In 2003 she announced her intention to promote and manage country music singers, including Queensland's Brian Letton, and in so doing she found a new place in the spotlight in rural Queensland and New South Wales. In this shared cultural space of class-marked musical practices and discourses of Australian "true blue" country life, country music sings in a double voice. With a fan base made up of both the male, conservative non-Indigenous and "Anglo" Australians held to be least sympathetic to particularly Indigenous rights (and perhaps most supportive of Hanson's conservative platforms), as well as aging Aboriginal activists and the communities and kin networks that make up an Aboriginal domain, the public events of country music festivals entail a potential for unexpected interaction and shared belonging that official policies of reconciliation sought to encourage in their most idealistic forms. It is that potential that Tiga, Matthew, and AJ all seek to capitalize on with their use of a shared genre and a sophisticated broadcast address that might gain a sympathetic ear from an audience that is held to support Hanson.

While Matthew, AJ, and the others took down the equipment and PA from the busking stage, I moved on to the Tamworth Town Hall to purchase tickets for the last installment of the Aboriginal showcase. Arriving late at the town hall, I found that all the prime seating was sold out, and I was forced upstairs to the long balcony running in a large U above the main floor. Tiga stood squarely in the middle of the hall. He had set up his laptop next to the mixing board and sound engineer for the afternoon performance, taking a direct feed from the board and importing an audio signal mixed for the space of the performance hall directly to his hard drive, to be later edited down and mastered in Triple-A's demountable studios. He stared intently at his screen as Roger Knox rolled through four hits, including a memorable "Koori Rose." Knox was followed by other Indigenous country luminaries. Warren Williams sang his then-current hit "Dreamtime Baby," and Jimmy Little sang a short set of five songs, dismissing the band and strumming his own accompaniment on an Australian-made Maton guitar—a favorite of Australian country guitar players and easily recognized by the characteristic point designed into its pick guard. For his final number he sang his early 1960s gospel country hit "Royal Telephone" and had the audience on its feet. Finally, Troy Cassar-Daly took the stage and sang numbers from his current release *Take the Long Way Home*, prefacing his performance with stories of his days as an aspiring singer, living in Tamworth's back blocks.

Later I went out with AJ and Noel and several others for a long night of pub crawling, following a packed schedule made up from AJ's picks of worthy entertainers. We started at the house 4AAA had rented, up a small rise from Tamworth's town center. We clambered into AJ's green Monaro, an Australian, V8-equipped muscle car built to seat four, now fitting seven. Radio blasting, AJ drove us into town for our first stop, a pub with more electronic poker machines than chairs, but with a live band onstage and affordable pitchers of beer. AJ moved through the room looking for mates, checking out the scene, while Noel told jokes to the rest of us at a table cluttered with schooners and pitchers of lager. The band here, a country outfit from Sydney, disappointed AJ and Noel, and soon we were on the move again, looking for the rest of the 4AAA crew and walking now, car safely parked.

I hurried to keep pace with AJ and Noel as we walked between Tamworth's numerous RSLs[11] and hotels spread out on a shallow rise above the fairgrounds and the Peel River, and AJ regaled me with stories of his recent victory as representative of the Waanyi Nation in a large, nonviolent occupation of the Century Zinc mine just outside Mt. Isa, near Queensland's border with the Northern Territory.[12] He described in vivid detail storming the mine's canteen, throwing his pack on a lunch table, and declaring the mine property of the Waanyi Nation. In the ensuing negotiations, these Waanyi activists used AJ's media talents to videotape their negotiations over the terms of continued resource extraction. Following this victory, AJ had been elected chair of the Aboriginal Corporation charged with representing the Waanyi, Ganggalida, and Garrawa peoples (all of whom have consolidated a legal identity as the Waanyi Nation in pursuit of a land claim; see NTRU 1998). The country music festival was his first chance to unwind from these tense weeks of action and celebrate a Waanyi victory in the country pubs of Tamworth. The already charged atmosphere of Tamworth's busy festival shows only amplified his recent success.

AJ soon turned us to the highlight of the evening, extolling the virtues of his mate's band—Kevin Bennett and the Flood. "Living legends, mate," AJ said, describing Bennett as a musician's musician. On entering the hotel where the Flood would play, AJ parted the crowd with Noel in tow and greeting mates as he went. The rest of us followed. As we worked or way up toward the stage and an adjacent bar, we collected the rest of 4AAA's crew. Given the energy and size of the waiting crowd, it was clear that we were far from alone in anticipating the Flood's performance. The audience seemed to consist largely of the festival's workers, the media crews, and musicians staying in Tamworth as a professional obligation. We had heard Paul Kelly play the previous day. Aside from internationally recognized rock performer Nick Cave, Kelly is perhaps the best-known Australian songwriter and recording artist of his generation. His songs "From St. Kilda to Kings Cross," "To Her Door," and "Sydney from a 747," for instance, are cherished by several generations of Australians who recognize themselves in the narrative topographies Kelly builds and who find themselves moved by the guitar-based rock grooves, as well as by a pathos that derives from both the narrative content and the prosodic, stereotypically Australian, masculine twang of Kelly's voice itself. Kelly is also known for his support of Aboriginal rights and causes, and he gave ample time to 4AAA's broadcast, sitting in their trailer for an interview and a short acoustic performance for 4AAA's microphones. But onstage Kelly was subdued, the audience quiet and seated, and the energy off.

By the time the Flood took their stage, however, the hotel garden was standing room only, with beer spilled on shoes and a packed dance floor as Aboriginal and Anglo Australians alike took to their feet dancing, laughing, and shouting. At the bar to the side of the stage AJ and I began with beer and talk, or, rather, shouting. AJ leaned in and yelled to me throughout the show about Kevin's career, his songwriting skills, how no one outside of Nashville could touch him, and how Bennett's band was the tightest, most polished group not just in Tamworth but in all of Australia. This was AJ as hyperbolic advocate for Australian country and rock music, opining and assessing aspects of the sound, the musicianship, and the songwriting much as he had critiqued the hip-hop at Bomb Shelter in Brisbane's Fortitude Valley, yelling then too to rise above the amplified music. And he was right: the Flood gave an electric performance.

I saw some of the other trainees and 4AAA DJs on the floor dancing. 4AAA's principle sound engineer KR was then still out on bail awaiting trial. He'd been accused of assaulting his younger cousin and was subject to an AVO, an Apprehended Violence Order that kept him not just from her, but also from half his family. He'd ridden here from Brisbane on a big, old, chopped-up Honda motorbike and seemed relaxed. He left his leathers on a bar stool while he danced with a young woman, herself a trainee in sound engineering at TEABBA. I didn't yet know it, but I wouldn't see much more of him after our trip. He would soon violate his AVO and be sent back to jail to await trial for the assault.

DS stayed at the bar; a spinal injury kept him from dancing. KR's incarceration would soon open a spot for DS to move more centrally into sound engineering. Several years younger than KR, and relatively new to 4AAA, DS rarely tangled with the police. He was invested in producing hip-hop and learning to engineer sound. He was also dedicated to the broader political project pursued at 4AAA. He brought an energy to production that blossomed as he grew more knowledgeable about the studio's technology. His serious health problems, a compressed vertebra, kept him at home now and again. In Tamworth the group took over a section of bar but also mingled with the crowds. They had been hard at work all week, broadcasting concerts, conducting interviews, setting up and taking down sound equipment. Noel and his girlfriend soon came and pulled AJ away from the bar and onto the dance floor, where they moved between dancing and shouting their appreciation of the band toward the stage, Kevin acknowledging AJ and Noel from the stage with a nod and a grin. DS's interests at Tamworth seemed more focused on the technology. Quieter than either AJ or KR, and less interested in country music than hip-hop and DJ-ing, he spent his time following Tiga, learning to record live sound. His listening, like Tiga's, took place as much through headphones, with eyes focused on a digital timeline, as it did from a bar or dance floor. Together, however, DS and AJ would translate their Tamworth experiences to radio sound as two sides of the broadcast coin, one technical and material, invested in transduction and technical skill, the other discursive and verbal, interested in a narrative account of musical value and expressive skill. AJ's capacity to talk music matched DS's capacity to hear aspects of frequency spectrum and timbre through digital audio's technical affordance.

Live performances matter greatly to making radio here, grounding CD and cassette recordings in experiential, ritualized audition and often taking particular recordings and reanimating them as performance for a live audience. They matter for radio producers insofar as to make radio is also to listen closely, with an ear for detail, for talent, and for what moves audiences, what draws people to dance, shout, and to feel something. Aboriginal scenes of listening to live music are often maximally participatory in this way, evoking appreciative shouts and cries and even efforts to converse with performers from in front of the stage monitors, efforts that often fail in the face of the loud sounds coming from the stage.[13] Live performance, that is, often meant the elicitation, or at least accommodation, of audience vocalization. The excess of expressivity cultivated in bars and concerts contrasts, however, with the care around the voice, the measured approach to crafting sound for broadcast that informed radio producers' attention to live sound and that animated studio production, to which I turn next.

Trainees: From Cultural Production to "Creative Industries"

Talking to younger trainees in one of the weekly sessions aimed at giving them some insight into announcing as both daily labor and political practice, AJ described his daily routine and an approach that echoes 4AAA's broader broadcasting ideology. Awake at 3:30 every morning, AJ runs through the shower and drives to the studios by 4. He then reads the paper, circling stories to share with listeners and developing conversation topics: "It's no good getting on the air and just talking about the songs—that's boring. So I'm always working really, reading the paper, watching the news for things to bring on the show." He added that he also keeps his monologues short to keep his audience from drifting away. Finally, AJ brings small stories to air, generally about Aboriginal history and often drawing from a Triple-A archive of Aboriginal historical events assembled in calendar form. AJ added, "I don't force it down their throat, just a little bit, and with music they like." He continued, "It's no good trying to argue with someone. If you try and force this stuff down people's throats you're never going to get anywhere.... This old fella once told me, if you're going to argue with someone, don't scream and get out of control. Keep your voice like this the whole time." AJ said this last with an even, prosodically flat, and very, very soft delivery. When he then relaxed this control, the dynamism in his speaking voice seemed exaggerated, its prosodic dynamics foregrounded after the even keel of his example. "Keep your voice steady and you'll not only probably win the argument, you'll probably get his trust and confidence too!"

One afternoon some weeks later, I followed 4AAA lead trainer, Matthew, to one of Triple-A's production studios, where he was to help trainees Trisha and Corey prerecord a presentation for that Sunday's youth program. We arrived to find a red light above the shut studio door, indicating that recording was in progress. When the light dimmed, we opened the door and entered, finding DS and Jeff preparing to listen to a presentation they had just recorded. We all listened to Jeff's "read" of a script, back-announcing a song and advertising a youth disco to be held the following week. Matthew praised Jeff for his read: "That's the best first read of any student at 4AAA thus far." He then moved to coach all of us on the use of the voice in a radio broadcast. "In order to keep it interesting, you need to pay attention to your intonation," he said. "Do you know this concept? Not slurring, not too fast, not too slow, but varied."

Such attention to the prosodic and pragmatic character of the voice and its mediated forms were pervasive at 4AAA. In the values associated with "professional" broadcasting and the timbre and prosody of the broadcast voice, in attention to the proximity of the microphone and the need to minimize the studio space in order to foreground the voice, and in attention to idiom and prosodic dynamics, the radio voice and 4AAA's outgoing signal were a focus of constant, formal attention. In part this was a clear effort to counter the broad stereotypes of Indigenous linguistic alterity so widely spread in Australia, and often in the demeaning, broadly racist forms I encountered in Tamworth. But Matthew and AJ, in encouraging reflexive attention to the voice and to its formal characteristics, also contributed to a broader discourse on sound and its mediation made explicit in the training activities and extending into the musical interests and music production of the trainees. This moved beyond a politics of representation and into a pragmatics of capacity building, encouraging linguistic flexibility on the part of students. The voice became, in this context, the overdetermined focus of combined efforts to persuade and reach a broad audience, counter negative stereotypes, and a more prosaic effort to increase employability and individual capacity.

For most students, training at 4AAA took place in the context of the pursuit of a nationally certified technical degree in broadcasting, journalism, sound production, or even advertising sales. 4AAA received funding to organize this training from Queensland's Department of Education and had thus become adjunct to a national system of degree-granting technical colleges. 4AAA trainees in residence in Brisbane received financial support through two primary commonwealth initiatives. "AbStudy," a government-funded program to provide support for Aboriginal and Torres Strait Islander people seeking secondary and tertiary education, supported a few of the trainees. But much more significant for 4AAA, and for Aboriginal media organizations across Australia, was the Community Development Employment Projects scheme (CDEP). Designed primarily to support the training and development of Aboriginal capabilities in remote areas where employment or apprenticeship opportunities were few, from its establishment in 1977 it has come to play an extremely large role in Aboriginal employment throughout Australia, including within large urban areas such as Brisbane (Altman 2007; Hunter and Gray 2013). While the financial support and promise of a certified competency were clearly significant factors motivating participation at 4AAA, so too was the potential for escape from gendered labor and non-Indigenous oversight that the trainees had experienced in other work and apprenticeship experiences.

Often trainees came to 4AAA after demoralizing experiences in other vocational training programs, physical labor, and/or apprentice work in various building trades or other kinds of gendered menial labor. Originally from Moree in northern New South Wales, Trisha described how she appreciated the work and the big change it was from the kinds of work she had been able to pursue in Moree, where occupation was strictly gendered. She described how the men in Moree were given CDEP jobs mowing lawns and landscaping, yet the women stayed in the community center and either sewed or, as she remembers it, stared out the window with nothing to do. Trisha's entry into 4AAA was occasioned through a work experience requirement at a local technical and further education college (TAFE).[14] "I wanted to learn about mechanics," she told me:

The whole family knows it, I know it. But you know, just the tiny bits of it. My brother was in spray painting, so I decided, yeah, I'll have a look. I don't care if don't get anywhere near it but I'm still going to have a look at it. And then, there was nothing that I could, I couldn't see anything, that I could—about that there. So I decided—then, you know, one of the TAFE teachers said, why don't you try Triple-A?

At 4AAA Trisha was trained to manage the constant task of updating the digital music library on which the station's broadcast depends. Working with software called Sound Forge, Trisha sat in Studio C, listening to music, "normalizing" it and "topping and tailing" each piece, that is, removing noise and signal spikes and clipping the beginning and ending of each digital song to leave just the right amount of silent lead-in to the music. Rather than being confined to gendered forms of office administration, at 4AAA Trisha was able to pursue a growing interest in music and technology.

Trisha came to Triple-A through the offices of state-assisted vocational training and job placement, ostensibly for a short visit. Once offered a job working one day a week importing music into Triple-A's digital library, Trisha soon applied for CDEP wages, a small sum that for two days of work provided Trisha with AU $170/week, supplemented by $30 to help defray living costs. "It's like a rent assistance help, which doesn't help at all!" she said angrily in one of our interviews. "And I'd rather never be on CDEP again. I said I wouldn't be on it again and I am." When I asked Trisha why she had gone back to CDEP she responded: "Because I wanted to stay here."

Clearly her CDEP wages were not reason enough to stay at 4AAA, but it became clear in further discussion with Trisha that the rewards of participation at 4AAA were many. She was able to reconnect with and learn something of her family by comparing notes with other trainees, staff, and management at Triple-A—many of whom know Moree and Trisha's relatives living there.

And if in the CDEP at Moree she faced days of unrelenting make-work, 4AAA soon had her working in a studio. In the end Trisha found the experience so rewarding that she dropped her TAFE office administration studies to remain working at 4AAA.

DS, also from Moree, was a popular, respected figure throughout 4AAA. In his early twenties and highly skilled with the various technologies that make up radio and sound production, DS came to radio after an accident while working as a laborer. This accident left him with a compressed disc and in a great deal of physical pain, and also marked the beginning of a spiral of daily drinking and depression. His mother's active involvement in Brisbane's Indigenous organizational field provided her with information on Triple-A's program, yet DS postponed joining as he pursued professional sound engineer training at a commercial vocational school in Brisbane. When this was slow to materialize, DS spoke on the phone with Matthew. When Matthew mentioned that they also would have the opportunity to learn multitrack mixing, DS signed up. A dedicated producer and charismatic figure, DS quickly took on a central role in the trainees' production work and after one year was able to manage most digital preproduction work that took place on 4AAA's sixth floor. He was also in line to learn much more involved technical work as an apprentice to professional technicians installing a new production studio on the sixth floor.

Many of the other trainees came to their studies at Triple-A after experiences not dissimilar to those of Trisha and DS. Jeff, for example, worked as a carpenter's apprentice but was kept from skilled work by a seemingly permanent post behind a wheelbarrow. Corey had been employed producing boomerangs for the tourist trade on the Gold Coast, which allowed his English employers to place a sticker on the pieces labeled "authentic Aboriginal boomerang." Echoing DS, Corey also stated that this seemed a betrayal of his community, and he disentangled himself to pursue broadcasting and a greater involvement with Brisbane's Murri community.

Training in the "Smart State"

This focus on vocational training in the cultural industries recalls the move in the 1990s to embrace the export of Australian cultural production, spelled out as policy in then Prime Minister Paul Keating's 1995 statement *Exports from a Creative Nation*. There Keating introduced an initiative to bolster Australian cultural production. Film, television, and multimedia productions were to be supported through international marketing, and the creative industries were to be given priority in the economic development of Australian exports.

> As we approach the conclusion of this millennium, Australians are realizing that our future largely depends on the quality and sophistication of the things that we make. In the coming years, nations will prosper or founder on the basis of the value they add to their products. And adding value requires the employment of creativity. (Keating 1995: 4)

This focus on added value had a second aspect as well that addressed Australia's international image and sought to develop its multicultural potential:

> Our creative sector is a significant national economic resource. But cultural exports also serve another function. As we approach the 21st century, we should be projecting a contemporary Australia to the world; tolerant and diverse, interesting, lively and enterprising. A nation at home with all of its constituent elements, and proud of its extraordinary Indigenous heritage. (Keating 1995: 5)

This has a ground as well in the importation into Australia of the framework of "Creative Industries." This term has its origins in a policy framework developed within the Blair government's Department of Culture, Media and Sport in the UK in the late 1990s—a time when a neoliberal paradigm found fuel in figures of the "information society" to figure cultural production as the premiere commercial activity and site of potential revenue extraction and national economic growth of the coming twenty-first century (Caves 2000; Miller 2004; Rossiter 2004).

In its Australian incarnation, cultural studies and media scholars brought together scholarship on popular culture and mass media technologies with a policy focus on amplifying investment in forms of creative labor. This is generally understood as an advocacy project by scholars and champions of the "creative industries" concept such as John Hartley and Stuart Cunningham. Indeed, their work encouraged projects geared toward promoting content production, and enabling Indigenous people and youth across Queensland to gain access to and experience with media technologies. This is evident in the ways in which "Indigenous Creative Industries" are aligned with a rethinking of the practical achievement of Indigenous autonomy and cultural development and in the ongoing relationship between scholars such as Hartley and Queensland's Indigenous activist and policy development community (cf. Hartley and McKee 2000).

Yet this move to embrace key neoliberal tropes from within the academy has not gone without its detractors. Toby Miller notes that the stress on consumption and creativity fails to address the "New International Division of Cultural Labor" that underwrites and obfuscates this intensified creation of surplus value, an ongoing global alienation of labor, and an amplified transnational transfer of resources that a creative industries, neoliberal perspective misrecognizes as liberatory (2004). Neil Rossiter echoes Miller, arguing that the creative industries are "a natural extension of the neoliberal agenda within education as advocated by successive governments in Australia since the mid-1980s," and he points to the alienation of creative labor as intellectual property that the paradigm advocates. Rossiter warns, further, that this "reinforces the status quo of labour relations within a neoliberal paradigm in which bids for industry contracts are based on a combination of rich technological infra-structures that have often been subsidized by the state (i.e. paid for by the public), high labour skills, a low currency exchange rate and the lowest possible labour costs" (2004: 5).

In spite of such vocal detractors, the programmatic efforts of "creative industries" do resonate strongly with a broadly circulating discourse of Indigenous autonomy, given its clearest articulation and most forceful argument in the writings of historian and Aboriginal activist Noel Pearson (2010; cf. Sutton 2011). Pearson asserts that the bureaucratic administration of Aboriginal self-determination has been socially destructive, and in his terms, the funding of Aboriginal communities and projects from the commonwealth purse has undermined Indigenous values of exchange and reciprocity. Welfare dependence, Pearson argues, is a consequence of these policies while true Aboriginal autonomy, participation in Australia's "real economy," and an improvement in the indicators of Aboriginal life chances are most likely to come about through Aboriginal initiatives to redefine the form of the Aboriginal corporation and economic development. As I suggest above, however, Pearson's arguments are only the most developed of a widely circulating discourse in which state welfare is held to be inimical to Aboriginal autonomy and in which a three-decade-old policy of "self-determination" has been supplanted by a paradigmatic conflation of "autonomy" and "enterprise" that divorces Aboriginal development and governance from state welfare and economic oversight.[15]

Pearson's ideas thus participate in a broad, neoliberal transformation of the institutional and discursive frames of Aboriginal governance and cultural production in Australia. The most public index of such shifts came in May 2004, when the Liberal government of Prime Minister John Howard moved to dissolve the Aboriginal and Torres Strait Islander Commission (ATSIC). Following the defeat of an appeal lodged by Indigenous senator Aden Ridgeway, Parliament upheld this decree in March of 2005. These moves surprised few in Australia, as the diminishing of ATSIC's role had been an aim of the Howard government since well before 2004. In a small, informal press conference held in Darwin in 2003, for example, Minister for Indigenous Affairs Philip Ruddock described the admiration he held for Pearson's Balkanu Cape York Development Corporation.

Aboriginal media campaigners had also been aware of a general shift away from a national body and toward "regional development corporations," and toward the privatization of service delivery to Indigenous communities and cultural development policy through contractual agreements between such corporations and the commonwealth. While sympathetic to the economic ideology underwriting these moves, many of my interlocutors also saw such shifts as spelling the end of collective representation as embodied in national representative organizations such as ATSIC.[16] Organizations such as Balkanu Cape York Development Corporation (chaired by Pearson's brother Gerhardt) and the Outback Digital Network put ideas of fiscal responsibility and entrepreneurial initiative at the center of their corporate and activist rationales. ATSIC's demise, then, came as a particularly forceful symbolic step in a process already well under way.

In Brisbane, this cluster of ideas and their institutional materialization clearly inflected the managerial practice and governing direction at 4AAA, and their efforts are often figured as a move to "get out from under the boot of welfare." Ironically, this has led 4AAA ever more fully into bureaucratic and state-run forms of auditing and accountability, in part motivated by Australia's move to export its cultural products and educational institutions. Through partnerships with academics and bureaucrats at the Queensland University of Technology (QUT) School of Business, and through proximity to "the 'world's first' Creative Industries faculty," run by Cunningham and Hartley, also at QUT, 4AAA was embracing a shift in the framing of Indigenous cultural production from "subsidized arts to emergent industries" (Keane and Hartley 2001: 13)—and thus seeking to shed a reliance on public funding in favor of market expansion. In short, the efforts to train youth at 4AAA were part of a larger effort to keep funding coming into the radio station, to diversify and take advantage of governmental and broader interests in Brisbane's public culture in "youth" and associated educational funding.

Auditing Creative Training

In light of such policy discourse, 4AAA had begun to seek funding outside of the then-dominant ATSIC grant process (which nonetheless continued to provide much of the station's funding). This included seeking the small amounts of community sponsorship permitted in their license, "one-off" project grants, and commonwealth and state funding such as the Creative Arts Training Initiative run by Queensland's Department of Employment and Training (DET). In accord with the recommendations and policy positions of cultural studies researchers at the Cultural Industries Research and Applications Centre at the Queensland University of Technology, 4AAA had sought to expand their work into broadcast training, supported by state-based training initiatives and by the broadening rationalization of vocational education begun in Australian in the mid-1990s. This entrepreneurial relationship to the state and to different sources of financial resources led them into increasingly frustrating conflicts with the state's educational apparatus. In the process of responding to a robust educational bureaucracy and its demands for verification of funding outcomes, the aims of the media organization could seem as though swallowed by the effort expended in fulfilling a governmental bureaucracy's mandate. It could seem as though the voice would never arrive, deferred by the need to document its emergence. This is biopolitics as bad faith, when governmental claims to encourage Indigenous "creative industries" are made over as disciplinary exercise for its own sake, when the aims of media production are turned from a concern with voice as sound to the statistical manifestation of its successful education. Here a specter of the voice emerged again, now through the frustrations I encountered among trainers. In order to satisfy governmental auditors, they needed to provide evidence of its education and elicitation.

At the end of 2002, 4AAA had just begun the process of becoming recognized by Queensland's DET as a Registered Training Organization. In 4AAA's case this recognition came through a submission to the Queensland State Government Industry Training Advisory Body for the Creative Industries, which in turn worked in conjunction with several other commonwealth and state bodies, in particular with a commonwealth-administered training advisory board called CREATE Australia (an acronym for Culture Research Education and Training Enterprise Australia). This commonwealth body also focuses on the "creative industries" and seeks to ensure that cultural production can proceed within a proper framework of standardized curricula, assessed with reference to the Australian Qualifications Framework (AQF) and twelve standards known as the Australian Quality Training Framework.

Matthew, Katherine, and Tiga spent much of their time helping to maneuver Triple-A's training body through this welter of acronyms and the audits that accompanied engaging the state in terms of an educational bureaucracy. For several months at the beginning of 2003 I assisted Matthew in preparing for an audit, conducted by CREATE Australia and meant to assess Triple-A's compliance with curricular standards.[17] We spent weeks building a database of documents that corresponded to a delivered "competency" and a step toward one or another certificate within the AQF hierarchy of recognized skill levels. These documents were to be filled out by students, signed by a trainer, and then filed as evidence of student progress.

Although Matthew and I worked to rationalize the training schedule and to construct a transparent curriculum for which Triple-A could be accountable, in the end auditors from CREATE found Triple-A to be "noncompliant." As Matthew later told me, at issue was the lack of documents attesting to student's progress through the TAFE-supplied curricular materials. Matthew was angry and frustrated—much of his work with students in February and March 2003 had been in preparation for the visit of these auditors, yet he found that the requirement to document each stage of training in order to leave a paper trail for auditors seemed inimical to the actual work of the station, to overlook the technical and vocational aspects of Triple-A's training as well as the cultural issues faced in an Indigenous environment.

For Matthew these latter issues encompassed both the sense that young Indigenous students were at risk for drug abuse, domestic violence, and incarceration, and that they were subject to different regimes of socialization and learning, which Matthew grouped as "oral culture"—learning by showing and telling as opposed to reading and writing. Yet while Matthew spent much of his day dealing with the regulatory regimes in which the station was suspended, he also saw his task as preparing these young Indigenous people so that they would be able to undertake the management tasks themselves. The process, that is, served state interests in auditing organizational "compliance" with Australian standards far more than student or instructor interests in training. But as such they had a measurable effect on the ways in which the voice itself became an assessable instrument within 4AAA. His training sessions thus often made explicit both their pedagogical goals and the institutional frameworks. In mid-February, some months before the CREATE Australia audit was to occur, Triple-A received five students from the small city of Rockhampton, visiting for a week of intensive training on 4AAA's equipment. Their first day coincided with a scheduled, weekly group training session. Matthew's explicit pedagogy makes this a good example with which to describe the training process and the explicit role of the state in framing this for young Murris.

Matthew opened the session by recognizing an Indigenous trainee who had just acquired his Certificate IV in Workplace Training, a technical pedagogy degree, and was now acting alongside Matthew to help coordinate Triple-A's training. This was announced as a step toward supplanting non-Indigenous trainers. Matthew then introduced one of the tools by which Triple-A attempted to monitor the progress of trainees—the training diary. Matthew placed the need for a diary, and the standards to which Triple-A was accountable, squarely in the context of an economy of educational exports. "We need to be, they tell us, more competitive," he began.

> There's a big export market in training. A few years ago Asians began to see Australia as a good place to come and study, and the government sees this as a place to get revenue. But they also saw the need to raise standards to an international level. To make sure [that this happens], they've developed twelve standards, and they're tough—you've got to be good to meet them. They're very dictatorial, and they're paper based. So we have to try and deal with the need for signatures and paper in what is at the end of the day an oral culture. I'm passing around one of the most important documents we have, the training diary. This allows us to show not only that you're here, but also to identify that your training was undertaken within those twelve guidelines.

Matthew continued the training meeting, drawing out a critical difference of Triple-A's program from other avenues, and one emphasized again and again by Murri trainees—the vocational aspect of training "on the job." As he told the students, "We're not a university, we're not a TAFE, we're not a school. This organization runs a radio station and a training program; real life, real time, vocational training." This was underlined as Matthew made explicit the range of training ongoing at 4AAA, encouraging the visiting students to get involved in a number of the six "streams" of production training on the sixth floor, all of which tied directly into 4AAA's broadcast production.

First, they might get involved helping to produce the youth program, *Girrabala*. For those with an interest in contemporary music, this would be ideal. Programming a magazine like this was difficult, however, since much of the music they would want to play would not be appropriate or would require editing prior to broadcast due to offensive language and or sexual themes.[18] The second stream of training was journalism, which required developing interviewing, critical thinking, and scriptwriting skills. The third stream, sales and administration, entailed selling on-air advertising space, generally to southeast Queensland Aboriginal organizations, and also required becoming familiar with the networks of Indigenous services and corporations in Brisbane while acquiring experience in telephone sales and networking. The fourth stream, presentation, involved working as a DJ, announcing for such programs as *Girrabala*, *The Job File*, *Stayin' Strong*, or the request program. The fifth and sixth streams, sound production and special events, required a more intense engagement with technology, and Matthew held DS up as Triple-A's role model—someone who worked with Triple-A management and engineers to begin to acquire the skills to mix and record, to put together and take down PA and remote broadcasting equipment at the many festivals and outdoor broadcasts Triple-A produces annually.

The following day the training continued—but now concerned more with bureaucratic regimes of the state's educational oversight. I found Matthew working with one of Triple-A's engineers-in-training, KR, as he filled in sections of his training diary. KR had played a big role in setting up the broadcast from Tamworth, including climbing up on top of the demountable studio and setting up the satellite dish. KR and Matthew sat in the front office, poring over KR's file in order to confirm that he had correctly completed the documentation that would attest to his certificate competencies. However, they were also making sure that 4AAA's competence as a training institution would be evident in KR's file. Matthew reminded KR that he had taken photographs of his work at Tamworth, particularly his work with the satellite dish—"It's fresh in your mind, and I've got evidence. Document that activity in your diary," Matthew told KR, "and we'll have that to show the auditors."

CHAPTER 5 | Speaking For or Selling Out?

Dilemmas of Aboriginal Cultural Brokerage

While Matthew and KR were struggling to meet the expectations of governmental auditors in southeast Queensland, an Aboriginal media association in the Northern Territory, the Top End Aboriginal Bush Broadcasting Association (henceforth TEABBA), was seeking to meet both Australian governmental and remote Indigenous expectations. TEABBA faced pressures from the state in the form of new policy directions that asked the association to seek commercial funding and to find ways to market their Aboriginal audience to advertisers. TEABBA, however, faced a problem insofar as marketing their audience also meant in part alienating that audience, making what formerly had been considered a constituency or collective "owner" of the institution itself into a product for sale. This shift made plain some of the fundamental constraints on the capacity of this organization's managers and media producers to maneuver within newly amplified expectations of entrepreneurial behavior by community cultural organizations. Much like producers at Brisbane's 4AAA, TEABBA's administrators and producers found themselves caught between governmental and ideological pressures to privatize formerly state-supported endeavors. But unlike 4AAA, TEABBA's audience is made up almost entirely of TEABBA's Indigenous members and constituents. These listeners are scattered among thirty-odd remote communities across the Top End of the Northern Territory and are largely remote from the dense population centers and the associated concentration of employment and consumption opportunities these are understood to offer. TEABBA thus found itself in a different dilemma from the urban organization I described in chapter 2, and this had consequences for the sounds and the social organization of its cultural production.

During my first week conducting research at TEABBA the association's general manager, Donna, and assistant manager, Gary, asked if I would be able to help them to develop an organizational "marketing and promotions prospectus." Donna and Gary had recently contracted a non-Indigenous adviser and consultant to draft a five-year plan for their organization, much of which was aimed at securing fiscal independence from the budgetary oversight of ATSIC—at that time still the principal funder of TEABBA's broadcasting and recording projects.[1] This strategic plan argued that TEABBA should accomplish this by "new business activity and new income generation." One of this adviser's key recommendations was that TEABBA put more effort into marketing and promotions, producing materials for circulation to commercial organizations and governmental offices that could foreground TEABBA's relationships with remote communities and figure these as a salable commodity. TEABBA was to sell its access to the Top End's Aboriginal communities as its chief asset.

In some ways this would have been consonant with the ways that TEABBA had long approached government agencies, acting as a broker between the service provision initiatives and policies of the Australian state and the interests and aims of TEABBA's member communities. Indeed, this was the rationale on which Aboriginal organizations across Australia were built during the 1970s and 1980s. Organizations like TEABBA were founded under the articles of the Aboriginal Councils and Associations Act (1976), a piece of the legislative architecture of self-determination that was designed to create representative Indigenous bodies that could allow the democratic participation of Aboriginal people in commonwealth policy formation and service delivery while also recognizing and enabling local Aboriginal priorities and local processes. In retrospect, the move across the 1990s and through the 2000s to reimagine Aboriginal media organizations as profit-making enterprises mimics the arc of Jürgen Habermas's historicization of the bourgeois public sphere in Europe, as publics built on political discourse became zones of spectacle and commodity circulation (see also Debord 1967; Wark 2013). This is where Habermas's (1989) argument resonates most closely with his Frankfurt School mentor, Theodor Adorno, in the sense that the constitution of the bourgeois public sphere that Habermas charts is increasingly banalized, joined together less by rational debate and more by the dynamics of consumer choice and commoditized experience. Such narratives, however, do not capture the complexity of public formation in the Northern Territory nor the mixing of pleasure, consumption, politics, and representation that Indigenous cultural production entails here. This chapter begins to open onto this complexity by charting the ways that the movement of TEABBA toward a market-based model of institutional reproduction was highly constrained by the very relations on which such market logics might rest.

Most immediately and materially TEABBA's broadcast signal did not address the city of Darwin itself, the home of its institutional headquarters and the commercial and administrative hub of the Northern Territory's Top End, but instead reached across a number of remote Aboriginal communities to Darwin's east and southwest. These communities are not the most obvious market for many Darwin businesses, the very businesses to which TEABBA was encouraged to turn in order to find its market. Further, as TEABBA pursued their new entrepreneurial path they not only had to find ways to market their "remote" Indigenous audience to Darwin city businesses, but also had to do so while avoiding the traffic in goods they felt to be detrimental to the well-being of those remote communities—primarily soft drinks such as Coca-Cola and various kinds of other sweetened drinks or fast food. Paul's iced coffee or Kentucky Fried Chicken, for instance, one a sugar-laden sweet, the other a deep-fried fast food, were seen as undermining the health and well-being of remote communities. So although remote Aboriginal communities did constitute a market for such commodities, Donna and Gary sought to refrain from participating in their traffic insofar as they felt such foods to participate in reducing life expectancy in remote communities through their contribution to diabetes, obesity, and liver and kidney disorders. In our initial meeting, then, Donna and Gary suggested some alternative possibilities that might be acceptable, including Toyota Troop Carriers, outboard motors, the shipping services of Perkins Barge (a company that serviced the waterside communities of Arnhem Land and the Gulf of Carpentaria), and travel on the numerous small airlines that form a core transportation infrastructure across the Top End. The list was short. And if the value of these communities as markets seemed limited, TEABBA's activist administrators were in no rush to open those markets further to the rapid cycles of novelty and obsolescence required by consumer capitalism—seeing their role as custodial and pastoral, diminishing the ravages of a broader settler commercial culture. This left TEABBA's staff looking more intensively to the governmental and community organizations who often seek to reach these communities through Aboriginal broadcast media.

I soon learned that there was a further, more intractable difficulty in that TEABBA's relationship with (and therefore access to) these communities was itself highly provisional and constrained by the very relations that made TEABBA of value to others. Through the shared ritual performance of funerals, smoking ceremonies, "welcomes to country," and the ascription of kinship relation that I describe below, TEABBA's workers are bound tightly to a series of remote communities by kinship and by shared experience. Within rubrics variously referred to as forms of "community consultation" or "cultural protocols," relatively urban Indigenous activists, advocates, and administrators sought to derive organizational direction from the communities they understood themselves to serve. Certainly this should be understood as coextensive with the efforts of many Aboriginal people in cities and towns to overcome a sense of divide between their own experiences and the experiences of those in remote northern and western communities. But more immediately and pragmatically, the participation and encouragement of ritual, kinship, and ceremonial ties emerged from efforts to encourage the participation of remote community people in TEABBA's organizational endeavor—to elicit a response and sense of responsibility from remote-dwelling people.

In both contexts of large, governmentally funded media associations such as TEABBA and in smaller entrepreneurial and project-oriented partnerships, making media has often been understood as a practice of producing relations (see Ginsburg 1994; cf. Michaels 1994). Further, the value of relations, of "linking up" (see my chapter 1), is a frequent refrain in the way that people talk about their work, and in practice, networks of kinship and networks of technology overlap and intermingle, making professional networks, media production, and personal relationships difficult to separate out as distinct entities. These are also often historically new kinds of relationship, built across forms of intra-Aboriginal and intercultural distance and difference. The work of making media, that is, creates relationships that exceed its stated aims and that also exceed the manifest politics of representation and "giving voice." This chapter details these relationships between Indigenous, Darwin-based cultural producers who manage and maintain the association, and the members of remote Aboriginal communities to which these producers broadcast—communities that alternately figure as constituents, directors, "countrymen," organizational capital, and beneficiaries of the association's cultural development work and broadcasting projects. I introduce and analyze some of the particular issues facing cultural brokers in northern Australia, figure the work of media production as a kind of cultural brokerage, and foreground some of the institutional and interpersonal difficulties involved in brokering Aboriginal cultural production.

Relationships across the Top End constrain TEABBA's producers and administrators by producing acute senses of responsibility and obligation in them, by which TEABBA's workers are themselves bound by a revered system of law, ancestral precedence, and Aboriginal cultural tradition, animated performatively through the pragmatics of ceremonial performance in the offices, parking lots, and studios managed by the association. TEABBA's producers felt themselves to have very little room to maneuver and very little capacity to ask things of the communities they felt themselves to serve. Indeed, they often sought to place themselves and their association at the disposal of member communities—even to the extent of placing themselves in conflict with the bureaucratic patrons to whom TEABBA was, ultimately, financially beholden.

On Responsibilization and Policy Shift

Responsibility is an oft-noted centerpiece of much neoliberal discourse, policy, and ideology. Indeed, the term "responsibilization" has traveled from Foucault's critical historical analyses of neoliberal governmentality to broader policy writings in both critical analytical and instrumental registers (Foucault 2009, 2011). In the widely read analyses of cultural geographers like David Harvey, as well as in a range of political writing, criminology, sociology, economics, and public policy, "responsibility" is understood as a key precondition for forms of neoliberal governmentality: this kind of government aims to devolve its operations and distribute power to individual citizen-subjects and requires forms of responsibility for their own conduct and care to be taken on by these citizen-subjects. Some historical comparison may help clarify what might be at stake in such figures. In Stephen Collier's account of post-Soviet Russian policy shift, neoliberal reforms "aimed to 'responsibilize' citizens not just as subjects of need, but as sovereign consumers making calculative choices" (2011: 8). Collier's work on post-Soviet infrastructure and his effort to understand neoliberal thinking as a form of critical, even utopian intervention provides a route to see how responsibility can figure so powerfully in the writings and public arguments of Indigenous activists and public intellectuals like Noel Pearson (2010). As both Collier's critical analytical account and Pearson's normative interventions in Australian Indigenous politics suggest, responsibility entails not just a relationship to oneself and one's biographical telos but also relationships with and stances toward others—relations that are susceptible to cultural and historical variation and, in situations of radical change, contact, or colonial violence, to ontological insecurity as well. It is this relationship between imperatives to "responsibilize" and states of ontological insecurity that preoccupy me here—forms of insecurity that derive, I will suggest, from the tensions between relations with remote people and requirements of governmental direction.

Such tensions are a frequent touchstone in discourse by anthropologists, linguists, and other culture workers living with and working for Aboriginal people, and they animated a public discussion in 2012 around the publication of a critique of such relations, Kim Mahoud's 2012 confessional narrative of white cultural brokerage in remote Aboriginal communities. Mahoud writes of her experiences through the satirical portrait of a committed non-Indigenous southerner, working with, and ostensibly for, Aboriginal people in an unnamed, fictionalized desert community. Mahoud's article was greeted enthusiastically by a range of posters to the Australian Anthropological Society listserv, and anecdotally by linguists, anthropologists, and other non-Indigenous people closely involved with communities in northern Australia, people who saw their experiences reflected in the poor treatment, manipulation, and even abuse suffered by the well-meaning "Kartiya" (a central desert term for "whitefella")—driven to death, "like a Toyota," as Mahoud puts it in her evocative title, "Kartiya Are Like Toyotas" (2012). Another evocation, though, can be seen in a different memoir of life with Aboriginal people, painter Rod Moss's account of his "friendships" in Alice Springs (2012). Moss evokes with humorous appreciation how his Aboriginal friend and interlocutor had "scored himself a whitefella friend"—using a different register to foreground the forms of both interest and affect that bind people together here. Each writer echoes decades of awareness that whitefellas can act as brokers in the towns, communities, and camps of northern Australia—avenues to valued resources, bearers of capacities and forms of comportment that can be of use to Aboriginal people in need of transport, food, and sometimes lodging or forms of remunerative labor (see especially Sansom 1980). And likewise, remote-dwelling, "traditional" blackfellas provide powerful sources of value to "well-meaning" (if occasionally, as Mahoud suggests, psychologically needy) whitefellas.

But what of Aboriginal cultural brokers? What of those people who share (or desire to share) with remote-dwelling Aboriginal communities a sense of emplaced identity, of corporeal substance, and the "special friendship" that Marshall Sahlins (2013) terms "kin relatedness," and who in northern Australia themselves often occupy key positions as cultural brokers? For these people, acting on behalf of remote communities entails seeking and negotiating a sense of identity and belonging, but also a sense of difference, and it occasionally throws up forms of radical alterity that can inhere in the space between bush and town. Indeed, relations between urban Aboriginal producers and remote-dwelling communities and kin groups can be trying, fraught with conflict and humbug as much as with identification, friendship, and love. It also means working within a particular crucible of bureaucratic and bodily discipline. Stuck behind computer screens, engaging in quarterly audits, surveys, and various kinds of accounting procedure, these cultural brokers' work-lives may only sporadically be punctuated by short, intensely social visits to remote communities, outstations, schools, churches, fishing spots, and occasionally sacred sites and favorite hunting grounds. Brokering Aboriginal media production merits attention to the particular phenomenology of such institutionally mediated social relatedness.

In part, the workaday world of Aboriginal media production is the product of a turbulent, bureaucratic environment under the intense strain of constant change. That change can be witnessed in the past decades' intense transformation of Aboriginal government, in which governmental organizations were transformed and the political map of the Northern Territory literally redrawn: power once invested in local councils now resides in shires and (where they are still in residence) local community "general business managers." The latter have been installed in communities to manage a shift from older Aboriginal administration to newer. But running through this governmental and institutional turbulence is a discursive framework of enterprise, responsibility, industry, and a host of associated contradictions and impossible demands—requests that brokers such as those who staff TEABBA fulfill seemingly contradictory imperatives.

One recurrent thread running through these transformations in Aboriginal policy, as I began to describe in the previous chapter, is a discourse of autonomy through enterprise and a broad figure of Aboriginal communities as increasingly "passive" recipients of welfare in need of new instruments of governance organized around exchange and reciprocity (cf. see Pearson 2000). These latter social processes—exchange and reciprocity—are historically understood as paradigmatically "Aboriginal," yet today find new meaning within a neoliberal framework as generic social dynamics wherein exchange, enlightened self-interest, and the workings of the market best adjudicate "stranger sociality" and citizenship within the "modern" Australian polity (cf. Taylor 2002; Warner 2002). And in Australia, as elsewhere, these kinds of relations and modes of citizenship are frequently reckoned through ideas of "responsibility."

Responsibility has been an overt touchstone of Aboriginal government in Australia since the election of the conservative Liberal Party, led by John Howard, in 1996. Under Howard's direction, policies of "mutual obligation" endeavored to tie welfare to the social participation of its recipients. In 2004 Howard appointed Amanda Vanstone as Indigenous Affairs minister, overseeing the dismantling of ATSIC, the democratically elected representative body established in 1989 to advocate at the commonwealth level for Aboriginal interests and to administer a range of Aboriginal policy initiatives. From this point, organizations such as TEABBA needed to negotiate their funding directly with a branch of the commonwealth government. This coincided with the public involvement of Indigenous advocates of welfare reform in policy development and funding decisions vis-à-vis Indigenous communities. Perhaps the most prominent among such advocates was Noel Pearson, whose self-published book *Our Right to Take Responsibility* (2000) garnered praise and cautious critique for its efforts to reconcile Indigenous autonomy and Aboriginal enterprise. In the first decades of the twenty-first century, then, enterprise and responsibility became the dominant and relatively unquestioned linchpins of Aboriginal development and autonomy.

Much as with Aboriginal media production in Queensland, in the Northern Territory this paradigm inflects intercultural relationships of exchange and advocacy in ways that speak to the dilemmas of producing Aboriginal culture in an era of global neoliberalism, but through organizations formed under governmental policies and institutional regimes of "self-determination." TEABBA, for example, was incorporated within the Aboriginal Councils and Associations Act (ACA) (1976) with the express purpose of aiding Aboriginal communities in their attempts to control the sorts of media to which they are increasingly subject.[2] Funding comes to TEABBA in its guise as a cultural development organization, facilitating the broadcasting activities and network capabilities of some thirty-odd remote Aboriginal communities. And although TEABBA may have a great deal of difficulty marketing their audience as commodity to Top End businesses, they still rely on their relationship with that audience as a very real kind of "cultural capital" in their dealings with state, commonwealth, and other Aboriginal agencies.

In 2004, with a shrinking annual grant award from ATSIC, increasingly frequent (at times quarterly) audit exercises, and with the encouragement of ATSIC field officers and other Aboriginal advocates, TEABBA found an increasing percentage of its budget met by organizations such as the Community Broadcasting Foundation (CBF) and Arts Northern Territory, and from contracts with commonwealth and Territory bureaucracies servicing the remote Aboriginal communities that made up TEABBA's networked audience.[3] However, the difficulties they faced in securing and retaining support in this fashion resulted in their embrace of a discourse of private enterprise, and a subsequent effort to refigure their work of cultural brokerage as an affair of the market. Even as the terms of Aboriginal cultural production continue to be refigured by a valorization of market rationality, "creative industries," and forms of what I here call responsibilization, TEABBA continues to broker incommensurable notions of "responsibility" between Australian bureaucratic institutions and remote Aboriginal regimes of value. I'll suggest first that this brokerage can be best understood not in economic or functional terms, but by reference to the value of social relations and their actual, everyday meaning for workers in organizations like TEABBA.

I begin here by locating TEABBA among a range of Aboriginal organizations and other industries in Darwin, the administrative capital of the Northern Territory. This description can begin to suggest the complexity of this space as an intra-Indigenous, cultural frontier in which knowledge of remote communities provides its own form of valued commodity. I conclude with a more detailed discussion of the career trajectories of several of TEABBA's key staff members, and their relationships to the remote Aboriginal community membership that figures as TEABBA's constituency, its capital, and at times as "countrymen" and even kin for TEABBA staff. In the final pages of this chapter I track some of these different kinds of imaginings of responsibility and practices of responsibilization, the related ways that certain kinds of relations are prioritized over others, and the problems this presents to Aboriginal organizations.

TEABBA's Darwin

Darwin sits along a large peninsula at the northernmost point of the Northern Territory, and due south of the Tiwi Islands off its coast. Founded in 1869 by an expedition under the command of G. W. Goyder, surveyor-general of South Australia, Darwin's early history was dominated by the relatively small-scale resource extraction of the Top End, including pearls from Darwin Harbor and gold from Pine Creek. Of equal concern during this period was the establishment of Darwin as a point of trade with Malaysia and the Dutch East Indies, due north. With respect to the former, the tropical regions around Darwin also were home to ill-fated ventures into rice and mango farming, along with cattle and other pastoral endeavors, and the region has been shaped by significant mining operations across the Top End. These have included uranium at Jabiluka in western Arnhem Land and at Rum Jungle due south of Darwin Harbor. A gold rush at Pine Creek during the 1870s led to the arrival of several thousand Chinese miners, and more recently, in the early 1960s, prospectors discovered enormous reserves of bauxite in northeast Arnhem Land. This last mining discovery led to large-scale industrial activity at Gove at the northeastern tip of Arnhem Land, and corresponding, concerted efforts on the part of Yolngu and other land rights activists to counter those operations (Williams 1986; cf. Attwood 2003 cf. Dewar 1992). Industrial resource extraction continues to shape the region's economy through the Gove area, as well as through a new natural gas refinery on Darwin Harbor itself. And over the past decade Darwin's population numbers have ballooned as the city has benefited economically from a countrywide mining boom driven by Asian exports of coal, gas, bauxite, and a range of other mineral resources (Knox 2013).

Despite the vast scale of industrial resource extraction at Darwin's figurative doorstep, the city is perhaps better known as the seat of Northern Territory government, as a tourist rest stop and gateway to Kakadu National Park, and as the administrative center of the Northern Territory's Aboriginal administration. Indeed, it might be better to figure Darwin as the epicenter of a "Northern Development" that emphasizes the Territory's tourist economy, trade relations with Asian ports, and the development of Aboriginal cultural production as a Territorian enterprise (cf. Altman 2003). As such, in Australia the city represents a frontier on a number of levels: its location directly between the Arafura and Timor Seas makes it the urban center of Australia's lengthy northern border with Indonesia and Southeast Asia, while its proximity to Arnhem Land, the Daly River region, and Kakadu also make it a frontier between a "remote" Aboriginal domain and more urban and suburban areas. And as Australia's national public concerns increasingly turn toward immigration and border control, Darwin has also grown in importance as a depot for those seeking to immigrate to Australia as refugees. The Paspaley family pearl dynasty, which built its fortunes through West Australia and later the Top End's rich pearling grounds, has now expanded its investment activities into privatized immigrant detention, building a fifteen-hundred-bed detention center at Wickham Point, thirty-five kilometers to Darwin's south, and leasing it to the commonwealth government to house migrants seeking refugee visas.

Darwin's largest employers are without doubt the commonwealth and Territory governments, and the city's population of some 120,000 people is largely made up of civil servants and their families, and military personnel from a number of Australia's defense forces (headquartered at Larrakeyah Barracks and the Royal Air Force Base in the geographical center of the city). A smaller group of families, however, constitute a diverse population of "Territorians" who have lived in or near Darwin for several generations, or who have moved there permanently as immigrants and "new Australians." This latter group includes Darwin's small Timorese and Malaysian communities and a sizable population of Greek immigrants. A much larger population of Aboriginal people and their families also call Darwin home. They have roots here through kin ties and family networks, but also as the result of past state policies that placed children and families in a number of compounds both within the city and on the nearby Tiwi Islands.

In spatial terms, much of Darwin's social complexity can be drawn out of the opposition between the Casuarina shopping mall at its easternmost point and the old town center to the west, at the end of the peninsula. During the temperate dry season, the open-air mall, the green esplanade overlooking Darwin Harbor, and the cafes, pubs, and restaurants of the city center are filled with an international collection of tourists and travelers, resting after long drives up the Stuart highway or days spent touring Kakadu National Park in western Arnhem Land. Five miles down Trower Road at the Casuarina shopping mall, and among the numerous military families shopping at the Coles supermarket or the Big W department store, Torres Strait Islander and Aboriginal Darwinites wander through the air-conditioned walkways of the Casuarina mall eating lunch in its food court alongside staff and students from Charles Darwin University. This is also near the Darwin Royal Hospital, Casuarina Beach, and the "long-grass camps" in the suburb of Tiwi, and as such is generally an area where Aboriginal visitors from remote communities across the Top End congregate when in Darwin. When the US Navy brings its ships to port, they generally give their crew shore leave, and both poles in Darwin's social landscape fill up with thousands of American sailors. Wandering the mall, whistling at girls on city streets, and filling Darwin's shops and nightclubs, the sailors can spend millions of dollars during their few days on shore.

For many Australians and other travelers, Darwin is a last comfortable stop at the frontier of white Australia. Darwin is as famous for having (barely) survived the damage of Cyclone Tracy in 1974 as for its extreme climate and sheer distance from Australia's southern capital cities (see Lea 2014). "Closer to Singapore than Sydney" is one well-worn aphorism describing Darwin's tropical, exotic location, and a mythic narrative marking both Cyclone Tracy and the bombing of Darwin Harbor during World War II receives continuous exposition on programming repeated daily on Darwin's tourist television channel. In Andrew McGahan's literary imagination, Darwin occupies an odd space on the mysterious northern frontier. His novel *1988* sites Darwin at the edge of Australia. Past the desert and beyond far North Queensland, it is a frontier beyond the imaginations of all but the most foolhardy young adventurers—in this case two characters bound for a remote weather station on the Cobourg Peninsula's Arafura coast, three-hundred-plus kilometers into the bush northeast of Darwin. Here Darwin figures as the seat of Aboriginal administration—a place through which one must travel to get to more remote, "traditional" places in the bush, but not a place one would want to stop in—it figures here, that is, as a colonial backwater, denigrated as a frontier neither properly urban nor properly Aboriginal.

This perspective on Darwin is not anomalous. A decade ago Kate Finlayson began a semiautobiographical account of her search for the "real Crocodile Dundee" in Darwin—where she keeps his saddlebags in the tropical shed of her suburban lot. Much to the chagrin of Darwin's settler residents, Finlayson's *A Lot of Croc* (2003) figures Darwin as a "white trash" administrative backwater, sweltering in the tropical heat just too far from the "salmon pink" desert for which she pines:

> Unlike the relative poverty of the rest of the Territory, the inner city of Darwin is abundant, rich and racist. It lives out none of the old pioneering dreams, preferring instead to put its energies into an overblown public service, urban development, cowboy politics and shady deals into Asia; priding itself on a no-nonsense redneck "butt-out" attitude to Aboriginal people, Southerners and the rest of the world. . . . Me and the fat cats, the do-gooders, drunks and developers all sit in Darwin, a white trash town sinking under tropical toyhouse inner-city developments built on cleared mangrove swamps and thick bog. (Finlayson 2003: 3–4)

This remains a widespread perspective on Darwin and the Top End—suburban, white, incompetent, disconnected from the concerns of "southerners"—that disappears the intensity and richness of Aboriginal life in Darwin and the substance of Aboriginal life that emerges in its suburban lots and office blocks. It

also disappears the intensity of intra-Indigenous and long-term relations between and among different groups in Darwin that have so marked its history.

Aboriginal Darwin

The vocal presence of the families and clans collectively identifying as the
Larrakia Nation immediately complicate this image of a white, colonial space.
For three decades the Larrakia have been highly vocal in seeking recognition as the traditional owners of the country on which Darwin sits (Day 1994;
Povinelli 2002; Wells 1995). And in addition to its status as the site of the
disputatious Larrakia Land Claim, many Australian anthropologists and other
researchers know Darwin as a center of commonwealth and Territory Aboriginal governance, as well as one of the last stops en route to more remote research
locations in Arnhem Land, the Port Keats region to the southwest, or the cattle
stations and Aboriginal communities of the Katherine region, Nitmiluk National Park, and the Victoria River district some three hours drive due south.
Many have cycled through its sprawling suburbs, and its harborside museum
has been an active agent in fostering an audience and market for Aboriginal
arts since the 1970s. Anthropologist Betty Meehan fondly recalls spending a
few memorable weeks at the Old Vic pub in downtown Darwin, enjoying the
company of hydrologists and jazz enthusiasts before embarking with Les Hiatt
by sail for fieldwork in Maningrida (Meehan 1997; cf. Hiatt 1965). This status
as regional metropole has meant that Aboriginal people themselves come to
Darwin from a range of communities across northern Australia, staying with
families in suburban houses or Territory-funded housing commissions that dot
Darwin's inner-city suburbs. They also come to visit the hospital, attend a board
meeting for one of the many Aboriginal-run organizations in town, or just to
socialize and drink on their way to somewhere else. Darwin can be a vibrant,
socially messy space of intra-Aboriginal social and political life.

Darwin also has long fostered labor and aboriginal political activism.
Between the 1930s and the 1960s, Australia's trade unionists and Aboriginal activists found common cause here (see Hardy 1968; Herbert 1938). In
1950 and 1951 Aboriginal workers staged strikes to demand better conditions
and wages, aided first by Fred Waters and later by the Northern Australian
Workers Union. Later, brothers Joe, Jack, and Val McGuiness drew on their
travel and experiences as union organizers and, with the aid of a number of
non-Indigenous supporters, formed a "half-caste association" to protest institutionalized discrimination.[4] In the 1960s similar efforts found a national

audience through the collective actions of writer Frank Hardy, trade union organizer Brian Manning, and the Gurindji men Dexter Daniels and Vincent Lingiari in the organization and strike of the Gurindji stock workers. Ten years later, activist-turned-anthropologist Bill Day encouraged and advocated for the Larrakia land claimant Bobby Secretary (Day 1994; Hardy 1968; Wells 1995).

Such scenes remain significant for another of Darwin's self-images, fostered annually through the return of dry season residents and the May Day concert on the city's foreshore, which brings together Aboriginal performance, Darwin's camp-dwelling Aboriginal people, and Australian labor politicians in a show of solidarity. The Darwin Royal Hospital and Berrimah Prison are also sites through which many residents of the Top End's remote communities circulate, and the city's pubs and parks have long been meeting places for Aboriginal visitors to town. For many Aboriginal people from the Top End's remote communities and smaller towns, then, coming to Darwin presents a different sort of encounter than that which Finlayson describes— one that leads to the pubs and fringe or long-grass camps of the city's beaches and parks. However, these are also often trips to visit family in hospital, for court appearances at Darwin's numerous judiciary bodies, or to sit in a meeting as member of the board for any number of Aboriginal organizations that have their headquarters in Darwin.

Darwin also has a long history of intra-Indigenous activism and cultural brokerage. The city remains a center of Aboriginal governance and cultural production, functioning in large part as the administrative center for the activity of a much wider area stretching from Port Keats down to Lajamanu in the west and across to Numbulwar and up into northeast Arnhem Land. Many of its bureaucratic organizations, Aboriginal corporations, and industries look past Darwin's sprawling suburbs and rural communities, though that is changing as this remote population's intense engagement with Darwin is increasingly recognized. The Northern Land Council, the Summer Institute for Linguistics (SIL), and the Aboriginal Resource and Development Service (ARDS) all have offices in Darwin and provide employment opportunities and reasons for many Aboriginal people from remote communities to come through town. In addition, the city's numerous boarding colleges, such as Nungalinya, St. John's, and Kormilda, all take Aboriginal boarders from across the Northern Territory for high school studies. The SIL employs Aboriginal people in its Bible translation projects. And the Arnhem Land Progress Association (ALPA) has offices in Darwin that function as the administrative center for a network of community stores spread right through Arnhem Land (ALPA 2003; Wells 1995).

TEABBA itself, with a membership spread across the Northern Territory, each year brings its remote Aboriginal membership to Darwin for a long weekend of meetings. While primarily aimed at electing the next year's membership and discussing TEABBA's production for the coming year, this is also an opportunity for visitors to catch up with mates and family from distant communities, to "run amok" in town with a shared cask of wine or a slab of beer, and to visit family in hospital or one of Darwin's several homes for the elderly. Less frequently, Darwin may also be a jumping-off point for Sydney, where some community members must also travel for meetings, or to Asia and Malaysia, and even as far as North America, where not a few have also traveled as cultural performers representing Aboriginal Australia through the offices of the Australia Council for the Arts.

Finally, Darwin is home to a growing population of Darwin-raised families who view this city with affection. In addition to both the Larrakia Nation and the many different groups of Aboriginal people who continue to travel through Darwin, the town has been historically a site to which Indigenous children were brought, placed alongside Larrakia families in institutions such as the Kahlin Compound or the Retta Dixon Children's Home (cf. Cummings 1990; see also Austin 1993 and Haebich 2000). For others taken to missions such as Garden Point on Melville Island, Darwin was a place where they were unceremoniously deposited on turning sixteen, and in which they were expected to take up jobs as laborers or domestic servants. For a few, Darwin's proximity to Garden Point meant that it also provided an important site of escape and the chance to imagine a life away from mission authorities.

A brief sketch of the Bennett family, who now stretch across three generations living in Darwin and whose younger members were key members of TEABBA's staff, can make this point more clear. Dolores Bennett grew up in the Garden Point mission on Melville Island, where she and her siblings were taken after removal from their family in western Australia during the 1940s. On turning sixteen she was turned out of the mission and sent to Darwin, where she met English expatriate Jim Bennett. In the coming months Jim and Dolores returned to the mission and used Jim's outboard skiff to remove Dolores's siblings from the mission. When mission staff subsequently came to the door of their Darwin home, Jim and Dolores turned them away and acted as guardians for Dolores's siblings before raising their own children in later years.

Such stories of removal and institutional upbringing are not uncommon for Aboriginal families. Jim Bennett's work as a tugboat operator, crocodile hunter, and father to five children put him within a relatively small but significant population of non-Indigenous Northern Territory residents who came north in the late 1940s and 1950s and stayed on to raise families and put down roots. The Bennett family now names an extended network of kin that stretch across three generations and have come to occupy significant space in Darwin's Indigenous (and non-Indigenous) communities, and such stories are told now by Dolores and Jim's children (who told them to me), as well as by the daughter of a second marriage between Jim and Joy Bennett, also an Aboriginal woman and member of the Stolen Generation who was taken from her family in Gurindji country to Darwin's south. Two of the Bennetts' children, Gary Bennett and Tracy Bennett, told a seemingly endless stream of other stories—many from their own experiences as children growing up in Darwin, living through Cyclone Tracy in 1974 and being sent to live with relatives in Adelaide and Alice Springs, being chased by a King Brown snake in the bush at Berry Springs, or mustering stock and digging wells during memorable weekends on properties to Darwin's south. As a student at Batchelor College's Indigenous media training program, and learning to make radio documentaries in a course in which Aboriginal students were encouraged to create works on the lives and stories of their elders, Tracy produced a radio documentary on Jim Bennett's years hunting crocodiles, recording stories told by Jim and other hunters, now in their senior years yet still living in Darwin. The Bennett family is perhaps somewhat singular for their keen ability to embrace and retell such stories of their parents' lives. In addition, their awareness of their different cultural background to the communities and "countrymen" that TEABBA represents also conditions their identification with remote countrymen and with the families that make up the Larrakia Nation.

Darwin is thus home to a number of quite distinct Aboriginal peoples, some of whom have had their families and kin relations radically altered by state intervention. Such people often have a complicated relationship to Darwin's colonial past, sharing an interest in and fascination with the colonial exploits of crocodile hunters, patrol officers, and community workers (who may be living family members, or family friends) as well as an identification with and respect for the histories and genealogies of their own and other Aboriginal histories. Here I hope to suggest that in addition to the families that make up the Larrakia, Darwin's traditional owners, there are various other

Aboriginal families with long histories of relationship with Darwin—people who would perhaps never feel entitled to lay a claim of traditional ownership but who nonetheless have come to understand their world as centered around its back blocks and rural lots. These people are central agents within a broad industry of Aboriginal cultural brokerage, seeking both relations with those from the bush and opportunities for meaningful, remunerative labor, the means to pay a mortgage or fund trips to ancestral country in the regions to Darwin's east and southwest.

The Top End Aboriginal Bush Broadcasting Association

Established in 1989 as a means to coordinate and make use of a range of new radio and video gear that had been delivered by the commonwealth, often unannounced, during the previous year as part of the Broadcasting for Remote Aboriginal Communities Scheme (BRACS), TEABBA now coordinates the technical and broadcast capability of media facilities across the Top End of the Northern Territory. TEABBA draws its membership from a wide range of Aboriginal communities and language groups from across the Top End. Although frequently identified as "Yolngu Radio" (figure 5.1),[5] TEABBA in fact draws a membership from Port Keats/Wadeye in the West, down to Lajamanu in the South, and over to the Arnhem Land communities of Numbulwar, Yirrkala, and Galiwin'ku in the East. Its broadcast languages thus include Burarra, Warlpiri, Yolngu Mata, Tiwi, Anandilyakwa, and Northern Territory Kriol.

For its first five years of operation TEABBA was housed in a building owned by Aboriginal educational institution Batchelor College, one hundred kilometers due south of Darwin. Called "Radio Rum Jungle" after the uranium mine that used to be sited at Batchelor, for this period TEABBA provided a broadcast to remote communities and served as an advocacy, technical, and training institution for Top End remote Aboriginal broadcasters. Its operations as a training facility were greatly aided by its location at Batchelor, which is home to a college aimed at providing tertiary education geared to the particular requirements of Aboriginal people living in remote northern Australia (Uibo 1993).[6] While branch campuses exist both in Darwin and in Alice Springs, the Batchelor campus boarded students for three-week-long courses up to eight times over the course of a year. Several of TEABBA's managerial staff completed diplomas in broadcasting and journalism through Batchelor's curriculum.

5.1 An old, dismantled satellite dish, repainted and planted beside TEABBA's drive.

Tracy Bennett, a broadcaster at TEABBA since finishing her high school diploma in 1993, recalled her first visit to the Batchelor studios and college campus. The year following her graduation, 1994, she was searching for work, ideally work that might sustain a long-term career.

Dad run into the manager of TEABBA at the time, and his family is an old Darwin family as well, so Dad knew his father and rah rah rah. They got into a conversation about how each other's families were, and Dad spoke of me and said, "Oh, my daughter's just left year twelve, and she applied for a job at the ABC to be a journalist in the radio section." And he [the manager] said, "Oh, I run an Indigenous radio station and we're looking for trainees, tell her to come and see me." So that's how it ended up happening.

We were based in Batchelor at the time. My dad drove me down—I think I was sixteen going on seventeen or had just turned seventeen. And my first thoughts when we arrived at Batchelor—it was an asbestos building falling apart, there was louvers—it was like our kitchen [at TEABBA] but worse, you know the louvers and the cobwebs. And there was all these countrymen sitting out the front smoking and just sitting on the concrete floor—it wasn't tidy! [laughter] There was paper everywhere, no filing system, and I just looked at it and went, "My god, what am I doing here!" And that's how I started and just went from there.

Tracy's comments capture both the sense in which Batchelor College runs in a relaxed fashion to accommodate the expectations of those accustomed to community life and also brings together Aboriginal people of diverse backgrounds and life experience. Tracy's initial shock at the run-down state of Batchelor's buildings and its "untidiness" soon gave way to respect for the ways in which Batchelor seeks to make countrymen comfortable and to provide education to Aboriginal people in a manner sensitive to their concerns.[7] In the following years, Tracy became a central figure in maintaining relationships between Darwin-based TEABBA staff and operations and the numerous countrymen and remote BRACS stations that make up TEABBA's current network.

In 1994 TEABBA also developed the capability to take a radio signal from any one of its member communities and then retransmit this over satellite to all the rest, or even across Australia through the National Indigenous Radio Service (NIRS). This capability was encouraged by TEABBA's technician at the time, Evan Wyatt, in discussion with FD, a founding and highly active board member from Galiwin'ku, and with anthropologist Jennifer Deger, who was then beginning PhD research on Indigenous video production in Gapuwiyak (see Deger 2006). Wyatt and FD endeavored to network Arnhem Land's communities drawing on satellite and telephonic communications technologies. Taking a signal by telephone through a codec tie-line, TEABBA then sent the signal on to Alice Springs and the Imparja studio's satellite connection. This was then retransmitted on the Optus 2 satellite for delivery to small receivers now installed in many Northern Territory remote communities.

Whose Voice Is It? TEABBA's Relationship to Its Constituent Communities

While the primary aims of Wyatt and FD were explicitly to foster forms of Yolngu expressive practice and social organization, in actual practice it is more accurate to foreground the roles of associations like TEABBA as an attempt to manage and advocate for the interests of heterogeneous communities within a broader institutional and cultural economy. A map on TEABBA's office wall showed thirty small Aboriginal flags spread across the Top End, each representing a remote radio station. Such stations come on and off the air, may be the domain of only one or two individuals, and when functioning may broadcast only within the community, or only during special occasions during sports festivals, concerts, or community "open days." Which end of this spectrum these stations fall on depends on a number of factors, including community interest, the support of the community clerk, the relationships among community producers, community administration, and a regional broadcasting organization.

Whether these BRACS facilities are nonfunctioning, are the domain of one or two individuals within a community, or are broadcasting in a number of languages on a daily basis, these facilities are not simply an extension or function of TEABBA. Rather, these individual BRACS facilities have independent licenses and their own "identity." For example, when a broadcast originates from Peppimenarti, it's the "Peppi" BRACS broadcasting on the TEABBA satellite network. And when FD goes onto the network from Elcho Island or Milingimbi, its geographic ambit, its call sign, its choice of language, and the requests it receives and relays will primarily direct themselves to the kin networks and social preoccupations of northeast Arnhem Land audiences (for further discussion of the significance of requests in this production see my chapter 1).

The organization's geographic mandate thus covers a number of distinct regions and diverse communities. And this is also its asset from the perspective of some organizations based in Darwin that seek to advertise their work or otherwise address a remote Aboriginal population. The station's call sign, "Your voice in the bush," can thus be read several ways, depending on the reader's position and interests. For those in government and various kinds of community work, from health education to commercial sales, TEABBA might be heard as their own voice, an urban or institutional voice that reaches out from Darwin to the bush. For remote listeners, however, the voice is their own, occasionally as the voice of an Aboriginal "bush" subject but also the voice of an advocate—a voice that speaks of and in their interests.

At times, however, the organization may become closely tied to one of its remote community constituents or remote regions. Thus for much of TEABBA's history there has been a tendency to identify this organization with the Yolngu of northeast Arnhem Land. The historical and cultural reasons for the identification of TEABBA as a "Yolngu" network are complex, but I can hazard several suggestions. First, with respect to the lateness and character of

Yolngu colonial contact and the ongoing significance of particularly Yolngu cultural practices, this group has maintained and indeed been able to nourish a collective identity based in a series of communities, clan groups, and shared languages (Keen 1994; Morphy 1991; Williams 1986). Dewar (1992) suggests that the history of Maccassan trade with Yolngu prepared these communities for their dealings with the drastic interventions of Australian settler colonialism, perhaps establishing preconditions for the exchange relationships Yolngu have sought with non-Yolngu throughout the twentieth century. And second, in part as a result of attention garnered during the Gove land rights case, Yolngu have been increasingly vocal and successful in their attempts at shaping the character of their relationship with non-Yolngu, using the value of their own cultural forms and practices, and often an anthropological interest in those practices, to find a footing in postcolonial negotiations over Indigenous belonging, cultural development, and cultural rights. As an example of this that directly relates to TEABBA, Jennifer Deger's ethnographic research led her into partnership with a particularly effective Yolngu man, and his charisma and energetic embrace of media work contributed, in part, to the "Yolngu-ization" of TEABBA as their partnership, and the energy he brought to media work, for a time directed TEABBA toward Yolngu cultural projects (Deger 2006).

TEABBA's manager at the time, Donna Garland, placed that perception within the broader, heterogeneous cluster of Aboriginal communities that TEABBA aims to serve and foregrounded the energetic response that Arnhem Land communities initially demonstrated around radio and other media:

> I think a lot of our members know that our radio is for them, not just for a particular group. And there came a time when there was people saying, well, "Oh, you know, it was only all happening in the Arnhem Land area." Well, that's because the Arnhem area were getting their act together, you know. We try to make it inclusive by translating in a lot of different languages, translating community announcements. And even to the point of making sure that our board members are representing, you know, across the board rather than just in one different area.

TEABBA is thus constituted by an extremely wide range of communities, from the northwestern coastal Daly River region (Wadeye / Port Keats, Palumpa, Nauiyu) across through western Arnhem Land and the towns and communities of Jabiru, Oenpelli, and Maningrida, and on to the five major communities that make up the core Yolngu settlements (Gapuwiyak, Galiwin'ku, Milingimbi,

Yirrkala, and Ramingining). This diversity has been both one of TEABBA's primary assets, and as I describe in the following chapter, something of a liability as well.

In the remainder of this chapter I look to describe the character of staff relationships with the remote communities and cultural producers of the Top End. For instance, TEABBA's manager, Donna, was not originally from Darwin. Her family hailed from Queensland, where she grew up in the towns and cane farms of the Ingham and Townsville areas. Like other media producers across Australia, including Tiga Bayles in community radio and Rachel Perkins in film, Donna comes from families involved in early Aboriginal rights activism. Her father was a labor activist who helped to organize a strike at Palm Island in the late 1950s (cf. Thaiday 1981). Exiled from Palm Island as a result, the family moved southeast, to Ingham and eventually Townsville.[8] I asked Donna how she became involved in media production:

> You remember those *National Geographic* magazines, those yellow ones? I remember my dad used to get them sent to him. We used to live on a cane farm in Queensland and that was sort of like our window to the outside world. We had no TV, anything like that, and I used to like the pictures in it. And I always thought to myself "I'd love to become a photographer for the *National Geographic* and do stories." You know, and that's where it started from. . . . I believe that the Queensland system in those days thought that OK, you're an Aboriginal student, Aboriginal girl, you wouldn't be able to make it in this type of world, so the only place you can make it is in an office. You know, that sort of thing. So they get us towards taking up shorthand and typing and that sort of thing. And, um, fuck shorthand! [laughter]

Like a number of other cultural producers in the Top End who came to their work through teaching (including M. Yunupingu, who taught school in Yirrkala prior to taking up leadership of the band Yothu Yindi, and George Burarrwanga, who was also acting as a teacher in Papunya prior to joining the Warumpi Band), Donna's initial interests found expression in career paths then only just becoming options for Aboriginal people.

> And through high school and that, then things started to change. When I was at high school we were—it was the "in" thing to become an Indigenous teacher. So everybody was going towards, you know, doing teaching and that sort of thing.

It was while at teacher's college that, you know, you get to read about other people who've gone on and done law, and who've gone on and done other things in a different type of career than what was "suited for Aboriginal people." So I thought about it, you know, I thought, "Oh this could be something where I could probably branch into, finish my teaching and go into journalism."

A few years later, she was contacted by Australia's social security organization, Centrelink:

I was on the dole then, but just doing voluntary work at this center, and then they contacted me, the Department of Social Securities it was then, or Centrelink. They contacted me and said, "There's a traineeship happening with a radio group, with an Aboriginal radio group, would you be interested in it?" And I thought, oh, well, you know, it could mean something.

And I started, I think it was a twelve-month training course with the Townsville Aboriginal and Islander Media Association [TAIMA]. And the trainer there was Bill Thaiday, you remember Bill? He was the trainer there. . . . That started my interest in radio up again. Having a teacher like Bill sparked that fire again for me. To the point where I finished my training with TAIMA, and worked with them until 1989.

Donna's training at TAIMA and her interest in journalism as a career led her to pursue tertiary education in Melbourne, moving through a preparatory course at Monash University, geared toward aiding Aboriginal students in their pursuit of postsecondary schooling, and subsequently she earned a spot at the Royal Institute of Technology in Melbourne following a course that would have led to a bachelor of arts in journalism.

I did a year of that and I got too homesick [laughing]. I think I was the only Aboriginal student in that whole course. I got that homesick I ended up leaving.

After a short period working as a sales executive for BAY FM in Geelong, a small industrial city south of Melbourne, Donna returned to TAIMA and to work in Aboriginal media. When the chance to take up a position as a TEABBA broadcaster arrived, Donna took the opportunity and moved to Darwin. Not long after Donna moved from broadcaster to management, filling the vacant general manager position with the encouragement of other staff.

Working for the Board

Ideally, TEABBA's managers and staff serve the board of directors, drawn from senior figures in the remote communities to which TEABBA directs its services. Association staff thus see their work as implementing a series of projects developed in consultation with the board itself at biannual board meetings. However, acquiring the input and direction of a board of directors made up of people from such distinct communities as, for example, Milikapiti, Peppimenarti, and Yirrkala is not an easy task. TEABBA's membership had long been used to having TEABBA run by its management without much consultation. Donna recalls the difficulties she faced on first taking up her position in 1997:

You know, I don't want to say that the previous managers weren't sort of asking the board what to do next. I don't know. They may have or may not have. But I found that talking to the directors—they didn't know what they wanted for the association.

And then when we all got together in a room, and I said to them, "If this association is yours, you need to take some control and be able to work out what you want to happen, what you want this organization to do in the next two or three years." You know? "Do you still want to stay where you are? Do you still want it to be just radio programs going out, do you want video, do you want, you know, all this other stuff?" There were some of them that had good ideas, but that's all it was. They were good ideas, but it was just left on the boardroom table.

That's what I set about doing: Making sure those ideas became reality for them, and making sure it happened within their time as directors so that, you know, if previously we'd have directors sitting on the board for a year, and if within that year nothing happened, they became disillusioned about TEABBA and where it was going.

For Donna, that entailed ensuring that visible outcomes reach back to the board members, and she sought to accomplish this in a number of ways, such as extending the tenure of board membership from one to two years, working to secure visible outcomes for projects, and soliciting an ongoing relationship and frequent contact with remote radio operators. Donna provided the example of a recording project, funded by Australia's Community Broadcasting Foundation (CBF), in which TEABBA technicians and an Aboriginal apprentice visited a number of communities to record Aboriginal gospel, country, and rock bands:

Two years ago, the directors brought up the idea of recording bands in the communities, and that's where we got all those CDs done. And, you know, I don't know how they felt, but just for at AGMs,[9] they can show, you know, well, this is what we directors got this staff to do, and this is our end product. So people thought, "Well, we are going somewhere, TEABBA is going somewhere." Rather than "Well, we were going to talk about this, and we were going to talk about that but we didn't have the money or we didn't get around to doing this" and that sort of thing. We wanted end product after projects that we did.

Donna continued by describing the difficulties that TEABBA's distance from any one particular community represents in terms of remaining governed by its board of directors:

You see how we try to contact our directors, and it's very hard to do that. And I've told the board this too. I've said, "It is very easy for me to forget about you out in the community and run this place as I see fit," I said, "but that's not what I'm about. I'm about letting you make the decisions, because in the long run it's you guys [the remote membership] that are going to have to stand up and say, yes, we did this whether it's right or wrong." I think once I said that it was quite easy. It is quite easy to run this organization by myself. They realize well, oh, they realize that, you know, "Well, we better start doing something about it so that we continue what the old people wanted, you know, that we have a radio service that would involve all the *Yolngu*" [all the people].

One way this involvement is secured is through close working relationships with the people who work as broadcasters in their own communities across the North and who occasionally take on more substantial roles in Darwin as well. One such person is Laurel, who perhaps more than others came to share a close and long-standing relationship with Donna and with other TEABBA staff. Historically, TEABBA has relied on just a handful of broadcasters and translators, each with their own very specific biographies, capabilities, and interests. The work of these BRACS community broadcasters should be classed as itself a kind of cultural brokerage, and I here sketch several partnerships and exchanges between remote Aboriginal people and TEABBA staff members as agents involved in brokering the participation of remote Aboriginal communities in their representation and governance.

While Donna, Tracy, and Gary all come to this from relatively urban and intercultural families, many Aboriginal people from remote communities have also been crucial mediators and brokers of this broader media world—and TEABBA's work would not be possible without the translation and travel of several key individuals in Arnhem Land. When anthropologist Jennifer Deger went to Gapuwiyak to conduct research on Aboriginal video and BRACS production, she found it necessary to take it upon herself to train Yolngu BRACS operators (2006). One of the women trained to produce radio by Deger was Laurel, who would go on to become one of TEABBA's primary community translators and broadcasters and a frequent presence in TEABBA's Darwin office. Laurel also became a preferred travel partner when TEABBA visited the remote community music and cultural festivals, sports carnivals, and community open days that structure TEABBA's annual round of broadcasting and Top End travel. Laurel's intimate knowledge of kin networks and clan affiliations and her ability to speak a large number of Top End Aboriginal languages were a tremendous asset to TEABBA.

From Laurel's perspective, working with TEABBA allowed her a great deal of mobility. Having come to Darwin after the failure of an arranged marriage, her association with TEABBA and her ongoing translation work elsewhere in Darwin allowed her a degree of distance and some room to maneuver with respect to the communities and kin networks with which she is embroiled. That mobility was not merely distance from home, however, in that working for TEABBA also involved travel to the numerous Arnhem Land communities across which her family is spread. Her work in media allows her a kind of social mobility that might otherwise be difficult to achieve.

Donna also relies on Tracy and Gary. Both were born and raised in Darwin but, like Donna, have very different backgrounds than the community membership and audience that are TEABBA's constituents. Gary comes to TEABBA after many years traveling the waterways of the Top End as an employee of Perkins Shipping. Alongside his three elder brothers, all encouraged to work on boats by their father, himself captain of a tug on Darwin Harbor for several decades, Gary worked for years on overseas merchant marine vessels, traveling with Perkins Barge Company to help rebuild the wharves and docks in East Timor during Australia's participation in its postreferendum reconstruction, and sailing back and forth along the coast of Arnhem Land, delivering stores to communities such as Galiwin'ku, Yirrkala, and Numbulwar. This work later gave way to administration and office management for a barge owned by his elder brother and eventually to what he saw as more secure work at TEABBA in 1997. Gary spent much of his life working within the transport infrastructure of the Top End and knows its remote communities well.

Through frequent telephone and radio contact with BRACS broadcasters across Arnhem Land, Tracy is perhaps more familiar with the everyday community politics, with the disagreements between clans and the location of individuals across a dense field of towns, remote communities, and outstations. Yet with this knowledge also comes a sense of obligation and responsibility, generally implicit but perhaps most easily seen when it becomes burdensome. For example, in 2003 Tracy's parents gave her a personalized license plate for her birthday reading "Tracy B." While this is a relatively popular item for Territory vehicle owners, and one can scan the classifieds in Northern Territory towns for popular customized plates for sale, for Tracy herself this turned out to be a not entirely welcome gift. Tracy already owned a distinctive, "flash" late-model Toyota four-wheel-drive, and with the addition of personalized plates her vehicle became instantly recognizable. Henceforth, in every community through which she drove her Toyota, as well as around town in Darwin, she was susceptible to being approached by "mobs of people," asking her for a lift, a favor, some money, or just stopping her to catch up on gossip.

Tracy's dismay at this gift indexed, in part, the extent to which she had become a recognized personality, embroiled in relationships across the Top End. She was someone that people can ask things of, socially recognizable both through institutional relations and ascribed kinship. In short, she had become incorporated into a wide network of exchange relationships, as are most media activists who cultivate relationships with the communities they serve. And while the character of such ascribed kinship and its entailed exchange relationship are not peculiar to Tracy, the great extent to which she was recognized by countrymen across the Top End is somewhat unusual. The responsibility entailed by this relationship with countrymen could become onerous here, entailing a particular difficulty in saying no—at least in saying no without being "humbugged to death," as Tracy would occasionally put it. And in town it could be worse, where she was frequently recognized by those "runamoks"—now relatives—on the grog.

In sum, Donna and the Bennett siblings are highly familiar with remote communities, identify with the cultural and political economic aspects of their marginality, and understand their work as a kind of advocacy and representational practice. And while much of this identification is due to a shared sense of Aboriginality and common occupational purpose, it also has dimensions that exist primarily at the level of social practice. These dynamics of investment and obligation suggest an everyday participation in forms of northern Australian Indigenous sociality and a practical knowledge of the obligations and responsibilities of relatedness. That participation exceeds office work and begins to draw workers like Tracy into the social lives of Aboriginal people living rough in town. Many of those people know Tracy not only from her radio work but also from her periodic trips to remote communities, her efforts to assist communities in maintaining a media service, and from her presence at funerals, smoking ceremonies, and community festivals across the Top End.

So while TEABBA's workers come to this culture work as work, as a means to a career, a paycheck, and a mortgage, they also come to understand it as a form of participation in an ethical domain that exceeds the means-ends instrumentality they may be asked to display in the context of a quarterly audit or justification of their culture work at TEABBA. And if TEABBA's culture workers occasionally feel sick to death of the "runamoks" they have to deal with in town and out bush, they are also touched deeply by what they come to share with the communities whose media culture they broker and whose "voice" and partnership they elicit and on which they rely. Indeed, what they experience together over years of this work is the stuff of life and of death. People die. People get sick. People have romantic relationships and drama and children. People acquire qualifications, occasionally find national fame. And people also "run amok" with grog, living rough in the long grass. People also just get on with the daily grind of running a media organization. Gary opens up the office early. Donna answers e-mails, takes phone calls, and signs checks, and in her downtime in the office might play video games on her notebook computer or talk with a friend or relative on the phone.

Such everyday tasks and rhythms structure the life of media work and are strung together between the big dramas of social life, the stories of fights and romance and political turmoil that trickle in from the bush, over the telephone or with a city-bound traveler. These days of bureaucratic exercise and the dominance of administrative paperwork carry their own dramas and lessons and rituals that instill a form of competence. They are seen and experienced both as kinds of rote labor and as broader, ritualized maneuvers. I conclude this chapter by presenting two cases, contrasting the banal, at times cynical exercises of bureaucratic labor and their counter in the forms of ritualized reverence and care that animate relationships between bush and town.

Conducting a Survey

In 2003 the Community Broadcasting Foundation of Australia (CBF), with funding from the commonwealth's Department of Communications, Information Technology, and the Arts (DOCITA), sought to gather statistical information from remote Indigenous media organizations across Australia. This information was to be gathered within a broader Community Broadcasting Database for the purpose of assessing the needs of remote area broadcasters, as well as providing information for further lobbying and development planning vis-à-vis commonwealth and state governments. A brief sketch of this process sheds light on the ways in which TEABBA's relationship to its remote constituents rests at the center of their operation. Negotiations with the CBF's representative, ML, concluded with a contract providing TEABBA with a large payment of about AU $28,000 for collecting statistical data related to programming, staffing, funding, and operations related to the BRACS communities for which they were responsible. Given the constraints of funding the survey, the information would be gathered primarily by BRACS association office staff over the phone, as opposed to taking a flight or day's drive to visit a community.

At TEABBA this meant multiple telephone calls to each of the twenty-eight communities on their list. The survey consisted of 108 questions related to remote community radio programming and funding. Questions ranged from relatively easy to answer, such as "What is the total budget for the BRACS station?," to relatively difficult, such as a detailed auditing of the sources for that budget—what percentages came from commercial sponsorship, state government, commonwealth government, and regional council. The general response to this question, on the rare occasion that TEABBA staff received an answer, would be that the regional council would be the sole funder (from their ATSIC budget), but the other questions in the survey would have little applicability and make little sense to the producers and community members in the communities. Equally difficult to assess were statistics on programming: "How many hours of adult contemporary music does your BRACS station program?," for example, or "How many hours of metal? Of Christian music? Of ethnic music?" It was next to impossible for TEABBA's staff (which included myself in a volunteer capacity at TEABBA) to acquire any of this sort of information over the telephone. Perhaps more to the point, these questions imported an industrial generic standard of commercial audience share to the communities in which such social distinctions meant little. Certainly these musics were played, and people listened a great deal to country, hip-hop, rock, and other pop genres. But the multiplication of genres and market share presumed by such generic marks and their quantification through such surveys found little purchase in the Northern Territory.

The effort to reach communities by telephone also faced other obstacles. First, reaching any particular community member on the telephone was very difficult. Occasionally TEABBA staff would reach particular BRACS operators on the first try, but more often they would spent weeks tracking them down, and in some communities might never reach them. Second, the extent to which funding had been set aside for a community's broadcasting operations was not always clear. If (for example) AU $7,000 had been allocated in the community's annual budget for expenditure on media equipment repair or music purchasing, often the bookkeeper who understood how to access and allocate such funds resided elsewhere, or sometimes that person had recently quit. In the latter instance, the new bookkeeper might not understand the budget completely, or might not view the media and broadcasting facilities as a significant funding obligation. Further, with a fiscal requirement that communities spend all the money in their grant-derived annual budget, town councils "might spend that BRACS budget on a fence for the back paddock," as Gary once suggested with a rueful chuckle. Communities needed to spend it while they could or see it rescinded at the end of the fiscal year, and further risk a reduced allocation in the following year's budget. And finally, calling up a town clerk who may not have maintained the same relationship with TEABBA staff as the BRACS operators do and asking detailed questions about their financial affairs not infrequently provoked hostile reactions.

After several months of telephone calls and little success in acquiring the necessary responses, Gary began to worry about completing the survey, frequently wondering aloud if TEABBA would be required to return their contracted fees to the CBF after expending so much effort (and telephone expenses) on the process. He also grumbled about the lack of response he was getting from countrymen, even those as closely tied to TEABBA as broadcasters in Galiwin'ku, Daly River, and Palumpa. Tracy suggested we fax a copy of the survey to each community council, along with a short cover note explaining that TEABBA hoped the information would lead to more funds through the CBF. At this point Gary also asked that staff document each survey-related call, fax, and contact made to demonstrate for ML at the CBF the great effort we had devoted to the survey.

Among my notes I have records of perhaps one hundred telephone calls and faxes we made over several months, of which only a handful received any response. One of those responses offers a stark comment on the quality of the data we were producing and its imbrication with longer-term relations and networks of fiscal interdependence. The town clerk at Ngukurr, a community in southeast Arnhem Land, faxed us back almost immediately, completing the survey with a series of zeros. The tenor of the survey's progress emerges from my brief notes:

> S. responded via fax on 08/20/2003, most answers are nil because they have lost their [BRACS] facilities in a fire and have not been given anything by local ATSIC or council to rebuild. S. extremely reluctant to discuss survey categories further by telephone. Nonetheless they do very much want it back up again and I have put them in touch with MA to see if we can do anything for them, but this will be impossible if they have insufficient funding.

For TEABBA staff, the exercise underlined a disjunction between their capabilities, the limited resources of any particular BRACS facility, and the expectations of the CBF. And increasingly, as time went by without responses from remote communities, TEABBA oscillated between resignation—what else could they expect?—and annoyance with both the CBF and with their constituent communities. We went through the motions nonetheless, but this became an occasion for complaint and an alienating process whose goal quickly switched from producing knowledge about remote broadcasting to the completion of this administrative task itself—the need to provide a tidy-looking end product for the CBF. In the end Gary and I collated results in a "melancholy dot pointed abstraction," to borrow a turn of phrase from Tess Lea (2008: 211).[10] Meanwhile Donna, fed up with the whole scenario, played video games and turned her attention to the organization's upcoming travel to Barunga and Yirrkala, in the bush, for annual festival broadcasts later in the year. Tracy's interests turned away from work and toward suburban property around Darwin: she was aspiring to use a commonwealth-supported, zero-down loan targeted to Aboriginal people to acquire a house. A sense of malaise crept into our workdays at TEABBA, and the work of the organization, to the extent that it had turned to satisfying the CBF's survey, became an exercise of institutional wish fulfillment, alienating all of us from the data at the core of our work.[11] That work, however, and the nonresult to which it led, was performed with exacting detail and exaggerated care to follow the survey's instructions to the letter.

In my own discussions with ML (which followed similar discussions between ML and TEABBA's managers), she expressed her understanding of the difficulties that collecting such data by telephone entailed and asked for our suggestions on how to better conduct such a survey in the future. The unanimous recommendation from within the organization was that the CBF hire a single worker, ideally from the regional BRACS coordinator, who should then visit each community prepared to spend several days speaking in person with BRACS operators, town clerks, and/or bookkeepers, as well as assessing the state of repair of their BRACS studio and fixtures. And when ML later responded testily at the lack of progress made by the end of the survey period, TEABBA staff put their relationships with community BRACS operators and remote communities at the foreground. That is, they reminded each other that while they needed to take seriously the requests and contracts made with organizations like the CBF, they could not force such information out of their remote community operators, nor could they expect hours of time from either those operators or community clerks and bookkeepers—all of whom TEABBA staff expected to be wrapped up with community politics and the exigencies and dramas of their everyday lives and occupations.

The course of this particular institutional exercise can underscore the constraints TEABBA staff at times felt as they brokered between a remote Aboriginal domain and the bureaucratic institutions of Aboriginal government. It also suggests how an effort to identify a subject population through statistical media—to elicit a response in the form of enumeration and information on consumer behavior—turned in on itself in a rote exercise that served bureaucratic rather than remote community interests and a point, in retrospect, where different desires and investments in securing evidence of an "Aboriginal voice" became clear (resonating also with the "audit culture" that troubled 4AAA's early efforts to multiply its sources of funding and expand its mission to include education). In the next section I invert this perspective to suggest the ways in which remote communities seek recognition from the state, and how they accomplish this by incorporating institutions like TEABBA into local regimes of value. The relationships between such communities and TEABBA proved an antidote to the bureaucratic roundabout that so frequently threatened to capsize the organization.

Ritual Involvements: Smokings, Sorry Business, and Intercultural Ceremony

The year just prior to my arrival, 2002, was a disastrous year at TEABBA. The organization lost its chairperson, BW, an important and much respected man from Gapuwiyak, to a sudden, unexpected illness. He had done much to revitalize remote media production in northeast Arnhem Land and was widely respected.[12] Toward the end of the year another tragedy struck when an automobile accident took the life of Donna's youngest daughter during a school retreat. Both losses were keenly felt. Donna's daughter died on a stretch of highway, BW from a heart attack, but both deaths were sudden and premature. Much of the malaise I felt creeping through the everyday work of the organization that year can be understood as echoes of grief, particularly for Donna's youngest daughter. In 2003 a smoking ceremony was held at TEABBA for a third, recently deceased member of TEABBA's board of directors, someone who like BW had served as its chair in the past. This ceremony was understood to also address Donna's daughter, who was this man's classificatory granddaughter. The event was complex, reckoning with the grief that lingered following the loss of multiple significant family members, and also with broader relationships between TEABBA and its remote membership.

The term "smoking ceremony" has come to signify a pan-Indigenous, ritualized performance involving the use of smoldering native plants, often gum but also various long grasses, to "cleanse" a building and the body in a range of ways. Some Yolngu gloss the function of a smoking ceremony as a kind of healing, cleansing the body of ill feelings, of sorrow, grief, even illness. Others see it as significant for cleansing a space of the spirits of a deceased person. Others still emphasize this ritual's capacity to make a space welcoming to Aboriginal people, and much as with the ritualized "welcome to country" (in which a representative of the place on which an event is held provides a recognition of Indigenous traditional owners and a welcome to those gathered), smoking ceremonies have become part of an Australia-wide, institutional apparatus of recognizing Aboriginal people. All of these generalized, relatively vague individual and institutional glosses were involved in the different smoking ceremonies held at TEABBA. Here, though, recognition is about relationship and responsibility—and it cuts both ways, placing obligation on both TEABBA culture workers and on their remote mob.

BW was a central character in introducing such ceremony to the work of TEABBA.[13] Tracy describes his distinction from their previous chair, FD, as due in part to their different statuses in Yolngu country. FD was a Christian and as such neither participated in the management of ceremony nor sought particular distinction within Yolngu country as a ceremonial leader per se. BW, on the other hand, was heavily involved in the management of ceremony and was encouraged in this through his work with two anthropologists, Peter Toner and Jennifer Deger, each of whom relied on BW for help in understanding quite different aspects of Yolngu ritual practice and cosmology (see Deger 2006). BW was also from Gapuwiyak, a community that began as a sawmill for the neighboring mission at Elcho Island but was refashioned by Yolngu seeking to establish a traditional community. Gapuwiyak residents today pride themselves for their ongoing attention to the distinction of Yolngu culture (Deger 2006).

As Deger has written at length, BW approached her with ideas for a project to use media forms in the production of Yolngu culture. BW had recently been exiled to Darwin following an alcohol-fueled argument with his brothers and BW's subsequent destruction of a clan *bathi* (sacred dili bag). BW's work with the BRACS and his concern with things cultural was part of what Deger calls a "tentative process of social rehabilitation" in which BW sought, in part, to regain favor in the eyes of community ceremonial leaders (2006: 47). Not long after beginning to work with Deger in the Gapuwiyak BRACS, BW was elected chair of TEABBA's remote board during a period of increased Yolngu dominance in the direction and projects that TEABBA undertook. As part of this work, BW also brought TEABBA staff into circuits of Yolngu kinship and ceremonial practice, adopting Donna, Tracy, and Deger. This was meant to involve TEABBA staff in ceremony and the "sorry business" of funerals and mortuary ceremonies—a practice of inclusion that has a great deal of precedent in Yolngu ritual practice, but that had been left to the side at TEABBA, in part due to FD's distance from ceremonial management and from the diverse groups of Aboriginal people to whom TEABBA was responsible.

It was only with what Tracy termed the "aggressive" chairmanship of the TEABBA's community member–populated board of directors by BW that forms of ritualized relationship began to inflect TEABBA's organizational practice through the extension of ceremony into Darwin itself. This began after what Tracy described as a period of particularly bad luck at TEABBA, during which several board members passed away. BW's response was to organize a smoking ceremony for TEABBA's offices, a practice of carrying smoldering leaves and dancing through the building to clear the space of malevolent spirits and the charge left by those, now deceased, who had once spent time there.

Because he had such a strong cultural presence, that's when the smoking ceremonies—you know, TEABBA had a lot of bad luck. Well, I see it as bad luck. I reckon that we were jinxed, and we had a smoking ceremony in here to clear the air of bad luck or something. He sort of instigated that, and that's, ever since then there's just been smoking ceremonies all the time. We had another board member pass away, he run the smoking ceremony for that, then he [BW] passed away and we had to have one for him, and then Eddie. Yeah, and you know like it just went on and on and on. . . .

He was one of the top men that used to organize, he was a music man. He was the boss of all of the dances and he'd run the ceremony, he was the manager of the ceremonies which is a really prestigious position. So with him having such a strong cultural, traditional, status in that thing, and he was younger too, a lot younger, and very outspoken. So things started to happen when he come along.

In addition, Donna, Tracy, and one of their friends (and their auntie) Laurel drove south to Barunga to participate in the funeral of a former board member. To Tracy's surprise, the collected dancers waited for their arrival, placing them at the center of a markedly intercultural Yolngu and Christian funeral in what Tracy remembers as a series of locations, beginning on the Barunga football oval but leading through the family's home, the church, and eventually the cemetery.

We walked over to [BW] where he was with his dancers. They slapped all this paint on us, and Laurel said, oh, you've got to come with me now. We had to follow them. The dancers went first, then us, then family, and then guests. . . .

And then we danced, everyone danced. And then after that it was to the church, a big procession to the church where speeches were made. And after that it was a procession to the cemetery, which was a long way down the back in the bush somewhere.

In 2002, with the loss of BW himself and of Donna's young daughter, TEABBA staff went through a further intense period of ceremony, traveling to BW's funeral in Gapuwiyak. This period extended into 2003 when a smoking ceremony featured as a central aspect of the remote festival held at TEABBA's grounds in Darwin.

The morning of the first day of the event saw the arrival of numerous small buses and four-wheel-drives. The dancers and relatives of the deceased man were on a flight from Snake Bay, which had been running late, as charter flights in the Top End often do. All morning long Aboriginal people from across Australia trickled into TEABBA's parking lot, buses and taxis disgorging clusters of visitors from central Australia and the Kimberly in western Australia, while TEABBA staff collected media makers visiting from Sydney, Melbourne, and Arnhem Land from the airport. I took TEABBA's four-wheel-drive truck to pick FD up from his hotel, and when we returned we found perhaps seventy people milling about in front of TEABBA's building, sipping tea and quietly waiting for the ceremony to begin. Not long after our return, the contingent of dancers arrived. Organized by former chair JP and her brothers, these dancers promptly congregated in front of TEABBA's main entrance, lit branches aflame in an old metal bin, and began to sing. After a few moments the group of islanders carried smoldering leaves into the building itself, and I joined Donna and Tracy and a few other TEABBA staff members in following them into the main offices, past reception and into the open-plan, partitioned work space. Once inside the singing became hoarser and louder, echoing through the cubicles and off TEABBA's cinder-block walls and high ceiling. Several women fell to their knees or leaned against the wall and, covering their heads, began to cry loudly. One sat in a cubicle, on the floor, arm against the polyester fabric of an office partition. Inside the lament was amplified, made louder by the enclosed and reverberant space, and punctuated by muffled sobs from within the partitions.

After perhaps five minutes of ritualized, grief-stricken wailing within the building itself, the dancers returned outside and, after another few minutes of dancing, asked everyone in attendance to form lines—one for women, and another for men. All of us were patted down with smoldering branches as we filed past. After several more minutes of the Tiwi dancers' performance around the still-smoking metal bin, and a loud thank-you voiced by JP's brother to the assembled audience, the event concluded.

While many such intra-Aboriginal public events and performances now include a ritualized "welcome to country," generally by the traditional owners of the area (at the video festival this was conducted by an elder Larrakia woman), the elaborate character and extensive participation this ceremony involved would seem somewhat unusual (though not unheard of) elsewhere in Australia. Yet it has become a routine aspect of TEABBA's ongoing relationship with its constituent communities. From Tracy's perspective, the rationale behind these smoking ceremonies is to maintain the interest of countrymen

5.2 Tiwi members of TEABBA dance at a smoking ceremony, 2003.

in coming into TEABBA, making countrymen comfortable and doing things "Yolngu way."

> If we didn't have them [the smokings], they just wouldn't be interested in coming in here. They'd make up all these excuses, "Oh too busy" or something, without them actually saying "No, I'm not coming in there because you haven't had a smoking ceremony!"

Such ceremonial recognition and incorporation also give shape to new kinds of intra-Aboriginal relations—relations that take on substance through the recursive performance of rituals such as these and in the ways that TEABBA's staff come to reflect on their meaning and value, turning to their constituents as kin, as "uncle" or "auntie."

In addition to the personalization of such relations, however, such rituals have a corporate aspect. In Darwin, these ritual forms also come to typify relations between communities and TEABBA as an institution and should thus be understood as a kind of bureaucratic ritual. Much as in ML's efforts to impel TEABBA's responsible conduct through the medium of cash and institutional indebtedness, here the remote mob and TEABBA's Aboriginal cultural brokers collude in reproducing their relatedness. For TEABBA's staff these ritualized performances remake the otherwise mundane space of a suburban office into a Yolngu space. Such rituals thereby successfully orient the interests and understandings of TEABBA's cultural workers as shared with those in the bush.

5.3 A ceremonial leader addresses individual participants in a smoking ceremony, 2003.

Ritual Media and Statistical Media: On Cultural Brokerage and "Responsibilization"

> The position of these "brokers" is an "exposed" one, since, Janus-like, they face in two directions at once. They must serve some of the interests of groups operating on both the community and the national level, and they must cope with the conflicts raised by the collision of these interests. They cannot settle them, since by doing so they would abolish their own usefulness to others. Thus they often act as buffers between groups, maintaining the tensions which provide the dynamic of their actions.
>
> —WOLF 1956: 1076

Eric Wolf's comments on cultural brokerage have at times seemed to me appropriate to the experience of TEABBA, whose continued existence in part depends on the tensions and opacities between a range of settler Australian agencies and the remote Indigenous communities that make up TEABBA's constituents and must transact forms of Indigenous alterity with a range of Territory and commonwealth agencies. Yet Wolf's writings also undervalue the kinds of reflexivity that such "Janus-faced" brokerage can entail, and the consequential reassessment of how the interests of these different agencies and constituents should be constituted. His economistic and functionalist account, that is, tends to preclude the meaning of such brokerage in particular historical circumstances. Looking to the particular tenor of the contrasting forces that press up against TEABBA's workers—not simply "interests" but also values, practices, and ontologies of space and time—one can see a resolution and negotiation between forms of bureaucratic "bad faith" and ritual commitment and relatedness. In the former, TEABBA's workers must produce the ends assigned them, despite their awareness that such ends—survey results, for instance—were produced under duress and could not be made to correspond to the places they know. In terms of the latter, TEABBA's producers were drawn into remote ritual economies, interpellated as representatives of an Aboriginal domain and as kin. Just as TEABBA workers find themselves having to reconcile statistical media and ritual media, they also find themselves caught between market rationality and the meaning of social relatedness in the Top End. These are the dilemmas that elicited my opening question: Can you market a relationship?

The institutional requirement that TEABBA provide "end products"— reifications of institutional purpose with little relation, in the end, to actual institutional practice—meant that at times the work of making media could seem subverted by a broader, interinstitutional preoccupation with responsibilization, the deferral of meaningful work with expressive sound to its representation in survey data and quarterly audits. In brokering the voice, TEABBA's workers were asked to broker responsibility. But ultimately it was their own responsibility that was most at stake, that was most under interrogation by state agencies and a preoccupation of the most well-meaning white managers in remote communities. This is the manifest reason that TEABBA's staff had such trouble with moves toward enterprise which asked that they alienate their remote membership as a marketable audience, a representation serving as capital in an exchange with producers of cola or cigarettes. But much as lamentation transformed the maximally institutional space of polyester-walled office cubicles, relations built through ritual recognition between TEABBA and its member communities proved more commanding and consequential than the compulsion of bureaucratic routine.

CHAPTER 6 | A Body for the Voice

In 2004 I caught a predawn flight with Donna from Darwin out to Nhulunbuy airport in northeast Arnhem Land. We were headed to Yirrkala,
a community famous in Australia for its politics. The Yolngu people
of northeast Arnhem Land are one of Australia's best-known Aboriginal peoples, celebrated in the Southeast for their political assertiveness,
their historical resilience in the face of intense mining activity over the
last half of the twentieth century, and their canny self-assurance on
a national stage. The Yolngu launched one of Australia's earliest and
perhaps best-known land rights cases, drawing on the support of Arnhem Land missionaries and finding a sympathetic audience through
the pages of Australian newspapers and on the screens of Australian
television sets as they contested mining company interest in their
lands through the highly visible Bark Petitions submitted to Australia's
Parliament. Although they lost that first land rights case, it is no exaggeration to see in Yolngu collective action and its renown one of the
catalysts for the broad political movement that led to two decades of
self-determination policy and great changes in the place of Aboriginal
Australians in settler-colonial Australia.

While Yirrkala is still a center of Aboriginal political life, it is also a
place to which many look for examples of the radical alterity from settler Australia that Aboriginal people can represent.[1] People here speak
in a number of dialects collectively termed Yolngu Matha, and in part
owing to their great distance from the colonial centers of Australia's
Southeast and the difficulty of accessing Arnhem Land's floodplains in

earlier decades of the twentieth century, they experienced colonial incursion and settlement much later than peoples to their south.[2] In the brilliance of their language, ritual, music, dance, and painting, Yolngu easily figure as maximally other in ways that excite the interests of Australians and many others around the world. But the culturally distinct group of clans and dialects that come together today as Yolngu can also be understood to emerge historically as a collective political subject through forms of postcolonial Indigenous and missionary advocacy, assisted by their settlement at a series of Methodist missions established across northeast Arnhem Land during the first half of the twentieth century, and drawn more starkly as a singular subject by the Yolngu response to the threat of the expropriation of their lands during the 1960s (see Atwood 2004; Morphy 1991; Williams 1986). How that subject should be thought of at the turn of the twentieth century was much in discussion in the Northern Territory in 2004 as a discourse of social pathology and crisis ramped up in the Australian press and as changing ideas of how Aboriginal people should be governed moved decisively from "self-determination" to something termed "mutual obligation" and individual capacity encouraged by opportunities for enterprise.

That morning, as we headed to Yirrkala, this broader ideological policy shift was but one animating ingredient in a contest between two very different media institutions, each one imbricated with Yolngu life in distinct ways. Donna and I were flying to a meeting in which representatives of Australia's Aboriginal administration talked with representatives of a Yolngu-language media program run by a Uniting Church–funded NGO in the Northeast. At stake was an understanding of the place of Yolngu exceptionalism and distinction vis-à-vis other Aboriginal groups in the Northern Territory: How and in what language should they be addressed by "Aboriginal media"? As a political subject? A cultural alter in need of salvation? Or a collection of individuals in need of better information?

To make media with Indigenous Australians in the Northern Territory is not only to broker between institutions and politics of the state and remote Indigenous communities; it is also to enter into an often turbulent field of cultural production in which different understandings of what media are and how they should be deployed implicate the very collective subject such media are understood to represent. In defining the aims of their institutional work, in making arguments about the necessity of funding, and in describing the character of their relationship with their constituent communities, Indigenous cultural brokers and representative institutions also make arguments about who their constituents are and how they are to be reckoned—by language, by country of affiliation or origin, or by need. Conflict and competition around such questions—questions about which institution can best represent what collective subject and what might be the best ways to imagine "media" or "communication" in that work—are rife in the making of Indigenous media. They subtend routine decisions in media associations' seasonal calendars and event planning and also loom large in the organizational calculus around grant applications and governmental funding. And that reckoning also implicates the ontology of media itself as different organizations figure their work through specific media ideologies and metapragmatic orientations toward actual voices in their mediation.

In pursuing this turbulence empirically this chapter circles around one particularly charged meeting, held in a remote community in northeast Arnhem Land. In focusing on such institutional politics the chapter explores the gravity of what are at times dismissed as "black politics," foregrounding the reflexivity and constant problematization of collective agency in which Indigenous cultural producers are themselves engaged as they negotiate the institutional domain of Indigenous cultural production. I sketch a particular, momentary institutional conflict in order to suggest that the subject of Aboriginal media is itself a negotiated achievement within a dynamic politics shaped in part by limited funding and institutional competition, and in part by historical tensions between highly local, enduring forms of identity and Aboriginal particularity and broader, pan-Indigenous modes of collective agency and identification. To suggest that the subject of Aboriginal media is a historically emergent entailment of institutionalized cultural production, however, should evoke not scandal, but an appreciation that the work of making media and producing the Aboriginal voice also means producing the bearer of that voice—making a collective Indigenous subject institutionally, administratively, and politically legible. It is in such politicized fields of cultural production that the very ground of communication itself can be seen to be contested and repeatedly opened to redefinition and negotiation.

In this chapter I follow a particular conflict between two organizations pursuing Indigenous media production, both of which had strong claims on the representation of northern Australian Aboriginal interests, but which also saw those interests in terms that differed starkly. One organization, the Aboriginal Resource and Development Service (ARDS), sought to redefine the address of Top End Indigenous radio, focusing on the Yolngu, a grouping of closely tied clans and languages in northeast Arnhem Land, and arguing for exclusive Yolngu-language broadcasting; the other, TEABBA, sought to represent and consider the interests of a collective subject drawn much more broadly from across the Top End's many remote communities and languages, including but not limited to the Yolngu. This conflict is telling: insofar as it revolves around what kind of "voice" an Aboriginal address should take, it also speaks to the kind of subject such a voice ought properly to address. And drawing from distinct institutional genealogies and political constituencies, the two organizations differed, if less overtly, over what "media" are and how they (ought) to work. Tied up closely with these differences were consequential matters of annual funding, institutional survival, and a shifting ideological rationale informing the production of culture more broadly in northern Australia.

The Field of (Indigenous) Cultural Production

Throughout the course of my fieldwork in the Northern Territory, a small, locally based radio project funded largely by the Uniting Church through its development corporation in northeast Arnhem Land sought to create a Yolngu-language radio service for the Top End, directing its broadcasting primarily to Yolngu people. The service was spearheaded by Richard Trudgen, an Anglo-Australian Yolngu advocate and employee of the Uniting Church living in Yirrkala, a Yolngu community adjacent to the mining town of Gove (Nhulunbuy) at the far northeastern tip of Arnhem Land. Trudgen was a self-described "fitter and turner" turned Yolngu advocate. He had originally come to Arnhem Land from New South Wales in 1975, taking a job as a maintenance worker at the community of Ramingining, another Yolngu community to the west and along the northern coast from Yirrkala. Trudgen's writings (2001) and online publicity recount how in the course of that first visit he came to care for the people and the place, subsequently turning his energies toward development work and advocacy on their behalf. Trudgen went on to become the CEO of ARDS and pursue a range of community development projects that included providing directed information on healthcare, political empowerment, and "cultural sustainability." Echoing the development communications writings of such scholars and policy advisers as Srinivas Melkote (Melkote and Steeves 2001), Trudgen described the centrality of good information for Yolngu development, information the Yolngu might use to make informed decisions about their own well-being. Concerned about what he saw as the dire situation of Yolngu people—the high rates of suicide and substance abuse and the general poor physical and mental health that afflict Yolngu communities—Trudgen saw media as a kind of delivery service, providing news and information in Yolngu Matha to Yolngu people. A steady diet of health advisories and political news would, he argued, transform how Yolngu understood themselves and the world around them and could thus change the ways they behaved as individuals.

Under his leadership, however, ARDS expressed interest in securing commonwealth funding for Indigenous media services, then distributed regionally in a grant-based system by the Aboriginal and Torres Straight Islander Commission (ATSIC), the representative body (since abolished) that distributed funding and audited grant projects. This project had the potential to materially disrupt the work of TEABBA by depriving them of funding, forcing them to compete for scarce resources within a small regional economy of commonwealth-funded cultural production, and potentially undermine the rationale by which ATSIC renewed TEABBA's funding. Both the ARDS radio project and TEABBA's network were eligible to receive funding from the Miwatj region ATSIC council. While this made up a large portion of TEABBA's funding income, the ARDS project had been supported primarily through donations secured via the Uniting Church's broader networks and southern member churches. Through sales of his book and church-based appeals in the South, Trudgen had garnered financial support to begin construction of an Arnhem Land Yolngu-language radio network, built independently of the apparatus of self-determination and of commonwealth funding. The arguments brought by Trudgen and the ARDS radio project to the Miwatj ATSIC council threatened to cut into TEABBA's funding resources and also to delegitimize TEABBA's work in northeast Arnhem Land among their Yolngu constituents. The perspective on Aboriginal media taken by ARDS, further, underscored crisis, employing a kind of humanitarian reason that allowed Trudgen and his organization to dismiss the political rationale around self-determination subtending TEABBA's broadcasting aims.

As these two institutions argued, the very ground of TEABBA's endeavor was rehearsed both within the office space of the radio studio and in a series of charged meetings between TEABBA and other cognate organizations, between TEABBA and its ATSIC funders, and between TEABBA and ARDS. A series of fault lines were probed here by the ARDS project, one between Yolngu distinction and exception vis-à-vis a broader Aboriginal domain, another around the potential of "communication" to intervene in Yolngu well-being, and a third about what kind of representational apparatus could best serve Indigenous interests in the Top End. These fault lines and the determined and careful negotiation by TEABBA's managers and Yolngu board members of this proposal by the ARDS network may speak to a broader anxiety in Australian public culture around "black politics" and the occasional dismissal of such politics as impossibly fraught by non-Indigenous people, as uncomfortably aggressive, violent, or troublesome (see also Cowlishaw 2004). To outsiders and to some within this field, such political differences and arguments are often figured as a problem that undermines the aims of Aboriginal institutions themselves. Indeed, non-Indigenous media makers occasionally involved with TEABBA and with other Yolngu organizations dismissed the political rambunctiousness of TEABBA's relations with other organizations as a distraction from the "real business" of making media.

In suggesting that such conflict should be considered not as endemic to but rather as generative of Top End media production and institutional sociality, I take inspiration from Pierre Bourdieu's (1993) interests in the particular inversions and dynamics of fields of cultural production—fields that interact with markets but may also retain their own rationalities and distinct logics of social value and prestige, and that exist as observable, analytically available entities by virtue of the struggle and shifting positions that participants within these fields negotiate (cf. Born 1995). In foregrounding those moments when the positions and ideals of these institutions found articulation in conflict, I aim to avoid privileging the relationship between a homogeneous Indigenous subject and settler state. Instead I focus on the interaction of new policy imperatives and paradigms with a relatively autonomous and internally fractious "field of (Indigenous) cultural production." This is also to problematize the durability of Indigenous media by focusing on the intra-Indigenous and intercultural institutions responsible for its ongoing production: How do these exist? What are the principles on which their durability and self-understanding are predicated? How do these very institutions maintain an identity and viability? And finally, how is the field itself reproduced?

In his well-known essay "The Field of Cultural Production" (1993), Bourdieu suggests that such durability is something to be explained: if apparent analytically, the coherence of such social and institutional fields ought not to be taken as given. In seeking to understand the question of their structural coherence and durability over time, Bourdieu famously argues that such fields exist as the product of struggle:

We are insisting that what can be considered a system for the sake of analysis is not the product of a coherence-seeking intention or an objective consensus (even if it presupposes unconscious agreement on common principles) but the product and prize of a permanent conflict; or, to put it another way, that the generative, unifying principle of this "system" is the struggle, with all the contradictions it engenders. (1993: 34)

For Bourdieu, further, this conflict carries a common prize grounded on what he terms "particular forms of belief" (1993: 34–35). This is not economic conflict; rather, it is based on the principles and values of the literary (or artistic or cultural) field under consideration. These thoughts on the constitution of literary and art worlds suggest asking precisely what is at stake as different cultural institutions in the Northern Territory vie with one another—both in efforts to achieve forms of consensus on the aims and objectives of Indigenous cultural production, and in efforts by specific institutions and individuals to maximize their own viability and the viability of the cultural practices they hold dear.

A further note of qualification is in order here. The term "community," as Frances Peters-Little has written (2000), can cover over a lot of very intense and contentious disagreement and robust discussion. Her historical and ethnographic challenge to the naturalization of the idea itself in Australia looks to the diversity of ideas about the concept and the collectives it names, foregrounding politics and controversy as unremarkable, even valued aspects of Aboriginal life. Here I foreground disagreement, exploring a moment of tension and difference in how Indigenous media were imagined across these different institutions, and focusing on the different normative arguments about language choice and the related ontological constitution of the Aboriginal subject that media in the Top End ought to address. This is not to diminish the stakes of such issues for people living in Aboriginal communities, but to raise the possibility that politics are at their very heart and that "robust discussion" is a valued and constitutive part of their character.

I begin with a portrait of the everyday kinds of conflict and negotiation that mark such fields of cultural production, kinds of struggle and negotiation that mark a great deal of the work of TEABBA as an institution seeking to represent a broad and heterogeneous Indigenous public. I then turn to a remarkable and consequential contest over audience and Indigenous patronage between TEABBA and the then-new ARDS radio service in northeast Arnhem Land, placing this within a broader institutional economy in which the constitution of an Indigenous public remains an unsettling site of contestation, reflection, and negotiation. These struggles in Indigenous media production largely revolve around relationships with different groups—between relatively urban and relatively remote, between institutions and communities, between Indigenous clients and Indigenous patrons, that are highly valued both in and for themselves and also as forms of symbolic capital and a necessary precondition of much cultural production in this part of the world. This is a field in which indigeneity is itself valued and can be figured as a kind of symbolic capital, but also, and in less instrumental terms, as an indeterminate end in itself, a self-sufficient value that underpins all "position-takings" and that emerges as a kind of excessive, durable category—indefinite in form and thus open to interpretation. It is not just the Indigenous "voice" that is up for grabs in this field, but also the capacity to define the collective subject to which that voice becomes ascribed. And at times, in arguments around such ascription, the field itself can seem up for grabs.

A Yolngu Media Service

Between April and October, TEABBA's work turned from the administrative and office-focused work of bureaucratic management to staging broadcasts from remote sports carnivals and festival events, assessing, maintaining, and repairing studios in the communities they represent, and otherwise visiting with communities and broadcasters who become harder to reach when the rains of the wet season close many Northern Territory roads, clog airstrips, and otherwise disrupt easy travel across the Top End. In this endeavor it retains something of its original mission as a facilitator, ensuring equipment functionality and also funding availability for remote Indigenous broadcasting. But TEABBA has also increasingly sought to participate in regional cultural festivals such as the Barunga festival, held in the Barunga community southeast of Katherine, and the Garma festival, held near Yirrkala in northeast Arnhem Land. Such festivals are occasions at which TEABBA produces a live broadcast from the event that is broadcast minimally over TEABBA's Top End network, and maximally across the country through the National Indigenous Radio Service. Their visits to Barunga and Garma also included efforts to promote their work among these festivals' diverse attendees, catching up with old friends, and spending time with TEABBA's own remote broadcasters and their extended families. At Garma this participation entails putting together a crew of four to six people, traveling over two days by four-wheel-drive from

Darwin to Nhulunbuy, hiring telephone lines and hotel rooms as temporary broadcast suites in Gove, and then spending the week producing broadcasts from the festival site. Such festivals thus represent both an extensive obligation and an intense, relatively brief period of amplified sociability that can occupy the organization for months in advance.

In 2003 TEABBA not only sought to acquire greater funding for these very expensive broadcasts—both through project grants and through commercial sponsorship—but also was scheduled to host the Annual Remote Indigenous Video Festival, an annual screening and celebration of remote documentary and dramatic video production. Through the early dry season TEABBA managers Donna and Gary planned to produce this video festival at the Garma site in Arnhem Land, drawing on the audience already in the region for Garma to maximize attendance at festival screenings. In addition to a large, intercultural audience of bureaucrats, policy makers, and potential funders, video screenings at the Garma festival also promised a larger remote-community Indigenous audience than could be expected to attend if the festival were held in Darwin. However, the organizers of the Garma Festival, the Yothu Yindi Foundation (YYF), asked that all non-Yolngu attendees pay a fee to attend. Though this fee was lower than the one for tourists, it proved too large of an obstacle for TEABBA to overcome. The total cost to transport equipment, staff, and a number of video makers to northeast Arnhem Land and pay their cost of attendance led TEABBA to relocate these screenings to its Darwin offices and nominate a much smaller contingent to travel out to Nhulunbuy for the festival.

This provided a glimpse of serious interinstitutional turbulence, as TEABBA's aims for Garma found an obstacle in the YYF organizers' desires to use attendance fees to help support the festival and further Yolngu-specific aims. TEABBA's management and workers felt it fundamentally important to attend this festival, to be present and in conversation with its organizers and its many other Indigenous and non-Indigenous participants, and also to follow through on their plans to broadcast news and events from the festival for their broader Top End Indigenous audience. Such broadcasts are important for TEABBA's collective endeavor on several levels. First, they form a primary mission of their production work insofar as they serve their constituent communities in publicizing and maximizing the profile of such festivals themselves—from the largest and most widely known (such as the Garma and Barunga festivals) to the smallest and most locally focused (e.g., a high school sports carnival or remote community-based battle of the bands). In supporting and publicizing such cultural performance events, TEABBA fulfills a charter function that its remote community board members highly value. But attendance at cultural festivals also serves TEABBA's own distinct institutional imperatives insofar as it maximizes the profile of TEABBA and demonstrates the group's relevance and centrality to the social life of the Top End. It is vital to attend and to be seen to attend. Indeed, to not be invited to broadcast from these events would be a serious blow.

More can be seen at issue, however, than either the YYF's financial bottom line or TEABBA's institutional profile. In addition, the representational and institutional raison d'être of each organization came into conflict. The Yothu Yindi Foundation has become a highly visible and highly successful representative of Yolngu interests in northeast Arnhem Land. It grew from the partnership of the successful Yolngu band Yothu Yindi and their manager, AJ, around a series of community development and Yolngu-focused forms of cultural production. Through national and international tours, successful recordings, music videos, and an increasingly visible presence in land rights and other forms of Australian cultural activism, Yothu Yindi had garnered perhaps the highest profile of all Aboriginal bands during the height of its success (from roughly the mid-1980s until the early 2000s). Over the course of this period, AJ and the Yolngu clan that dominated Yothu Yindi consolidated this success through the Yothu Yindi Foundation—an organization that aimed to advocate for Yolngu interests and, beginning in 1999, sponsored the Garma Festival itself, garnering the support of Territory, commonwealth, and commercial sponsorship. Politicians, high-profile activists, academics, and businesspeople joined a large contingent of tourists for five days each dry season in a festival that celebrated all things Yolngu and provided a dedicated space for discussing broader issues of concern to Indigenous people, policy makers, and academics. In short, the YYF and the Garma festival are markedly Yolngu agencies, distinct from but running adjacent to the broadcasting and development focus of ARDS and TEABBA, ARDS dedicated primarily to furthering Yolngu development interests from within the ambit of the Uniting Church, and TEABBA prioritizing the shared needs of its diverse Aboriginal membership. TEABBA's video festival and TEABBA's dedication to its broader, regional constituency took a back seat both to the financial interests represented by Jackson and the YYF's board of directors, largely made up of Yolngu members of the Gumatj clan, and to the Garma festival's emphasis on all things Yolngu.

Even as TEABBA juggled its dry season calendar to accommodate both attendance and remote broadcasting from the Garma site and the production of a separate video festival, the negotiations with other institutional interests in Garma continued. As preparations continued, the Central Australian Aboriginal Media Association (CAAMA) signaled its interests in broadcasting from the Garma site. Arnhem Land falls within TEABBA's broadcast region, and although ultimately TEABBA's manager felt it important to collaborate with CAAMA rather than express frustration, it seemed a breach of protocol. TEABBA's managers saw CAAMA's intentions as a direct challenge, as undermining their position vis-à-vis their constituent communities. Ultimately, this minor conflict was resolved when CAAMA agreed to host its shows on TEABBA's signal—when the organizations resolved to collaborate rather than compete. These kinds of negotiations and minor tensions are a frequent, and frequently surmounted, feature of interinstitutional life in the Top End. There are many, many Indigenous organizations with different mandates, seeking to represent different groups of Aboriginal people, and with different ideas about how best to do this and how best to secure their funding over subsequent grant cycles. Yet as I suggested in the previous chapter, 2003 and 2004 witnessed some broad shifts in the logic by which media production needed to justify itself to funders, and in the channels and governmentally endowed bodies providing that funding.

As if these two large projects (a large cultural festival and a large video festival) were not already enough to keep TEABBA staff busy, both organizing and producing the events themselves and negotiating their relationship to other interested, representative institutions of cultural production, throughout 2003 they reluctantly found themselves in an increasingly oppositional and competitive position relative to a new radio service seeking to represent Yolngu people, and thus potentially reducing the funding available for TEABBA's own projects. In January 2003, a community announcement posted in the *Northern Territory News* caught Gary's attention. The notice advised readers of the application by the Aboriginal Resource and Development Service (ARDS) to begin operating a shortwave network in northeast Arnhem Land. This was to operate in a dialect of Yolngu Matha and aimed to provide information on current events, health, and politics in a voice and idiom that Yolngu people could understand and identify with. For Gary this was surprising and somewhat alarming. Founded as a partnership between Aboriginal activists and remote community media producers such as FD, TEABBA considers itself the primary representative of Aboriginal media interests in northeast Arnhem Land. TEABBA fought hard for commonwealth funding administered through the offices of ATSIC, the Aboriginal and Torres Strait

Islander Commission. In the four years leading up to the 2002–2003 financial year, TEABBA had already seen this funding halved and had been forced to continually justify and demonstrate its fiscal responsibility through a period of quarterly audits. These twin pressures of reduced funding and increased auditing had taxed their capacity to focus on production work itself insofar as they were so busy administering and accounting for the meager resources they had secured through ATSIC granting processes.

ARDS can be best figured as the development corporation of Australia's Uniting Church, but in practical terms the organization is identified in the Northern Territory with Trudgen. After two decades of work as both fitter and turner[3] as well as advocate and missionary in Yolngu communities, Trudgen has become a respected, if somewhat controversial public figure in the Northern Territory. His policy-oriented work *Why Warriors Lie Down and Die* (2001) rests on two pillars: first, that welfare dependency has been the primary cause of Aboriginal despair, and second, that this despair is compounded by the lack of communication between Yolngu and non-Indigenous Australians. Its focus on development and on the centrality of transparent and free access to information as a means to allow Yolngu to orient their behavior in line with healthier lives drew clear parallels with the efforts by UNESCO and a range of development organizations to equate free and open access to information with the technological imaginary of media, the promise of a technological response to a wide series of problems in the so-called Third World and within international development institutions themselves (e.g., UNESCO). At the time of writing, the ARDS service provides Yolngu-language news, public service programming, and entertainment to the six primary communities that make up Yolngu country, the more remote outstations and homelands scattered throughout northeast Arnhem Land, and the major population centers of Darwin and Palmerston.

Historically, the ARDS radio project should also be understood as part of the locally valued place of missions and missionary advocacy in northeast Arnhem Land. Missionization in Arnhem Land is largely an early twentieth-century development. Methodist missions frequently took on the role of advocating for Aboriginal interests in the region. For instance, they played a central role in mitigating the incursion of resource extractors beginning in the early 1960s and in later efforts to secure land rights for Yolngu people (see Williams 1986). The reverend Edgar Wells, superintendent of the Mission at Yirrkala, played an instrumental role in helping Yolngu men draft the famous Bark Petition—a statement of sovereign claim to the country of Blue

Mud Bay and in opposition to the introduction of bauxite mining without consultation with that country's traditional owners (Attwood 2004). This history of mission advocacy and involvement in Yolngu lives continues at an institutional level in a broader sense as well, with the Arnhem Land Progress Association running a network of community stores, and supporting an air service that connects the communities of Arnhem Land. Trudgen's work is overtly aligned and institutionally coextensive with this long history and extensive institutional network of missionary enterprise and advocacy, now on behalf of the Uniting Church, and aligned closely with Yolngu theologian and "cross-cultural missionary" Rev. Dr. Djiniyini Gondarra.[4] The ARDS radio service and other outreach and advocacy endeavors should be seen, then, as the corporate heirs to the missionary work of the early twentieth century.

One perspective to derive from these interlinked institutions and individuals is that the distinction and cultural singularity of Yolngu has become entwined with the institutional biography of the Uniting Church and a series of missions and individual missionaries who have dedicated their careers and lives to Yolngu advocacy. Indeed, the core of Trudgen's efforts are spun around his interest in retaining a particular Yolngu distinction—a linguistic and territorially distinct cultural group in Australia who might retain that distinction through, in part, the judicious and targeted use of a Yolngu-language media service. In this endeavor, Trudgen's position and broader advocacy can be seen as an extension of missionization in the Top End that has taken on a role of advocating for the value of Yolngu culture in and for itself. And for Trudgen, the distinct history and cultural singularity of Yolngu interests are manifest in the voice as language. The rhetorical and figurative language of his writings, then, avoid tropes of giving voice and instead focus on provisioning—offering information in a form by which it might be best consumed. And this means that radio programming must speak to Yolngu in Yolngu Matha, in Yolngu language.

ARDS radio is of a piece with this latter argument in its aim to provide basic information on issues such as health and hygiene, economics, and world events—but in Yolngu language. ARDS had already been working with crafting Yolngu-language accounts of major health issues afflicting Yolngu, such as diabetes and kidney disease, and sought to put such accounts on the air through their radio service. Its feasibility report figured this issue as an endeavor to "unlock social capital" in Arnhem Land. Under a subheading titled

"Keys to Human Capacity Building," the report expands on the abstract rationale behind the need for a particularly Yolngu radio service:

When it comes to human capacity building and creating social capital,
there are two essential keys: purpose and communication. Loss of purpose
emerges when people become confused and do not have enough information about the world around them to take control of their own lives and develop their own future. Without good communication, clear purpose is but
a faint and distant hope. Without clear purpose, human endeavor stops.
    Human capacity building cannot happen without good communica-
tion. Good communication happens when information is provided in a
way that allows it to be understood. This can only happen in the people's
own language, which is the medium they use to communicate, think and
construct knowledge.

Building on figures of the misery and anomic despair that have become
almost a reflex in much description of remote Australia, the report also subtly
pivots on the characterization of Yolngu as "confused" and without purpose;
its subtext, as will become clearer below, rests on figures of individual con-
fusion and listlessness and on individualizing the Yolngu subject. Trudgen's
actual program is thus highly specific, geared toward Yolngu communities
and the value of education for social development, yet operates through similar assessment of the lack of endeavor and listlessness of life in remote communities, while also seeing an answer in unlocking Yolngu social capital and
enterprising character.
    So while TEABBA acts in the Northern Territory as an institutionalized
arm of Aboriginal rights activism, ARDS can also be seen as an agent of
Yolngu interests, drawing on a history of missionary advocacy in pursuing a
liberal program of producing individuals capable of rational, self-maximizing
choice. My own sense, and that of my interlocutors at TEABBA, was that
Trudgen's aims individualized the difficulties of Aboriginal people as failures
grounded in their flexibility and capacity to accommodate biomedical understandings of affliction and etiology, an individualization that marginalized
and minimized the political efforts that underwrote much early Indigenous
media production. Indeed, Trudgen seemed unconcerned with the broader
history and context of Aboriginal political struggle for rights and recognition that led to the establishment of institutions such as TEABBA, Radio Larrakia, CAAMA, and many others. Trudgen argued, further, that the broader

institutional networks of Aboriginal activism neglected the specific needs of Yolngu in linguistic, cultural, and biomedical terms. Trudgen's sense of Yolngu exceptionalism vis-à-vis a broader Aboriginal political struggle joined the humanitarianism of ARDS efforts to challenge TEABBA's pan-Indigenous representational endeavor.

Perusing the numerous, enthusiastic letters of recommendation and support granted to the ARDS service and circulated as an appendix to their project report (ARDS 2002), it was clear that their plan appealed to a wide spectrum of Northern Territory commercial and governmental interest. As TEABBA's manager in 2003, Donna was in broad agreement with this assessment of the dire situation of Yolngu communities and with the suggestion that more radical efforts were required to improve Yolngu health and well-being. Many Indigenous activists and advocates also were in strong agreement with this rejection of the "welfare-capitalist" aspects of self-determination. However, like Aboriginal historian and advocate Noel Pearson, Donna saw the answer in terms of Indigenous entrepreneurship and self-representation and saw Trudgen's initiative as an imposition and as too narrowly focused on Yolngu goals. As I discuss below, I identify this difference as the primary fault line between the approach of TEABBA and ARDS. Where TEABBA sought to provide Aboriginal representation across the region and across language groups, Trudgen worked with ARDS to help Yolngu people in particular, foregrounding their singularity and distinction from other Aboriginal Australians, but also aiming to instrumentalize Yolngu-language media for highly local aims.

TEABBA's immediate response to the January community announcement noticed by Gary was to compose a letter advising the Australian Broadcasting Authority (and Trudgen) of their service, and asserting their willingness to contribute their expertise and aid in Trudgen's efforts to produce Yolngu radio. The letter went on to note that Trudgen might be able to take part in their service with the programming he intended to offer (and for which Donna expressed great admiration). That response was to lead to more discussion, but not immediately. Throughout 2003 the significance of the ARDS development fell away in the face of more immediate concerns with writing project grants and maintaining the broadcasting equipment across their member communities. When mention of the ARDS radio service did arise in TEABBA's offices, as often as not Donna or Gary sought to frame this less in terms of how it affected their own programming, and more in terms of how it might be beneficial to Yolngu, and how TEABBA might be able to provide support for a new Indigenous broadcaster in their region. Their emphasis returned again and again to how TEABBA might help Yolngu, minimizing the existential threat this development held for TEABBA as an organization. Nonetheless, the implicit tensions between the aims and historical understandings of staff in these two organizations, one emerging from a pan-Aboriginal institutional apparatus of self-determination and the other from a history of missionary advocacy on behalf specifically of Yolngu people in Arnhem Land, became increasingly apparent by the close of the year.

The following September a report on the delivery of media services to northeast Arnhem Land arrived by post at TEABBA's Coconut Grove offices. This had been occasioned by competing funding requests for Indigenous radio production in the Miwatj Region of Arnhem Land, an administrative jurisdiction that includes Yirrkala and a number of other Yolngu communities to Darwin's east. In addition to TEABBA's annual submission, ATSIC had also received an application from ARDS for funding to help in the establishment of their new network. Completed by WB, a Dutch intern at the Nhulunbuy offices of the Aboriginal and Torres Strait Islander Service (ATSIS, the newly created, and subsequently short-lived financial counterpart established to carry out the fiscal aspects of ATSIC policy) with the help of GD, a young Yolngu man interested in radio production, the report sought to assess the current state of the BRACS and, taking on a development role, to assess "alternative ways of providing broadcasting services to the region" and to maximize the results of ATSIC expenditure.

On receiving the report, TEABBA's managers expressed dismay. Not only did the developmental aspects of the report seem to overstep ATSIS's role as financial arm for ATSIC policy; it also elided a long history of Indigenous media endeavors in the region and overtly expressed interest in sidelining that work. For staff in Darwin, that the report overlooked the ongoing contributions and support of one of TEABBA's founding members, FD (at the time living not far away in the community of Milingimbi) added insult to injury. In part this inattention reflected the relatively shallow experience of a new ATSIS bureaucrat with little background in Indigenous media issues, but also the politics of patronage. Where FD had long provided TEABBA with a local point of access to Arnhem Land's Yolngu communities, ARDS worked more closely with a second man, the widely known Uniting Church minister Rev. Dr. Djiniyini Gondarra. TEABBA's response to WB's report relied on TEABBA's long-standing role as BRACS coordinator and their ability to telephone Darwin's ATSIC office (distinct from the offices in Gove) and register their complaints. In the event, the Gove ATSIS offices did call a public meeting of "BRACS Stake-holders" in order to, they stated, acquire community input and the input of other institutions with an interest in the BRACS program in Arnhem Land.

A Meeting in Yirrkala

Held in Yirrkala in November 2003, the meeting was managed by the young ATSIS intern, WB, who coauthored the Miwatj regional BRACS report with his Yolngu research associate, GD. Attending were representatives from a number of Yolngu BRACS as well as from other interested community organizations (such as health clinic and the "sport and recreations" officers), as well as the primary "stakeholders"—Richard Trudgen of ARDS, and Donna and I joined by TEABBA's technician.

In the predawn darkness, as we drove to the airport through a quiet, sleeping Darwin for our early flight across Arnhem Land, Donna explained to me that the large legal briefcase she carried contained TEABBA's service records for each and every member community in the Top End. Not only did she intend to educate ARDS and the Miwatj ATSIS officers on the facilities already in existence, she also intended to press a case for the relevance of TEABBA and to seek additional funds for equipment maintenance and capital infrastructure—areas of the BRACS network long neglected by ATSIC funders. In coming to Yirrkala Donna hoped to illuminate what infrastructure already existed, to make TEABBA's own past and current work known, and also to suggest ways that TEABBA might be able to help ARDS with their project.

The meeting got under way just past 10 A.M. The ATSIS intern orchestrating the meeting, and coauthor of the Miwatj BRACS Report, outlined its conclusions. He began with a description of the moribund character of BRACS broadcasting in northeast Arnhem Land, and conjectured that for Yolngu, watching DVDs and playing video games received much more enthusiastic attention than the BRACS programming. He then performed a scripted interaction between the researcher and a fictive composite community resident to demonstrate the report's conclusions, performing each role for the audience:

A lot of people from, say, health clinics, schools, sport and rec programs, they came to us and asked us "Well, what's this BRACS about?"

"Oh, it's like a local radio station, local television station."

"Could you use that to, like, broadcast to the community maybe health information or information about culture, information about economics, information about law?"

"Yeah!"

"Oh, we've been looking for that forever. We've got all this information we want to get out into the community, and we been looking for a way to get that out into the community. We never knew BRACS could do that for us."

In this performed dialogue WB figured a failed and invisible BRACS—a broadcaster invisible and inaudible to the very communities it exists to reach. While many of my interlocutors would agree with this assessment, its assertion in this context has a rhetorical end, framing a problem that requires action, action that the organizations represented by WB are well positioned to pursue. WB continued:

> So, hang on, that might be a really important find. So we started talking to community members. Like, "Would you listen to BRACS if BRACS brought you, in language, information about local sports, information about health in language, information about money in language, information about law in language?"
>
> A lot of people sort of sat up and said "Yeah, that's the sort of information we've been looking for. And we sometimes get that on the ABC or SBS [Special Broadcasting Service]. But it's all in English, it's all difficult. We don't really understand. And often it's like living in Sydney or living in Melbourne. Not about living in Gapuwiyak? So, um, yeah, it's not really relevant to us."
>
> So we figured, well, perhaps that's why people aren't listening. If we can get BRACS to broadcast materials about health, economics, law, culture, sports, local things, in the local language, produced by local people, probably BRACS would become a lot better program.

This discussion, as might be imagined, quickly touched on a sore nerve for BRACS producers who heard WB's proposal from the awareness that BRACS producers have sought to create just such programming, but that they have also historically received highly limited financial and institutional support in their efforts to do so. This negative figure of a failed and invisible broadcast service was strongly contested. In the Miwatj meetings these concerns were given voice by TEABBA cofounder FD, code-switching between English and Yolngu Matha.

> First up, it sounds *manymuk*. It sounds *manymuk* all this talk, but the bottom line is *rupiyah*. Some of us been with BRACS for *years ga bayngu*

rupiyah. You look at us some, we gone gray. We got three hundred dollars a fortnight.

No but true, it sounds good for you people to say things, but *napurru*—we, we are the ones who are suffering here. You want us to do programs on BRACS, whether video or no, you got to support us. We need the support. It sounds good but you got to look at *napurrunha*—you gotta look at *nappurrunha* side—because very, very important now when somebody come up with a good idea, you gotta support BRACS now.[5]

FD's statement argues a number of points, beginning with his assertion that after so many years of good intentions and good ideas, ATSIC and the commonwealth should put their money where their mouth is—which is to say, pay BRACS operators a proper salary. Making explicit the paltry sum provided by CDEP wages, merely three hundred Australian dollars per fortnight, FD then urged WB, and by implication ATSIS and the ARDS radio planners, to consider "our" side, switching to the exclusive first-person plural to rhetorically say "ours, not yours"—a term that he expected WB, who had been studying Yolngu (and rhetorically code-switching himself throughout the meeting), to understand. That is, you have to look at this situation from a Yolngu perspective.

Donna returned to these themes later in the meeting and identified a further source of the moribund character of BRACS production in northeast Arnhem Land in the lack of recognition and respect that Aboriginal producers received from other media organizations. The vast majority of media produced in remote communities continued to be produced by outsiders—professional crews who would visit communities and complete productions with no cognizance or recognition of the BRACS facilities or staff.

As Donna argued:

BRACS operators need to be recognized in the community *as* a community worker. Not just as someone who goes into an air-conditioned room because it's too hot outside, to play music. They need to be recognized BRACS operators. . . . One of the things we want to push, that TEABBA wants to push, is that any outside media, anyone who visits that community, that should be their first stop.

In part such statements can be seen as elicited by WB's introduction and his characterization of the BRACS program as moribund, particularly in light of the perceived challenge presented by the ARDS radio development. Donna's position reckoned invisibility as socially produced, as a form of structural marginalization made worse by the dismissive disregard of outsiders.

WB's comments thus set the stage for a contest around recognition and responsibility. However, when Trudgen took the stage, he presented a different perspective than many had been expecting, refocusing the meeting around several key proposals. Seconding WB's observation that the BRACS was failing as a scheme for Yolngu media production, Trudgen foregrounded two aspects of the existing BRACS organization that necessitated a new Yolngu radio service: the first organizational, in that commonwealth-supported projects administered by ATSIC had historically proven untenable, and the second in terms of the actual content of BRACS broadcasting. The tendency for the BRACS network, managed by TEABBA from Darwin, to retransmit programs from the ABC, Imparja, CAAMA, or 4AAA in Brisbane, he suggested, failed Yolngu by neglecting their particular media needs in favor of a broader regional Aboriginal network. Code-switching between English and Yolngu Matha, Trudgen expanded on these ideas:

> Just think of it this way. Education at the moment is putting in to east Arnhem Land something like about 26 million education dollars. At least 18 million of that, 18 mil', is going to Yolngu schools. As we know from all the statistics, it's not working very well—not working very well at all. What we want to do is create a classroom of not just twenty *djambarpuy*, or thirty *djambarpuy*.[6] We want to create a classroom of eight thousand Yolngu. One classroom, eight thousand Yolngu. . . .
>
> Now if we can't get some of this money, I don't think, we'll not even try. Now that's what part of the problem with media to Aboriginal communities in the past is that we kept on going to places like ATSIC, ATSIC, ATSIC, ATSIC—we call, [but] ATSIC saying no more, no more, no more. We have to start now, thinking, in business terms, how we can get other moneys that are out there. For instance—Alcan, for instance.[7] Alcan takes out of here how many million dollars a year, how many millions and millions of dollars?
>
> And we know it's killing the people back here. We know it's killing the people. So we're going to go to them a different way and hit them hard. But we're going to hit them hard with facts. It's no good going to them saying "Oh please, please help us." We gotta go with real story, real hard story and hit them right here between the eyes.
>
> And it's what we're trying to do with this one, and it's causing a fair bit of trouble, everyone's racing around and some people are saying "They're

criticizing, they're criticizing." Yeah, we are criticizing—because people are dying on the ground.

Trudgen here partakes of a form of humanitarian reason in the context of a broader social and moral crisis, turning the attention of his auditors away from the political stakes of "voice" and toward information. If people are "dying on the ground," he implies, there can be no more conversation. But Trudgen also surprised the room by shifting the parameters of the discussion in another sense as well. Rejecting the idea of taking any ATSIC money, Trudgen described his intention to work with the BRACS facilities, to complement and improve on their work. Noting limiting aspects of TEABBA's extended commitment, across numerous regions, language groups, and communities, Trudgen also recognized the benefits of the BRACS program, the significance of operators like FD and others, as well as the long-standing relationships and mutual respect they held in common.

> I see there's no competition here in the sense between us and people like TEABBA because I see TEABBA covering five or six language regions. Five or even six language regions. When I look at the map, because I'm involved in education, I always worry about language. Because I know we don't study all that "English way," we study him halfway. When you're talking to the doctor, half-half you understand, and the other half-half you haven't a clue what he's talking about. Now that's important because that ends up killing you, hey? And so many of my friends are already dead 'cause when they tried to listen to the doctor they didn't fully understand. Even the [Yolngu] health worker, tries to listen to the doctor, they don't fully understand the doctor apparently. Now that's not a criticism of Yolngu, that's just speaking reality, that's the truth.

In these terms, Trudgen sees ARDS as an extension of BRACS, as addressing its failings through an aggressive localism, a language-centered focus on Yolngu communication. For Trudgen, to make Yolngu radio is to foreground the limits of a regional approach, to foreground the shortcomings of a model that takes as its ambit a pan-Aboriginal domain.

In spite of Trudgen's relatively conciliatory tone regarding the BRACS facilities, ARDS did represent a challenge to the BRACS in the implicit assertion that the bureaucratization of Indigenous media, its institutional expression through ATSIC initiatives and ATSIS reports, has failed in making media central for community cultural development and social welfare. What Trudgen also asserted, in his written work as well as in his statements at Yirrkala in 2003, is that a broad, intra-Aboriginal radio network was failing Yolngu by failing to keep them informed on critical developmental matters of health and national politics. While TEABBA sought to represent Aboriginal people across such local distinctions and to address Yolngu as one of a broad array of Indigenous peoples, ARDS and its supporters in the Miwatj offices of the newly formed ATSIS instead saw the singularity and boundedness of Yolngu as both a signal value and an obstacle that could be overcome with "good information," and thus stressed the need for a particularly Yolngu service.

In this instance, what also becomes clear in attending to debates over the proper ways in which to both represent and serve Yolngu media needs is the power of enterprise and development to displace competition between local and regional models of Aboriginal representation. Trudgen's rhetorical move away from ATSIS support is coded as enterprise but emerges as a confrontation with commercial industry. Both frames were appreciated by his audience and, as such, defused the tensions that had slowly been building in the room. By submerging a potential conflict over one funding source into a broader, commonsense agreement on the need for radical action with respect to Yolngu well-being, Trudgen reconciled these different organizations. Yet he also redirected the meeting's focus from a conflict between activists and media producers such as Donna Garland, and Yolngu advocates such as Trudgen himself, over an implicit proposal to replace pan-Aboriginal representation with market relations. Ultimately, however, the audience for these presentations were BRACS radio presenters, ATSIS financiers, and Yolngu community council members and elders who could provide the symbolic capital and local support for these different projects. Even while Trudgen suggested a reconciliation, and that mollified TEABBA representatives, the contest was both structural, about the fiscal position of each organization, and also metapragmatic—an argument about what media should do, how one ought to conceive of their proper subject, and which organization was better equipped to represent Aboriginal interests in northeast Arnhem Land.

From Discourses of Enterprise to New Funding Arrangements: The Demise of ATSIC

Sweeping changes in the institutional infrastructure of Indigenous media came to a head in the last months of my research with the abrupt abolition of ATSIC, Australia's premiere organ of Indigenous representation and the principal conduit of state funding for Aboriginal cultural production. This marked the culmination of two decades in which the Australian state's relationship to Aboriginal people underwent a broad trend toward entrepreneurial cultural policy rationales, a move toward the privatization of "culture" and its traditional diacritics, which many scholars correlate with a more global neoliberal turn (Comaroff and Comaroff 2001; Miller 2002; Povinelli 2011). This echoed the meetings between ARDS and TEABBA in Yirrkala, combining the rhetoric of crisis and intervention with a reorientation of political authority. No longer, the Liberals declared, could the politicking continue at the expense of Aboriginal development and opportunity. This was an overt redirection of Aboriginal policy from the aims of political agency and representation and toward developmentalist and "pragmatic" concerns with economic inclusion through what was locally termed a "mainstreaming" of Aboriginal funding.

ATSIC had faced broad and bipartisan opposition from its very inauguration under the Labor Party government of Prime Minister Bob Hawke in 1990. The organization aimed to provide a national, democratically elected representative body for Aboriginal Australians, but also was designed as a mechanism for service delivery and for administering funding to Aboriginal corporate bodies and developmental projects. As such it combined the aims of self-determination policies to create an Aboriginal voice in national policy formulation with a governmental role in service delivery and project assessment and auditing. ATSIC faced a range of challenges and criticisms from its beginnings through to its demise in 2004. These included critiques that the nationally elected board of commissioners was unconcerned with the more regional and specific concerns of ATSIC's thirty-five regional councils; that the commission relied too heavily on a professional, non-Indigenous administrative arm to both provision Aboriginal projects and services and to audit those same services; and that those audits were increasingly and inappropriately onerous. TEABBA, for instance, found itself needing to perform quarterly audits over several years to account for the expenditure of an ATSIC grant budget that made up the vast majority of its annual income. This meant that its staff potentially spent more time demonstrating the legitimate acquittal of their funding than they did in pursuing the projects for which that funding had been granted in the first instance. Certainly this was the perspective adopted by media workers. That ATSIC might be abolished was thus greeted with both skepticism and anxiety, and occasionally hope that it might be replaced by more effective, less fraught sources of project funding.

In June 2004 I attended a pair of further meetings with TEABBA in Darwin and in Katherine to assess the coming funding implications of these changes in institutional support. In a broader context of critique around the arbitrariness of the Liberal-National coalition's abolition of ATSIC, TEABBA's managers and staff in fact seemed optimistic that their position might improve should they be taken out from under the umbrella of the Aboriginal and Torres Strait Islander Commission and placed within the funding purview of a more "mainstream" governmental department. They operated, they felt, with the strong support of their member communities and addressed a broad regional audience. This sense of support had been bolstered in their visits to Yirrkala and in discussions with FD and other Yolngu members. Surely this patronage would be enough to sustain their relevance and significance in a new policy era. Indeed, moving to a mainstream organization might lessen the political infighting and competition within ATSIC for attention and funding. It also might mean that they were less subject to the intense auditing and suspicion that seemed to accompany ATSIC funding. In sum, from TEABBA's perspective, this change could mean less politics, less oversight, and a higher measure of independence for TEABBA's staff.

In addition, as I suggest in chapter 5, while TEABBA's management had some difficulty in imagining their audience as a market and generating funds based on this objectification and commoditization of that market, they nonetheless broadly inhabited the discourse of enterprise then ascendant in Indigenous policy. A nearly universal feature of contemporary Australian policy discourse is the proposition that state-funding without "reciprocity" has undermined Indigenous sociality by consolidating Indigenous communities in "outback ghettos" (Pearson 2010; Sutton 2011).[8] This has led some to seek new means of encouraging and enabling Indigenous participation in a broader Australian and cosmopolitan economy and society, and resonates with a broader policy framework of "mutual obligation," which seeks a return from citizens for welfare payments. The implication of such figures for Northern Territory cultural policy and the discursive ground of Aboriginal representation is the desire to cultivate an Aboriginal citizenry capable of responsible investment and participation in a "Northern Development." Both figures share a foundation in the ability of exchange to elicit participation, and both suggest a broader move in Australian cultural policy and the character of a "good" public from what a politics of recognition (based on cultural difference) to what might be termed, following Rowse (2002), a politics of participation (based on economic rationale of reciprocity and mutual obligation).[9]

In the meetings with ATSIC about the shifts in funding arrangements that I attended with Donna, a great deal of concern centered on how Aboriginal organizations could remain autonomous and accountable to their communities—but also on how they might continue in the face of radical shifts in policy at a national level—policies that figured Aboriginal sociality in the language of both crisis and a (paradoxical) privilege—the "privilege" of welfare without the requirement of recompense. Much of the initial anxiety in the face of these changes concerned other organizations—and how these new arrangements might in fact augment their position in a contentious field of cultural production. Indeed, as Donna drove us to the first meeting, she confided that in fact she embraced the meeting as a way to "find out what's going on"—to gain some insight into the structures and broader shifts to this field by making them as transparent as possible. Donna's agility in imagining routes for her organization in the context of radical shifts in the material and political administration was measured by a concern with the particularity of TEABBA's project, to "give voice" in a material sense, to empower Aboriginal producers both in a national context and in the context of their own communities.

Her investment in this project, reaffirmed in our meetings with ARDS, pointed to a foundational issue in this field, the relationship of institutions of cultural production to their Indigenous constituents. This inflected media production by shifting both how producers imagined their audiences and how they sought to secure and figure their local patronage. These relationships were also the ones that were muddied by a "mainstreaming" push toward enterprise in Indigenous cultural production, as I suggest in the previous chapter. The machinery of relationship was being reconfigured and reimagined in this new policy landscape, and this caused the most serious kinds of anxieties within the institutions where I worked, while also presenting new ways to imagine kinds of partnership and enterprise.

These distinct organizations, each of which emerged from very different institutional and historical trajectories, one from Aboriginal activism (TEABBA) and a second from missionary work in Arnhem Land (ARDS), are agents within a quite complicated field of Indigenous cultural production. Their struggles as much as their collaboration help to constitute what I have come to understand analytically as a "field of (Indigenous) cultural production" in which the modes of capital and value producing strategies that Bourdieu terms "position-takings," and the meanings of those positions taken, owe a great deal to local concerns with cultural brokerage, to growing faith in the value of "enterprise," and to the value of "audience" as itself a form of symbolic capital. This suggests that within this field of (Indigenous) cultural production, concerns with enterprise and entrepreneurship animate fundamental concerns with audience and local struggles that are historically quite unique and relate to the positioning of diverse institutions within an emergent Indigenous public. And these struggles are not external to this field of cultural production; rather, they constitute the field itself.[10]

Consolidation

Today both ARDS and TEABBA thrive within a radically altered field of cultural production. In part this rests on the continued distinction of their grounds of possibility, one emerging from a history of missionary advocacy, the other from a history of Aboriginal activism. ARDS ultimately created a small radio service that addresses the core Arnhem Land Communities of Yirrkala, Gapuwiyak, Milingimbi, Galiwin'ku, and Ramingining as well as a number of outstations and the towns of Nhulunbuy and Darwin. The focus of their broadcast work is resolutely a mix of "traditional" Yolngu-language song-cycles and development-focused educational programming in Yolngu languages. They do not embrace the commercial and cosmopolitan forms so popular on TEABBA's broadcasts. In addition, their success—even as it has been funded by a range of commonwealth and Territory public agencies— has had little impact on TEABBA's programming. By 2011 and 2012 TEABBA had come to be a major force in representing the media concerns of many remote Aboriginal communities in the Top End. Their radio programming had gained listeners around the country; their video production program had grown and helped to fill the programming requirements of a new National Indigenous Television Service. And as importantly, TEABBA gained tacit recognition from the Northern Territory's political parties and major corporations. Their producers were placed on the lists of invitees at special events and their studios are a routine stop on the tour circuits of campaigning local politicians, Indigenous and non-Indigenous alike. Yet this status was far from secure in 2003 and 2004. At this time, as the field was undergoing a huge shift, the organization's very survival seemed at risk. Donna's efforts to "find out what was going on" should be seen as canny interventions to secure TEABBA's positions within a broader, turbulent field of Indigenous cultural production.

This turbulence also meant that during my research in northern Australia the body to which the voice of black Australia might be ascribed was itself a point of constant negotiation and tension. Any claim to speak for or speak about Aboriginal people in the North faced possible contestation through a particular economy of representation in which the dynamics of cultural production and institutional funding met a broader political instability and a radical shift in the rationale underlying Aboriginal government—a move away from a status quo that had emphasized self-determination and autonomy and toward a new faith in enterprise and economic participation as those values against which policy must be measured. Here these politics entailed a need to defend, reflect on, and argue about the constitutive character of the corporate Aboriginal subject for which my interlocutors spoke. To do so was also to make a metapragmatic argument. When Donna or FD argued about the value of remote communications policies that had emerged from self-determination, they also made not only an implicit argument about the relative inclusivity or exclusivity of a cultural address, but also a more ontological argument about how to characterize the subject of such representation and mediatized address. These are instances of contest and contradiction that made the voice subject to metapragmatic reflection and political debate, raising the relationship between voice and (cultural) body to institutional awareness and inflecting forms of activist voice consciousness in Aboriginal northern Australia. It is in such argument that the voice's mediatization emerges as a metapragmatics, and where an aporia in the liberal equation of voice with agency, interiority, and representative power becomes apparent.[11] Donna's response to the challenge presented to TEABBA's aims by ARDS very different vision of Yolngu cultural singularity and exceptionalism was to underscore the value of Aboriginal broadcasters' professional capacity—to foreground agency and recognition as ingredient to the project of making media Indigenous, but also to call attention to the ways this required extra-institutional forms of recognition, bolstered by a broader media world who should, she argued, attend to the professional status of Yolngu broadcasters as peers. In this a fault line became apparent between ARDS's focus on development and communication as "information" and TEABBA's project of producing voice and inserting Indigenous agents into an apparatus of media production relations.

Voice here is the focus of institutional labor, negotiation, competition, at times outright conflict. But in focusing here on the field of cultural production to which the Aboriginal voice is central, it becomes clear that to produce the voice one must also produce its bearer—recognized institutionally, culturally as either "Indigenous" or "Yolngu," and even interpersonally by peers as a professional. In northern Australia the proper character and bearer of the voice both remain sites of contestation, something at once presumed by particular modes of address as distinct as "Yaka Bayngu"'s musically mediated cosmopolitan appeal to a broad, heterogeneous NT audience (chapter 1), ARDS's efforts to foreground the Yolngu as a congress of culturally equipped individuals in need of "information" in order to maximize their capacity for self-preservation, what Trudgen might term their "purpose," or TEABBA's interests in bolstering the recognition and authority accorded to remote media workers in northeast Arnhem Land, seeing the ground of their capacity in such recognition.

CONCLUSION

An Immanent Alterity

In exploring the political forces gathering around sound and the voice in Indigenous Australia, this book has sought to bring an ethnographic ear to the political ontology of audio media. Its chapters underscore how such media entail a fundamental excess, a potentiality that draws together cultural intimacy, modes of Indigenous self-abstraction, and questions of liberal recognition as bureaucratic discipline. The first chapters' interests in a social poetics of affecting sound in country music and radio requests thus seek to evoke those sedimented forms of acoustic sociality in which intimacy and Indigenous self-abstraction double one another in sound. This is to listen to this world with an ear for the densities and evocative, musical modes of interpellation and social value it has come to entail as sound. Later chapters sought to demonstrate that this sound world should also be considered an accomplishment built through the negotiation of settler-colonial interest and institutional contest. Focusing on the institutionalization and bureaucratic rationalization of Indigenous audio media suggests that this sound world does more than simply echo an Indigenous agency; it also gathers to itself powerful, at times incommensurable agencies and interests. Attention to the power of vocal sociality and affecting sound does suggest the complexity of the politics this can entail, but I have foregrounded something of the slippery character of mediatized sound in order to explore how the voice in Indigenous Australia has been solicited by diverse historical actors, and in an effort to understand the voice's power in relation to both its unsounded, tropic potency and its sounded, musical materiality.

In part the institutionalization of audio media has meant that the mediatization of sound might be read as reducing all sound to a tropics of voice, the latter a key value by which the institutions I've introduced here purchase their continued subvention and support and by which the iterability of the Indigenous voice can be acquired as a value by the state. This requirement that audio media sound as Aboriginal voice has also meant that this voice can arrive in media institutions through its bureaucratic and discursive avatars, as statistic, as visual representation on a digital timeline, or as figurative appeal to "express oneself"—the voice indexed by its registration or solicitation, but not heard. Yet to focus on such deferral exclusively would be to downplay the historical durability and power of voice as meaningful sound, the power of musical media to stir memory, compel identification, and produce relatedness, to move bodies and catalyze deep feeling. Both in its institutional apparitions and in its sounded materiality, mediatized sound also impels the de- and renaturalization of Aboriginal expressivity, throwing my interlocutors back onto the kinds of struggle that become audible in audio media. The voice has been so important to this story, then, as that place where meaning, musical media, and power converge but also as a stumbling block where they find their limit, where the outcome of politics are underdetermined, and where work in sound entails reflection on sound's power as well as on a transitive relationship between sound and social subject. It is this tension between relating to and through sound and negotiating its deferral and denaturalization that I figure as an emergent politics of desire animating Indigenous and settler Australians alike in their engagements with the voice.

The trope of the emergent is a powerful corrective in ethnographic writing to the possibility of misidentifying stasis in forms of ethnographic representation, but the pace of historical transformation in northern Australia, and the central place of Indigenous Australians to that change, merits further reflection on my use of it here. In closing I want to underscore the incredibly rapid pace at which this politics moves and into which my Indigenous interlocutors are thrown. What appears systematic or structural in fields of cultural production, Pierre Bourdieu writes, is not the aim of objective, singular intention but rather both the "product and prize of a permanent conflict" (1993: 34): The gravity of this characterization, which emerges from Bourdieu's account of French literary culture, also speaks to the existential insecurity that policy shifts can introduce on the ground in northern Australia, and that occasion a well-known local figure of speech that characterizes the work of coping in such environs as "rolling with the policy punches." To call this emergent is not simply to nominate my interlocutors as historical agents, then, but in addition is to see history here as a running fight in which the stakes are the definition of the field itself. As I have attempted to suggest in the latter half of this book, this field of cultural production can feel like a board game in which, at indeterminate intervals, someone smacks the table, sending chips, dice, cards, and drinks into the air, rearranging the game and its rules, demanding that one start anew. Two conjoined forces condition this character of Indigenous cultural production in sounded media. One relates to the shifting rationale of Aboriginal government in Australia, a steady critique of self-determination and a corresponding shift to imagine arts and culture as industry and enterprise that have marked the past two decades of Aboriginal media funding and administration. The other has to do with the continued transformation of northern Australia's media infrastructure by digital media, mobile phones, MP3 compression protocols, the corporate social media of Facebook and YouTube, and by the related coconstitution of this media world by privatized forms of commercial cultural production. I conclude by evoking these changes, the ways they bound this field of cultural production and involve my interlocutors, under three terms: Intervention, Alterity, and Relation.

Intervention

In 2007 the Australian commonwealth, in the final months of a conservative, Liberal coalition government, upended the apparatus of self-determination in the Northern Territory by announcing the Northern Territory Emergency Response (NTER). This named a series of actions that together were termed colloquially "the Intervention" and which responded to a sense of crisis on the part of the Liberal coalition then governing Parliament. The most proximate instigation of the NTER was a report commissioned by the Northern Territory government describing the rampant sexual abuse and neglect of Aboriginal children in remote communities, titled *Ampe Akelyernemane Meke Mekarle* (*Little Children Are Sacred*) (Rex and Wild 2007).[1] In referring the immediate cause of its actions to this report the government framed its intervention as a humanitarian response to crisis, a crisis the Intervention's designers suggested had been exacerbated by policies of self-determination and an alleged welfare dependence that this was held to have entailed.

The NTER applied to seventy-three remote communities across the Northern Territory and introduced a series of legal restrictions aiming to address the immediate concern with children, while also transforming the government of Aboriginal people more generally. These restrictions included curtailing the sale and consumption of alcohol and pornography; new controls over welfare payments and the ways they might be spent; changes in the financial government of remote communities, including installation of commonwealth-directed government business managers; enforced school attendance; and the compulsory leasing of community lands to outsiders.[2] It also initially included mandatory medical examinations, conducted by military doctors, for all Aboriginal children in these communities, a proposition quickly dropped from the list of policies after the military itself objected.[3] The NTER also entailed the temporary suspension of the Racial Discrimination Act of 1975, legislation that prohibits inequitable treatment on the basis of racial criteria[4] and that would have made many of these measures, which so overtly targeted Aboriginal people on the basis of their Aboriginality, unconstitutional. The intervention also accompanied large shifts in the electoral map and jurisdictional organization of Northern Territory local government. Eight large shire councils were established to take the place of local community councils, and these became new administrative centers for political decision making. In combination with the introduction of the official position of the Government Business Manager at the community level, political and fiscal authority were decisively moved to non-Indigenous agents installed by commonwealth decree. As of this writing, the NTER and the range of measures it introduced have resulted in no prosecutions for child sexual abuse, yet many of its specific juridical and administrative interventions remain in place under new titles and have occasionally been expanded by subsequent Labor governments. Taken together, the intervention's primary accomplishment has, perhaps, been the criminalization and amplified stigmatization of Aboriginal men as sexual abusers and Aboriginal women as their enablers.

The NTER also unfolded in the press as a media event, created by the Liberal Party political machine in the run-up to a hotly contested election (Hinkson 2010; Howard-Wagner 2012). Newspaper headlines and talk show panels alike expressed concern for the well-being of Aboriginal children, while entire communities were accused of colluding in making small children available to older men (see, for instance, Graham 2015). On television and radio, in newspapers and online, Aboriginal men were figured as criminal, painted with the broadest brush as both cause and consequence of a social pathology. Newspapers and television reports from both Murdoch-owned newspapers (*The Australian*, the *Northern Territory News*, the *Daily Telegraph*) and Fairfax Media (the *Sydney Morning Herald*) published reports that bordered on the tabloid—focusing on the "rivers of grog" that now seemed so evidently to flow through Indigenous communities, and on the sexual violence and indolence that was felt to plague these places. Longer-form essays and platforms for public intellectual discourse also canvassed and critiqued these frameworks (see Altman and Taylor 2008; Morris and Lattas 2010). Northern Territory–based journalist Paul Toohey, for instance, critiqued the Intervention itself while painting a picture of Northern Territory communities as overrun with grog, drugs, and pornography, and affirmed the high rates of school truancy and a collapse of accountability of Aboriginal people to the law (2008). He rehearsed the scandal of small children watching pornography and acting out its scenarios with their toddler siblings and of violent men bashing their female partners within an inch of their lives. These accounts led him to sympathize with the minister for Aboriginal affairs, Mal Brough, in effect affirming the crisis to which he responded, even as Toohey critiqued the military character and electoral politics that seemed to impel its sudden, ill-considered implementation and the lack of consultation with Aboriginal communities this had entailed.

Toohey's account was in some ways exceptional, differing from much other reporting in seeming to address Aboriginal as well as settler Australian readers. And yet in the current moment there could hardly be a more profound difference between a settler public media that has great difficulty in imagining Aboriginal people as subjects of a media address, other than to register them as the object of scandal, and media made by Indigenous people, which has itself only expanded its successes both through the films and musics that I've explored in previous chapters and also through television, online, the art world, and a range of other expressive and artistic domains. For instance, as I write, a television program based on a remote Aboriginal radio station is in production in Alice Springs. The show is an ensemble-led situation comedy, titled eponymously for the fictive radio station itself, 8MMM ("mercenaries, missionaries, and misfits") and drawing narratively on the collision of "well-meaning whitefellas" and Aboriginal producers. At the time of writing the series pilot has not yet aired, yet the précis and promotional material suggest that it will make comedic fodder of the efforts of white managers to "save Aboriginal people from themselves." It seems fitting to me that the program self-advertising as the first Aboriginal written and directed comedy series takes as its subject matter the work of making radio—lampooning both the "misguided whitefellas" running the station and the Aboriginal media workers aiming to get their voices on the air. Radio's remediation as history takes a turn here toward a comedy of errors in which whitefellas and Aboriginal people must work together.

Although designed to upend the policy infrastructure of self-determination, the NTER has also, paradoxically, had beneficial consequences for some media institutions built within that older policy apparatus. TEABBA's recording, radio, and video projects had often chafed at the tensions and obstacles entailed by a representational project funded by short-term grants and overseen by an auditing regime suspicious of the very mission it oversaw. The Intervention itself further disturbed those forms of government that enabled media to work across the Territory, taking authority and spending power away from community councils and local governments and investing that power in new, larger regional shire councils and in the community general business managers whose positions had been legislated by the NTER itself. But the Intervention has also led to some idiosyncratic possibilities for new projects. By 2011, when I followed up on this question with TEABBA's current managing director it became clear that the new rules and new political structures entailed by the Intervention and associated electoral changes had included some positive ramifications for TEABBA. The stories he told outlined TEABBA's renaissance—the amplified resonance of its work across the Top End that had unfolded after 2007. In dealing with Shire councils and business managers in Arnhem Land, for instance, some remote communities found their broadcasting equipment locked away, forgotten by new business managers with no institutional memory or incentive to explore the possibilities of media making in the context of what was most frequently figured as a crisis. The manager thus described some places where broadcasting equipment now lies unused, locked away in storage sheds for which only white community business managers had keys. But he also described places such as Maningrida, where incoming business managers and shire council members brought new energy and appreciation for Indigenous broadcasting and media production. Here media that historically had been relatively moribund found an influx of energy, financial support, and interest from a new crop of public servants tasked with reform.

As important as the biopolitics of governmental intervention have been for Indigenous people in the Northern Territory and for how we apprehend the government of Indigenous media, it has been joined by the ongoing transformation of media infrastructure in the Northern Territory. In 2011 the introduction of the 3G network across northeast Arnhem Land expanded the reach and relevance of mobile phone technologies for Aboriginal people (Deger

2013). This has meant that music videos, texting, and photography enter even further into people's everyday lives across the Northern Territory, both complicating and enriching the media worlds in which Aboriginal people are immersed. Country music, hip-hop, and the radio voice now emerge from car radios and cell phones, iPads and desktop computers, and boom boxes tethered to solar-powered generators in far-flung outstations. In addition to the work of media associations such as TEABBA and CAAMA, networks of government-supported communications infrastructure allow the digital circulation of a range of sounds, traveling as commodity, click bait, and MP3s on inexpensive mobile phones.

From new offices at the southern edge of Darwin, bordering on the suburban communities of Palmerston, TEABBA took on several new, young DJs who embraced social media, the widespread availability of mobile phones, and the improved access to digital media in libraries and schools across the Territory. These DJs began conducting request programs in which Twitter and Facebook were employed alongside the telephone and the radio, assembling a technically dense "live" address in which radio found remediation online. These new producers also began to build a name for themselves, cultivating a local celebrity built through both radio production and social media by generating Facebook and Twitter profiles that advertised TEABBA and their own vocal personas. Facebook and YouTube thus join radio, not replacing its reach but remediating its power such that the shout-out and the call-in take digital form, resting alongside photography and video on small cell phones. To account for the power of Aboriginal audio media today in Arnhem Land and the Daly River region, as well as in Sydney and Brisbane, requires accounting for its remediation and the reflection on the voice that such remediation can entail.

Alterity

I began this book outlining three metapragmatic imperatives that drive Indigenous concerns with the voice in the production of Aboriginal audio media: that it represent a corporate Aboriginal agentive subject, that it sound black, and that it link people up, giving shape through forms of public affect and social deixis to a collective and black Australian sovereign. These imperatives are driven by a sense of the tremendous consequences of the voice's mediatization for Aboriginal claims to autochthony, distinction, and sovereignty, and they differently animate local engagements with audio media as technology, as commodity, and as political instrumentality. They are also frequently a point of disagreement, the focus of what some Australians might term, in ironic dissimulation, a "robust discussion." In tracing out aspects of the voice's mediatization, the politics of sounding black, and the affective resonance and pragmatic power of linking up, I found a new appreciation for the robustness of critique and political engagement in the studios and offices I've come to know—not as a contentious externality to media production, but rather as its constitutive dynamic. Indigenous media institutions were built on the foundation of a political refusal: a refusal to celebrate the bicentennial of Australia's First Fleet, to cherish the deeds of a settler colony's national ancestors, or to acquiesce to narratives that disappear Aboriginal people from contemporary Australian concerns. As actual places, radio stations and recording studios also have worked to give Aboriginal political life an institutional locus, a focal point for work on sound: boardrooms, courtyards, and studios where a collective subject could be staged as the locus of such refusal. They have thus embodied, both in their sounds and in their physical sites, a refusal of a settler media that saw Indigenous Australians largely in the doubled logics of primitivism and instrumental reason, as nonmoderns to be celebrated or mourned, or as a demographic problem requiring radical governmental intervention.

Yet as Patrick Dodson (2009) writes, "Aboriginal politics" frequently appear in the settler Australian press as scandal, evidence of the fallibility of Indigenous claims. This book has sought to analyze discursive, musical, and institutional aspects of Indigenous media production—occasionally placing argument and disagreement at its center—with precisely the obverse understanding of such political life, seeing it as a key for understanding something not just of the emergence but also the distinction and durability of Indigenous media. To put it another way, one might characterize the institutional fray of Indigenous cultural production, its at times intense and contentious political life, as generative of this field itself—in which what Bourdieu terms the "struggles" and "position-takings" one can find across these different sites and moments themselves constitute the field and give evidence of its particular autonomy, its characteristic difference and distinction. This is to suggest that Indigenous media production is neither simply in opposition nor in accord with the interests of the settler state but has become a relatively autonomous domain, with its own intra-institutional dynamics, distinct concerns, and consequential and particular history (cf. Myers 2002).

One aspect of this domain's distinction, as it were, is a marked effort to negotiate and lend value to forms of difference inhering within Aboriginal

Australia itself. The voice here can thus be a particularly charged thing, something that draws inordinate attention, concern, and care in its production, as well as appreciation and wonder—something that draws people to reflect on its contours. In a visual metaphor it might be a sparkling kaleidoscope, a flash of brilliance that prompts interest and argument. This focus on voice involves what one might call, following Roman Jakobson (1960), the aesthetic or poetic function of communication, a focus on form itself, on "the grain of the voice" (Barthes 1977), and on prosodic, material features of vocal performance. Poetic function and phatic function thus double up in forms of kinship address tied to a country song. It is often, in such moments, a place where an Aboriginal collective subject is most palpable, a historical accomplishment made present as meaningful sound. This is the first level at which a metapragmatic focus on the appropriateness and consequential character of mediatized speech and song comes into focus in the studios and stations of northern Australia and where mediatization matters as a form of poesis. It's here that a metapragmatics of media making takes shape as sound, where voice consciousness takes shape as vocal practice, and where media's provocation exceeds its specific discursive or musical content. That is, beyond political discourse or genre, the voice's mediatization draws attention to the affecting and sensuous character of music and language as sound.

In more abstract terms this voice consciousness amplifies the voice's denaturalization, drawing analytic attention to a metapragmatics of mediatization.[5] The constant unpacking and citing of the voice, the care around its production in media, music, and other forms of both expressive and institutional life, join a more general apprehension around Indigenous vocal expressivity that greeted me in radio and music studios across the North, and suggests how a particular voice consciousness animates forms of intra-Indigenous difference. In Aboriginal Australia audio technologies—radio stations, microphones, and CD backing tracks that stage the voice—should be understood then as a kind of supplement not just for individual expressivity, but for a broader political subject whose agency has long been figured through tropes of voice and voicing, but whose voice takes the shape it does in part as the consequence of a range of particular and highly politicized media work—in radio, in music studios, and on film—and in a range of particular governmental and institutional histories.

The producers I know thus often reflect on what it means to "get it right" when telling stories about Aboriginal people, and they include in this not just the desire to tell a true story but also to tell a story that accounts for issues of ownership, respect, consultation, and the ways in which the subjects of many radio, film, and video productions also make up the audience for that work. Such attunement to metapragmatic issues of authority and voice are evident at many levels, in forms of musical citation, media representation, and in the everyday politics of Aboriginal institutions. Many times in the course of my fieldwork, when asking direct questions and seeking to elicit commentary on Aboriginal social life, my interlocutors would sense that they were speaking for something beyond their individual person, that their response required a kind of representative character, and they might then fall back on highly scripted, stereotyped, and formulaic kinds of speech. For instance, in 2011 I spoke with a night patrol officer in Darwin, a woman tasked with overseeing the harm reduction efforts of Darwin's traditional owners, the Larrakia. I was conducting a recorded interview, using a portable digital recorder that rested on the desk between us. In representing the institutionalized interests of the organization for which she worked, carefully minding the microphone and my questions, she spoke entirely—over a period of an hour—in extended quotations of the literature that the organization had produced for public consumption. I could readily tell this was a practiced representation, yet only afterward, listening to our recorded interview and perusing the pamphlets and materials I had been given to take with me, did I realize the very great extent to which she had stayed with the script, quoting those pamphlets extensively and exactingly from memory in her comments. In this instance I first experienced this close citation as a rebuke of my questions, in contrast with the seeming warmth and openness with which they had been received. But after brief reflection I acknowledged that my questions, on the politics of intra-Aboriginal government and harm reduction efforts by the Larrakia Nation, indeed asked for an authoritative, collective response and one that would speak in the voice of a corporate body.

Such fundamental concerns with the voice animate social life in northern Australia and are amplified in the music and radio studios in which I worked as a locus of reflexive consideration; the frequent de- and renaturalization of the voice as an index of self, and a consequent de- and re-naturalization of how that self itself might be thought. I initially felt the need to get past such charged, formulaic sorts of speech, to get to know the "real person" that such speech seemed designed to obfuscate or protect. And to be sure, I did get to know people, I did enter into other kinds of conversation and talk, speaking with people about their lives, aspirations, and media work in ways that did not so clearly rely on such formulas. But the degree to which Indigenous interactions with both outsiders and with one another revolved around such quotation and reliance on collective speech seemed remarkable. Such quotation, as Miyako Inoue's work suggests (2006), can itself entail that which it cites, giving life to those historical subjects who are made manifest, in part, through the deictic function of reported speech. And just as clearly in Fanon's Algeria at midcentury as in the Northern Territory communities where many of my interlocutors work at the beginning of the twenty-first, audio media themselves both interpellate listeners and report speech, staging forms of collective life and cultural worlds that they at once presume and entail.[6] The everyday work of tying speech to bodies in northern Australia implicates institutions as well, vying for position and the success of their particular projects within this often rambunctious institutional field.

Together I see these features of Aboriginal media as driving a form of immanent alterity, in which the differences I encountered derive value and durability from the mediatized field of cultural production itself as much as they do from a cultural past or traditional ground of cultural alterity. The work of making such media makes the content of Aboriginal distinction an overt concern, one that enters into the expressive practices and working lives of my interlocutors in a central way, requiring of my interlocutors a certain reflexivity and sense of self-awareness about the substance of Indigenous distinction vis-à-vis a settler colony as well as other kinds of black identity in other colonial and postcolonial domains. The voice is one highly charged site where such alterity is both problematized and produced in forms of everyday practice. The capacity of media's machines to generate such alterity and lend it value is the complement of their power to produce relations and make such relations knowable through their aural doubling.

Relationship

I close with an account of a hunting trip that at first seemed to take me far from the music and radio studios I'd come to study. During the dry season of 2004, Tracy, her five-year-old niece, and I drove TEABBA's four-wheel-drive to the small community of Palumpa, several hours southwest of Darwin in the Daly River region.[7] We traveled to Palumpa nominally to repair some technical equipment and provide a lesson to the community manager on the technical operation of the community's broadcast service. But this trip also exercised relationships between generations of kin in Darwin, and the extension of those relations into the country and between urban Aboriginal producers and their remote interlocutors in the northwestern Northern Territory. Tracy's cousin Colin was teaching in the community, and this was a chance to bring niece and cousins together for a few days, to join Colin's friends and new relations in this community. I have been at pains to suggest at several moments in this book that making media here is as much about the relation between crafting kinds of kinship and identity across forms of intra-Indigenous difference as it is about the reproduction of a particular Indigenous distinction and difference from a broader settler Australian polity. In these terms media enable a range of relations across generations and across historically resonant forms of intra-Indigenous difference. These relations are the rewards of linking up, of embracing the vocal uncanny and the alterity of speaking for another as the very ground of sociality itself.

For workers in media organizations like TEABBA, social ties to communities across the Top End shape fundamentally the meaning of the work they do as cultural producers. Work in such organizations can become the ground of possibility for a range of other kinds of relations and forms of social life. This was a trip to examine the tie-line and radio broadcasting gear housed in Palumpa's BRACS station. Tracy would train the community's nominated radio producer in some technical aspects of the broadcasting gear, and would also have a close look at the gear itself, assessing whether further technical attention would be required to get the station up and running. In addition to her school-teaching cousin, Tracy also had other long-standing ties to some of the older people there who had worked with TEABBA in the past. This also then was a chance to introduce Tracy's niece to the Palumpa mob, give her an early introduction to some features of bush life, and to go hunting for geese—a prized treat for the Christmas season just a few months in the future. In short, a trip to repair the radio gear doubled as a chance to go hunting with old friends from the community and to begin involving her niece in this broader social world.

After a long morning on the road we spent the late afternoon and evening in the community's radio studio, a cement room with radio and television retransmission gear stacked in its center. The radio and broadcasting gear was in a small, locked room at the back of a large, tin-roofed, cement-floored structure. "Ooh, disco!" Tracy remarked as we walked through the hall, littered with colored paper and dirt, walls seemingly still vibrating from the previous night's dance party. Once inside the broadcasting room Tracy ran through the equipment, checking for malfunction and demonstrating for the community manager and an Indigenous broadcaster the few tasks needed to take control of the local broadcast, inserting a local radio show in place of the regional broadcasts coming from TEABBA's Darwin studio. Tracy's niece sat in a plastic chair in the corner, bored. I struggled to keep up with Tracy's demonstration, watching her run through the wall of satellite and communications gear that made up the community's BRACS station.

The centerpiece of the trip for Tracy, her niece, and the group of men hanging around outside the BRACS studio was the hunt. The next morning we clambered into two Toyota Troop Carriers and drove north out of the community. We first drove slowly along a track through some dense gum trees adjacent to the community itself. Tracy and I sat in the second car, behind her niece and her cousin Colin, an old man, and a very young boy in the first car. After a signal from the first truck we stopped, and Tracy and I watched as the old man stepped out of the passenger side with a small-caliber rifle, aimed into the bush, and fired. He missed the kangaroo he'd seen moving in the bush, so we drove on, repeating this exercise several more times before exiting the gum trees and moving onto an immense, clear escarpment. These were the Plains of Peppimenarti, made famous in the eponymous country song by Slim Dusty. I'd been hearing about this place for some time, on the radio and in that yodeling cowboy song, a tune that celebrates Aboriginal stockmen, bringing custom and the fun of chasing bullocks together in a romantic, musical celebration of a place famed for its community-owned cattle station.

Tracy and I shared grins and shouts over the engine's roar and the wind coming in the open windows as a group of wild horses overtook the Toyotas, manes flying behind them. The old men up front led us across the plains to a storied baobab tree sitting alone beside a dry creek bed. One of the men had seen evidence of wild pigs here the week before, and Colin hoped for a shot at one. There was no sign of pigs on this visit, so despite the men's disappointment, we moved on, Tracy pointing out the horses, still moving along the plains in the distance. Ahead Colin spotted the bustling and brief flights of a large cluster of wild ducks, gathered on the floodplain around an enormous tree, itself alone in the middle of a sea of long grass. Colin climbed down from his truck holding a shotgun. He closed in on the birds, took aim, and then shot twice. As the ducks took flight, he reloaded and shot again, then looked back and shouted to the young boy, who lurched out from beside the Troopie, running after Colin and helping to collect armfuls of fallen birds, many still struggling. The rest of us followed, moving more slowly but joining in, scooping up dead and wounded fowl and stuffing them into the rear compartment of the Troop Carrier.

C.1–C.3 Ducks flee from shotgun fire, Palumpa,
Northern Territory, 2004.

Back at Palumpa, the real work commenced as Tracy's niece and I joined others around the back of the Troop Carrier. We were each handed a duck and taught to wring the bird's neck before skinning it, holding firmly around the long neck and spinning the body clockwise, using its weight to break the neck. We then used sharp kitchen knives to carve a ring around its throat, tracing a line through tough skin and feather. Colin showed us how a strong grip would allow one to peel the feathered skin back from the body, pulling it away with a series of sharp tugs as though it were a close-fitting wrapper. We worked our way, laboriously, through the birds left (some still struggling) in the rear of the truck. I found myself working to match the efficiency and intent determination of Tracy's young niece, who showed no signs of squeamishness as she dug into the task. The skinned fowl were then split into two bunches, one to circulate through the community itself, redistributed by our host—the old man who directed our Troopies—and the other to be brought back to Darwin for the freezers of Tracy and Colin's extended families.

That night the community clerk had us all around to his house for a beer (banned by this community's local council but allowed in the white manager's house). He lectured Colin on the cost of the hunt: the liters of petrol, the bullets, and the time spent didn't add up, he argued, when compared to the frozen or fried chicken you could buy at the community store. To Colin and Tracy, though, that argument missed the value of one's own meat in the freezer, the chance to share around a large bounty with one's relations in the community, to show a small girl the proper way to kill and dress a bird, and the thrill of guns and the chase across the plains. Like the work Tracy came to do on the community's media equipment, "meat" was not the only thing at issue here. Rather, it was the relations activated in the chase itself and in the gifting of frozen carcasses and the celebration that followed. A short trip to train a media worker and inspect some broadcasting equipment here turned into a three-day visit, with hunting and parenting animating a range of social relations to the community, to a cousin from Darwin and that cousin's relations in Palumpa, and to the media crew in the community and to the community clerk himself, then responsible for Palumpa's day-to-day financial and administrative tasks. It was also an occasion to bring Tracy's niece into the presence of these people, to allow for her education in hunting and dressing wild birds, participating in a broader kin network through the distribution of food. Making media here, then, was also a means to a different end, to social relatedness itself.

There are other relations to which one might attend in this story, with wild birds, and their subsequent transformation into meat, with the complicated local relations to country and the gum-strewn plains across which our afternoon unfolded (those relations mediated by histories of missionization and enterprise in the Daly River region), and also between Troop Carriers, rifles, and women and men and kids—the technologies of mobility and power by which the hunt made a corporate body from a collection of very different people, countrymen (and kids) from community, Indigenous Darwinites (and kids), and of course a white anthropologist. But the transformation of the fowl from animal to food to gift meant a shift from bird to meat to medium of social reproduction—not so much in the necessity of hunted meat and its procurement, but in the ways that such meat carries this relation, makes it an object both of reflection and, now, argument—a place to pause and teach and talk about things shared but also a thing to defend. In this it's not dissimilar to what audio media amplify in those avatars of the voice that double sociality and make it available for reflection, for thought and also for surveillance, argument, or critique.

Aboriginal people frequently are compelled to think and talk about such practices and are occasionally made to defend them. This puts Indigenous Australians in particular kinds of reflexive relationship to practices central both to political life and to forms of everyday social reproduction and kinship relation—hunting and shooting, or making radio and listening to music. In retrospect I am struck by the great attention to production involved in our afternoon. The two moments that I remember most strongly, that scarcely require reference to my field notes, are discussions about petrol and bullets, critiques of the economy of the hunt from a white manager, and the work of making the carcasses into mobile gifts. This particular hunt should be understood as completely entangled with broader networks of media and mobility, with the technical management of audio media that here provided Tracy's alibi for a visit. Here the sociality of hunting cannot easily be separated from media making as cultural production. In both people often must stop and reflect, justify, and argue or even perhaps take a new tack, as Colin did when faced with the critiques of a white community manager, as Gary did when facing a particularly difficult survey, and as Donna did in the face of a missionary radio service with different ideas. This book has sought to better understand the political stakes of such reflection as a politics of aspiration, and to understand the ways such a politics takes shape in sound.

NOTES

Prologue

1 Throughout the text of this book I use pseudonyms to refer to my interlocutors. In a few instances where individuals are highly public figures, I retain their proper names.

2 Aboriginal Australia is filled with institutions, and acronyms are a local way of keeping track of the many Indigenous and governmental corporations. TEABBA is the first of many I will introduce in this book, and is spoken as "*Tee*-ba." I have retained these organizational names in the text and provide a glossary of acronyms to assist readers as they move through the chapters to follow.

3 *Yidaki* is the term in a number of Arnhem Land languages for what is called in Australian English a didgeridoo.

4 Mauboy's career took a positive turn the following year when she finished as the runner-up in the popular television program *Australian Idol*. Her initial audition for the program was an a capella rendition of Whitney Houston's "I Have Nothing," sung outdoors for a panel of celebrity judges. The stylization of her voice had radically shifted as the country sounds of the previous year—characterized by the cry break and the flat twang—were supplanted by a broad, controlled vibrato and melismatic flourishes.

5 For analyses that reflect on the interanimation of Aboriginal activism with broader concerns around cultural imperialism see Ginsburg 1994, 1995, 1997 and Michaels 1994; cf. Langton 1993.

Introduction

1 Papua New Guinea was governed by Australia from 1902 until its independence in 1975.

2 Batty's unpublished PhD dissertation provides a detailed account of the governmental interests in Indigenous media during the 1970s and is informed in part by his role as cofounder of the Central Australian Aboriginal Media Association (2005). Tim Rowse places Coombs and the rise of Aboriginal corporate representation at the center of the project of self-determination underscoring Coombs's investment in listening to Indigenous Australia in forms of dialogic relation rather than imposition (Rowse 2000).

3 Coombs is perhaps the most prominent of such non-Indigenous activists. He joined senior diplomat Barrie Dexter and anthropologist W. E. H. Stanner on the Council for Aboriginal Affairs, an advisory body established in the wake of a 1967 constitutional referendum that affirmed the authority of Parliament to craft law with respect to Aboriginal people. This authority had previously been vested in states and, significantly, Parliament had been expressly forbidden from crafting such legislation. The referendum and the council's subsequent efforts are understood today to mark the beginning of the era of self-determination as official commonwealth policy.

4 In addition to Peters's analysis, Mladen Dolar (2006) and Adriana Cavarero (2005) provide distinct critiques of a medium-focused account of voice, one based on its status as psychic object, the other on its irreducibly embodied character.

5 Durham Peters glosses these categories as "power, medium, art, organ, and eros" (2004:88).

6 See Latour 1993 for an analogous account of modernity as "purification" and "hybridization."

7 I have been assisted in this analysis by several writers who offer either exegetical analysis or critique of Lacan's writings on voice (Copjec 1996; Dolar 2006; Gordon 1997; Stokes 2010). Dolar's attention to Jacques Derrida's historicization of speech in its relation to writing, for instance, thus privileges the antinomial character of "voice" and "speech/writing"—noting the privileged but elusive and always deferred character of the former, its relationship as exception or constitutive externality to the seeming coherence and containment of the latter.

8 The resonance of this figure with the work of Mikhail Bakhtin will be apparent to many readers. My interest here, however, rests in the ways that the "social voice" that exercises much of Bakhtin's work on heteroglossia and dialogism can also be opaque, underdetermined in its shape and historical development, the outcome of contest (see Stokes 2010; cf. Copjec 1996; Povinelli 2003).

9 I find Slavoj Žižek's critique of the relation Michel Foucault posits between sex and sexuality helpful in figuring the shared territory of voice in Australia. For Žižek, Foucault "overlooks" a fundamental antagonism in the relation between sex and the various discourses and practices which constitute sexuality: "'sex' is therefore not the universality, the neutral common ground of discursive practices which constitute 'sexuality,' but rather *their common stumbling block*, their common point of failure" (Žižek 1992: 124, emphasis in original). Likewise, "voice" is

not the "neutral" territory shared by Indigenous people and government through a series of practices and institutions dedicated to "voicing", but rather a point of shared interest and divergence, their common stumbling block.

10 On an anthropology of hope see Miyazaki 2004 and Robbins 2013. For critical accounts of hope as reimagined from the ground of endurance and potentiality, see Povinelli 2011; see also Holbraad, Pedersen, and Viveiros de Castro 2013.

11 Here the forms of desire and aspiration in question are at once those of my Indigenous interlocutors, of various representatives and agencies of the settler state, and also of anthropology through its ethical commitment to the agency and otherness of its interlocutors (Gordon 1997). See also Holbraad, Pedersen, and Viveiros de Castro 2013 and Stevenson 2014 on recognizing the otherness of the other.

12 The mediatization of voice has long been a productive avenue for ethnographic and critical theoretical interests in the study of sound and technology, as scholars debate the place of the voice in cultural production, as at once a principle, embodied phenomena and the most proximate fulcrum of social life (Feld et al. 2004), and also as an intensely mediated site of ideological investment and metaphorical elaboration (Weidman 2006; Dolar 2006; Chion 1998). This conversation spans work on the voice in opera and the phonograph (Koestenbaum 1993), the relationship of audio technologies to a "sonic afro-modernity" and radical black aesthetics (Moten 2003; Weheliye 2005), the "ideologies of voice" that emerge as voice and violin stage one another in South Indian musical performance (Weidman 2006), and the way FM radio provides new expressive avenues for Nepali speech (Kunreuther 2014). Such scholarship suggests the power of technology to inform technique and to both amplify and reify the voice as icon of identity, expression of interiority, and a fundamental index of self-presence (cf. Derrida 1976; Dolar 2006).

13 Allen Weiss (1995) thus approaches the radio voice's historical apprehension through the mediatization of the voice-body relation and the "indissociability of techne and psyche." For Weiss this is not to leave the body behind in a focus on mediatized sound, but to ask how the radio voice is made to relate to body, granting both a phantasmic character in the face of their techno-social dispersal: "There exists a point, unlocalizable and mysterious, where listener and radio are indistinguishable. We therefore seek that realm where the voice reaches beyond its body, beyond the shadow of its corporeal origins, to become a radically original sonic object" (1995: 7).

14 This logic is also implied in Brian Larkin's analysis of what he terms the "colonial sublime": the use of a range of media infrastructure as both the magical might of colonial power and its modern promise (2008).

15 The key text in such work is David J. Bolter and Richard Grusin's *Remediation* (1998). While they are concerned primarily with visual representation, their attention to the generative relation between interests in crafting immediacy and a

reflexive hypermediation that draws attention to technologies and techniques of mediation themselves proves generative in the radio and music studio, where the voice is itself de- and renaturalized as a form of media, an index of identity, and a medium of affective, collective life. To think the voice in this register, then, is to foreground its remediation in terms of an oscillation between involvement and distanciation.

16 Ana Maria Ochoa's (2014) history of the relation between voice and ear in late colonial and early postcolonial Colombia, though manifestly interested in the shifting ontological and epistemological ground that listening to the archive may make available, provides a powerful account of the emergence of a mediatized voice—a sounded voice inscribed for circulation, and this in a moment in which voices can be imagined as requiring as yet uninvented portable recording devices. She cites a North American traveler, Isaac F. Holton, who recalls the sounds of Colombian barge workers for his mid-nineteenth-century travelogue: "Their cry was tremendous. Oh for some method incapable of exaggeration, like the photographic process, to record it and compel belief!" (in Ochoa 2014:39).

17 Rosalind Morris (2000) and Miyako Inoue (2006) each provide remarkable monograph-length studies that lend historical and ethnographic nuance to this way of reckoning mediatization, the former focused on the opening up of a problematics of loss, a concern with misplaced origins, and the latter addressing the hypostatization of a gendered category from its mediatized voice.

18 Jennifer Deger (2006) offers a sophisticated analysis that draws on this mode of media's capacity to "present" rather than simply "represent." Her work, however, focuses on the local, Yolngu interest in forms of cultural process and cosmology that media production abetted in its capacity to make present Indigenous ancestral power and precedent.

19 This unsettling character resonates differently across a wide range of literatures interested in exploring forms of haunting and the uncanny. Ken Gelder and Jane Jacobs (1998) write of the repressed violence of colonial history and its emergence as an uncanny possible presence of the sacred for settler Australians. Avery Gordon (1997) writes compellingly of the different ways that the "sociological imagination" might entertain such ghosts, to see in them an absence that can register both loss and the past and also, simultaneously, "a future possibility, a hope" (61–62).

20 Peter Limb (2008) and Gary Foley (2001) differently single out the 1971 Springboks tour as galvanizing Aboriginal Australian senses of solidarity and identification. Where Limb suggests its catalyzing effect, Foley places the Springbok's tour in the context of a tumultuous year for Sydney's "black power group" that included the opening of the Aboriginal Medical Service in Redfern, an institution that gave concrete form to the ideals of "the young Redfern radicals who had created it," and a game-changing speech by activist Paul Coe to an anti-Vietnam rally at Sydney, calling out the hypocrisy of white protests against Vietnam, yet blindness to Aboriginal dispossession (Foley 2001).

21 These particular analytics for questioning global pop travel through the twin foundational critical texts of Paul Gilroy's *The Black Atlantic* (1993) and Eric Lott's *Love and Theft* (1994), which sketch some broad coordinates for understanding Afro-diasporic musics and minstrelsy as driving engines of not just American but of a global popular culture (cf. McLary 1998).

22 Kodwo Eshun's (1998) posthuman manifesto and Alexander Weheliye's (2002) critical engagement with the category's presumptions each theorize the post-human by staging its conditions of possibility vis-à-vis black cultural production (2002). Both also prioritize sounding over speaking and foreground facets of timbre, beat, and vocal synthesis in their efforts to problematize a white liberal subject that they argue covertly continues to animate a posthuman imaginary (see also Veal 2007). In so doing they build a critical counternarrative to a Eurocentrism in Heidegger's writing and in its reinterpretation by Kittler (1994). Closer to the ground of Indigenous media, the writing of novelist Alexis Wright (2013) opens a fictional window on a northern Australia whose apocalypse has already come, exploring relations between humans and their nonhuman alters in what might be termed a critical Indigenous futurism.

23 While key texts in this literature include Gilroy 1993 and Hebdige 1987, I have been assisted in thinking critically with this scholarship by George Lewis's writings on the racialized distribution of composition (1996, 2008) and by Steven Feld's (2012) critique of the reprimitivization of Ghanaian musicians (and "Africa" more broadly) in jazz scholarship.

24 Scholarly works that begin to trace the complex travels of such Afro-diasporic forms beyond the Atlantic include Jones 2001 and Condry 2006.

25 The poem's full text is archived with Noonuccal's collected papers in the University of Queensland's Fryer Rare Books Library. I thank Hilary Emmett for assistance in procuring this text.

26 It is in this sense that Faye Ginsburg discusses Aboriginal media as a practice of "mediation" (drawing on the sense of this term most closely linked to the notion of "intermediary") and foregrounds the activities of those Indigenous cultural activists she terms "border crossers" (Ginsburg 1991: 106).

27 There is a rich scholarship on this phenomena best represented perhaps by the long-term research on film and television of Faye Ginsburg (1991, 1993, 1994, 2002, 2012). See also Batty 2003, 2005; Langton 1993; Michaels 1994; Molnar and Meadows 2001; Wilmott 1984.

28 One of Fred Myers's more arresting examples of this revolves around a request for cigarettes (1989: 20).

29 This situation emerged in part from the advocacy of Alan Lomax and his efforts (supported by the Library of Congress) to curate the diversity of American folk music traditions as recorded and broadcast audio, and to thereby encourage a conversation on American identity (Szwed 2011). For accounts of *isicathamiya*, a South African popular music, and its relation to radio airplay see Gunner 2012.

In Peru, see Fisher 2004. Discussions of the American and Canadian developments can be found in Guralnick 1994 and Szwed 2011.

30 I have, however, found Cody's recent literature review (2011) to be a helpful and recent reorientation to such questions.

31 See, for instance, Chris Anderson 1995 and Myers 1986 and 2004 for central Australia; Morphy 1991 and Williams 1986 for northeast Arnhem Land.

32 For further discussions see Chris Anderson 1995; Berndt 1962; Deger 2004; Ginsburg 1994, 1995; Michaels 1994; Myers 2002.

33 For further accounts of such negotiations see Bryson 2002; Corn 2009; Deger 2004, 2013; Ginsburg 1994, 1995; Myers 2004; Toner 2003, 2005.

34 Myers 2004 provides a particularly striking monograph-length account with respect to the emergence and remarkable international success of Indigenous fine art.

35 The capacity to selectively distribute by virtue of firewalls and password-protected access has also informed the construction of databases of traditional cultural knowledge (see Christen 2008; Christie 2008).

Chapter 1: Mediating Kinship

1 Adorno's famous analysis of the miniaturization that the symphony undergoes in its broadcast amplifies the sense that this equation with the advertisement means a profound transformation of symphonic power, from dynamic expansiveness in the singular realization of the work to its reification and replication as broadcast commodity (Adorno 1990).

2 As the volume of programming has grown, as stations come to share the burden of content production, and as digital technologies come to automate many aspects of production, these stations increasingly operate twenty-four hours a day, seven days a week.

3 Helmreich (2007) offers a provocative argument for thinking sound and mediation ethnographically, positing "transduction" as a more ethnographically perspicacious concept metaphor for forms of sonic mediation than "soundscape" or "immersion." Transduction comes to apply both to the mediation of sound and the kinds of "turbulence" that characterize forms of ethnographic knowledge production.

4 Michaels was appointed to an Australian Institute for Aboriginal Studies research project to "assess the impact of commercial TV on Aboriginal communities" (Michaels 1990). He did so through work both on the ways that Warlpiri people watched television, the distinctive aspects of their interpretive perspective, and on the ways that Warlpiri people produced TV, organizing much as they would for ritual production and sharing the work between "owners" and "managers" (Michaels 1994). Michaels and Kelly became high-profile advocates for the support for Indigenous broadcasting before Michaels's death in Brisbane in 1990 (see Michaels 1994, 1997).

5 Of those Aboriginal people in prison, the overwhelming majority serve short terms (80 percent under three months, 90 percent under six months) for offenses related to driving, the possession of illegal drugs, the possession of stolen goods, and/or assault and domestic violence (Krieg 2006; MacDonald 1996).

6 Media theorists such as Friedrich Kittler (1999) might turn such logic around, arguing perhaps that the language of media networks has birthed contemporary figures of kinship and its relational possibilities. Edwards and Strathern (2000) offer analyses that figure kinship's calibration with forms of technology in more dialectical terms, and here I resist the temptation to figure either media or kinship as historically or ontologically foundational.

7 I draw this term from Edwards and Strathern, whose work refers to the ways in which networks "co-mobilise different orders of phenomena" (2000: 162).

8 Ginsburg argues an analogous point in her discussion of Aboriginal visual media and their "embedded aesthetics" (1994). For Ginsburg, Aboriginal producers placed an emphasis on the social relations that media as a practice entails and sustains. Ginsburg terms this orientation "embedded aesthetics" in order to "draw attention to a system of evaluation that refuses a separation of textual production and circulation from broader arenas of social relations" (1994: 368; see also Salazar and Cordova 2008).

9 In the Northern Territory, where Indigenous people account for 29 percent of the total population, Aboriginal people account for 77 percent of the prison population (ABS 2002, 2004).

10 As of 2011, mobile phones receive much better coverage in the remote Northern Territory as Australia's 3G network has been expanded to include many Indigenous communities. The consequences of increased telecommunication have yet to be studied systematically, but see Deger 2013 for a brief exploration of the relationship between mobile phones and photography and video and Mansfield 2014 for an account of the significance of mobile telephone technologies for music circulation in the remote northwestern Northern Territory.

11 For a more detailed discussion see Lisa Stefanoff's extended interview with Thornton (2006).

12 "Youse" is an Australian colloquial plural of "you."

13 "Bre," "Bourke," and "Gunyah" refer to the New South Wales country towns of Brewarrina, Bourke, and Enngonia.

14 Chloe Hooper provides a novelized journalistic account (2008) that focuses on anxieties about wildness and the mimetic relation between white projections of violence and police presumptions of its necessity in their work.

15 Helpful material on the Stolen Generations can be found in Attwood 2001; Cummings 1990; Haebich 2000; Read 1999.

16 The suspension of Australia's 1975 Racial Discrimination Act, which prevented inequitable treatment under overtly racial criteria, has been one of the more reviled measures of the so-called Intervention.

17 This may be traced historically to the extensive reach of classificatory forms of kinship reckoning in Aboriginal Australia (Sutton 1998).

18 This can be usefully contrasted with the work of Gerd Baumann on the Southhall use of kin terms in crafting and concretizing forms of intraethnic relatedness as friendship (1995). Where Baumann saw the power of kin terms in their application across cultural boundaries, for my interlocutors in northern Australia it is in the sense that the kinds of kinship they value and reproduce are distinct—are more precisely not shared (with settler Australians)—that they become valuable as an icon of Indigenous distinction and singularity.

19 For distinct elaborations of this idea see Merlan 1981; Myers 1986; Povinelli 2002; Schneider 1972; Schwab 1988.

20 I have heard people express their aboriginality not just by reference to such specific relations, but also by oblique reference to figures of classificatory kinship, by which one's relationship to any other Aboriginal person, in principle, can be described in kin terms. This becomes a means for many Aboriginal (and non-Indigenous) people to figure Aboriginal Australia as a "kin-based" society, in contradistinction to the "stranger relationality" presumed to govern public affairs in settler Australia (see also Gelder and Jacobs 1998; Warner 2005).

21 One of Elvis's best-known recordings is his "Jailhouse Rock," written by Jerry Leiber and Mike Stoller and released as a single in 1957. Johnny Cash, on the other hand, is remembered for his 1955 single "Folsom Prison Blues," and equally for a live performance at Folsom Prison in 1968, recorded and subsequently released as a full-length live album, *Johnny Cash at Folsom Prison* (1968).

22 Producers at 4AAA are also attentive to the broad appeal of country music for non-Indigenous Australians and at times figure their broader broadcasting endeavor in part around this shared appeal. In these moments they describe their work as a practice of antiracist representation built on the popularity of country music to recruit a maximally diverse audience of both Aboriginal and settler Australians.

23 See Rowse 1993 for a historical critique of the application of Goffman's analytical constructs to Aboriginal missions and reserves.

24 Such work further argues that the kinds of publics convened may depend on ideologies of immediacy and transparency surrounding broadcast media (Morris 2000). The perceived limits to a mediatized "immediacy" have also been explored by Silverstein (2008) in his discussion of radio-mediated Sufi devotional practice.

25 A growing body of ethnographic and media studies work places such concerns in a sensory register (Seremetakis 1996; Hirschkind 2006; cf. Buck-Morss 1996). Much as I intend here, this scholarship understands "affects and sensibilities" as foundational for kinds of public deliberation more frequently figured in terms of rational, instrumental reason, and places the public vehicles of such affect at the center of their attentions.

1 Among many connections, the famous soul and funk record label Stax was founded in 1957 by country fiddler–turned-banker Jim Stewart (Gordon 2013). In 1959 he was joined by his elder sister, Estelle Axton, in the company Satellite Records, later renamed with the combination of the first two letters of their surnames as Stax.

2 David Samuels's (2004, 2009) work with San Carlos Apache and Kristina Jacobsen-Bia's (2009, 2014) research in Navajo country provide historical and ethnographic accounts of the particularity of country's Native significance, emphasizing the centrality of radio media to the movement of country musics across reservation lands and, in Jacobsen-Bia's work (2009), the musicalization of radio's sonic signature. Byron Dueck's (2013) work in Winnipeg extends these interests to the "civil twilight" that marks spaces of alcohol and country music consumption alike.

3 Straw here calls for popular music studies to look to relationships between "musical localism" and translocal alliances and processes, industrial/commercial or otherwise. His full quotation reads: "Basing a politics of local or Canadian music on the search for musical forms whose relationship to musical communities is that of a long-term and evolving expressivity will lead us to overlook ways in which the making and remaking of alliances between communities are the crucial political processes within popular musics" (1991: 370).

4 While Samuels (2009) notes the ways a similar question—"How is it possible for Native North Americans to so deeply appreciate the music of those most identified with their exploitation?"—acts to alienate Native North American engagements with country, my question here is not "How can Aboriginal people love a music that is not their own?" but, rather, "How did country become their own?" How that is, does country become tradition?

5 Notable exceptions to this include Beckett 1993, Ottoson 2006 and Walker 2000.

6 Slim Newton rose to fame in the early 1970s with his hit single "Red Back on the Toilet Seat." The song continues to figure as an Australian classic in country performance.

7 I draw Williams's recollections from Egan's episode of the television program *Frontiers Down Under*, titled "Country Outcasts" and produced in 1979.

8 Jeremy Beckett, personal communication, May 2007.

9 I thank Ian Bedford and Jeremy Beckett for their recollections and insights into Young's music and popularity.

10 Young's renown extended to a national folk scene when Beckett's early recordings of Young were released on the Australian label Wattle Records (Beckett 1993; cf. Gilbert 1974; Walker 2000).

11 I thank Clint Walker for alerting me to the significance of cassette tape distribution in Charley Pride's popularity. As he put it to me in 2013: "The records were

actually available, in Charley's case, because he was with a big, big major label, RCA, . . . and another thing there is that in the '70s into the '80s, RCA was really big on cassettes, and cassettes were the way music was consumed in the bush in Australia."

12 In publicity interviews, Chris O'Dowd was quick to note that he had grown up with soul music, channeled in Ireland through the enormous success of the 1991 film *The Commitments*.

13 Some observers in the United States see in such overuse a caricature of melisma.

14 Clutsam was a well-known composer and performer in London, but his professional career began in Australian and New Zealand blackface and minstrel tours as a pianist at the turn of the century. In the 1950s and 1960s a number of African American singers including Harry Belafonte, Odetta, and Marian Anderson traveled through, meeting with Pastor Doug Nicholls and, as Ann Curthoys puts it, seeking out Aboriginal people (2010). Robeson himself visited Sydney in the last months of 1960. While this visit was occasioned by a profitable Australian and New Zealand concert tour, Robeson and his wife, Eslanda Robeson, sought out and met with both Trade Unionists and Aboriginal activists such as Faith Bandler, herself a former singer and longtime fan and admirer of Robeson (Curthoys 2010; Juddery 2015).

15 Orpheus McAdoo, an early member and director of the Fisk Jubilee Singers, and impresario of groups including the Virginia Concert Company and Jubilee Singers, passed away in Sydney in 1900 and is buried in Waverly Cemetery in Sydney's eastern suburbs.

16 On "diasporic intimacy" see Boym 1998 and Feld 2012.

17 This technique can be heard in a pared-down form on Otis Redding's breakout 1962 single "These Arms of Mine," one of Stax's first hits on their subsidiary label Volt. Redding's Stax contemporaries recall the "tear" in Redding's voice as a principal means by which his singing resonated as soulful (see Robert Gordon 2013).

Chapter 3: From the Studio to the Street

1 I thank Faye Ginsburg for this observation (personal communication, October 2013).

2 "Not hearing the Voice, the listener would sometimes leave the needle on a jammed wave length or one that simply produced static, and would announce that the voice of the combatants was here. For an hour the room would be filled with the piercing, excruciating din of the jamming. Behind each modulation, each active crackling, the Algerian would imagine not only words, but concrete battles. The war of the sound waves, in the gourbi, reenacts for the benefit of the citizen the armed clash of his people and colonialism" (Fanon 1994 [1965]: 87–88).

3 This is, of course, a fundamental problematic of vocal mediation that has been productively explored in contexts of mediumship (Morris 2000; Siegel 1998,

2006) as well as in historical and philosophical tracts that thematize Western concerns with voice, presence, interiority, and the sociality of communication (see Bakhtin 1981; Derrida 1976; Dolar 2006; Durham Peters 1999).

4 This will be recognized by many readers as the distinction in Marx queried by Gayatri Spivak (1988) positing the difficulty of locating the subaltern subject of voice in the first instance, insofar as a command to speak is historically entangled with a politics of subaltern relation.

5 For an analogous account of institutionalized avant-garde music production as an intensively visual endeavor, see Born 1995.

6 The ethnographic material in this section is discussed in a different analytical framework in Fisher 2010.

7 These latter primarily valued country music, and often figured this genre as a kind of shared territory—a common ground between Indigenous communities and the supposedly "redneck" white listeners who also tuned in to 4AAA.

8 *Gammon* is an Aboriginal English term that can be variously glossed as "fake," "untrue," or "broken." For further discussion of this important term see Fisher 2010.

9 *Bruz* is a vocative pronoun conjoining both "cousin" and "brother" frequently heard in the Aboriginal English of southeast Queensland.

10 The ARIA awards in Australia are national industry awards roughly equivalent to the North American Grammy Awards.

11 The full text of "The Black Commandments" can be found in Noonuccal's archived papers at the University of Queensland's Fryer Rare Books Library. It reads:

1. Thou shall gather thy scattered people together.
2. Thou shalt work for black liberation.
3. Thou shalt resist assimilation with all thy might.
4. Thou shalt not become a black liberal in white society.
5. Thou shalt not uphold white lies in black society.
6. Thou shalt take back the land stolen from thy forefathers.
7. Thou shalt meet white violence with black violence.
8. Thou shalt remove thyself from a sick white society.
9. Thou shalt find peace and happiness in a stable black society.
10. Thou shalt think black and act black.
11. Thou shall be black all the rest of thy days.

12 This shift from campaigns around race and Black Power toward the politics of land rights and autochthony is canvassed in detail in Attwood 2003 and Williams 1986.

13 The "proximity effect" refers to the amplification of lower frequencies when placing a microphone closer to a sound source. This is a feature of microphone use and placement that producers may take advantage of in recording some voices or instruments, or seek to minimize in recording others.

14 Although I am drawn to this figure by moments at which particular subjects are unsettled by the forms their own voices take, this is not primarily a psychoanalytic account. If, in Freud's writings (1990 [1919]) the uncanny names a feeling of alterity within the self as a return of the repressed, here I describe an alterity that owes more to the technologically plastic character of mediatized speech and a social and historically informed ambivalence around black lingo than to an "originary violence" or repression (cf. Derrida 1976).

15 In his analysis of public affect in Turkish popular song, Martin Stokes (2010) describes the voice as a paradigmatic form of Lacan's *objet petit a*. Both of and other to the voicing body, the voice cannot be simply "quilted" into the symbolic order and thus becomes a "quasi-independent object of aesthetic attention and erotic quest" (2010: 7). As objects of amplified interest and anxiety, voices thus generate discourse. As Stokes does for popular music in Turkey, I have focused here on studio talk and the mediatized voice as amplifying the voice's already reflexive social life, and I have situated that talk historically with respect to recent transformations of Aboriginal public culture.

16 The broadest Australian response has been the Special Broadcasting Service, which has a focus on multicultural broadcasting and, in Ang's terms, a mandate to make cultural diversity "a matter of public representation" (2008: 3).

17 Recordings of these projects gained a great deal of attention in 2002 when students from Wilcannia performing as Wilcannia Mob won a Deadly (a prestigious Indigenous award similar to an Oscar or Grammy) for their track "Down River," which also received extensive airplay on community and mainstream stations around Australia.

18 Eisenstein's feature films are singled out as characteristic: "The particular characteristics of the screen as a cognitive organ enabled audiences not only to 'see' this new collective protagonist, but (through eidetic reduction) to 'see' the idea of the unity of the revolutionary people, the collective sovereignty of the masses, the idea of international solidarity, the idea of revolution itself" (Buck-Morss 1996: 52).

19 Like Kittler, Buck-Morss also makes an epistemological claim, suggesting that the camera as "prosthesis of perception" provides Husserl's phenomenological *epoché* with its unacknowledged prototype. "The objective, historically transient reality which he wants to bracket *out* of the cogitatio penetrates precisely into that realm of 'reduced' mental acts where he thought himself most secure (Buck-Morss 1996: 58, italics in original).

Chapter 4: From Radio Skid Row to the Reconciliation Station

1 For a comprehensive discography of this period of Aboriginal recording see Gibson 1994 and Walker 2000.

2 Us Mob were a band managed by 4AAA's manager Tiga Bayles, whom I introduce in this chapter and whose 1981 performance tour of New South Wales was chronicled in the filmic documentary travelogue *Wrong Side of the Road* (1981).

3 The ABC investigative journalism magazine *Four Corners* followed up a *Courier-Mail* newspaper story, broadcasting an investigative report in 1987 that alleged widespread corruption within Queensland's police. This led to further media attention and, eventually, to the selection of G. E. "Tony" Fitzgerald, QC, to head the inquiry.

4 An effort to understand the value of art and to critique its radical separation from gross material concerns, so powerfully articulated by Bourdieu's diagnosis of the field of cultural production as the "economic world reversed" (1993), also redefines creative work as labor. Fred Myers tracks similar tendencies in the emergence of Aboriginal fine art, noting a recurrent effort to make such cultural production self-sufficient, commercially viable and thus independent of government subvention (see Myers 2002).

5 "Smart State" is the title of Queensland's cultural development policy, aimed at "maximizing" Queensland citizens' opportunities to participate in the "new economy." Creative Nation is a similar, national policy introduced in the 1990s by Prime Minister Paul Keating.

6 Rennie and Featherstone (2008) provide a concise account of the advent of the National Indigenous Television Service (better known in Australia as NITV) that canvasses the institutional history of Indigenous media activism.

7 Collins's conflation of Skid Row and Radio Redfern also points to the close operating relationship between these organizations, one that has tended to be backgrounded in historical recounting in recognition of a political stance that foregrounds Aboriginal agency behind the establishment of Radio Redfern.

8 In performance this story achieves a powerful effect through the opposition of Us Mob, a markedly flamboyant and gregarious rock band, with the image of a buttoned-down Bowls league, dressed all in white, an upright pillar of white Australian community politics and privilege.

9 "Ute" here is short for "utility truck", an Australian colloquial reference to the country's ubiquitous flatbed pickup trucks.

10 See chapter 3 for an extended discussion of this scheme and its ongoing significance.

11 Returned Servicemen's Leagues are a fixture of many Australian towns and suburban neighborhoods. They often offer a fixed-price dinner, gaming rooms, and a bar, although wealthier RSLs might also have pools, playgrounds, restaurants, and larger entertainment venues.

12 These actions took place in November and December 2002. They received a great deal of coverage in the Australian press and found a public spokesperson in Murrandoo Yanner.

13 This can also make some forms of live performance difficult. Enrec's manager and producer/engineer, Steve Newton, recalled that Charley Pride once quit an Alice Springs show in midstride. The noise and rambunctious appreciation of the audience drove him from the stage: "Have you ever been to a Charley Pride concert?"

Newton asked. "It's the quietist concert you've ever heard in your life. It's almost conversation level, so that people can sing along with him, it's just unbelievable."

14 TAFE is a network of vocational schools that provides educational services geared toward what, in Australia, are termed trades. Plumbers, mechanics, and electrical engineering are all courses in which one can be certified. This framework has expanded greatly to include sound production and software design, photography, and community development work. TAFE provides the institutional background for the certification process that Triple-A employed in turning toward an educational endeavor.

15 This often seemed to refigure the relationship between Aboriginal organizations and the state, rather than doing away with state support. The Cape York Digital Network (CYDN), an organization affiliated with Pearson's Balkanu Cape York Development Corporation and with the Outback Digital Network, has sought to build an enterprise that can bring employment to remote Cape communities through broadband video link-ups. A CYDN public relations officer and former manager of the Tanami Network in Central Australia argued that the main client of this corporation would be the various agencies of Queensland and commonwealth government (interview with author, Cairns, December 4, 2002). While this continues commonwealth financing of Indigenous community services, it refigures that relationship in terms of exchange, enterprise, and corporate client relations.

16 These are complex issues. ATSIC has not been universally mourned by Aboriginal organizations and activists. Indeed, its imperfect realization of the ideals of a generation of Aboriginal activists and policy makers such as H. C. Coombs led many to see in ATSIC something of a paper tiger (see Rowse 2000). Further, allegations of mismanagement and misappropriation of ATSIC funding have been lodged from across the spectrum of both non-Indigenous and Indigenous perspective. Nonetheless, many of the charges of mismanagement leveled at ATSIC belong with other "mainstream" organizations.

17 These standards, rationalized across a number of different educational institutions in the mid-1990s as the "Australian Qualifications Framework," provide a loose goal for trainees' education. Certificates I–IV and diplomas roughly correspond to vocational certificates and associate's degrees in the United States, and 4AAA sought to become qualified to grant such certificates in areas such as journalism, workplace training, broadcasting, sound engineering, and radio presentation.

18 DS subsequently gave me an example of the latter, describing how he manipulated the sound of the vocal track on a hip-hop song, singling out swear words and profanity and reversing these segments to make the profanity sound "backward," thus unintelligible. In this way he made the recording retain its edge yet now sound "clean," appropriate for broadcast.

Chapter 5: Speaking For or Selling Out?

1 ATSIC has since been dissolved and replaced by mainstream commonwealth organizations such as the Department of Communications, Information Technology, and the Arts (DOCITA).

2 In its daily practice, however, this has often meant ensuring that these communities continue to receive both public and commercial television broadcasts of Channel 7 and the ABC. From some perspectives this has been the grand irony of BRACS—i.e., that a discourse of cultural maintenance has ensured that television programming from major, mainstream broadcasters reaches remote communities uninterrupted, often within the rubric of rights of access to the same communications services received by non-Indigenous Australians.

3 With the demise of ATSIC and the transfer of granting responsibilities from ATSIC to the "mainstream" DOCITA, the stress on autonomy through enterprise, perhaps ironically, came under increased attack, with a DOCITA field officer telling TEABBA in no uncertain terms that they must not "commercialize" while on the "commonwealth dollar."

4 Joe McGinness credits Xavier Herbert, an Australian novelist and longtime resident of Darwin, with the idea of a "Euro-Australian League" to press for Aboriginal rights as an early instigation for this association (McGinness 1991: 23; see also Herbert 1938).

5 Its service includes northeastern Arnhem Land and the five primary Yolngu communities of Yirrkala, Galiwin'ku, Gapuwiyak, Ramingining, and Milingimbi.

6 Batchelor was founded as a vocational training center for Aboriginal students, initially focused on training Aboriginal teaching assistants for remote community schools. It was located at Batchelor, an hour south of Darwin, as a means of centralizing a number of older training programs that had to that point been located in Darwin in such institutions as Kormilda College. As Uibo suggests, "This was beginning to prove unsatisfactory, because of the movement of students between accommodation locations and work places on a daily basis. There were transport problems, and student absences were difficult to monitor—remembering that the (adult) students were almost always from remote communities and so not used to the regulated lifestyle of a larger town" (1993: 8–9). The move away from Darwin thus also sought to address anxieties about the movement of remote Aboriginal trainees, an issue that remains of concern for the Northern Territory government and Aboriginal organizations.

7 Like 4AAA in southeastern Queensland, though to a lesser degree, TEABBA also seeks to provide training to young Aboriginal people in Darwin. For example, between 2001 and 2003 TEABBA employed an apprentice to work with their technical staff. The apprentice, TH, drew on this apprenticeship as part of his studies toward a diploma in broadcast engineering. TH grew up in Adelaide River, a small town several hours south of Darwin where his German father settled following World War II. TH's mother is an Aboriginal woman from Yarralin, in the Victoria River

district of the Northern Territory, although TH has only visited family there infrequently. He has spent far more time in Darwin, attending Kormilda College as a boarder for his high school years, then living with his girlfriend and her family in the suburb of Coconut Grove while working at TEABBA.

8 William Thaiday's son Bill Thaiday has also become a senior media activist and remote media organizer in Australia, and during my period of fieldwork acted as the chair for the Indigenous Remote Communications Association. In my talks with Donna about her experiences growing up in Queensland, and her interest in media production, Bill emerges as a central figure to whom she has connections through the early labor activism of their respective parents: "With Bill, I can sit and talk to him for ages, you know? His family and my family—in the 1950s my dad and his dad, they kicked up a stink, they all used to live on Palm Island, which was a penal colony. And they kicked up a stink about wages, so they went on strike and it was like, 'Hey, hang on, these Aboriginal people should be working!' And they went on strike. . . . And in the middle of the night the police came from Townsville and took my dad and my mum and a couple of my older sisters and brothers I think, and his [Bill Thaiday's] dad and them, and shifted them all to Warrabinda. And they were kicked off the island and were told never to go back to Palm Island."

9 Annual General Meetings (AGMs) are a feature of every Aboriginal corporation formed under the Aboriginal Councils and Associations Act. For TEABBA they require flying up to forty people to Darwin for a long weekend of meetings, reports, and planning for the year ahead.

10 With Lea, I would underscore that I do not see here a simple instance where care is replaced by bad faith; rather, such bad faith plagues the bureaucratization of care, and the work of making media means constantly wrestling with the agency of institutional momentum itself. In this context, bad faith might better be figured through Peter Sloterdijk's double entendre of cynical reason (Sloterdijk 1987), a kind of tactical affect toward authoritative discourses and institutional processes. For recent discussions of such tactics in an ironic mode see Boyer and Yurchak 2010; see also Boyer 2005 and Yurchak 1997, 2005.

11 Retrospectively working through this episode (and others like it), I have been struck as well by the uncanny resonance of this with Alain Corbin's (1998) account of the shifting soundscape of late eighteenth- and early nineteenth-century French countryside. He documents the great resistance, bafflement, and generalized disjunction between centralized efforts to govern bells and bell ringing, to enumerate and evenly distribute the secular peals of bells across a national territory, and various divergent, nostalgic, and otherwise variegated attachments of town and country communities to those bells and their pealing.

12 Jennifer Deger (2006) provides a book-length account of his work.

13 For many Aboriginal Australians, the names and other representations of the deceased (including audio recordings of speech and music) are removed from circulation. Laurel, for example, has undergone several name changes in recent

years as individuals with whom she shared a proper name have passed away. In her book-length account of BW's work, Deger refers to her friend and primary field informant by his proper name, a decision she locates with respect to his family's degree of comfort with this representational practice and by reference to his own high profile. Due to the circumspect ways in which TEABBA staff continued to refer to this individual as "our former chairman" or, rarely, by his clan surname, Wunungmurra, I have opted to refer to him by his initials, BW, and to refer readers to Deger's work for further discussion of his accomplishments.

Chapter 6: A Body for the Voice

1   The highly visible cultural alterity of the Yolngu has often been made to serve as an icon of a broader, Australian national singularity.

2   I make this observation with some trepidation and reservation: the consequences of Australian settlement for Yolngu have been nothing if not severe.

3   "Fitter and turner" is a colloquial term for the role of handyman contracted out to many remote communities.

4   Gondarra was then the Yolngu director of the Arnhem Land Progress Association (ALPA), a thirty-year-old project to turn community stores into an Aboriginal enterprise (see Wells 1993). ALPA's public slogan, printed on its letterhead and in promotional materials, reads "Unity through Enterprise." For more on Gondarra's biography, training, and ministry see Magowan 2007: 154–184.

5   Rendered without Yolngu code-switching, my transcription reads as follows: "First up it sounds good. It sounds good all this talk, but the bottom line is money. Some of us been with BRACS for years, but still there is no salary. You look at us, we've gone gray. . . . We get three hundred dollars a fortnight. No but true, it sounds good for you people to say things, but we [Yolngu Matha first-person plural exclusive]—we, we are the ones who are suffering here. [If] you want us to do programs on BRACS, whether video or no, you [have] got to support us. We need the support. It sounds good [what you've been suggesting], but you have to look at it from our [Yolngu] side—because it's very, very important when someone comes up with good idea. You gotta support BRACS now."

6   People who speak *djambarpuyngu*, a Yolngu Matha dialect.

7   Alcan is the corporate owner of the bauxite mine at Nhulunbuy, just outside Yirrkala.

8   In drawing out these similarities between the Liberal emphasis on retooling the welfare state to enable market participation, on the one hand, and the emphasis of those like Pearson who seek to enable Aboriginal responsibility, on the other, I do not intend to reduce the distinct differences between them. Pearson has gone on to critique the Howard government's withdrawal from Indigenous programs and in particular their efforts to curtail the application of Native Title, while at the same time (as I detail in chapter 1) the current Liberal government has gone

to great lengths to promote the resonance of Pearson's ideas with their own as they dismantle the apparatus of self-determination.

9 Pearson figures exchange as a particularly Aboriginal practice that has been distorted by the "'gammon' economy of passive welfare" (2001), which is to say, by the welfare-capitalist governmental practice of "giving" without requiring a return. For Pearson, exchange now lives on in some North Queensland communities primarily in the social-pathological obligation to share "grog," contributing to a social epidemic of alcoholism. This approach to Indigenous policy in particular emerges from a sense of despair at welfare-capitalist programs that, in spite of optimistic beginnings, have come to be understood as a cause of Indigenous misery rather than the path to its alleviation.

10 Fred Myers (2002) writes of the unique position in the market for Aboriginal painting as fine art of the "art advisor"—someone who must broker between (minimally) two distinct interests and regimes of value—that of the communities of painters and histories of both practical and aesthetic interest alive in particular (and distinct) places such as Papunya, Yayayi, or Maningrida and of the desires and demands of galleries, collectors, and government funding bodies. The interaction of these distinct agents, he demonstrates, constitutes the field itself.

11 Laura Kunreuther's (2014) discussion of the fissures in this ideology of voice as it emerges tied to FM radio in Nepal provides comparative ground to begin thinking about the remediation of vocal power across different technological apparatuses, there figuring status of FM radio technology against a Nepali history of AM radio.

Conclusion

1 The title derives from the Arrernte language of central Australia.

2 Altman and Russell (2012) chronicle seven areas for reform implemented in the months following the NTER's announcement. In addition to those listed above, other reforms included increased policing; housing and tenancy reform; and dissolving the permit system that required visitors to receive permission through regional land councils prior to traveling to remote communities.

3 This provision was among the first to be discarded, as critics and participants quickly saw it as too difficult in both ethical and practical terms to examine every Aboriginal child in the Northern Territory.

4 Specifically, quarantining Indigenous welfare payments was considered construable as discriminatory. Prime Minister John Howard famously described this provision as a "constitutional nicety" that stood in the way of a successful governmental intervention. The act was reinstated in 2010 with the expansion of such quarantine provisions to some non-Indigenous recipients.

5 I have been assisted in thinking through the relation between these different theoretical understandings of voice by Dolar (2006) and the historical attention to the relation between metapragmatic and psychoanalytic understandings

of speech broached by Inoue (2006). As Inoue writes: "Whereas Derrida (1976) shows us how the voice grounds the full presence of the subject here and now, Lacanian voice is that which undermines it" (2006: 68, n. 47).

6   This is one way I read Inoue's account of the "vicarious language" that one may not speak but that one "hears" in a novel's reported speech, a speaking toy doll, or a television program (2006).

7   Palumpa began as a mission-run cattle station for Murrinhpatha-speaking people moving to be closer to their traditional country, and it retains kinship- and language-based ties to the larger coastal community of Wadeye, approximately forty kilometers to the west.

REFERENCES

ABS (Australian Bureau of Statistics). 2002. *National Aboriginal and Torres Strait Islander Social Survey*. ABS Catalogue, 4714.0. Canberra: ABS.

ABS (Australian Bureau of Statistics). 2004. *Prisoners in Australia*. ABS Catalogue, 4517.0. Canberra: ABS.

ABS (Australian Bureau of Statistics). 2011. *Prisoners in Australia*. ABS Catalogue, 4517.0. Canberra: ABS.

Adorno, Theodor. 1990. The Form of the Phonograph Record. *October* 55: 56–61.

Adorno, Theodor. 2009. *Current of Music*. Edited by Robert Hullot-Kentor. London: Polity.

Agha, Asif, ed. 2011. *Mediatized Communication in Complex Societies*. Special issue, *Language and Communication* 31(3).

Aird, Michael. 2001. *Brisbane Blacks*. Southport, Queensland: Keeaira Press.

ALPA (Arnhem Land Progress Association). 2003. *Unity through Enterprise: Annual Report 2002–2003*. Darwin: Arnhem Land Progress Association.

Althusser, Louis. 2001 [1971]. *Lenin and Philosophy, and Other Essays*. Translated by by Ben Brewster. New York: Monthly Review Press.

Althusser, Louis. 2005 [1965]. *For Marx*. London: Verso.

Altman, Jon. 2001. "Mutual Obligation," the CDEP Scheme, and Development: Prospects in Remote Australia. In F. Morphy and W. G. Sanders, eds., *The Indigenous Welfare Economy and the CDEP Scheme*, pp. 125–134. Canberra: Centre for Aboriginal Economic Policy Research. Australian National University Press.

Altman, Jon, and Susie Russell. 2012. Too Much Dreaming: Evaluations of the Northern Territory Emergency Response Intervention 2007–2012. Centre for Aboriginal Economic Policy Research, Australian National University, https://journal.anzsog.edu.au/userfiles/files/2012Issue3Final.pdf, accessed August 11, 2015.

Altman, Jon, and John Taylor. 2008. A Drift towards Disaster. *The Australian,* July 11, 2008.

Anderson, Benedict. 1983. *Imagined Communities: Reflections on the Origin and Spread of Nationalism.* New York: Verso.

Anderson, Chris, ed. 1995. *Politics of the Secret.* Sydney: Oceania.

Anderson, Patricia, and Rex Wild. 2007. *Ampe Akelyernemane Meke Mekarle "Little Children Are Sacred": Report of the Northern Territory Board of Inquiry into the Protection of Aboriginal Children from Sexual Abuse.* Darwin: Northern Territory Government.

Anderson, Warwick. 2006. *The Cultivation of Whiteness: Science, Health, and Racial Destiny in Australia.* Durham, NC: Duke University Press.

Ang, Ien. 2008. *The SBS Story: The Challenge of Cultural Diversity.* Sydney: University of New South Wales Press.

Armstrong, Robert Plant. 1972. *The Affecting Presence: An Essay in Humanistic Anthropology.* Urbana: University of Illinois Press.

Attwood, Bain. 2001. "Learning about the Truth": The Stolen Generations Narrative. In B. Attwood and F. Magowan, eds., *Telling Stories: Indigenous History and Memory in Australia and New Zealand,* pp. 183–212. Crows Nest, New South Wales: Allen and Unwin.

Attwood, Bain. 2004. *Rights for Aborigines.* Crows Nest, New South Wales: Allen and Unwin.

Austin, T. 1993. *I Can Picture the Old Home So Clearly: The Commonwealth and "Half-Caste" Youth in the Northern Territory, 1911–1939.* Canberra: Aboriginal Studies Press.

Awkward, Michael. 2013. "The South's Gonna Do It Again": Changing Conceptions of the Use of "Country" Music in the Albums of Al Green. In Diane Pecknold, ed., *Hidden in the Mix: The African American Presence in Country Music,* pp. 191–203. Durham, NC: Duke University Press.

Bakhtin, M. M. 1981. *The Dialogic Imagination: Four Essays.* Austin: University of Texas Press.

Bakhtin, M. M. 1986. *Speech Genres and Other Late Essays.* Austin: University of Texas Press.

Barthes, Roland. 1977. The Grain of the Voice. In Stephen Heath, ed., *Image Music Text,* pp. 179–189. New York: Hill and Wang.

Barthes, Roland. 1980. *Camera Lucida.* New York: Hill and Wang.

Batchelor College. 1988. *A Proposal to Develop Batchelor College as an Institute of Aboriginal Tertiary Education: A Response to the Commonwealth Government's Green Paper on Higher Education.* Darwin: Batchelor College.

Batty, Philip. 2003. *Governing Cultural Difference: The Incorporation of the Aboriginal Subject into the Mechanisms of Government with Reference to the Development of Aboriginal Radio and Television in Central Australia.* PhD diss., University of South Australia.

Batty, Philip. 2005. Incorporating the Aboriginal Self into the Mechanisms of the State: The Government Development of Aboriginal Broadcasting. In Luke Taylor, Graeme Ward, Graham Henderson, Richard Davis, and Lynley Wallis, eds., *The Power of Knowledge and the Resonance of Tradition*, pp. 169–181. Australian Institute for Aboriginal and Torres Strait Islander Studies, 2005.

Baumann, Gerd. 1995. Managing a Polyethnic Milieu. *Journal of the Royal Anthropological Institute* 1(4): 724–741.

Beck, Ulrich. 2010. *Cosmopolitan Vision*. New York: Polity.

Beckett, Jeremy. 1993. "I Don't Care Who Knows": The Songs of Dougie Young. *Australian Aboriginal Studies* 2: 34–38.

Beckett, Jeremy. 1996. Against Nostalgia: Place and Memory in Myles Lalor's "Oral History." *Oceania* 66(4): 312–322.

Bell, Sharon. 1990. Filming Radio Redfern: "Riding to Success on the Backs of Blacks"? *Media Information Australia* 56: 35–37.

Bell, Wendy. 2008. *A Remote Possibility: The Battle for Imparja Television*. Alice Springs: IAD Press.

Benjamin, Walter. 1968 [1936]. The Work of Art in the Age of Mechanical Reproduction. In Hannah Arendt, ed., *Illuminations*, pp. 217–251. New York: Schocken Books.

Benjamin, Walter. 1999 [1931]. Little History of Photography. In Michael Jennings, ed., *Selected Writings*, vol. 2: *1927–1934*. Cambridge, MA: Harvard University Press.

Benjamin, Walter. 2015 [1931]. *Radio Benjamin*. Edited by Lecia Rosenthal. New York: Verso.

Berland, Jody. 2009. *North of Empire: Essays on the Cultural Technologies of Space*. Durham, NC: Duke University Press.

Berndt, Ronald. 1962. *An Adjustment Movement in Arnhem Land, Northern Territory of Australia*. Paris: Mouton and Company.

Bessire, Lucas, and Daniel Fisher, eds. 2012. *Radio Fields: Anthropology and Wireless Sound in the 21st Century*. New York: New York University Press.

Bolter, David, and Richard Grusin. 1999. *Remediation*. Cambridge, MA: MIT Press.

Born, Georgina. 1995. *Rationalizing Culture*. Berkeley: University of California Press.

Born, Georgina. 2004. *Uncertain Vision: Birt, Dyke and the Reinvention of the BBC*. London: Secker & Warburg.

Born, Georgina. 2005. Musical Mediation: Ontology, Technology and Creativity. *20th Century Music* 1(2): 7–36.

Born, Georgina, ed. 2013. *Music, Sound, and Space: Transformations of Public and Private Experience*. Cambridge: Cambridge University Press.

Bornstein, Erica, and Peter Redfield, eds. 2010. *Forces of Compassion: Humanitarianism Between Ethics and Politics*. Santa Fe: School for Advanced Research

Bourdieu, Pierre. 1993. *The Field of Cultural Production*. New York: Columbia University Press.

Boyer, Dominic. 2005. *Spirit and System*. Chicago: University of Chicago Press.

Boyer, Dominic. 2007. *Understanding Media: A Popular Philosophy*. Chicago: Prickly Paradigm Press.

Boyer, Dominic, and Alexei Yurchak. 2010. American Stiob: or, What Late-Socialist Aesthetics of Stiob Reveal about Contemporary Political Culture in the West. *Cultural Anthropology* 25(2): 179–221.

Boym, Svetlana. 1998. On Diasporic Intimacy: Ilya Kabakov's Installations and Immigrant Homes. *Critical Inquiry* 24(2): 498–524.

Briggs, Charles. 2007. Mediating Infanticide: Theorizing Relations between Narrative and Violence. *Cultural Anthropology* 22(3): 315–356.

Briggs, Charles, and Daniel Hallin. 2007. Biocommunicability: The Neoliberal Subject and Its Contradictions in News Coverage of Health Issues. *Social Text* 25(4): 44–66.

Bryson, Ian. 2002. *Bringing to Light: A Brief History of Ethnographic Filmmaking at the Australian Institute for Aboriginal Studies*. Canberra: Aboriginal Studies Press.

Buck-Morss, Susan. 1996. The Cinema Screen as Prosthesis of Perception. In Nadia Seremetakis, ed., *The Senses Still*, pp. 54–62. Chicago: University of Chicago Press.

Buckmaster, Luke. 2009. Interview with Warwick Thornton, Writer/Director of *Samson and Delilah*. *Crikey*, May 12, 2009, http://blogs.crikey.com.au /cinetology/2009/05/12/interview-with-warwick-thornton-writerdirector-of -samson-delilah/.

Buddle, Kathleen. 2008. Transistor Resistors: Native Women's Radio in Canada and the Social Organization of Political Space from Below. In Pam Wilson and Michele Stewart, eds., *Global Indigenous Media: Cultures, Poetics, and Politics*, pp. 128–144. Durham, NC: Duke University Press.

Butler, Brendan SC. 2001. Is the Standing Commission of Inquiry a Successful Model for Anti-Corruption Commissions? Presentation to the International Society for the Reform of Criminal Law Conference, August 27, 2001, Canberra.

Calhoun, Craig, ed. 1992. *Habermas and the Public Sphere*. Cambridge, MA: MIT Press.

Carsten, Janet, ed. 2000. *Cultures of Relatedness: New Approaches to the Study of Kinship*. Cambridge: Cambridge University Press.

Carsten, Janet. 2004. *After Kinship*. Cambridge: Cambridge University Press.

Cavarero, Adriana. 2005. *For More Than One Voice: Toward a Philosophy of Vocal Expression*. Stanford, CA: Stanford University Press.

Caves, Richard. 2000. *Creative Industries: Contracts between Art and Commerce*. Cambridge, MA: Harvard University Press.

Chion, Michel. 1998. *The Voice in Cinema*. Translated by Claudia Gorbman. New York: Columbia University Press.

Christen, Kimberly. 2006. Tracking Properness: Repackaging Culture in a Remote Australian Town. *Cultural Anthropology* 21(3): 416–436.

Christen, Kimberly. 2008. *Aboriginal Business: Alliances in a Remote Australian Town*. Santa Fe: School of American Research Press.

Christie, Michael. 2008. Digital Tools and the Management of Australian Aboriginal Desert Knowledge. In Pam Wilson and Michele Stewart, eds., *Global Indigenous Media: Cultures, Poetics, and Politics*, pp. 270–306. Durham, NC: Duke University Press.

Cody, Francis. 2011. Publics and Politics. *Annual Review of Anthropology* 40: 37–52.

Collier, Stephen. 2011. *Post-Soviet Social: Neoliberalism, Social Modernity, Biopolitics*. Princeton, NJ: Princeton University Press.

Comaroff, Jean, and John Comaroff, eds. 2001. *Millennial Capitalism and the Culture of Neoliberalism*. Durham, NC: Duke University Press.

Condry, Ian. 2006. *Hip Hop Japan: Rap and the Paths of Cultural Globalization*. Durham, NC: Duke University Press.

Copjec, Jean. 1996. *Read My Desire: Lacan against the Historicists*. Cambridge, MA: MIT Press.

Corbin, Alain. 1998. *Village Bells: The Culture of the Senses in the Nineteenth-Century French Countryside*. New York: Columbia University Press.

Corn, Aaron. 2009. *Reflections and Voices: Exploring the Music of Yothu Yindi with Mandawuy Yunupingu*. Sydney: Sydney University Press.

Couldry, Nick. 2008. Mediatization or Mediation? Alternative Understandings of the Emergent Space of Digital Storytelling. *New Media Society* 10(3): 373–391.

Cowlishaw, Gillian. 2004. *Blackfellas, Whitefellas and the Hidden Injuries of Race*. London: Wiley-Blackwell.

Cowlishaw, Gillian. 2009. *The City's Outback*. Sydney: UNSW Press.

Cummings, Barbara. 1990. *Take This Child . . . : From Kahlin Compound to the Retta Dixon Children's Home*. Canberra: Aboriginal Studies Press.

Cunningham, Stuart. 2002. From Cultural to Creative Industries: Theory, Industry, and Policy Implications. *Media Information Australia Incorporating Culture and Policy* 102: 54–65.

Curthoys, Ann. 2010. Paul Robeson's Visit to Australia and Aboriginal Activism. In Frances Peters-Little, Ann Curthoys, and John Docker, eds., *Passionate Histories: Myth, Memory and Indigenous Australia*, pp. 163–184. Canberra: Australia National University Epress.

Day, Bill. 1994. *Bunji: A Story of the Gwalwa Daraniki Movement*. Canberra: Aboriginal Studies Press.

Debord, Guy. 1994 [1967]. *Society of the Spectacle*. New York: Zone Books.

Deger, Jennifer. 2006. *Shimmering Screens: Making Media in an Aboriginal Community*. Minneapolis: University of Minnesota Press.

Deger, Jennifer. 2013. The Jolt of the New: Making Video Art in Arnhem Land. *Culture, Theory and Critique* 54(3): 355–371.

Dent, Alexander. 2009. *River of Tears: Country Music, Memory, and Modernity in Brazil*. Durham, NC: Duke University Press.

Derrida, Jacques. 1998 [1967]. *Of Grammatology.* Translated by Gayatri Spivak. Baltimore: Johns Hopkins University Press.

Dewar, Mickey. 1992. *The "Black War" in Arnhem Land.* Canberra: North Australia Research Unit, Australian National University.

Dodson, Patrick. 2009. Introduction to Sarah Maddison, *Black Politics.* Crows Nest, New South Wales: Allen and Unwin.

Dolar, Mladen. 2006. *A Voice and Nothing More.* Cambridge, MA: MIT Press.

Donald, James. 2008. "As It Happened . . .": Borderline, the Uncanny and the Cosmopolitan. In Jo Collins and John Jervis, eds., *Uncanny Modernity: Cultural Theories, Modern Anxieties,* pp. 91–111. New York: Palgrave Macmillan.

Dousset, Laurent. 1997. Naming and Personal Names of Ngaatjatjarra-Speaking People, Western Desert: Some Questions Related to Research. *Australian Aboriginal Studies* 2: 50–54.

Du Bois, W. E. B. 1903. *The Souls of Black Folk.* New York: Dover.

Dueck, Byron. 2013. Civil Twilight: Country Music, Alcohol and the Spaces of Manitoban Aboriginal Sociability. In Georgina Born, ed., *Music, Sound, and Space: Transformations of Public and Private Experience,* pp. 239–256. Cambridge: Cambridge University Press.

Durham Peters, John. 1999. *Speaking into the Air: A History of the Idea of Communication.* Chicago: University of Chicago Press.

Durham Peters, John. 2004. Voice as Modern Media. In Doris Kolesch and Jenny Schrödl, eds., *Kunst-Stimmen,* pp. 85–100. Berlin: Theater der Zeit Recherchen.

Dussart, Françoise. 2004. Shown but Not Shared, Presented but Not Proffered: Redefining Ritual Identity among Warlpiri Ritual Actors (1990–2000). *Australian Journal of Anthropology* 15(3): 253–266.

Dusty, Slim, and Joy McKean. 1996. *Another Day, Another Town.* Sydney: Pan Australia.

Edwards, Jeanette, and Marilyn Strathern. 2000. Including Our Own. In Janet Carsten, ed., *Cultures of Relatedness: New Approaches to the Study of Kinship,* pp. 149–166. Cambridge: Cambridge University Press.

Eshun, Kodwo. 1998. *More Brilliant Than the Sun: Adventures in Sonic Fiction.* London: Quartet Books.

Fanon, Frantz. 1994 [1965]. *A Dying Colonialism.* New York: Grove.

Fanon, Frantz. 2008 [1952]. *Black Skin, White Masks.* New York: Grove.

Fardon, Richard, and Graham Furniss, eds. 2000. *African Broadcast Cultures: Radio in Transition.* Westport, CT: Praeger.

Fassin, Didier. 2011. *Humanitarian Reason: A Moral History of the Present.* Berkeley: University of California Press.

Feld, Steven. 1994. From Schizophonia to Schizmogenesis: The Discourses and Commodification Practices of "World Music" and "World Beat." In C. Keil and S. Feld, *Music Grooves.* Chicago: University of Chicago Press.

Feld, Steven. 2000. A Sweet Lullaby for World Music. *Public Culture* 12(1): 145–171.

Feld, Steven. 2012. *Jazz Cosmopolitanism in Accra: Five Musical Years in Ghana*. Durham, NC: Duke University Press.

Feld, Steven, Aaron Fox, Thomas Porcello, and David Samuels. 2004. Vocal Anthropology: From the Music of Language to the Language of Song. In Alessandro Duranti, ed., *A Companion to Linguistic Anthropology*, pp. 322–345. Malden, MA: Blackwell.

Finlayson, Kate. 2003. *A Lot of Croc: An Urban Bush Legend*. Sydney: Vintage Books / Random House Australia.

Fisher, Daniel. 2004. Local Sounds, Popular Technologies: History and Historicity in Andean Radio. In Jim Drobnick, ed., *Aural Cultures*, pp. 207–218. Montreal: Walter Phillips Gallery / YYZ Books.

Fisher, Daniel. 2010. On Gammon, Global Noise, and Indigenous Heterogeneity. *Critique of Anthropology* 30(3): 265–286.

Fisher, Daniel. 2012. Running Amok or Just Sleeping Rough? Long-Grass Camping and the Politics of Care in Northern Australia. *American Ethnologist* 39(1): 171–186.

Fisher, Daniel. 2013. Becoming the State in Northern Australia: Urbanisation, Intra-Indigenous Relatedness, and the State Effect. *Oceania* 83(3): 238–258.

Fitzgerald, C. E. 1989. *Commission of Inquiry into Possible Illegal Activities and Associated Police Misconduct*. http://www.cmc.qld.gov.au/about-the-cmc/the -fitzgerald-inquiry, accessed June 3, 2014.

Flew, Terry. 2014. Creative Industries—a New Pathway. *InterMEDIA* 2(1): 11–13.

Foley, Charmaine, and Ian Watson. 2001. *A People's Movement: Reconciliation in Queensland*. Southport, Queensland: Keeaira Press.

Foucault, Michel. 1991 [1978]. Governmentality. In Graham Burchell, Colin Gordon, and Peter Miller, eds., *The Foucault Effect: Studies in Governmentality*, pp. 87–104. Chicago: University of Chicago Press.

Foucault, Michel. 2009. *Security, Territory, Population: Lectures at the Collège de France, 1977–1978*. New York: Picador / Palgrave Macmillan.

Foucault, Michel. 2011. *The Government of Self and Others: Lectures at the Collège de France, 1982–1983*. New York: Picador / Palgrave Macmillan.

Fox, Aaron. 2004. *Real Country: Music and Language in Working-Class Culture*. Durham, NC: Duke University Press.

Fraser, Nancy. 1992. Rethinking the Public Sphere: A Contribution to the Critique of Actually Existing Democracy. In Craig Calhoun, ed., *Habermas and the Public Sphere*, pp. 109–142. Cambridge, MA: MIT Press.

Freire, Paolo. 1973. *Education for Critical Consciousness*. New York: Seabury.

Freud, Sigmund. 1990 [1919]. The Uncanny. In *Art and Literature*. Vol. 14, *The Penguin Freud Library*, edited by Albert Dickson and translated by Alix Strachey, pp. 335–376. Harmondsworth, UK: Penguin.

Gaonkar, Dilip, and Elizabeth Povinelli. 2003. Technologies of Public Forms: Circulation, Transfiguration, Recognition. *Public Culture* 15(3): 385–397.

Garde, Murray. 2013. *Culture, Interaction and Person Reference in an Australian Language: An Ethnography of Bininj Gunwok Communication*. Amsterdam: John Benjamins.

Gelder, Lawrence, and Jane Jacobs. 1998. *Uncanny Australia: Sacredness and Identity in a Postcolonial Nation*. Melbourne: Melbourne University Press.

Gershon, Ilana. 2010. *The Breakup 2.0*. Ithaca, NY: Cornell University Press.

Gilbert, Kevin. 1977. *Black Like Me: Blacks Speak to Kevin Gilbert*. Melbourne: Allen Lane.

Gilroy, Paul. 1991. Sounds Authentic: Black Music, Ethnicity and the Challenge of a "Changing" Same. *Black Music Research Journal* 11(2): 111–136.

Gilroy, Paul. 1993. *The Black Atlantic: Modernity and Double Consciousness*. Cambridge, MA: Harvard University Press.

Gilroy, Paul. 2010. *Darker Than Blue: On the Moral Economies of Black Atlantic Culture*. Cambridge, MA: Harvard University Press.

Ginsburg, Faye. 1991. Indigenous Media: Faustian Contract or Global Village? *Cultural Anthropology* 6(1): 92–112.

Ginsburg, Faye. 1994. Embedded Aesthetics: Creating a Discursive Space for Indigenous Media. *Cultural Anthropology* 9(3): 365–382.

Ginsburg, Faye. 1995. The Parallax Effect: The Impact of Aboriginal Media on Ethnographic Film. *Visual Anthropology Review* 11(2): 64–76.

Ginsburg, Faye. 1997. From Little Things, Big Things Grow: Indigenous Media and Cultural Activism. In R. Fox and O. Starn, eds., *Between Resistance and Revolution*, pp. 118–144. New Brunswick, NJ: Rutgers University Press.

Ginsburg, Faye. 2012. Australia's Indigenous New Wave: Future Imaginaries in Recent Aboriginal Films. Gebrands Lecture #2, Fonds Voor Etnologie in Leiden, http://www.fel-leiden.nl/wp-content/uploads/Gerbrandslecture-2-Faye-Ginsburg1.pdf, accessed June 2, 2014.

Ginsburg, Faye, Lila Abu-Lughod, and Brian Larkin, eds. 2002. *Media Worlds*. Berkeley: University of California Press.

Ginsburg, Faye, and Fred Myers. 2006. A History of Aboriginal Cultural Futures. *Critique of Anthropology* 26(1): 27–45.

Gitelman, Lisa. 2006. *Always Already New: Media and the Data of Culture*. Cambridge, MA: MIT Press.

Goffman, Erving. 1961. *Asylums*. New York: Anchor.

Goffman, Erving. 1981. *Forms of Talk*. Philadelphia: University of Pennsylvania Press.

Gordon, Avery. 1997. *Ghostly Matters: Haunting and the Sociological Imagination*. Minneapolis: University of Minnesota Press.

Gordon, Robert. 2013. *Respect Yourself: Stax Music and the Soul Explosion*. New York: Bloomsbury.

Graham, Chris. 2015. Bad Aunty: Seven Years On, How ABC Lateline Sparked the Racist NT Intervention. *New Matilda*, June 21, 2015. https://newmatilda.com/2015/06/21/bad-aunty-seven-years-how-abc-lateline-sparked-racist-nt-intervention.

Gunner, Elizabeth, Dina Ligaga, and Dumasani Moyo, eds. 2012. *Radio in Africa: Publics, Cultures, Communities*. Johannesburg: Wits University Press.

Guralnick, Peter. 1994. *Last Train to Memphis: The Rise of Elvis Presley*. Boston: Back Bay.

Habermas, Jürgen. 1989. *The Structural Transformation of the Public Sphere*. Translated by Thomas Burger and Frederick Lawrence. Cambridge, MA: MIT Press.

Haebich, Anna. 2000. *Broken Circles: Fragmenting Indigenous Families 1800–2000*. Fremantle: Fremantle Arts Centre.

Hall, Stuart. 1993. What Is This "Black" in Black Popular Culture? *Social Justice* 20(1/2): 104–114.

Hall, Stuart. 1996. Race, Articulation and Societies Structured in Dominance. In *Sociological Theories: Race and Colonialism*, pp. 305–345. UNESCO.

Hardy, Frank. 1968. *The Unlucky Australians*. Sydney: Goldstar.

Harkness, Nicholas. 2014. *Songs of Seoul: An Ethnography of Voice and Voicing in Christian South Korea*. Berkeley: University of California Press.

Hartigan, John. 1999. *Racial Situations: Class Predicaments of Whiteness in Detroit*. Princeton, NJ: Princeton University Press.

Hartley, John, and Stuart Cunningham. 2001. Creative Industries: From Blue Poles to Fat Pipes. In Malcolm Gillies, ed., *The National Humanities and Social Sciences Summit, Position Papers*. Canberra: Department of Education Science and Training.

Hartley, John, and Alan McKee. 2000. *The Indigenous Public Sphere: The Reporting and Reception of Australian Indigenous Issues in the Australian Media*. Oxford: Oxford University Press.

Hayward, Philip. 2003. *Outback and Urban: Australian Country Music*. Vol. 1. Gympie, Queensland: Australian Institute of Country Music.

Hebdige, Dick. 1987. *Cut n' Mix: Culture, Identity and Caribbean Music*. London: Routledge.

Heidegger, Martin. 2008 [1962]. *Being and Time*. New York: Harper Perennial.

Heilbut, Anthony. 1997 [1971]. *The Gospel Sound: Good News and Bad Times*. New York: Limelight Editions.

Helmreich, Stefan. 2007. An Anthropologist Underwater: Immersive Soundscapes, Submarine Cyborgs, and Transductive Ethnography. *American Ethnologist* 34(4): 621–641.

Herbert, Xavier. 1938. *Capricornia*. Sydney: Angus & Robertson.

Herzfeld, M. 1997. *Cultural Intimacy: Social Poetics in the Nation-State*. New York: Routledge.

Hesmondalgh, David. 2006. Bourdieu, the Media, and Cultural Production. *Media, Culture and Society* 28(2): 211–231.

Hiatt, Les. 1965. *Kinship and Conflict: A Study of an Aboriginal Community in Northern Arnhem Land*. Canberra: Australian National University.

Hill, Jane H. 1995. The Voice of Don Gabriel: Responsibility and Self in a Modern Mexicano Narrative. In Dennis Tedlock and Bruce Mannheim, eds., *The Dialogic Emergence of Culture*, pp. 97–147. Urbana: University of Illinois Press.

Himpele, Jeff. 2008. *Circuits of Culture: Media, Politics and Indigenous Identity in the Andes.* Minneapolis: University of Minnesota Press.

Hinkson, Melinda. 2004. What's in a Dedication? On Being a Warlpiri DJ. *Australian Journal of Anthropology* 15(2): 143–162.

Hinkson, Melinda. 2010. Media Images and the Politics of Hope. In J. Altman and M. Hinkson, eds., *Culture Crisis*, pp. 229–247. Melbourne: Arena.

Hinkson, Melinda. 2014. *Remembering the Future: Warlpiri Life through the Prism of Drawing.* Canberra: Aboriginal Studies Press.

Hirschkind, C. 2006. *Ethical Soundscape: Cassette Sermons and Islamic Counterpublics.* New York: Columbia University Press.

Hjarvard, Stig. 2013. *The Mediatization of Culture and Society.* New York: Routledge.

Hodgson, Jay. 2010. *Understanding Records: A Field Guide to Recording Practice.* New York: Continuum.

Holbraad, Martin, Morten Axel Pedersen, and Eduardo Viveiros de Castro. 2013. The Politics of Ontology: Anthropological Positions. Fieldsights—Theorizing the Contemporary, Cultural Anthropology Online, January 13, 2014, http://culanth.org/fieldsights/462-the-politics-of-ontology-anthropological-positions.

Hooper, Chloe. 2006. The Tall Man: Inside Palm Island's Heart of Darkness. *The Monthly*, March. http://www.themonthly.com.au/monthly-essays-chloe-hooper-tall-man-inside-palm-island039s-heart-darkness-185, accessed May 10, 2013.

Hooper, Chloe. 2008. *The Tall Man.* Melbourne: Penguin Australia.

Howard-Wagner, Dierdre. 2010. From Denial to Emergency: Governing Indigenous Communities in Australia. In Didier Fassin and Mariella Pandolfi, eds., *Contemporary States of Emergency*, pp. 217–239. New York: Zone.

Howard-Wagner, Dierdre. 2012. Reclaiming the Northern Territory as a Settler-Colonial Space. *Arena* 37/38: 220–240.

Hughes, Charles L. 2013. You're My Soul Song: How Southern Soul Changed Country Music. In Diane Pecknold, ed., *Hidden in the Mix: The African American Presence in Country Music*, pp. 283–305. Durham, NC: Duke University Press.

Hullot-Kentor, Robert. 2009. Editor's Introduction: Second Salvage: Prolegomenon to a Reconstruction of *Current of Music*. In Theodor Adorno, *Current of Music*, pp. 1–39. Cambridge: Polity Press.

Hunter, Boyd, and Matthew Gray. 2013. Continuity and Change in the Community Development Employment Projects Scheme (CDEP). *Australian Journal of Social Issues* 48(1): 35–56.

Inoue, Miyako. 2003. The Listening Subject of Japanese Modernity and His Auditory Double: Citing, Sighting, and Siting the Modern Japanese Woman. *Cultural Anthropology* 18(2): 156–193.

Inoue, Miyako. 2006. *Vicarious Language.* Berkeley: University of California Press.

Ivy, Marilyn. 1995. *Discourses of the Vanishing: Modernity, Phantasm, Japan.* Chicago: University of Chicago Press.

Jacobsen-Bia, Kristina. 2009. Rita(hhh): Placemaking and Country Music on the Navajo Nation. *Ethnomusicology* 53(3): 449–477.

Jacobsen-Bia, Kristina. 2014. Radmilla's Voice: Music Genre, Blood Quantum, and Belonging on the Navajo Nation. *Cultural Anthropology* 29(2): 385–410.

Jakobson, Roman. 1960. Closing Statement: Linguistics and Poetics. In Thomas Sebeok, ed., *Style in Language*, pp. 350–377. New York: Wiley.

Jameson, Fredric. 1990. *Postmodernism, or, the Cultural Logic of Late Capitalism.* Durham, NC: Duke University Press.

Johnston, Elliot, QC. 1991. *Royal Commission into Aboriginal Deaths in Custody National Report.* Vol. 1. Adelaide: Royal Commission into Aboriginal Deaths in Custody.

Jones, Andrew. 2001. *Yellow Music: Media Culture and Colonial Modernity in the Chinese Jazz Age.* Durham, NC: Duke University Press.

Juddery, Mark. 2015. Faith Bandler: Activist, Author and Inspiration. *The Australian.* http://www.theaustralian.com.au/news/features/faith-bandler-activist-author-and-inspiration/story-e6frg6z6-1227219201740, accessed February 13, 2015.

Kahn, D., and G. Whitehead, eds. 1994. *Wireless Imagination: Sound, Radio, and the Avant-Garde.* Cambridge, MA: MIT Press.

Keane, Michael, and John Hartley. 2001. *From Ceremony to CD Rom: Indigenous Creative Industries in Brisbane.* Brisbane: Economic Development Branch, Brisbane City Council Creative Industries Research and Applications Centre.

Keating, Paul. 1995. Exports from a Creative Nation. *Media Information Australia* 76: 4–6.

Keen, Ian. 1994. *Knowledge and Secrecy in an Aboriginal Religion.* Oxford: Clarendon.

Kennedy, Gayle. 2003. Thanks Slim, from Me and My Mob. You Wrote the Soundtrack to Our Lives. *Sydney Morning Herald*, September 26, 2003. http://www.smh.com.au/articles/2003/09/25/1064083124507.html.

Kittler, Friedrich. 1994. Observations on Public Reception. In Diana Augaitis and Dan Lander, eds., *Radio Rethink: Art, Sound and Transmission*, pp. 75–85. Banff: Walter Phillips Gallery.

Kittler, Friedrich. 1999. *Gramophone, Film, Typewriter.* Stanford, CA: Stanford University Press.

Knox, Malcolm. 2013. *Boom: The Underground History of Australia, from Gold Rush to GFC.* Melbourne: Viking.

Koestenbaum, Wayne. 1993. *The Queen's Throat: Opera, Homosexuality, and the Mystery of Desire.* New York: Da Capo.

Kosnick, Kira. 2007. *Migrant Media: Turkish Broadcasting and Multicultural Politics in Berlin.* Bloomington: Indiana University Press.

Kowal, Emma. 2008. The Politics of the Gap: Indigenous Australians, Liberal Multiculturalism, and the End of the Self-Determination Era. *American Anthropologist* 110(3): 338–348.

Krieg, Anthea Susan. 2006. Aboriginal Incarceration: Health and Social Impacts. *Medical Journal of Australia* 184(10): 534–536.

Kunreuther, Laura. 2014. *Voicing Subjects: Public Intimacy and Mediation in Kath-mandu.* Berkeley: University of California Press.

Lacan, Jacques. 2004. *Ecrits: A Selection.* New York: Norton.

Langton, Marcia. 1993. *"Well, I heard it on the radio and I saw it on the television":* *An Essay for the Australian Film Commission on the Politics and Aesthetics of Filmmaking by and about Aboriginal People and Things.* North Sydney, New South Wales: Australian Film Commission.

Larkin, Brian. 2008. *Signal and Noise: Media, Infrastructure, and Urban Culture in Nigeria.* Durham, NC: Duke University Press.

Latour, Bruno. 1991. Technology Is Society Made Durable. In *A Sociology of Monsters: Essays on Power, Technology and Domination,* pp. 103–131. New York: Routledge.

Latour, Bruno. 1993. *We Have Never Been Modern.* Cambridge, MA: Harvard University Press.

Lea, Tess. 2008. *Bureaucrats and Bleeding Hearts.* Sydney: University of New South Wales Press.

Lea, Tess. 2014. *Darwin.* Sydney: University of New South Wales Press.

Lee, Benjamin, and Edward LiPuma. 2002. Cultures of Circulation: The Imaginations of Modernity. *Public Culture* 14(1): 191–213.

Levin, Thomas, and Michael von der Linn. 1994. Elements of a Radio Theory: Adorno and the Princeton Radio Research Project. *Musical Quarterly* 78(2): 316–324.

Lewis, George. 1996. Improvised Music after 1950: Afrological and Eurological Perspectives. *Black Music Research Journal* 16(1): 91–122.

Lewis, George. 2008. *A Power Stronger Than Itself: The* AACM *and American Experimental Music.* Chicago: University of Chicago Press.

Limb, Peter. 2008. The Anti-Apartheid Movements in Australia and Aotearoa / New Zealand. In Sifiso Ndlovu, eds., *The Road to Democracy in South Africa,* vol. 3: *International Solidarity,* pp. 907–982. Pretoria: SADET/Unisa Press.

Lott, Eric. 1994. *Love and Theft: Blackface Minstrelsy and the American Working Class.* Oxford: Oxford University Press.

Macdonald, David. 1996. Aboriginal Deaths in Custody and Aboriginal Incarceration: Looking Back and Looking Forward. Australian Institute of Criminology. http://www.aic.gov.au/media_library/conferences/other/mcdonald_david/1996 -11-dic.pdf, accessed August 12, 2015.

Maddison, Sarah. 2009. *Black Politics: Inside the Complexity of Aboriginal Political Culture.* Crows Nest, New South Wales: Allen and Unwin.

Magowan, Fiona. 2007. *Melodies of Mourning: Music and Emotion in Northern Australia.* Crawley: University of Western Australia Press.

Mahoud, Kim. 2012. Kartiya Are Like Toyotas. *Griffith Review* 36: 43–59.

Mansfield, John. 2014. Listening to Heavy Metal in Wadeye. In Amanda Harris, ed., *Circulating Cultures: Exchanges of Australian Music, Dance and Media,* pp. 239–262. Australian National University Press.

Martin Barbero, Jesus. 1993. *Communication, Culture and Hegemony: From the Media to Mediations*. Newbury Park, CA: Sage.

Masco, Joseph. 2006. *The Nuclear Borderlands: The Manhattan Project in Post-Cold War New Mexico*. Princeton, NJ: Princeton University Press.

Maxwell, Ian. 2003. *Phat Beats, Dope Rhymes: Hip Hop Down Under Comin' Upper*. Middletown, CT: Wesleyan University Press.

Mazzarella, William. 2003. *Shovelling Smoke: Advertising and Globalization in Contemporary India*. Durham, NC: Duke University Press.

Mazzarella, William. 2004. Culture, Globalization, Mediation. *Annual Review of Anthropology* 33: 345–367.

McGahan, Andrew. 1995. *1988*. New York: St. Martin's.

McGahan, Andrew. 2000. *Last Drinks*. Crows Nest, New South Wales: Allen and Unwin.

McGinness, Joe. 1991. *Son of Alyandabu: My Fight for Aboriginal Rights*. St. Lucia: Queensland University Press.

McLary, Susan. 1998. *Rap, Minimalism, and Structures of Time in Late 20th Century Culture*. Lincoln: University of Nebraska Press.

McLuhan, Marshall. 1964. *Understanding Media: The Extensions of Man*. New York: McGraw-Hill.

McMillan, Andrew. 1988. *Strict Rules*. London: Hodder and Stoughton.

Meehan, Betty. 1997. Irreverent Recollections of the Making of an Anthropologist. In F. Merlan, J. Morton, and A. Rumsey, eds., *Scholar and Skeptic: Australian Aboriginal Studies in Honour of L. R. Hiatt*, pp. 11–28. Canberra: Aboriginal Studies Press.

Meintjes, Louise. 2003. *Sound of Africa! Making Music Zulu in an African Recording Studio*. Durham, NC: Duke University Press.

Melkote, Srinivas, and Steeves. 2001. *Communication for Development in the Third World*. London: Sage.

Merlan, Francesca. 1981. "Egocentric" and "Altercentric" Usage of Kin Terms in Manarayi. In J. Heath, F. Merlan, and A. Rumsey, eds., *Languages of Kinship in Central Australia*, pp. 125–140. Oceania Linguistic Monographs, 24. Sydney: University of Sydney Press.

Merlan, Francesca. 1998. *Caging the Rainbow*. Honolulu: University of Hawaii Press.

Michaels, Eric. 1986. *The Aboriginal Invention of Television in Central Australia 1982–1986*. Canberra: Australian Institute of Aboriginal Studies.

Michaels, Eric. 1994. *Bad Aboriginal Art: Tradition, Media, and Technological Horizons*. Minneapolis: University of Minnesota Press.

Michaels, Eric. 1997. *Unbecoming*. Durham, NC: Duke University Press.

Miller, Toby. 2004. A View from a Fossil: The New Economy, Creativity and Consumption—Two or Three Things I Don't Believe In. *International Journal of Cultural Studies* 7: 55–65.

Miller, Toby, Nitin Govil, John McMurria, and Richard Maxwell. 2001. *Global Hollywood*. London: British Film Institute.

Mills, Mara. 2012. Media and Prosthesis: The Vocoder, the Artificial Larynx, and the History of Signal Processing. *Qui Parle: Critical Humanities and Social Sciences* 21(1): 107–149.

Mitchell, Tony. 2006. The New Corroboree. *Meanjin* 65(1): 20–28.

Miyazaki, Hiro. 2004. *The Method of Hope: Anthropology, Philosophy, and Fijian Knowledges.* Stanford, CA: Stanford University Press.

Mobray, Martin, and Kate Senior. 2006. A Study in Neo-conservative Populism: Richard Trudgen's *Why Warriors Lie Down and Die. Australian Journal of Anthropology* 17(2): 216–229.

Molnar, Helen, and Michael Meadows. 2001. *Songlines to Satellites: Indigenous Communication in Australia, the South Pacific, and Canada.* Annandale, New South Wales: Pluto Press.

Morphy, Howard. 1991. *Ancestral Connections: Art and an Aboriginal System of Knowledge.* Chicago: University of Chicago Press.

Morris, Barry, and Andrew Lattas. 2010. Embedded Anthropology and the Intervention: On Cultural Determinism and Neo-liberal forms of Racial Governance. *Arena Magazine* 107: 15–20.

Morris, Rosiland. 2000. *In the Place of Origins: Modernity and Its Mediums in Northern Thailand.* Durham, NC: Duke University Press.

Moss, Rod. 2012. *The Hard Light of Day: An Artist's Story of Friendships in Arrernte Country.* St. Lucia: University of Queensland Press.

Moten, Fred. 2003. *In the Break: The Aesthetics of the Black Radical Tradition.* Minneapolis: University of Minnesota Press.

Mrázek, Rudolf. 2002. *Engineers of Happy Land: Technology and Nationalism in a Colony.* Princeton, NJ: Princeton University Press.

Murray, Neil. 1993. *Sing for Me Countryman.* Rydalmere, New South Wales: Sceptre.

Murray, Neil. 2014. Cry When We're Gone. In Christian Ryan, ed., *The Best Music Writing under the Australian Sun,* pp. 181–194. Melbourne: Hardie Grant Books.

Myers, Fred. 1982. Always Ask: Resource Use and Landownership among the Pintupi of Central Australia. In N. Williams and E. Hunn, eds., *Resource Managers: North American and Australian Hunter-Gatherers.* Boulder: Westview.

Myers, Fred. 1986. *Pintupi Country, Pintupi Self.* Berkeley: University of California Press.

Myers, Fred. 1989. Burning the Truck and Holding the Country: Pintupi Forms of Property and Identity. In Edwin N. Wilmsen, ed., *We Are Here: Politics of Aboriginal Land Tenure,* pp. 15–42. Berkeley: University of California Press.

Myers, Fred. 2002. *Painting Culture: The Making of an Aboriginal High Art.* Durham, NC: Duke University Press.

Novak, David. 2010. Cosmopolitanism, Remediation, and the Ghost World of Bollywood. *Public Culture* 23(3): 40–72.

Novak, David. 2013. *Japanoise: Music at the Edge of Circulation.* Durham, NC: Duke University Press.

Ochoa, Ana Maria. 2014. *Aurality: Listening and Knowledge in Nineteenth-Century Colombia*. Durham, NC: Duke University Press.

O'Connor, Justin. 2011. The Cultural and Creative Industries: A Critical History. *Ekonomiaz* 78(3): 24–45.

O'Regan, Tom, ed. 1990. Communication and Tradition: Essays after Eric Michaels' *Continuum*. *Australian Journal of Media and Culture* 3(2).

Osborne, Peter. 2013. *Anywhere or Not at All: The Philosophy of Contemporary Art*. London: Verso.

Ottoson, Ase. 2006. Improving Indigenous Music Makers. In Tess Lea, Emma Kowal, and Gillian Cowlishaw, eds., *Moving Anthropology: Critical Indigenous Studies*. Darwin: Charles Darwin University Press.

Pazderic, Nicola. 2004. Recovering True Selves in the Electro-Spiritual Field of Universal Love. *Cultural Anthropology* 19(2): 196–225.

Pearson, Noel. 2000. *Our Right to Take Responsibility*. Cairns: Noel Pearson and Associates.

Pearson, Noel. 2001. On the Human Right to Misery, Mass Incarceration and Early Death. Dr. Charles Perkins Memorial Oration, University of Sydney, October 25, 2001. http://sydney.edu.au/koori/news/pearson.pdf.

Pearson, Noel. 2009. *Up from the Mission: Selected Writings*. Fremantle: Black Inc. Press.

Pecknold, Diane, ed. 2013. *Hidden in the Mix: The African American Presence in Country Music*. Durham, NC: Duke University Press.

Petersen, Nicolas. 1993. Demand Sharing: Reciprocity and the Pressure for Generosity among Foragers. *American Anthropologist* 95(4): 860–874.

Peters-Little, Frances. 2000. *The Community Game: Aboriginal Self-Definition at the Local Level*. AIATSIS Research and Discussion Paper Number 10/2000. http://www.aiatsis.gov.au/_files/research/dp/DP10.pdf.

Phillips, Richard. 2009. "Cinema is a lie that tells the truth about life": Warwick Thornton Discusses *Samson and Delilah* with the wsws. *World Socialist Web Site*. https://www.wsws.org/en/articles/2009/05/inte-m14.html, accessed August 14, 2015.

Pinch, Trevor, and Frank Trocco. 2004. *Analog Days: The Invention and Impact of the Moog Synthesizer*. Cambridge, MA: Harvard University Press.

Poirier, Sylvie. 2008. Reflections on Indigenous Cosmopolitics-Poetics. *Anthropologica* 50(1): 75–85.

Porcello, Thomas, and David Greene, eds. 2005. *Wired for Sound: Engineering and Technologies in Sonic Culture*. Middletown, CT: Wesleyan University Press.

Povinelli, Elizabeth. 2002. *The Cunning of Recognition*. Durham, NC: Duke University Press.

Povinelli, Elizabeth. 2003. Sexuality at Risk: "Psychoanalysis Metapragmatically." In Tim Dean and Christopher Lane, eds., *Homosexuality and Psychoanalysis*, pp. 387–411. Chicago: University of Chicago Press.

Povinelli, Elizabeth. 2006. Finding Bwudjut: Common Land, Private Profit, Divergent Objects. In Tess Lea, Emma Kowal, and Gillian Cowlishaw, eds., *Moving Anthropology: Critical Indigenous Studies*, pp. 147–166. Darwin: Charles Darwin University Press.

Povinelli, Elizabeth. 2011. *Economies of Abandonment: Social Belonging and Endurance in Late Liberalism*. Durham, NC: Duke University Press.

Price, Monroe. 1994. Satellite Broadcasting as Trade Routes in the Sky. *Public Culture* 11(2): 387–403.

Read, Peter. 1999. *A Rape of the Soul So Profound: The Return of the Stolen Generation*. Crows Nest, New South Wales: Allen and Unwin.

Read, Peter, and Coral Edwards. 1989. *The Lost Children: Thirteen Australians Taken from Their Aboriginal Families Tell of the Struggle to Find Their Natural Parents*. New York: Doubleday.

Rennie, Ellie, and Daniel Featherstone. 2008. The Potential Diversity of Things We Call TV: Indigenous Community Television, Self-Determination, and the Advent of NITV. *Media Information Australia* 129: 52–66.

Robbins, Joel. 2013. Beyond the Suffering Subject. *Journal of the Royal Anthropological Institute* 19: 447–462.

Robson, Frank. n.d. New Waves: Radio 4AAA Is a Station Run by Aborigines, Some of Whom Were Once Street Kids. *Sydney Morning Herald*.

Roitman, Janet. 2013. *Anti-Crisis*. Durham, NC: Duke University Press.

Rossiter, Ned. 2004. Creative Industries, Comparative Media Theory, and the Limits of Critique from Within. *Topia: A Canadian Journal of Cultural Studies* 11: 21–48.

Roth, Lorna. 2005. *Something New in the Air*. Montreal: McGill-Queens University Press.

Rowse, Tim. 1992. *Remote Possibilities: The Aboriginal Domain and the Administrative Imagination*. Casuarina, NT: Australian National University, North Australia Research Unit.

Rowse, Tim. 1993. *After Mabo: Interpreting Indigenous Traditions*. Melbourne: Melbourne University Press.

Rowse, Tim. 2000. *Obliged to Be Difficult: Nugget Coombs' Legacy in Indigenous Affairs*. Cambridge: Cambridge University Press.

Rowse, Tim. 2002. *Indigenous Futures: Choice and Development for Aboriginal and Torres Strait Islander Australia*. Sydney: University of New South Wales Press.

Rowse, Tim. 2007. The Problem of Indigenous Jurisdiction. In Jon Altman and Melinda Hinkson, eds., *Coercive Reconciliation: Stabilize, Normalize, Exit Aboriginal Australia*, pp. 47–61. North Carlton, Victoria: Arena.

Ruby, Jay. 2000. *Picturing Culture: Explorations of Film and Anthropology*. Chicago: University of Chicago Press.

Sahlins, Marshall. 2013. *What Kinship Is . . . and Is Not*. Chicago: University of Chicago Press.

Salazar, Juan Francisco, and Amalia Cordova. 2008. Imperfect Media and the Politics of Indulgence Video in Latin America. In *Global Indigenous Media: Culture, Poetics, and Politics*, pp. 39–57. Durham, NC: Duke University Press.

Salecl, Renata, and Slavoj Žižek, eds. 1996. *Gaze and Voice as Love Objects*. Durham, NC: Duke University Press.

Samuels, David. 2004. *Putting a Song on Top of It: Expression and Identity on the San Carlos Apache Reservation*. Tucson: University of Arizona Press.

Samuels, David. 2009. Singing Indian Country. In Tara Browner, ed., *Music of the First Nations: Tradition and Innovation in Native North America*, pp. 141–160. Champaign: University of Illinois Press.

Sansom, Basil. 1980. *The Camp at Wallaby Cross: Aboriginal Fringe Dwellers in Darwin*. Canberra: Australian Institute for Aboriginal Studies Press.

Schaeffer, Pierre. 2012. *In Search of a Concrete Music*. Berkeley: University of California Press.

Schafer, R. Murray. 1993 [1977]. *The Soundscape: The Tuning of the World*. Rochester, VT: Destiny Books.

Schneider, David M. 1972. What Is Kinship All About? In Priscilla Reining, ed., *Kinship Studies in the Morgan Centennial Year*, pp. 32–63. Washington, DC: Anthropological Society of Washington.

Schulz, Winifried. 2004. Reconstructing Mediatization as an Analytical Concept. *European Journal of Communication*. 19(1): 87–101.

Schwab, Jerry. 1988. Ambiguity, Style and Kinship in Adelaide Aboriginal Identity. In Ian Keen, ed., *Being Black: Aboriginal Cultures in Settled Australia*, pp. 77–95. Canberra: Aboriginal Studies Press.

Sconce, Jeffrey. 2000. *Haunted Media: Electronic Presence from Telegraphy to Television*. Durham, NC: Duke University Press.

Seremetakis, C. Nadia, ed. 1996. *The Senses Still: Perception and Memory as Material Culture in Modernity*. Chicago: University of Chicago Press.

Shryock, A. 2004. Other Conscious/Self Aware: First Thoughts on Cultural Intimacy and Mass Mediation. In A. Shryock, ed., *Off Stage, On Display: Intimacy and Ethnography in the Age of Public Culture*, pp. 3–30. Stanford, CA: Stanford University Press.

Siegel, James. 1998. *A New Criminal Type in Jakarta: Counter-Revolution Today*. Durham, NC: Duke University Press.

Siegel, James. 2006. *Naming the Witch*. Stanford, CA: Stanford University Press.

Silverstein, Brian. 2008. Disciplines of Presence in Modern Turkey: Discourse, Companionship and the Mass Mediation of Islamic Practice. *Cultural Anthropology* 23(1): 118–153.

Simpson, Audra. 2014. *Mohawk Interruptus: Political Life across the Borders of Settler States*. Durham, NC: Duke University Press.

Sloterdijk, Peter. 1987. *Critique of Cynical Reason*. Minneapolis: University of Minnesota Press.

Smith, Benjamin, and Frances Morphy, eds. 2007. *The Social Effects of Native Title: Recognition, Translation, Coexistence*. Centre for Aboriginal Economic Policy Research Monograph No. 27. Canberra: Australian National University Epress. http://press.anu.edu.au/wp-content/uploads/2011/05/whole_book28.pdf, accessed December 29, 2014.

Smith, Graeme. 2005. *Singing Australian: A History of Folk and Country Music*. Melbourne: Pluto.

Sommer, Doris. 1993. *Foundational Fictions: The National Romances of Latin America*. Berkeley: University of California Press.

Spitulnik, Debra. 2002. Mobile Machines and Fluid Audiences: Rethinking Reception through Zambian Radio Culture. In Faye Ginsburg, Lila Abu-Lughod, and Brian Larkin, eds., *Media Worlds: Anthropology on New Terrain*, pp. 337–354. Berkeley: University of California Press.

Spitulnik Vidali, Debra. 1998. Ideologies in Zambian Broadcasting. In B. B. Schieffelin, K. Woolard, and P. Kroskrity, eds., *Language Ideologies: Practice and Theory*, pp. 163–188. Oxford: Oxford University Press.

Spitulnik Vidali, Debra. 2012. "A House of Wires upon Wires": Sensuous and Linguistic Entanglements of Evidence and Epistemologies in the Study of Radio Culture. In L. Bessire and D. Fisher, eds., *Radio Fields: Anthropology and Wireless Sound in the 21st Century*, pp. 250–267. New York: New York University Press.

Spivak, Gayatri. 1988. Can the Subaltern Speak? In Cary Nelson and Lawrence Grossberg, eds., *Marxism and the Interpretation of Culture*, pp. 271–313. Urbana: University of Illinois Press.

Sreberny-Mohammadi, A., and A. Mohammadi. 1994. *Small Media, Big Revolution*. Minneapolis: University of Minnesota Press.

Stanner, W. E. H. 1937. Aboriginal Modes of Address and Reference in the North West of Australia. *Oceania* 7(3): 301–315.

Stefanoff, Lisa, and Warwick Thornton. 2006. Making Whites Obsolete. *Meanjin* 65(1): 114–121.

Sterne, Jonathan. 2003. *The Audible Past: Cultural Origins of Sound Reproduction*. Durham, NC: Duke University Press.

Sterne, Jonathan. 2013. *MP3: The Story of a Format*. Durham, NC: Duke University Press.

Stevenson, Lisa. 2014. *Life Beside Itself: Imagining Care in the Canadian Arctic*. Berkeley: University of California Press.

Stewart, Kathleen. 1988. Nostalgia—a Polemic. *Cultural Anthropology* 3(3): 227–241.

Stokes, Martin. 2007. On Musical Cosmopolitanism. Paper No. 3 for the Macalester International Roundtable, Institute for Global Citizenship, Macalester College. http://digitalcommons.macalester.edu/cgi/viewcontent.cgi?article=1002 &context=intlrdtable, accessed September 5, 2015.

Stokes, Martin. 2010. *The Republic of Love: Culture Intimacy in Turkish Popular Music*. Chicago: University of Chicago Press.

Strathern, Marilyn. 1988. *The Gender of the Gift*. Berkeley: University of California Press.

Straw, Will. 1993. Systems of Articulation, Logics of Change: Communities and Scenes in Popular Music. *Cultural Studies* 5(3): 361–375.

Sutton, Peter. 2003. *Native Title in Australia: An Ethnographic Perspective*. Cambridge: Cambridge University Press.

Sutton, Peter. 2011. *The Politics of Suffering*. Melbourne: Melbourne University Publishing.

Szwed, John. 2010. *Alan Lomax: The Man Who Recorded the World*. New York: Viking.

Taussig, Michael. 1993. *Mimesis and Alterity: A Particular History of the Senses*. New York: Routledge.

Taylor, Charles. 2002. Modern Social Imaginaries. *Public Culture* 14(1): 91–124.

Thaiday, Willie. 1981. *Under the Act*. Townsville, Queensland: NQ Black.

Thompson, Emily. 2002. The *Soundscape of Modernity: Architectural Acoustics and the Culture of Listening in America, 1900–1933*. Cambridge, MA: MIT Press.

Thorner, Sabra. 2010. Imagining an Indigital Interface: Ara Irititja Indigenizes the Technologies of Knowledge Management. *Collections: A Journal for Museum and Archives Professionals* 6(3): 125–146.

Toner, Peter. 2003. Melody and the Musical Articulation of Yolngu Identities. *Yearbook for Traditional Music* 35: 69–95.

Toner, Peter. 2005. Tropes of Longing and Belonging: Nostalgia and Musical Instruments in Northeast Arnhem Land. *Yearbook for Traditional Music* 37: 1–24.

Toohey, Paul. 1996. *God's Little Acre*. Melbourne: Duffy and Snelgrove.

Toohey, Paul. 2008. Last Drinks: The Impact of the Northern Territory Intervention. *Quarterly Essay* 30: 1–101.

Trudgen, Richard. 2001. *Why Warriors Lie Down and Die*. Darwin, NT: Arnhem Land Resource and Development Services.

Tsing, Anna Lowenhaupt. 2005. *Friction: An Ethnography of Global Connection*. Princeton, NJ: Princeton University Press.

Uibo, Michael. 1993. The Development of Batchelor College, 1972–1990. Unpublished MEd Thesis, Faculty of Education, Northern Territory University.

Veal, Michael. 2007. *Dub: Soundscapes and Shattered Songs in Jamaican Reggae*. Middletown, CT: Wesleyan University Press.

Virilio, Paul. 1989. *War and Cinema: The Logistics of Perception*. New York: Verso.

Walker, Clinton. 2000. *Buried Country*. Sydney: Pluto Press.

Wark, McKenzie. 2013. *The Spectacle of Disintegration: Situationist Passages Out of the 21st Century*. New York: Verso.

Warner, Michael. 2005. *Publics and Counterpublics*. New York: Zone Books.

Wear, Rae. 2002. *The Lord's Premier: Johannes Bjelke-Petersen*. St. Lucia: University of Queensland Press.

Weatherburn, Don. 2014. *Arresting Incarceration: Pathways out of Indigenous Imprisonment*. Canberra: Aboriginal Studies Press.

Weber, Samuel. 1996. *Mass Mediauras: Form, Technics, Media.* Stanford, CA: Stanford University Press.

Weheliye, Alexander. 2002. Feenin': Posthuman Voices in Contemporary Black Popular Music. *Social Text* 20(2): 21–47.

Weheliye, Alexander. 2005. *Phonographies: Grooves in Sonic Afro-Modernity.* Durham, NC: Duke University Press.

Weidman, Amy. 2006. *Singing the Classical, Voicing the Modern: The Postcolonial Politics of Music in South India.* Durham, NC: Duke University Press.

Weiss, Allen S. 1995. *Phantasmic Radio.* Durham, NC: Duke University Press.

Wells, Samantha. 1993. *Taking Stock: Aboriginal Autonomy through Enterprise.* Darwin: Australian National University, North Australia Research Unit.

Wells, Samantha. 1995. *Town Camp or Homeland? A History of the Kulaluk Aboriginal Community.* Darwin: Australian Heritage Commission.

West, Cornel. 1990. The New Cultural Politics of Difference. *October* 53: 93–109.

Wild, Rex, and Pat Anderson. 2007. *Ampe Akelyernemane Meke Mekarle (Little Children Are Sacred).* Board of Inquiry into the Protection of Aboriginal Children from Sexual Abuse.

Williams, Nancy. 1986. *The Yolngu and Their Land: A System of Land Tenure and the Fight for Its Recognition.* Canberra: Australian Institute for Aboriginal Studies Press.

Williams, Raymond. 1975. *The Country and the City.* Oxford: Oxford University Press.

Wilmott, Eric. 1984. *Out of a Silent Land.* Department of Aboriginal Affairs.

Wolf, Eric. 1956. Aspects of Group Relations in a Complex Society: Mexico. *American Anthropologist* 58: 1065–1078.

Wright, Alexis. 2013. *The Swan Book.* Artarmon, New South Wales: Giramondo.

Yurchak, Alexei. 1997. The Cynical Reason of Late Socialism: Power, Pretense, and the *Anekdot. Public Culture* 9: 161–188.

Yurchak, Alexei. 2005. *Everything Was Forever, Until It Was No More: The Last Soviet Generation.* Princeton, NJ: Princeton University Press.

Zeitlyn, David. 1993. Reconstructing Kinship, or, The Pragmatics of Kin Talk. *Man* (n.s.) 28(2): 199.

Žižek, Slavoj. 1992. *Enjoy Your Symptom! Jacques Lacan in Hollywood and Out.* New York: Routledge.

INDEX

Page numbers in italics refer to illustrations.